America, Russia, and the Cold War
1945–1996

America in Crisis

A series of books on American Diplomatic History

Editor: *Robert A. Divine*

H. W. Brands: *Since Vietnam:*
The United States in World Affairs, 1973–1995

H. W. Brands: *Into the Labyrinth:*
The United States and the Middle East, 1945–1993

Robert A. Divine: *The Reluctant Belligerent:*
American Entry into World War II

George Herring: *America's Longest War:*
United States and Vietnam, 1950–1975

Burton I. Kaufman: *The Korean War:*
Challenges in Crisis, Credibility, and Command

Walter LaFeber: *America, Russia, and the Cold War, 1945–1996*

H. Wayne Morgan: *America's Road to Empire:*
The War with Spain and Overseas Expansion

Daniel M. Smith: *The Great Departure:*
The United States and World War I, 1914–1920

Gaddis Smith: *American Diplomacy during the Second World War,*
1941–1945

America, Russia, and the Cold War 1945–1996

EIGHTH EDITION

Walter LaFeber
Cornell University

The McGraw-Hill Companies, Inc.

New York   St. Louis   San Francisco   Auckland   Bogotá   Caracas
Lisbon   London   Madrid   Mexico City   Milan   Montreal   New Delhi
San Juan   Singapore   Sydney   Tokyo   Toronto

McGraw-Hill

A Division of The McGraw·Hill Companies

For Sandra

AMERICA, RUSSIA, AND THE COLD WAR 1945–1996

This book is printed on recycled acid-free paper containing a minimum of 50% recycled de-inked fiber.

2 3 4 5 6 7 8 9 0 DOC DOC 9 0 9 8 7

ISBN 0-07-036064-2

This book was set in Palatino by ComCom, Inc.
The editor was Monica Freedman;
the production supervisor was Elizabeth J. Strange.
The cover was designed by Wanda Lubelska.
Project supervision was done by Spectrum Publisher Services, Inc.
R. R. Donnelley & Sons Company was printer and binder.

Library of Congress Cataloging-in-Publication Data

LaFeber, Walter.
America, Russia, and the Cold War, 1945–1996 / Walter LaFeber. — 8th ed.
     p.   cm. — (America in crisis)
Rev. ed. of: America, Russia, and the Cold War, 1945–1992.
Includes bibliographical references and index.
ISBN 0-07-036064-2
1. United States—Foreign relations—Soviet Union.   2. Soviet Union—Foreign relations—United States.   3. United States—Foreign relations—Russia.
4. Russia—Foreign relations—United States.   5. World politics—1945–
6. Cold War.   I. LaFeber, Walter. America, Russia, and the Cold War, 1945–1992.
7th ed. c1993.   II. Title.   III. Series.
E183.8.S65L34   1997
327.73047'09'045—dc20   96-34844

Foreword

"The United States always wins the war and loses the peace," runs a persistent popular complaint. Neither part of the statement is accurate. The United States barely escaped the War of 1812 with its territory intact, and in Korea in the 1950s the nation was forced to settle for a stalemate on the battlefield. At Paris in 1782, and again in 1898, American negotiators drove hard bargains to win notable diplomatic victories. Yet the myth persists, along with the equally erroneous American belief that we are a peaceful people. Our history is studded with conflict and violence. From the Revolution to the Cold War, Americans have been willing to fight for their interests, their beliefs, and their ambitions. The United States has gone to war for many objectives—for independence in 1775, for honor and trade in 1812, for territory in 1846, for humanity and empire in 1898, for neutral rights in 1917, and for national security in 1941. Since 1945 the nation has been engaged in two wars in Asia, a relatively brief conflict in Korea, and a longer and more tragic encounter in Vietnam.

This volume on the Cold War is part of a series of books designed to examine in detail critical periods relating to American involvement in foreign wars. Since the first edition appeared in 1967, Professor LaFeber has carefully revised his account to explain the course of the Cold War as it moved from periods of intense crisis and confrontation to times of relative stability. In this latest edition, he pays special attention to the dramatic events that began in the fall of 1989 with the collapse of communism in Eastern Europe, symbolized by the tearing down of the Berlin Wall, through the failed coup in the Soviet Union in August 1991, which convinced all but diehard skeptics that the Cold War was indeed finally over. As a result, he is now able to examine the entire course of the rivalry between the United States and the Soviet Union, from its origins in the aftermath of the

Second World War through the remarkable interaction of two of the most unlikely collaborators in recent history—Ronald Reagan and Mikhail Gorbachev.

Robert A. Divine

Preface

For the eighth edition, changes and additions have been made in nearly every section of the book. Because of the Woodrow Wilson International Center's remarkable Cold War History Project, under Jim Hershberg's direction, new materials from Russian and Chinese archives have become available especially to supplement the section covering 1945–1953. Recently published memoirs and declassified documents have also allowed a rewriting of some events in the 1950s, the Lyndon Johnson presidency, and the Reagan presidential years. The final chapter, on post-1989 to the present, has been extensively rewritten and updated, while the bibliography includes newly published work.

Two other changes, at least in emphasis, have been made. The first edition of this book argued that U.S. foreign and domestic policies were linked, and that the latter usually shaped the former. That link has too often been lost in intervening editions, and this thesis is now reemphasized. It is also briefly overviewed in the final chapter. The other change is more focus on Soviet-Russian developments, in part so that the book will be truer to its title, in part because post-1991 events are unfortunately demonstrating that U.S.-Russian problems and confrontations did not end with the formal closing of the Cold War. Especially because of internal changes, Russia is again emerging as the nation posing the most important challenges to the United States.

Many friends have offered materials and advice that have shaped this edition. These friends include Cornell colleagues Joel Silbey, Richard Polenberg, Michael Kammen, Tim Borstelmann, Tom Christensen, Glenn Altschuler, Peter Katzenstein, and George Kahin; former students (now successful in their own various careers) David Maisel, Evan Stewart, Eric Edelman, Dan Fried, Sheila Heslin, Carol Kuntz, Jim Siekmeier, Frank Costigliola, Douglas Little, Bob Hannigan, Anne Foster, Lorena Oropeza, Kirk Dorsey, Sayuri Shimizu, Shannon Smith, David Green, Mark Lytle, Amy Davis, Holly Isdale, Jeffrey Cowan, and, in a different category, David Langbart of the National Archives; professional colleagues Milton Leitenberg of the University of Maryland, Paul Dukes of University of Aberdeen (Scotland), and Frank Kofsky of California State–Sacramento; Academicians N. N. Bolkhovitinov of the Russian Academy of Sciences and Tom Schoonover of Southwest Louisiana University; and, as always, decades-old friends Marie Underhill Noll, Lloyd Gardner, Thomas McCormick, Martin Sklar, and Bob Divine, who is the editor of this series. Dennis Bilger of the Truman Presidential Library and David Humphrey, formerly of the Lyndon Johnson Presidential Library and now with the Department of State Historical Office, are owed much by all scholars who study the post-1945 years, especially by the present author. For special reasons, I also thank Stephen Weiss of New York City.

I am grateful to the following reviewers for their comments: Albert Berger, University of North Dakota; Sidney Fine, University of Michigan; and David Healy, University of Wisconsin–Milwaukee.

The students and teachers who continue to find this book useful have made a new edition possible. I am indebted to the readers who have sent criticisms and other comments about earlier editions. LizAnne Rogovoy, Rebecca Gaslow, Karin Tamis, and Kathryn Comerford were exemplary research assistants. I owe a great deal to the McGraw-Hill staff, particularly Monica Freedman. Thanks also to Kathleen Riley-King, who did the copy editing, and to Mercedes Jackson, production editor. As always, Sandra and Scott LaFeber, Suzanne and Tom—and Matthew—Kahl, Bill and Hilde Kahl, and Hurley and Peg Gould have made it all worthwhile.

Acknowledgments to the First Edition

Robert Divine of the University of Texas, the editor of this series; Gaddis Smith of Yale; Myron Rush of Cornell; and Lloyd Gardner of Rutgers have immeasurably helped this manuscript by reading it in its entirety and making many constructive criticisms. To Lloyd Gardner and to Thomas McCormick of the University of Pittsburgh, William Appleman Williams of the University of Wisconsin, Fred Harvey Harrington, President of the University of Wisconsin, and Robert Bowers of Hanover College, I owe considerably more than mere thanks for professional advice. Knight Biggerstaff of Cornell read many of the sections on Asia and improved them greatly. William Gum of Wiley has been the most helpful and long-suffering editor that an author could wish for. Nancy Unger, also of Wiley, made this a better volume by taking care of the editorial work on the maps.

Tom Rogers, Coordinator of Research at Cornell; Frank Long, Vice President of Research at Cornell; Stuart Brown, Dean of Cornell's College of Arts and Sciences; and Sandy Cheney, Associate Dean of that college, have literally made this book possible by providing the research funds that enabled me to investigate materials in various libraries and to have the manuscript typed. I particularly thank Mrs. Nancy Bressler of the Princeton University Library staff for making the Dulles and Baruch papers so easy to use and also for expediting the clearance of my notes through the Dulles Committee. Phillip Brooks and Phillip Lagerquist were very helpful at the Truman Library. I am, of course, primarily obligated to the fine library staff at Cornell, particularly to Giles Shepherd and Evelyn Greenberg. Herman Phleger, General Nathan Twining, and Sherman Adams graciously consented to allow the use of the quotations from their oral history interviews in the Dulles manuscripts at Princeton. Mrs. Robert Ludgate and Mrs. John Quincy Adams of Ithaca typed the manuscript with great care.

I thank those persons who either supplied me with research materials or somewhat narrowed the boundaries of my ignorance by talking with me about the Cold War: David Brion Davis, Walter Pintner, Michael Kammen, and Richard Polenberg, all professors at Cornell in the Department of History; Andrew Hacker, Clinton Rossiter, John Lewis, and George Kahin in the Cornell Government Department; Paul Marantz, a graduate student in government at Harvard; David Maisel, an undergraduate at Cornell; Raymond G. O'Connor, professor and chairman of the History Department at Temple University; Professor Barton Bernstein of Stanford; Professor Athan Theoharis of Wayne State University; John Windmuller, professor in the Industrial and Labor Relations School of Cornell; and George Kennan of the Institute for Advanced Study at Princeton. I am particularly indebted to Professor Carl Parrini and the History Department at the University of Northern Illinois for allowing me to try out some of my ideas about the Cold War at their N.D.E.A. Institute in the summer of 1966. The dedication is to a person who has yet to lose a war—either hot or cold—and this has been fortunate for me.

Walter LaFeber

To my wife, Sandy

Contents

Introduction: The Burden of History (to 1941)   1

1. Open Doors, Iron Curtains (1941–1945)   7

2. Only Two Declarations of Cold War (1946)   30

3. Two Halves of the Same Walnut (1947–1948)   49

4. The "Different World" of NSC-68 (1948–1950)   74

5. Korea: The War for Both Asia and Europe (1950–1951)   99

6. New Issues, New Faces (1951–1953)   125

7. A Different Cold War (1953–1955)   145

8. East and West of Suez (1954–1957)   169

9. New Frontiers and Old Dilemmas (1957–1962)   192

10. Southeast Asia—and Elsewhere (1962–1966)   220

11. A New Containment: The Rise and Fall of Détente (1966–1976)   252

12. From Cold War to Old War: Reagan and Gorbachev (1977–1989)   283

13. A New World Order—Or the Age of Fragmentation? (1989–)   327

Bibliography for Additional Reading   373

Index   387

About the Author   409

Maps

How the Soviet Union Was Formed   xiii

U.S. and U.S.S.R. Overseas Commitments at the
  Height of the Cold War   xiv–xv

Divided Germany in a Divided Europe, 1946   18

Japan, Korea, China, and Russia after World War II   32

Iran, Turkey, Greece, and Russia, 1946–1948   36

Conflict in Korea, 1950–1953   103

The Middle East and the Suez Crisis, 1956   184

Central and South America, 1954–1990   207

Southeast Asia, 1971   218

A 1980s Soviet View   269

The Middle East, 1967, 1979   275

The Near East in Upheaval, 1980   293

Turning Points in Eastern Europe, 1989   336

Areas of Discontent, 1988–1994   348

The Bosnian Crisis, 1995–1996   355

How the Soviet Union Was Formed
Years of admission as full members of the union.

Lithuania, Latvia and Estonia
1940 (as a result of the Hitler–Stalin pact)

Russia
1922

• St. Petersburg
• Moscow

Vladivostok

Byelorussia
1922

Ukraine
1922

Moldavia
1940

Georgia
1922

Armenia
1922

Azerbaijan
1922

Uzbekistan
1924

Turkemenia
1924

Kazakhstan
1936

Kirghizia
1936

Tadzhikistan
1929

Source: U.S.S.R. Facts and Figures Annual

U.S. and U.S.S.R. OVERSEAS COMMITMENTS
at the HEIGHT of the COLD WAR

United States and its treaty alliances

Soviet Union and its treaty alliances

◆ Principal overseas bases of the United States

● Principal overseas bases of the Soviet Union

INDIAN OCEAN

◆ Diego Garcia

AFGHAN

PAKIST

THAILAND

CHINA

MONGOLIA

WARSAW PACT
BULGARIA
CZECHOSLOVAKIA
E. GERMANY
HUNGARY
POLAND
RUMANIA
SOVIET UNION

PHILIPPINES

U.S.–NATIONALIST CHINA DEFENSE TREATY

U.S.–SOUTH KOREA DEFENSE TREATY

U.S.–JAPAN DEFENSE TREATY

AUSTRALIA

MICRONESIA (U.S.)

PACIFIC

SEATO (1954–1977 with residual 1954 Manila Pact ties remaining with the Philippines and Thailand.)

AUSTRALIA	PAKISTAN
BRITAIN	PHILIPPINES
FRANCE	THAILAND
NEW ZEALAND	UNITED STATES

NEW ZEALAND

AFRICA

EGYPT

IRAQ
SYRIA
GREECE
TURKEY
ALBANIA
BULGARIA
RUMANIA
YUGOSLAVIA
HUNGARY
CZECHO-
SLOVAKIA
POLAND
ITALY

SPAIN
PORTUGAL
FRANCE
W. GERMANY
BELGIUM
NETHERLANDS
BRITAIN

E. GERMANY
DENMARK
NORWAY
ICELAND

GUINEA

Equator

ATLANTIC OCEAN

SOVIET UNION

VIETNAM

North
Pole

Alaska

OCEAN

Hawaii

CANADA

UNITED STATES

MEXICO

CUBA
PANAMA

SOUTH AMERICA

NATO

BELGIUM	GREECE	NETHERLANDS
BRITAIN	ICELAND	NORWAY
CANADA	ITALY	PORTUGAL
DENMARK	LUXEM.	TURKEY
W. GERMANY	SPAIN	UNITED STATES

INTER-AMERICAN TREATY
24 NATIONS

America, Russia, and the Cold War
1945–1996

Introduction:
The Burden of History
(to 1941)

The Cold War has dominated American life since 1945. It has cost Americans $8 trillion in defense expenditures, taken the lives of nearly 100,000 of their young men and women, ruined the careers of many others during the McCarthyite witch hunts, led the nation into the horrors of Southeast Asian conflicts, and in the 1980s triggered the worst economic depression in forty years. It has not been the most satisfying chapter in American diplomatic history.

These tragedies can be understood—and, it is hoped, some future disasters averted—only by understanding the causes of this struggle between the United States and Russia. The conflict did not begin in 1945 or even with the communist victory in Russia during 1917. The two powers did not initially come into conflict because one was communist and the other capitalist. Rather, they first confronted each other on the plains of north China and Manchuria in the late nineteenth century. That meeting climaxed a century in which Americans had expanded westward over half the globe and Russians had moved eastward across Asia.

Until that confrontation the two nations had been good friends. Whenever conflicts arose (as over settlements in California and Alaska), the Russians retreated before the demands of U.S. expansionists. Encounters outside the New World, however, could not be settled so easily. Americans swept across a continent while sending out tentacles of trade that quickly seized upon Asia as the great potential market for their magnificently productive farms and factories. By the 1890s Russia, after five centuries of expansion, controlled a grand continental empire containing (like the United States) peoples of many cultures. Americans believed that a "manifest destiny" of supernatural force directed their conquests. The Russians similarly viewed their czar, or emperor, as an instrument of God's will.

But the two nations also differed sharply. The American empire was decentralized, or "federal," with states and outlying territory enjoying considerable freedom. The Russian empire was tightly centralized, with an army of bureaucrats working antlike for the czar (and, later, a small Communist party elite in Moscow). Russian officials agreed that only rigidly enforced order from above could preserve the nation. Such bureaucracies are not renowned for imagination and originality. (In part because of the resulting uncreativity, Russia, both before and after 1917, necessarily borrowed technology and new industrial methods from the West.[1]) The oppressive bureaucracy also was brutal, especially in the post-1880 era when it condemned political dissenters to Siberian prison camps and accelerated pogroms against Russian Jews. Anti-Russian feelings spread across the United States. Congress threatened to cut trade with the czar. Mark Twain caught the mood when he exclaimed that if the regime could be ended only with dynamite, "then thank God for dynamite."

And Americans were also finding another fault with their former friends. The United States honored not bureaucracies, but businesspeople who moved across the oceans to profit in open world marketplaces. Russians, however, moved across land, not water. They developed an empire that was more political than commercial. After annexing land in Asia, they tried to control it tightly by closing the markets to foreign businesspeople with whom they could not compete. This highlighted the problem between the two countries in the 1890s: the United States believed its prosperity increasingly required an "open door" to trade in China's rich province of Manchuria, but the Russians were determined to colonize and close off parts of Manchuria. Two hostile systems confronted each other, much as they would during 1945 in Eastern Europe, and for many of the same reasons.

From the 1890s until 1917 the United States tried to contain Russian expansion, usually by supporting Japan, which, for its own purposes, also wanted an open Manchuria. President Theodore Roo-

---

[1]Robert Wesson, "Soviet Russia: A Geopolitical View," *Survey*, XVII (Spring 1971): 1–13.

sevelt exemplified American sentiments: the Russians "are utterly insincere and treacherous; they have no conception of the truth . . . and no regard for others." As for the czar, he was "a preposterous little creature." More to the point, TR feared that Russia was trying to "organize northern China against us."[2]

These views did not change even in 1914 when the czar allied with England and France against Germany. Colonel Edward House, President Woodrow Wilson's closest adviser, starkly outlined the alternatives that were to haunt Americans throughout the twentieth century: "If the Allies win, it means the domination of Russia on the continent of Europe; and if Germany wins, it means the unspeakable tyranny of militarism for generations to come."[3] Either way the United States would lose.

The traditional Russian danger grew more threatening in late 1917. Vladimir Lenin's Bolshevik movement used the devastation, chaos, and poverty caused by World War I to overthrow the Russian government and establish a Soviet. The ever-expanding czarist empire now possessed an ideological force, Marxism, that was supposedly driven by historical law and dedicated to world revolution. Between 1918 and 1920 Woodrow Wilson dispatched more than 10,000 American soldiers as he cooperated with Allied attempts to overthrow Lenin by force, and, simultaneously, tried to prevent an invading Japanese army from colonizing and closing off Siberia. The President finally contained the Japanese, but the Allied intervention was a disaster. In the short run many Russians fled from the foreign troops to support Lenin. In the long run Soviet leaders did not forget that the intervention seemed to confirm their belief that "capitalist encirclement" aimed at strangulating the communist regime.

At the Versailles Peace Conference in 1919, the Allies sought another approach. With the shadow of Lenin darkening every discussion, the Western powers tried to isolate the Soviets by creating such buffer states as Poland, Rumania, Czechoslovakia, and Yugoslavia in Eastern Europe. As a young, embittered American official named Walter Lippmann phrased it, the Allies created a military *cordon sanitaire,* when peace required a "sanitary Europe," that is, a prosperous,

---

[2]Quoted in William Henry Harbough, *Power and Responsibility: The Life and Times of Theodore Roosevelt* (New York, 1961), p. 277.
[3]Quoted in Arthur S. Link, *Wilson: The Struggle for Neutrality, 1914–1915* (Princeton, 1960), p. 48.

less militarized area that could build a more attractive and equitable society than Lenin could devise.[4] (In 1947, as dean of American journalists, Lippmann would again condemn American postwar policy, and again be rejected by Washington officials.)

Attempting to isolate the Soviets, Woodrow Wilson refused to open diplomatic relations. Sounding like Theodore Roosevelt discussing the czar, Wilson declared that Lenin's government "is based upon the negation of every principle of honor and good faith." But others refused to follow his lead. England began trading with Russia in 1921. A year later the two outcasts, Russia and defeated Germany, signed a treaty of cooperation. Though shocking Americans by condemning religion and private property, the Soviets were apparently here to stay.

The United States by no means ignored the Bolsheviks. An American relief mission distributed over $60-million worth of aid to starving Russians in the 1920s. When Lenin announced in 1921 that he would welcome foreign capital for reconstruction projects, Secretary of Commerce Herbert Hoover believed this meant communism was collapsing. Hoping that Americans could control as well as profit from a more capitalist Russia, Hoover encouraged businessmen to look upon Russia as an "economic vacuum" that, like all vacuums, invited invasion. They responded. Ford, General Electric, and Westinghouse were among the many major firms that invested millions of dollars. Young W. Averell Harriman also took the plunge. Heir to a great railway fortune, Harriman began to develop a billion-dollar manganese concession in Russia during 1926. When his venture ran into financial trouble, the Soviets freed him from his contract. (Harriman found them less cooperative when Franklin D. Roosevelt named him U.S. ambassador to Russia during World War II.) Meanwhile, between 1925 and 1930 Soviet-American trade rose to over $100 million, well above the prewar figure.

The economic relationship was suddenly transformed after 1928, but not as Hoover had hoped. When Lenin died in 1924, Joseph Stalin used his control of the Soviet party bureaucracy to boost himself to the top. Son of a cobbler, educated at (and expelled from) an Orthodox theological seminary, and frequently arrested before 1917 for revolutionary activities, Stalin and his brutality had so alienated Lenin

---

[4]Walter Lippmann, *New Republic* (March 22, 1919), supplement.

that the Soviet leader had nearly broken off personal relations. Lenin's death solved that potential problem; then Stalin brilliantly played faction against faction to defeat his opposition. In 1928 he enhanced his power by announcing five-year plans for rapid economic development. These schemes required a tightly run, self-sufficient society. The communist call for worldwide revolution became less important to Stalin than unchallenged personal power and a rebuilt Russia strong enough to withstand "capitalist encirclement."

American-Russian trade consequently dropped just as the United States entered the worst depression years. Many businessmen pressed the newly elected President, Franklin D. Roosevelt, to recognize Russia formally. He did so in November 1933, but only after overcoming, or ignoring, strong anti-Soviet feeling from his own State Department, as well as from the American Legion, Roman Catholic Church leaders, the Daughters of the American Revolution, and the American labor movement. Justifiably concerned that the Russians might not be warmly welcomed, Roosevelt scheduled the arrival of the Soviet delegation at the same time his countrymen raucously celebrated the end of Prohibition.

Stalin welcomed recognition, but not for economic reasons. He wanted American help against the Japanese army that began rampaging through Manchuria in 1931. Roosevelt refused to respond to the Russian appeal. The State Department even assured the Japanese in 1933 that recognition of Russia should not be taken as a threat against Japan.[5] Until World War II the United States never deviated from this policy. Twice in the next five years, in 1934 and 1937, American officials rejected Soviet requests for joint policies against Japan and Nazi Germany. The administration received strong support from many American liberals, even former communists, who grew disillusioned as Stalin began bloody purges of his political enemies. After the war these liberals would not forget their earlier disenchantment with communism, "the God who failed."

By 1938 Stalin's relations with the Western powers were disintegrating. The climactic blow occurred that year at the Munich conference, when the French and British appeased Hitler by giving Germany part of Czechoslovakia. At the Communist party's Eighteenth Con-

---

[5]Stanley K. Hornbeck to Secretary of State Cordell Hull, October 28, 1933, and Hornbeck to William Phillips, October 31, 1933, 711.61/333, Archives of the Department of State, Washington, D.C. (Hereafter cited NA, followed by Record Group number.)

gress in early 1939, Stalin declared that the West hoped to turn Hitler east toward war with the Soviets. This would not happen, he indicated, for although "new economic crises" in the capitalist world made inevitable another "imperialist" war, this time Russia would not pull Western "chestnuts out of the fire."[6] Making much of a terrible situation, Stalin stunned the West in late August 1939 by signing a nonaggression pact with Hitler. The two dictators agreed to divide Poland and the Balkans. A week after the treaty was negotiated, Hitler began World War II by invading Poland.

During the next eighteen months Russian-American relations hit bottom. The Soviet invasion of Finland secured a strategic buffer for Stalin but simply confirmed to Americans that Russia brutalized small neighbors. In early 1941, however, Hitler tired of negotiating with the Russians and decided to take Eastern Europe fully into his own hands. On June 22 Nazi armies swept into the Soviet Union in history's greatest military operation.

The State Department debated for twenty-four hours before issuing an announcement that condemned the Soviet view of religion, declared that "communistic dictatorship" was as intolerable as "Nazi dictatorship," said nothing good about the Russians, but concluded they must be helped since Hitler posed the larger threat. Harry S Truman, Democratic senator from Missouri, bluntly expressed his and many other Americans' feelings: "If we see that Germany is winning we should help Russia and if Russia is winning we ought to help Germany and that way let them kill as many as possible, although I don't want to see Hitler victorious under any circumstances."[7]

It was not the best spirit with which to start a new partnership. But such statements only climaxed half a century of Russian-American enmity. Possessing drastically different views of how the world should be organized, unable to cooperate during the 1930s against Nazi and Japanese aggression, and nearly full-fledged enemies between 1939 and 1941, the United States and the Soviet Union finally became partners because of a shotgun marriage forced upon them by World War II.

[6]Myron Rush, ed., *The International Situation and Soviet Foreign Policy: Key Reports by Soviet Leaders from the Revolution to the Present* (Columbus, Ohio, 1970), pp. 85–96.
[7]*The New York Times*, June 24, 1941, p. 7.

CHAPTER 1

Open Doors, Iron Curtains (1941–1945)

A honeymoon never occurred. Despite exchanges of military information and nearly $11 billion of American lend-lease supplies sent to Russia, conflicts quickly erupted over war strategy and plans for the postwar peace.

As the Nazis drove deeper into Russia in 1942, Stalin desperately asked President Roosevelt and British Prime Minister Winston Churchill to open a bridgehead in Western Europe. Soviet Foreign Minister V. M. Molotov, according to one observer, knew only four words of English: "yes," "no," and "second front." Twice Roosevelt promised an invasion. Twice he and Churchill reneged. Believing they lacked the power to attack Western Europe, they instead invaded North Africa and Italy. These campaigns stalled the opening of the second front until mid-1944. By then the Russians had themselves driven back the Nazis, although at tremendous cost.

Stalin's suspicions multiplied as he asked Roosevelt and Churchill to agree that postwar Russia should include the Baltic States and parts of Poland, Finland, and Rumania. These areas had belonged to czarist Russia and had been reclaimed by Stalin in 1939 with the Nazi-Soviet pact. In 1943 Roosevelt told an unhappy Stalin that millions of U.S. voters of Baltic ancestry made it impossible for him to recognize Soviet claims to Latvia, Lithuania, and Estonia—although Roosevelt added that he certainly "did not intend to go to war with the Soviet Union on this point." Roosevelt hoped to delay discussion on other territorial issues until after the war.

That was a fateful decision. By 1945 the Red Army stood astride Eastern and much of Central Europe. Roosevelt and Churchill, moreover, would have to discuss Stalin's demands in a strikingly different world, for the Allies were destroying Germany and Japan, two nations that historically had blocked Russian expansion into Europe and Asia.

American policymakers soon discovered an even greater problem. Their own policy was contradictory. Neither Roosevelt nor his successor, Harry S Truman, ever reconciled the contradictions. That failure was a major cause of the Cold War. The contradiction contained an economic and a political factor.

Washington officials believed another terrible economic depression could be averted only if global markets and raw materials were fully open to all peoples on the basis of equal opportunity. American domestic requirements, moreover, dictated such a policy. The world could not be allowed to return to the 1930s state of affairs, when nations tried to escape depression by creating high tariff walls and regional trading blocs that dammed the natural flow of trade. If that recurred, Americans could survive only through massive governmental intervention into their society. If the government dominated the economy, however, it would also regulate individual choice and perhaps severely limit personal freedom.

"In the event of long-continued unemployment," Vice President Henry Wallace warned, "the only question will be as to whether the Prussian or Marxian doctrine will take us over first." Such alternatives could be avoided only if Americans realized, in the words of Assistant Secretary of State Dean Acheson, that "we cannot expect domestic prosperity under our system without a constantly expanding trade with other nations." As one official noted, "The capitalistic system is essentially an international system," and "if it cannot function internationally, it will break down completely." For these reasons the United States required an open world marketplace after the war.[1]

In August 1941, at the Atlantic Conference held off Newfoundland with Churchill, Roosevelt moved to implement this policy. In Article III of the Atlantic Charter, the two leaders declared that after the war all peoples should have the right "to choose the form of government under which they will live." Article IV added the economic side to that principle: all states should enjoy "access, on equal terms, to the trade and to the raw materials of the world which are needed for their

[1]Henry Wallace, Herbert Hoover, et al., *Prefaces to Peace* (New York, 1943), p. 413; Lloyd C. Gardner, *Economic Aspects of New Deal Diplomacy* (Madison, Wis., 1964), p. 344; testimony of Secretary of the Treasury Fred Vinson, *The New York Times*, March 6, 1946, p. 8.

economic prosperity."[2] That "need" for Americans grew incredibly during the next four years. Their industrial output rose 90 percent. This economic power, developed while other industrial nations were decimated by war, also assured Americans they would be in the most advantageous position to race for "access, on equal terms" in world trade.

The Ghosts of Depression Past and Depression Future thus shaped American postwar objectives. But those objectives were political as well as economic. Closed economic blocs not only hurt trade but easily developed into political blocs. Friction between such blocs caused world wars. That was precisely what had occurred during the 1930s when the British, Germans, Japanese, and Russians had warred on one another economically, then militarily. As State Department economic adviser Will Clayton declared, "Nations which act as enemies in the marketplace cannot long be friends at the council table."[3]

In 1944 the United States tried to ensure that the postwar marketplace would be friendly. An international conference at Bretton Woods, New Hampshire, created a World Bank (the International Bank of Reconstruction and Development) and the International Monetary Fund (IMF). The World Bank would have a treasury of $7.6 billion (and authority to lend twice that amount) to guarantee private loans given for rebuilding war-torn Europe and for building up the less industrialized nations. The IMF possessed $7.3 billion to stabilize currencies so that trade could be conducted without fear of sudden currency depreciation or wild fluctuations in exchange rates, ailments which had nearly paralyzed the international community in the 1930s. The United States hoped these two agencies would reconstruct, then stabilize and expand world trade. Of course, there was one other implication. Voting in the organizations depended on money contributed. Since Americans would have to contribute the most, they would also control the World Bank and IMF.

American policy from the Atlantic Charter through the Bretton Woods conference seemed well thought out. Financier and self-appointed adviser to Presidents and congressmen, Bernard Baruch caught the spirit in early 1945: if we can "stop subsidization of labor and sweated competition in the export markets," as well as prevent

---

[2]U.S. Department of State, *Foreign Relations of the United States* [henceforth *FRUS*], *1941*, I (Washington, 1948): 366–368.
[3]Quoted in Lloyd Gardner, *Architects of Illusion* (Chicago, 1970), p. 123.

rebuilding of war machines, "oh boy, oh boy, what long-term prosperity we will have."[4] Like Dorothy, Americans seemed on their way to a happier land of Oz, with their immense economic power serving as ruby slippers. But, like Dorothy, they soon encountered witches—not just one, but wicked witches from both West and East.

In the West the French and British had realized since the 1920s that they could no longer compete with the efficient American industrialists in an open marketplace. During the 1930s the British had created their own economic bloc to shut out American goods. Churchill did not believe he could surrender that protection after the war, and he watered down the Atlantic Charter's "free access" clause before agreeing to it. Yet American officials were determined to break open the empire. Combined, British and American trade accounted for more than half the world's exchange of goods. If the British bloc could be split apart, the United States would be well on the way to opening the entire global marketplace.

A devastated England had no choice. Two wars had destroyed its principal industries that paid for the importation of half the nation's food and nearly all its raw materials except coal. The British asked for help. In 1945 the United States agreed to loan $3.8 billion. In return, weary London officials promised to dismantle much of their imperial trading bloc. Will Clayton, who negotiated the agreement, confided to Baruch, "We loaded the British loan negotiations with all the conditions that the traffic would bear."[5]

France received the same treatment. For nearly two centuries French and American interests had clashed in both the Old and New Worlds. During the war French mistrust of the United States was personified by General Charles de Gaulle, president of the French Provisional Government. De Gaulle bitterly fought American officials as he tried to maintain his country's colonies and diplomatic freedom of action. These officials in turn saw de Gaulle as pro-British and a political extremist; one State Department officer even called him "this

[4]Baruch to E. Coblentz, March 23, 1945, Papers of Bernard Baruch, Princeton University Library, Princeton, N.J.
[5]"Memorandum for Mr. Baruch," from Clayton, April 26, 1946, Baruch Papers. For the background, see Warren F. Kimball, "Lend-Lease and the Open Door . . . 1937–1942," *Political Science Quarterly,* LXXXVI (June 1971): 232–259.

French Adolf."[6] In 1945 de Gaulle had to swallow his considerable pride to ask Washington for a billion-dollar loan. Most of the request was granted; in return France promised to curtail governmental subsidies and currency manipulation which had given advantages to its exporters in the world market.

The United States was freeing itself to deal with the witch of the East, the Soviet Union.[7] As it did, the contradictions within American policy became stunningly apparent. On the one hand, Washington demanded an open Europe. As a top official later explained, the State Department wanted all Europe "west of the Russian border . . . established as a cooperative continental system economically unified in certain major particulars."[8] On the other hand, Stalin had constantly demanded that Roosevelt and Churchill recognize the Soviet right to control large parts of Eastern Europe. For Stalin the Russian "sphere" would serve as a strategic buffer against the West and could also be exploited economically for the rapid rebuilding of the Soviet economy. Making his intentions clear, Stalin refused to sign the Atlantic Charter until he added provisions that emasculated Articles III and IV.[9]

As early as 1942, therefore, Roosevelt faced the choice: he could either fight for an open postwar world (at least to the Russian borders) or agree with his ally's demands in Eastern Europe. If he chose the first alternative, Russian-American relations would probably erode until the joint effort against the Axis might collapse. At the least, Americans and Russians would enter the postwar world as enemies.

[6]H. F. Matthews to Ray Atherton, June 25, 1943, Papers of William Leahy, Box 4, Library of Congress, Washington, D.C.

[7]Unfortunately, the "wicked witch" analogy is not far-fetched. Louis Halle, a member of the State Department Policy Planning Staff in the late 1940s, recalled that throughout this era until "almost the end of 1962," the West lived under the terror of "the Moscovite tyranny that was spreading from the East." For those who wished to understand such fears, Halle recommended reading J. R. R. Tolkien's trilogy, *The Lord of the Rings,* which Halle believed "enshrines the mood and emotion of those long years." *The Cold War as History* (New York, 1967), p. 138.

[8]Adolf Berle, "Diplomacy and the New Economics." In E. A. J. Johnson, ed., *Dimensions of Diplomacy* (Baltimore, 1964), pp. 93–95.

[9]Martin F. Herz, *The Beginnings of the Cold War* (Bloomington, Ind., 1966), pp. vii–viii.

(As it was, a mistrustful Stalin secretly considered a separate peace with Hitler as late as mid-1943.[10]) If Roosevelt chose the second alternative, he would undermine American hopes for the triumph of the Atlantic Charter principles, thus destroying the chances for postwar peace and American prosperity. Not that the United States required Eastern European markets. But a stable, prosperous world did require a healthy Europe, and that meant a united Europe with its eastern sectors providing food and western areas the industrial products. Each depended on the other. As the State Department informed Roosevelt in early 1945, European stability "depends on the maintenance of sound economic conditions and reasonable prosperity in all parts of the Continent."[11] Besides, a dangerous precedent could be set. If Stalin got away with building his own sphere in Europe, Churchill, de Gaulle, and others might try to rebuild their blocs.

Faced with this agonizing dilemma, Roosevelt at first suggested to the Soviets that the postwar world should be stabilized by "four policemen"—the United States, Russia, Great Britain, and China. The Soviets were delighted, for they understood this plan to mean they would be the policeman patrolling Eastern Europe. By late 1943, however, State Department officials were changing Roosevelt's mind. The "four policemen" concept could not be reconciled with a unified, open world. Areas patrolled by one policeman could too easily become closed spheres controlled by one power. Roosevelt began to stall, then to modify the idea. As he delayed, the Red Army started its sweep across Eastern Europe in 1944. Stalin understood what was happening. "This war is not as in the past," he told fellow communists. "Whoever occupies a territory also imposes on it his own social system" as far "as his army can reach."[12]

Churchill also understood. In October 1944 he deserted Roosevelt's policy of delay and flew to Moscow to make a deal. He promised to recognize Soviet domination in Rumania and Bulgaria. In return, Stalin agreed that England could control Greece. Thus Churchill protected the Mediterranean lifeline of the British Empire while acknowledging Russia's "first say" in certain Eastern European nations. With accuracy, and sarcasm, Churchill warned Stalin

---

[10]Vojtech Mastny, "Stalin and the Prospects of a Separate Peace in World War II," *American Historical Review*, LXXVII (December 1972): 1365–1388.

[11]*FRUS: The Conferences at Malta and Yalta, 1945* (Washington, 1955), pp. 235–236.

[12]Milovan Djilas, *Conversations with Stalin* (New York, 1961), p. 114.

that the deal had better be expressed "in diplomatic terms and not . . . use the phrase 'dividing into spheres,' because the Americans might be shocked."[13]

When he learned of the agreement, Roosevelt was shocked anyway, but worse was to come. In February 1945 the Big Three met at the Russian Black Sea resort of Yalta to shape the postwar world. An acrimonious debate erupted over the future of Poland. Throughout 1943–1944 Roosevelt had indicated he understood the need for a Polish government that would (unlike that government in the interwar years) be friendly toward Russia. But he was not prepared for Stalin's moves in early 1945. The Soviets had recognized a communist-dominated regime before the Yalta meetings began. FDR and Churchill demanded that pro-Western Poles be included in the government. The three men finally agreed that the regime must be "reorganized on a broader democratic basis." Admiral William Leahy, Roosevelt's chief military aide, accurately observed that the agreement was "so elastic that the Russians can stretch it all the way from Yalta to Washington without technically breaking it." Since the Red Army occupied Poland, however, this was the best FDR could do. He did try to make the agreement less elastic by proposing a "Declaration of Liberated Europe." This provided that each of the three powers would pledge cooperation in applying the self-determination principle to newly liberated nations. The Russians amended the declaration until it was virtually meaningless. Again, FDR had to accept the remains.[14]

Stalin left Yalta doubtless believing his allies had at least acquiesced to his domination over Eastern Europe. That must have been a relief, for throughout much of the war his policy had also been pulling in two directions. The Soviet dictator insisted on his own sphere but to this point had carefully not explained to his partners what Russian control implied. To have done so might have angered the Allies,

---

[13]"Record of Meeting at the Kremlin, Moscow, October 9, 1944," PREM 3, 434/47, Public Record Office, London, England. I am indebted to Professor Lloyd Gardner of Rutgers—New Brunswick and Professor Warren Kimball of Rutgers—Newark for calling my attention to this document. In much the same way, the United States excluded the Soviets from any authority in liberated Italy; see Gabriel Kolko, *The Politics of War, 1943–1945* (New York, 1968), pp. 37–39.

[14]*FRUS: Yalta*, pp. 234–235, 668–669, 677–678, 898. The important work on these developments is Lloyd C. Gardner, *Spheres of Influence: The Great Powers Partition Europe, From Munich to Yalta* (Chicago, 1993).

slowed American deliveries of war matériel, and perhaps even led to a separate deal between the West and Germany. (After all, why should Stalin have expected capitalist scruples to be more elevated than his own?) With the Red Army so close to total victory, he did not want any last-minute diplomatic bungling. Yalta seemed to remove that danger.

But Stalin miscalculated. Two weeks after the conference adjourned, the Soviets turned the screws on Rumania by demanding that the king appoint a communist-controlled government. Rumanian soldiers, the Soviets recalled, had marched with the Nazis into Russia in 1941. Churchill, moreover, had agreed to turn his back on Rumania in return for Stalin's ignoring Greece. But the United States claimed that Stalin was breaking the Declaration of Liberated Europe. The American case was difficult to argue, and Molotov picked it apart.[15] This was not, however, a mere debate: control of Eastern Europe was at stake.

A crisis developed when Russia refused to allow any more than three pro-Western Poles into the eighteen-member Polish government. For Americans, Poland became the test case of Soviet intentions. As Secretary of State Edward Stettinius observed, Poland, not Rumania, was *"the big apple in the barrel* and we should concentrate on that." The analogy obviously implied that one rotten apple could spoil all the others. On April 1 Roosevelt gravely warned Stalin that the Soviet plan could not be accepted. On April 5 Averell Harriman, U.S. ambassador to Russia, insisted to FDR that Stalin must not be allowed to establish "totalitarianism," for "unless we are prepared to live in a Soviet-dominated world, we must use our economic power to assist countries naturally friendly to us."[16] Writing to Churchill about the crisis the next day, Roosevelt referred to yet another weapon: "Our armies will in a very few days be in a position that will permit us to become 'tougher' than has heretofore appeared advantageous to the war effort."[17]

Within a week Roosevelt was dead. The new President, Harry S

[15]Daily Staff Summary, March 1, March 19, March 28, 1945, Lot File, NA, RG 59.
[16]"Record," volumes III, IV, 11–17 March 1945. Papers of Edward Stettinius, University of Virginia Library, Charlottesville. Italics in original. "Special Information for the President," from Stettinius, April 5, 1945, Lot File 53 D 444, NA, RG 59.
[17]Roosevelt to Churchill, April 6, 1945. In Francis L. Loewenheim, Harold D. Langley, and Manfred Jonas, eds., *Roosevelt and Churchill* (New York, 1975), p. 705.

Truman, inherited a decayed alliance. FDR had not discussed foreign policy (or much else) with him. As Vice President, Truman referred to himself as a "political eunuch." But his affection for Russia had not noticeably increased since 1941. After Roosevelt appeared before Congress to put a good face on the difficulties at Yalta, journalists asked Truman what he thought of the speech. "One of the greatest ever given," he replied—and then joined them in laughter.[18]

Truman entered the White House a highly insecure man. ("I felt like the moon, the stars, and all the planets had fallen on me," he told reporters.) And he held the world's most responsible job in a world that was changing radically. Truman tried to compensate for his insecurity in several ways. First, he was extremely jealous of his presidential powers and deeply suspicious of anyone who challenged those powers. Truman made decisions rapidly not only because that was his character but also because he determined "the buck stopped" at his desk. There would be no more sloppy administration or strong, freewheeling bureaucrats as in FDR's later years.

Second, and more dangerously, Truman was determined that these decisions would not be tagged as "appeasement." He would be as tough as the toughest. After only twenty-four hours in the White House, the new President confidently informed his secretary of state, "We must stand up to the Russians," and he implied "We had been too easy with them."[19] In foreign-policy discussions during the next two weeks, Truman interrupted his advisers to assure them he would certainly be "tough."

His determination was reinforced when he listened most closely to such advisers as Harriman, Leahy, and Secretary of the Navy James Forrestal, who urged him to take a hard line. Warning of a "barbarian invasion of Europe," Harriman declared that postwar cooperation with the Soviets, especially economically, must depend on their agreement to open Poland and Eastern Europe. In a decisive meeting on April 23, Secretary of War Henry Stimson argued with Harriman. Stimson declared that peace must never be threatened by an issue such as Poland, for free elections there were impossible, Russia held total control, and Stalin was "not likely to yield . . . in substance."[20]

---

[18]Margaret Truman, *Harry S Truman* (New York, 1973), pp. 220–222.
[19]"Private Calendar Notes, 4/13/45," Box 224, Stettinius Papers.
[20]Diary, April 23, 1945. Papers of Henry Stimson, Yale University Library, New Haven, Conn.

Stimson was not an amateur; he had been a respected Wall Street lawyer and distinguished public servant for forty years, including a term as Herbert Hoover's secretary of state.

But Truman dismissed Stimson's advice, accepted Harriman's, and later that day berated Soviet Foreign Minister Molotov "in words of one syllable" for breaking the Yalta agreements on Poland. Truman demanded that the Soviets agree to a "new" (not merely "reorganized") Polish government. An astonished Molotov replied, "I have never been talked to like that in my life." "Carry out your agreements," Truman supposedly retorted, "and you won't get talked to like that."[21]

The next day Stalin rejected Truman's demand, observing that it was contrary to the Yalta agreement. The dictator noted that "Poland borders with the Soviet Union, what [sic] cannot be said of Great Britain and the United States." After all, Stalin continued, the Soviets do not "lay claim to interference" in Belgium and Greece where the Americans and British made decisions without consulting the Russians.[22] In June Truman reluctantly accepted a compromise when Stalin included several more pro-Western Poles in the government. Americans hoped that political recognition of the new regime would allow them to use their economic power to open Poland "to a policy of equal opportunity in trade, investments and access to sources of information."[23] But the Poles refused to open the door to the dollar. Stimson had been correct. Truman's toughness had only stiffened Russian determination to control Poland.

An "iron fence" was falling around Eastern Europe, Churchill blurted out to Stalin in mid-1945. "All fairy-tales," the Soviet leader blandly replied. But it was partly true. The crises over Rumania and Poland only raised higher the fence around those two nations. In other areas, however, the Soviet approach varied. A Russian-sponsored election in Hungary produced a noncommunist government. In Bulgaria the Soviet-conducted elections satisfied British ob-

---

[21]Harry S Truman, *Memoirs, Volume One* (Garden City, N.Y., 1955), p. 82. This precise exchange was possibly created by Truman's imagination. These words are not reported on the official records of the conversation. They doubtless suggest, nevertheless, the tone of what Truman did say.

[22]*FRUS, 1945*, V (Washington, 1967): 263–264.

[23]*FRUS: The Conference of Berlin*, I (Washington, 1960): 262–264; "Memorandum for the President," June 27, 1945, Lot File 53 D 444, NA, RG 59.

servers, if not Americans. Stalin agreed to an independent, noncommunist regime in Finland if the Finns would follow a foreign policy friendly to Russia. An "iron fence" by no means encircled all of Eastern Europe. There was still room to bargain if each side wished to avoid a confrontation over the remaining areas.

But the bargaining room was limited. Stalin's doctrine and his determination that Russia would not again be invaded from the west greatly narrowed his diplomatic options. So too did the tremendous devastation of the war. Rapid rebuilding under communism required security, required access to resources in Eastern and Central Europe, and continued tight control over the Russian people. The experience of war was indelible. Russians viewed almost everything in their lives through their "searing experience of World War II," as one psychologist has phrased it.[24] The conflict had destroyed 1700 towns and 70,000 villages and left 25 million homeless. Twenty million died; 600,000 starved to death at the single siege of Leningrad.

During those terrible years Stalin had shrewdly asked his countrymen not to sacrifice themselves for communism (in whose name, after all, millions had been executed or placed in Siberian prisons during the 1930s), but for "Mother Russia." Little evidence exists, however, that Stalin privately changed his own peculiar brand of Marxist-Leninist doctrine. This was crucial, for all Soviet leaders cloaked their policies with this doctrine, using it not only in determining foreign policy but also in rationalizing their own power and in silencing internal dissent. To outside observers, therefore, doctrine acted as a weather vane; once officials decided upon policy, they publicly justified it with appropriate doctrine, and the doctrinal changes indicated the policy changes.

Stalin's doctrine during the spring of 1945 differed little from the views he had uttered about Western "imperialists" in 1939. The wartime alliance apparently did not dent his outlook, or if it did the Western attempts to open Eastern Europe rekindled his earlier fears. Consistency of Soviet doctrine also resulted from the remarkably stable membership of the politburo (the policymaking body of the Com-

---

[24]Ralph K. White, "Images in the Context of International Conflict." In Herbert C. Kelman, ed., *International Behavior* (New York, 1965), p. 271.

DIVIDED GERMANY IN A DIVIDED EUROPE, 1946

Former frontiers, 1937

Annexed by Russia, 1939–1945

States which became Communist, 1945 to 1948

The Iron Curtain from 1948

● Moscow

U. S. S. R.

OCCUPIED BY POLAND

(Formerly Germany)

POLAND

RUSSIAN ZONE

Berlin

AIR ROUTE

Bremen

AIR ROUTE

CZECHOSLOVAKIA

BRITISH ZONE

Frankfurt

U.S. ZONE

Bonn

FRENCH ZONE

NETHERLANDS

LUX.

BELGIUM

FRANCE

SWITZERLAND

U.S. ZONE

U.S. Zone

British Zone

French Zone

Occupied by Poland

Russian Zone

FINLAND

Leningrad

NORWAY

SWEDEN

ESTONIA

LATVIA

LITHUANIA

Pinsk

DENMARK

Hamburg

Berlin

E. GERMANY

Warsaw

POLAND

Frankfurt

W. GERMANY

CZECHOSLOVAKIA

Vienna

Budapest

GREAT BRITAIN

London

NETHERLANDS

BELGIUM

Bonn

LUXEM.

Paris●

FRANCE

SWITZ

AUSTRIA

HUNGARY

ROMANIA

Bucharest

Belgrade

YUGOSLAVIA

BULGARIA

Sofia

ITALY

Rome●

ALBANIA

GREECE

TURKEY

Athens

Communist activity 1946–1949

SPAIN

Madrid●

PORTUGAL

English Channel

munist party's Central Committee). The politburo's membership in 1945 almost exactly resembled that of 1939 when the Nazi-Soviet pact was signed. The leadership's view of Western democracy, capitalist encirclement, the inevitability of further capitalist wars, the sources of imperialism, and the impossibility of disarmament evidently changed little between 1939 and 1945. In April 1945 Stalin told fellow communists that another war was only a matter of time. The Germans "will recover, and very quickly," he warned. "Give them twelve to fifteen years and they'll be on their feet again. And that is why the unity of the Slavs is important."[25]

During 1945 the triumphs of the Red Army and the growing tension over Eastern Europe led Stalin to tighten his control over Soviet life. Special schools opened to teach the dictator's doctrine; "Mother Russia" gave way to "Glorious Stalin." The Red Army received special attention. It had been exposed to corrupting "bourgeois" influence in Central Europe and had grown too rapidly for Stalin to impose rigid political control. He raised his close associate Lavrenti Beria, chief of the dreaded secret police, to the rank of marshal of the Red Army and promoted himself to generalissimo. Army officers, holding the only power capable of challenging Stalin, slowly disappeared from public view. By the summer of 1945 his authority was unquestioned.[26]

Some scholars have examined Stalin's acts of 1928–1945, pronounced them the work of a "paranoid," and concluded that the United States had no chance to avoid a cold war since it was dealing with a man who was mentally ill. That interpretation neatly avoids confronting the complex causes of the Cold War but is wholly insufficient to explain those causes. However Stalin acted inside Russia, where he had total control, in his foreign policy during 1941–1946 he displayed a realism, a careful calculation of forces, and a diplomatic finesse that undercut any attempt to explain away his actions as para-

[25]Djilas, *Conversations with Stalin*, p. 114; John S. Curtiss and Alex Inkeles, "Marxism in the U.S.S.R.—The Recent Revival," *Political Science Quarterly*, XLI (September 1946): 349–364; Frederick C. Barghoorn, "Great Russian Messianism in Postwar Soviet Ideology," in Ernest J. Simmons, ed., *Continuity and Change in Russian and Soviet Thought* (Cambridge, Mass., 1955), p. 541. A fine study of this problem is Paul Marantz, "The Soviet Union and the Western World: A Study in Doctrinal Change, 1917–1964," unpublished doctoral dissertation, Harvard University, 1971.

[26]Alexander Werth, *Russia at War* (New York, 1964), pp. 943–945; Raymond L. Garthoff, *Soviet Military Policy, A Historical Analysis* (New York, 1966), pp. 42–44.

noid.[27] If he and other Soviets were suspicious of the West, they were realistic, not paranoid: the West had poured thousands of troops into Russia between 1917 and 1920, refused to cooperate with the Soviets during the 1930s, tried to turn Hitler against Stalin in 1938, reneged on promises about the second front, and in 1945 tried to penetrate areas Stalin deemed crucial to Soviet security.

American diplomats who frequently saw Stalin understood this background. In January 1945 Harriman told the State Department, "The overriding consideration in Soviet foreign policy is the preoccupation with 'security,' as Moscow sees it." The problem was that Americans did not see "security" the same way. They believed their security required an open world, including an open Eastern Europe. No Western diplomat has been found who declared in 1945–1947 that Stalin showed signs of mental illness. Some actually argued that hard-line "boys" within the politburo forced him to be tougher with the West than he wished.[28] That was inaccurate. Stalin set policy and the policy was consistent. Only timing and tactics varied.

In dealing with foreign Communist parties, Stalin's priority was not world revolution but, once again, Russian security and his own personal power. In 1943 he had made a goodwill gesture by disbanding the Comintern (the organization which directed overseas Communist parties from headquarters in Moscow). It was only a gesture, however, for Stalin determined to control these parties for his own purposes. In 1944–1945 he ordered the powerful French Communist party to cooperate with the Western Allies rather than attempt to seize power. Wanting above all else Anglo-American acquiescence to his acts in Eastern Europe, Stalin restrained the French communists before they became dangerously overambitious.

Similarly, a leading French communist, Jacques Duclos, blasted the American Communist party in the spring of 1945 for moving too close to the New Deal, and ordered it to create a separate identity—

---

[27]Adam B. Ulam, *Stalin* (New York, 1973), pp. 685–686. The most popular expression of Stalin's supposed paranoia is in Arthur Schlesinger's essay, most easily found in Lloyd C. Gardner, Arthur Schlesinger, Jr., and Hans J. Morgenthau, *The Origins of the Cold War* (Waltham, Mass., 1970), pp. 72–73.

[28]*FRUS: Yalta*, pp. 450–451; "Mr. Macmillan to Foreign Office," 21 March 1945, FO 371 N3097/1545/38, Public Record Office, London; *FRUS: Berlin*, I: 13. For new evidence on the internal Soviet debate, 1943–1945, see Vladimir O. Pechtanov, *The Big Three After World War II*. Cold War International History Project, Woodrow Wilson Center (Washington, D.C., 1995), pp. 1–25.

but then advised working within the American political system. "Nothing prevents a Communist Party from adapting its electoral tactics to the requirements of a given political situation," observed Duclos. The State Department, however, informed Truman that Duclos's advice required the government "to treat the American Communist movement as a potential fifth column." Traditional American fear of communist ideology reinforced the administration's dislike of Stalin's actions in Eastern Europe. Such fear at home was hardly warranted. Fifty thousand, or half the membership in the U.S. Communist party's Political Association, left the group by 1946.[29] Ironically, Americans began their feverish search for communists at the same time the Communist party had to begin its own search for members.

By mid-1945 Stalin's policies were brutally consistent, while Truman's were confused. The confusion became obvious when the United States, opposed to a sphere of interest in Europe, strengthened its own sphere in the Western Hemisphere. Unlike its policies elsewhere, however, the State Department did not use economic weapons. The economic relationship with Latin America and Canada could simply be assumed. During the war these two areas had fed cheap raw materials to the U.S. industry. After the struggle, and despite promises to the contrary, Washington neglected its neighbors while sending goods and money to rebuild Europe.

But Latin America was not neglected politically. A young assistant secretary of state for Latin American affairs, Nelson Rockefeller, and Senator Arthur Vandenberg (Republican from Michigan) devised the political means to keep the Americas solidly within Washington's sphere. Their instrument was Article 51 of the U.N. Charter. This provision was largely formulated by Rockefeller and Vandenberg at the San Francisco conference that founded the United Nations in the spring of 1945. The article allowed for collective self-defense through special regional organizations to be created outside the United Nations but within the principles of the charter. In this way, regional organizations would escape Russian vetoes in the Security Council. The United States could control its own sphere without Soviet interference.

[29]*Daily Worker*, May 24, 1945, pp. 7–9; *FRUS: Berlin*, I: 267–282; Joseph R. Starobin, *American Communism in Crisis, 1943–1957* (Cambridge, Mass., 1972), pp. 74–120.

Intimately acquainted with Latin America because of his family's investments (especially in Venezuelan oil), Rockefeller wanted Russia excluded so that North and South America could be economically integrated and developed without outside interference. He also understood that unless the United States "operated with a solid group in this hemisphere" it "could not do what we wanted to do on the world front."[30] Vandenberg had other reasons. Although he was known as a 1930s "isolationist" who became an "internationalist" in 1945, it is questionable how far he actually turned.

The portly, white-haired senator exemplified the truism that Americans tend to become political "isolationists" when they cannot dominate international affairs and "internationalists" politically when they can. (They have been economic and cultural "internationalists" since the seventeenth century.) Rarely have Americans been prepared to bargain or to compromise their freedom of action. They have joined such organizations as the United Nations when they could control them. Throughout the war Vandenberg gradually left his earlier political "isolationism" because he believed the United States would have the power to internationalize the Atlantic Charter freedoms. These principles, he proclaimed in early 1945, "sail with our fleets. They fly with our eagles. They sleep with our martyred dead." And they must be had by all, including Eastern Europeans. But the Yalta agreements shocked him. Terming the Polish settlement "awful," he doubted that the United Nations, burdened with the Soviet veto in the Security Council, could enforce the Atlantic Charter. The Western Hemisphere could nevertheless be protected. When he and Rockefeller finished with Article 51, they thought they had obtained the best of both worlds: exclusive American power in the New and the right to exert American power in the Old.

The obvious confusion in that approach was pinpointed by Secretary of War Stimson when he condemned Americans who were "anxious to hang on to exaggerated views of the Monroe Doctrine and at the same time butt into every question that comes up in Central Europe." Almost alone, Stimson argued for an alternative policy. Through bilateral U.S.-U.S.S.R. negotiations (and not negotiations

---

[30]David Green, *The Containment of Latin America* (Chicago, 1971), p. 234.

within the United Nations, where the Russians would be defensive and disagreeable because the Americans controlled a majority), Stimson hoped each side could agree that the other should have its own security spheres. But as he had lost the argument over Poland, so Stimson lost this argument. Truman was prepared to bargain very little. He might not get 100 percent, the President told advisers, but he would get 85 percent. Even in Rumania, where the Russians were particularly sensitive, the State Department secretly determined in August 1945, "It is our intention to attain a position of equality with the Russians." When, however, the Americans pressed, the Soviets only tightened their control of Rumania.[31]

Not even Stimson, however, could suggest a solution for Germany, the biggest problem of all. Throughout 1943–1945 Roosevelt had wavered between virtually destroying the nation (he even once mentioned mass castration) and allowing Germany to reindustrialize under tight controls. Stimson and Secretary of State Cordell Hull fought for the latter policy. They believed world recovery depended on a strong, industrialized Europe. That required at its heart, as it had for a century, a rebuilt Germany. Roosevelt—typically—never made a clear choice.

For his part, Stalin agreed when Roosevelt suggested dismemberment, but the Russian cared more about taking reparations (in the form of industrial machines and goods) out of Germany. In this way he could rebuild Russian industry while killing off any possibility that Germany could again threaten Russia in the foreseeable future. Stalin also insisted upon territorial changes. He wanted the Poles to have part of eastern Germany as compensation for the land they were being forced to give Russia in eastern Poland. At first Churchill and Roosevelt had not objected to this demand, but by 1945 they opposed the new German-Polish boundary. They rightly feared this simply masked communist control of eastern Germany.

At the Potsdam conference, held outside captured Berlin in July 1945, Truman and Secretary of State James Byrnes offered Stalin a deal. The West would de facto recognize the new Polish-German boundary. The Russians could also take reparations out of their own

---

[31]"Memorandum for the Secretary," August 20, 1945, Lot File, Staff Officers' Summary, NA, RG 59.

occupation zone of eastern Germany, an area primarily agricultural. But in the three Western occupation zones (controlled by the Americans, British, and French) the Soviets could have only 25 percent of the reparations; about half of those would have to be paid for with foodstuffs from the Russian zone. With considerable grumbling, Stalin accepted the deal. The United States had finally made the choice: it would not rush to dismember Germany but would hold tightly to the nation's western industrial heartland and methodically rebuild the shattered German economy. Of course there was one other implication. An economic division of Germany could lead to a political division. The deal laid the basis for an eastern and a western Germany.

Although Truman did not obtain his "85 percent" at Potsdam, en route home he received the news that a weapon of unimaginable power, the atomic bomb, had obliterated Hiroshima, Japan, on August 6. Eighty thousand had died. This was some 20,000 fewer than had been killed by a massive American fire bombing of Tokyo earlier in the year, but it was the newly opened secret of nature embodied in a single bomb that was overwhelming. Roosevelt had initiated the atomic project in 1941. He had decided at least by late 1944 not to share information about the bomb with the Soviets, even though he knew Stalin had learned about the project. By the summer of 1945 this approach, and the growing Soviet-American confrontation in Eastern Europe, led Truman and Byrnes to discuss securing "further *quid pro quos*" in Rumania, Poland, and Asia from Stalin before the Russians could share the secret of atomic energy.

Truman and his advisers, however, never figured out how to use the bomb to obtain concessions they wanted from the Soviets. At Potsdam the President had used the cool approach. After hearing that the test atomic device had worked at Los Alamos, New Mexico, Truman nonchalantly informed Stalin that the United States possessed a new destructive weapon, but did not mention what it was. Stalin instantly understood but acted so nonchalant himself that Truman was uncertain whether the Soviet leader grasped the President's remark. Stalin, however, understood so well that he immediately instructed the chief of the supersecret Soviet atomic project to speed up the work. The chief responded that he lacked both electrical power and the equipment needed to clear forests for the laboratories. Stalin quickly ordered electricity used by civilian areas to be switched to the nuclear project, then he sent two tank divisions to clear the forests. Just hours after the atomic age began, its arms race was accelerating.[32]

Truman dropped the bomb on Hiroshima for at least three reasons. First, the weapon had been developed with the expectation that it would be used. The primary target had been the Nazis, but when Germany surrendered in May 1945, the target automatically became Japan. Given the ferocious fighting of early 1945, when in months Americans suffered more casualties in the Pacific than they had during the previous years of warfare in that theater, Truman's more difficult decision would have been *not* to use the bomb. Second, the planned late-1945 invasion of Japan would be costly. Using the bomb would reduce, if not remove, the need for paying such costs in American blood. Third, a diplomatic object was apparent. Stalin had promised at Yalta to invade Japanese strongholds in Manchuria approximately three months after the war with Germany ended—that is, sometime in August. In early 1945 U.S. officials had been much relieved that the Soviets would help fight the Japanese. By midsummer, however, Truman and Byrnes no longer wanted Stalin's armies too close to Japan. On August 8 the Soviets declared war on the Japanese and invaded Manchuria. The next day a second atomic bomb destroyed the city of Nagasaki. If reasons existed for laying the first bomb on Hiroshima, few observers since have found reasons for dropping the second—unless the reasons were that Truman simply did nothing to stop it (he did then order no more to be dropped without his express instructions) and that the Soviet invasion, in the eyes of top U.S. officials, required a quick Japanese surrender.

On August 10, 1945, the Emperor overruled his military and Japan began peace negotiations. After several more heavy U.S. Air Force conventional raids took thousands of Japanese lives, Tokyo and

---

[32]This and the following two paragraphs are drawn from Anatoly Dobrynin, *In Confidence* (New York, 1995), p. 23; Martin J. Sherwin, "The Atomic Bomb and the Origins of the Cold War . . . ," *American Historical Review,* LXXVIII (October 1973): 945–968; Barton Bernstein, "The Atomic Bombings Reconsidered," *Foreign Affairs,* 74 (January 1995), pp. 135–152; the collection of important essays in *Diplomatic History,* 19 (Spring 1995), pp. 197–365; and Gar Alperovitz, *The Decision to Use the Atomic Bomb and the Architecture of an American Myth* (New York, 1995), especially pp. 303–311, 484–489. The material in these three paragraphs is also based on chapter 7 of Walter LaFeber, *The Clash: United States Relations with Japan from the 1850s to the Present* (New York, 1997), where further citations are listed.

Washington worked out surrender terms during August 14–15. Those terms could probably have been settled earlier if, as Stimson urged, Truman had said that the Japanese Emperor could remain (although shorn of his divine status). Byrnes, however, warned that if Truman made such a compromise, the American people would damn the President. In the end, the President accepted the retention of the Emperor. That acceptance and the Soviet declaration of war on August 8 largely convinced the Emperor and his advisers—who greatly feared that the armies of their historic enemy, Russia, might impose a communist system on their home islands if the war continued—to make peace. Soviet troops were never able to move into the main Japanese home islands. Stalin vigorously protested when Truman excluded the Russians from any real power in occupied Japan. The Japanese, including their Emperor, however, were going to be subject only to U.S. wishes.

The bomb "is the greatest thing in history," Truman boasted. Nor was he sorry he had used it. Noting the "unwarranted attack on Pearl Harbor," the President explained to a journalist, "When you deal with a beast you have to treat him as a beast."[33] On August 19 Admiral Leahy announced over national radio that the United States possessed a more powerful navy than any other two fleets in existence, the best-equipped ground force in the world, the "largest and most efficient air force," and "with our British allies, the secret of the world's most fearsome weapon." Clearly, Americans held most of the high cards as World War II ended. That same month Secretary of State Byrnes publicly announced the stakes for which the game would be played.

"Our international policies and our domestic policies are inseparable," he began. "Our foreign relations inevitably affect employment in the United States. Prosperity and depression in the United States just as inevitably affect our relations with the other nations of the world." Byrnes expressed his "clear conviction that a durable peace cannot be built on an economic foundation of exclusive blocs . . . and economic warfare." Specifically he warned: "In many countries . . . our political and economic creed is in conflict with ideologies which reject both of these principles." Byrnes concluded: "To the

---

[33]Quoted in Lisle A. Rose, *Dubious Victory: The United States and the End of World War II* (Kent State, 1973), p. 363.

extent that we are able to manage our domestic affairs successfully, we shall win converts to our creed in every land."[34] John Winthrop had not expressed it more clearly 300 years earlier at Massachusetts Bay. Only now the City Upon a Hill, as Winthrop called it, was industrialized, internationalized—and held the atomic bomb.

But the Soviets refused to budge. Byrnes and Molotov agreed on little at a Foreign Ministers conference in the autumn of 1945. Inside Russia the threat of "capitalist encirclement" was trumpeted. Ominous rumors spread that Stalin would respond by further regimenting the Soviets with more five-year plans. Stimson, about to retire from the War Department, made one final attempt to stop an East-West confrontation. In a September 11 memorandum to Truman, Stimson prophesied "that it would not be possible to use our possession of the atomic bomb as a direct lever to produce the change" desired inside Eastern Europe. If Soviet-American negotiations continue with "this weapon rather ostentatiously on our hip, their suspicions and their distrust of our purposes and motives will increase." He again urged direct, bilateral talks with Stalin to formulate control of the bomb and to write a general peace settlement.[35] Stimson's advice was especially notable because several months before he himself had hoped to use the bomb to pry the Soviets out of Eastern Europe. Now he had changed his mind.

Truman again turned Stimson's advice aside. A month later the President delivered a speech larded with references to America's monopoly of atomic power, then attacked Russia's grip on Eastern Europe. Molotov quickly replied that peace could not be reconciled with an armaments race advocated by "zealous partisans of the imperialist policy." In this connection, he added, "We should mention the discovery of . . . the atomic bomb."[36]

With every utterance and every act, the wartime alliance further disintegrated. Stalin understood and regimented the Russian people for the struggle. Americans did not yet understand. Public and congressional opinion followed, not shaped, presidential and State De-

[34]Raymond Dennett and Robert K. Turner, eds., *Documents on American Foreign Relations,* VIII (1945–1946) (Princeton, 1948): 601–602.

[35]See Henry Stimson and McGeorge Bundy, *On Active Service in Peace and War* (New York, 1948), pp. 638–650.

[36]*Department of State Bulletin,* XIII (October 28, 1945): 653–656; V. Molotov, *U.S.S.R. Foreign Policy* (Shanghai, 1946), pp. 7–8.

partment policy. Harriman and other officials had defined the issues and called for a tough policy before Congress or its constituents knew about an "iron fence." In this, as in most foreign-policy issues, the executive branch could create a public opinion for policies it believed were in the national interest.[37] American interest was not threatened by a possible Soviet invasion of Western Europe. As the State Department informed Truman in June 1945, the Russians "are not too greatly concerned about developments in Western Europe so long as the Western European countries do not show signs of ganging up on them."[38]

A U.S. intelligence report spelled out Stalin's military problems in a stunning analysis of November 1945. The report listed Soviet military weaknesses and "the time required to remedy" them so that the U.S.S.R. would be "willing to risk a major armed conflict":[39]

1. War losses in manpower and industry (15 years)
2. Lack of technicians (5–10 years)
3. Lack of a Strategic Air Force (5–10 years)
4. Lack of a modern navy (15–20 years for a war involving major naval operations)
5. Poor condition of railway and military transportation systems and equipment (10 years)
6. Vulnerability of Soviet oil, rail, and vital industrial centers to long-range bombers
7. Lack of atomic bomb (5–10 years, possibly less)
8. Resistance in occupied countries (5 years or less)
9. Quantitative military weakness in the Far East—especially naval (15–20 years)

The report concluded that Russia would be unlikely to chance a major war for at least fifteen years. Since half the transport of the standing Soviet army was horse-drawn (and would remain so until 1950), fifteen years seemed a safe estimate.

Thus at the outset of the Cold War, Truman's problem was certainly not the threat of Soviet invasion of Asia or Europe. Nor was it

[37]For a good analysis of this general problem, see Bernard Cohen, *The Public's Impact on Foreign Policy* (New York, 1973), especially pp. 155–156 on Acheson.
[38]*FRUS: Berlin,* I: 264.
[39]A superb analysis is in Matthew A. Evangelista, "Stalin's Postwar Army Reappraised," *International Security,* VII (Winter 1982–1983): 121–122.

American public opinion. The problem lay in Eastern Europe, where Stalin militarily roped off the region—and thus directly challenged the Atlantic Charter principles and the growing belief in Washington that the American system could only work globally. The division of Germany was set. Poland and Eastern Europe sank behind an "iron fence." The question now became this: how would the world's most powerful nation respond to these frustrations of its dreams for the postwar world? And there was a related question: when they responded, how would Americans use their tremendous power—not least their new atomic bomb? Some recalled the words of the famous nineteenth-century science-fiction writer Jules Verne: "The end of the earth will be when some enormous boiler . . . shall explode and blow up our globe. And [the Americans] are great boilermakers."[40]

[40]Paul Boyer, *By the Bomb's Early Light* (New York, 1985), p. 248.

CHAPTER 2

Only Two Declarations of Cold War (1946)

In late 1945 General George Patton, as heroic a figure to some Americans in the 1990s as in the 1940s, addressed eight-year-olds in a Sunday school class. "You are the soldiers and nurses of the next war. There will be another war," Patton assured the children. "There has always been."[1]

During 1946 war became more imminent than even Patton had expected. In Manchuria, Iran, Turkey, and Europe, the American and Russian military forces confronted each other. Several times they approached flash point. The crisis did not develop quite so far in China, but that situation was nevertheless critical, for the United States was losing a position in the western Pacific won during the war with American blood.

Harry Truman determined to maintain that position. "The future foreign interests of the United States will be in the Western Hemisphere and in the Pacific," he told an adviser in September 1945. The President believed Asian interests depended upon strengthening the Nationalist Chinese regime of Chiang Kai-shek. Chiang was to replace Japan as the stabilizing force in the area. And then there would also be economic benefits. By working through Chiang, Washington officials believed they could develop not only the great China market but other Asian countries as well. For more than a century Yankee tradesmen had pursued the mirage of that market. It now finally seemed real. A billion Asian customers would be of considerable help in avoiding another economic depression. John Carter Vincent, the State Department's expert on China, encouraged restoration of postwar trade "with all the speed we can generate. We are endeavoring to get

---

[1]Quoted in L. Wittner, *Rebels Against War . . . 1941–1960* (New York, 1969), p. 98.

businessmen back into China for their sake and for China's sake."[2] Whether a China could be created that would be both strong and friendly to Western interests was a question the West had avoided facing for a century.

This ambitious policy banged immediately into a major obstacle. Chiang's control was being chipped away by communist forces led by Mao Ze-dong. Although outnumbered five to one in 1945, Mao's army had increased dramatically since 1935 when Chiang had isolated it in northern China. At the end of World War II, the communists controlled one-fifth of China and more than 105 million people. Chiang's regime, meanwhile, was shot through with corruption, squandered more than a billion dollars of American aid, and drove the peasants (who comprised four-fifths of the population) into Mao's hands. Of special importance, the Nationalists could not control a roaring inflation that shot prices up some 2000 percent between 1937 and 1945, nearly wiping out the middle classes.

Intent on preventing a Communist China, Roosevelt, then Truman, developed a policy that first aimed at separating Mao from the Soviets. In 1945 FDR obtained Stalin's promise to deal with Chiang, not Mao. In return for this pledge and his promise to enter the war against Japan, Stalin received substantial territorial concessions: the lease of Port Arthur as a Soviet naval base, internationalization of the port of Dairen, joint Sino-Soviet operation of the Chinese Eastern and South Manchurian railroads, possession of southern Sakhalin and the Kurile Islands (then held by Japan), and a plebiscite to be held in Outer Mongolia (which in October 1945 voted under Soviet supervision to become independent of China and move closer to Russia by the amazing score of 483,291 to 0). Chiang and Stalin agreed to most of these terms in a Treaty of Friendship and Alliance. The State Department and such periodicals as Henry Luce's *Time-Life* publications, which kept close watch over American interests in Asia, cheered the treaty.

Only Mao was bitter. He later recalled that "Stalin tried to prevent the Chinese Revolution by saying . . . we must collaborate with Chiang." Soviet policy was clear. Stalin preferred a chaotic, divided China that would not threaten Russia rather than a united China

---

[2]"Seymour to Foreign Office," 24 November 1945, FO 371 F11517/36/10, Public Record Office, London.

JAPAN, KOREA, CHINA, and RUSSIA AFTER WORLD WAR II

PACIFIC OCEAN

KURILE ISLANDS
(To Russia)

N. SAKHALIN

S. SAKHALIN
(To Russia)

JAPAN
(controlled by the U.S.)

Tokyo

Hiroshima

Nagasaki

Vladivostok

(Soviet Naval Base)

Divided by U.S.–U.S.S.R.
agreement

—38°

KOREA

U. S. S. R.

Trans-Siberian Railroad

Joint U.S.S.R.–
Chinese
control

Chinese Eastern Railroad

MANCHURIA
(Chinese)

Harbin

South Manchurian Railroad

Port
Arthur
Dairen

Shanghai

OUTER MONGOLIA
(Russian)

(Chinese–Russian Naval Base)

Peking

CHINA

under either Chiang or Mao. As head of a giant nation, Mao could particularly challenge Stalin within the communist world.[3]

With Mao's regime apparently isolated, the State Department moved to the next goal: ending the civil war by forcing Mao and Chiang into a coalition that Chiang could control. But Chiang refused to be locked into the same room with the communists. He had more direct methods. When asked about the danger of Russian-Chinese communist cooperation, Chiang replied "there is nothing to worry about" because he "was going to liquidate Communists."[4] Knowing that approach would not work, Truman pressured Chiang to accept the coalition idea.

Chiang-Mao talks broke down over whose army would control Manchuria, a key industrial area occupied by Japan since 1931. In the autumn of 1945 the problem became more complicated and ominous when Russian armies moved into Manchuria to disarm the Japanese, then remained to carry out what officials on the scene termed "scientific looting" of industrial machinery for the rebuilding of Russian industry.[5] Mao and Chiang raced to control Manchuria. Mao won, despite Truman's attempt to help Chiang by keeping Japanese soldiers in place against the communists until Chiang's troops could move into position. The President even dispatched 50,000 American soldiers to help Chiang push northward. Soon 100,000 Americans were in China.

With Chiang's position eroding, Truman sent General of the Army George Marshall on his famous mission to reconcile Chiang and Mao in order, in the general's words, to avert "the tragic consequences of a divided China and of a probable Russian reassumption of power in Manchuria, the combined effect of this resulting in the defeat or loss of the major purpose of our war in the Pacific."[6] Few Americans dissented from Marshall's analyses of the potential Russian danger.

By late February 1946 Marshall had worked out an agreement, including a cease-fire. This was the closest the United States or the Chinese themselves would come to a peaceful settlement. By mid-April

---

[3]Seymour Topping, *Journey Between Two Chinas* (New York, 1972), p. 54.
[4]Daily Staff Summary, February 26, 1945, Lot File, NA, RG 59.
[5]"Memorandum for the President," September 17, 1945, OSS Memoranda for the President, Donovan Chronological File, Box 15, Truman Library.
[6]Quoted in Tang Tsou, *America's Failure in China, 1941–1950* (Chicago, 1963), pp. 355–356.

the arrangement had collapsed. Marshall later placed much blame on Chiang for this disaster, since the latter insisted on taking Manchuria by force. The American, however, also noted that toward the end of the negotiations the communists were unwilling "to make a fair compromise," particularly on the disposition of their army.[7]

Believing he could defeat the communists militarily and that the United States had no alternative but to provide him with all the arms he required, Chiang refused Marshall's suggestions for further compromise. The Chinese leader sadly miscalculated. As the State Department had feared, Mao's armies obtained a treasure when, in March and April 1946, Soviet occupation troops in Manchuria suddenly withdrew, leaving behind vast stores of Japanese arms and equipment for the communist forces. Chiang launched a major military offensive into Manchuria. At first he was successful, then his army overstretched its supply lines. By late 1946 Mao was successfully counterattacking.

As the military tide began to turn, even worse lay in wait for Americans. They would suffer for their involvement with Chiang. American officials warned that "widespread resentment" by the Chinese people "which cannot be openly expressed is being turned almost entirely against the U.S." Even the American troops were being pressured to leave. It was a terrible dilemma. If the United States remained, it would be "an immediately available target . . . for . . . Chinese xenophobia." On the other hand, Chiang required American aid. "If we break" with him, a top White House adviser observed, "the result will be that we will have no friends in either of the Chinese factions and no friends in China."[8]

Marshall cut through to the core of the problem. If Americans tried to save Chiang they would "virtually [have] to take over the Chinese government. . . . It would involve the [United States] in a continuing commitment from which it would practically be impossible to withdraw" and could make China "an arena of international conflict."[9] Neither Truman nor Marshall would get sucked into that kind

[7]For Marshall's later assessment and hope for a liberal middle way for China, see Department of State, *U.S. Relations with China* (Washington, 1949), pp. 686–689.
[8]Daily Staff Summary, January 8, 1947, Lot File, NA, RG 59.
[9]Daily Staff Summary, January 8, 1947, Lot File, NA, RG 59; Leahy Diaries, Box 5, August 12, 1946, Leahy Papers; Akira Iriye, *The Cold War in Asia* (Englewood Cliffs, N.J., 1974), p. 166.

of war. The President tried to cover his retreat after late 1946 with a small aid program for Chiang, but Truman was pulling out of China. He and Marshall could only hope that the revolution would not be completed "for a long time."

Stalin shared that hope. Indeed, Truman could downgrade China precisely because the Russians had withdrawn from Manchuria and were behaving throughout Asia. On the other hand, viewing international events in the context of the American-Soviet confrontation forced Washington officials to give top priority to European and Middle Eastern affairs. As China dropped down the American priority list in 1946, these two elements—Washington's determination to counter all Soviet threats, and total commitment to keeping Western Europe within the American camp—fused and exploded into a dramatic crisis in the Middle East.

For nearly a century the Middle East had formed the lifeline of the British and French empires. More recently it provided the Western world with oil. American companies had moved into a dominating position in the petroleum industry. To protect this vital area, the British, Russians, and Americans had agreed in 1942 to occupy Iran jointly. They further agreed to withdraw six months after the conflict ended. Several times during the war Churchill and Roosevelt assured Stalin that Russia, which bordered Iran, would have its interests protected in the postwar settlement. By 1944, however, the State Department was developing a tough policy to fight Soviet claims.[10]

By early 1946 most of the British and American forces had withdrawn, but the Russians stalled. They demanded oil concessions approximating those obtained by the British. The Soviets then supported a revolt of the Azerbaijanian population in northern Iran. The State Department panicked. The Russians seemed on the move everywhere, a top official warned, not only in the east and west but through this "third barrier" in the south. They threatened to "sweep unimpeded across Turkey . . . into the Mediterranean and across Iran . . . into the Indian Ocean."[11]

Washington officials decided on a two-pronged policy. First they

---

[10]The best analysis is Mark Lytle, "American-Iranian Relations 1941–1947 and the Redefinition of National Security," unpublished doctoral dissertation, Yale University, 1973, especially chapters III–VI.
[11]*FRUS, 1946, Near East,* pp. 1–5.

IRAN, TURKEY, GREECE, and RUSSIA, 1946–1948

Oil Fields

SOVIET UNION

CASPIAN SEA

•Tehran

IRAN

Persian Gulf

Azerbaijan Province

IRAQ

SAUDI ARABIA

BLACK SEA

Istanbul

TURKEY

SYRIA

LEBANON

ISRAEL (1948)

JORDAN

EGYPT

Dardanelles

Athens

GREECE

MEDITERRANEAN SEA

YUGOSLAVIA

took the Iranian case to the United Nations. The opening session of the new Security Council was thus poisoned by a bitter exchange between the Soviets and Americans. Second, when Russian tanks rumbled toward the Iranian border in early March, Secretary of State James F. Byrnes smacked one fist into his other hand and declared, "Now we'll give it to them with both barrels." Byrnes sent a message to the Soviets that they must withdraw from the country. In late March Iran and Russia announced that the Red Army would leave and a joint Iranian-Soviet oil company would be formed subject to ratification of the Iranian Parliament (the Majlis). The Iranian army then put down the Azerbaijan revolt. Several months later the Majlis rejected the oil company. Russia had suffered a major diplomatic defeat.

Another setback quickly followed in Turkey. This crisis had grown from historic Russian-Turkish antipathy, Soviet determination to gain joint control of the strategic Dardanelles Straits (the key link between the Mediterranean and Soviet ports on the Black Sea), and Stalin's inherited Georgian trait of hating everything Turkish except tobacco. In early 1945 he revived an ancient Russian demand for partnership with the Turks to control the straits. Again, during the war FDR and Churchill had assured Stalin that Russia was "justified" in having access to the Mediterranean, particularly since Turkey had collaborated with Hitler.[12] And again, as in Iran, by 1945 the British and Americans had changed their minds. They were determined to keep the Soviets away from the Mediterranean.

Quiet diplomatic probing by both sides followed until August 1946, when Stalin sent a note to Turkey which Under Secretary of State Dean Acheson interpreted as a Soviet attempt to dominate Turkey, threaten Greece, and intimidate the remainder of the Middle East. Acheson advised a showdown with the Russians before the fall of Turkey led to the collapse of "the whole Near and Middle East," then even "India and China." Here, as in the Iranian crisis, American officials justified their policy on the basis of what would later be termed the "domino theory." This theory rested on the assumption that Stalin, like Hitler, was intent on unlimited conquest. That assumption was another vivid demonstration that using a false histor-

---

[12]Adam Ulam, *Expansion and Coexistence* (New York, 1968), pp. 430–431; "Record of Meeting at the Kremlin," 9 October 1944, PREM 3, 434/7, Public Record Office, London.

ical analogy is one of the most dangerous forms of argument. Soviet policy in 1946 and Hitler's ambitions of 1938 were not comparable. But few officials (or historians) wished to point that out at the start of the Cold War.

Harry Truman saw nothing wrong with Acheson's view. "We might as well find out whether the Russians were bent on world conquest now as in five or ten years," the President asserted.[13] So he informed the Soviets that Turkey would continue to be "primarily responsible" for the straits. The State Department then reinforced an American naval unit (including marines) which had been sailing in the Mediterranean since early spring. The *Franklin D. Roosevelt,* the most powerful American aircraft carrier, moved into the area. By the autumn of 1946 Soviet pressure on Turkey had eased. A tough Washington response had kept the dominoes upright.

Stalin probably believed that, because of its wartime sacrifices and geographic location, Russia had as much right to Iranian oil and control of the Dardanelles as any other power. Thwarted in these areas, in February 1946, Stalin brought charges in the Security Council against the British repression of the Greek rebellion and British and Dutch attempts to suppress revolution in Indonesia. The bitterest outburst occurred three months later at the Paris Foreign Ministers conference. Molotov gave the Soviet view of what was occurring:

> Nineteenth century imperialism may be dead in England, but there are new twentieth century tendencies. When Mr. Churchill calls for a new war and makes militant speeches on two continents, he represents the worst of 20th century imperialism. . . . Britain has troops in Greece, Palestine, Iraq, Indo-China and elsewhere. Russia has no troops outside of security zones and their lines of communication. This is different. We have troops only where provided by treaties. Thus we are in Poland, for example, as our Allies are in Belgium, France and Holland. I also recall that Egypt is a member of UNO [the United Nations]. She demands that British troops be withdrawn. Britain declines. . . . What shall we say of UNO when one member imposes its authority upon another? How long can such things go on?[14]

[13]James Forrestal, *The Forrestal Diaries,* Walter Millis, ed. (New York, 1951), p. 192; Thomas Paterson, *Soviet-American Confrontation* (Baltimore, 1973), pp. 192–193.
[14]Arthur H. Vandenberg, Jr., ed., *The Private Papers of Senator Vandenberg* (Boston, 1952), pp. 277–278.

During early 1946 Stalin and Churchill issued their declarations of Cold War. In an election speech of February 9, the Soviet dictator announced that Marxist-Leninist dogma remained valid, for "the unevenness of development of the capitalist countries" could lead to "violent disturbance" and the consequent splitting of the "capitalist world into two hostile camps and war between them. War was inevitable as long as capitalism existed. The Soviet people must prepare themselves for a replay of the 1930s by developing basic industry instead of consumer goods and, in all, making enormous sacrifices demanded in "three more Five-Year Plans, I should think, if not more."[15] There would be no peace, internally or externally. These words profoundly affected Washington. Supreme Court Justice William Douglas, one of the reigning American liberals, believed that Stalin's speech meant "The Declaration of World War III." The *New York Times* front-page story of the speech began by declaring that Stalin believed "the stage is set" for war.[16]

Winston Churchill delivered his views at Fulton, Missouri, on March 5. The former prime minister exalted American power with the plea that his listeners recognize that "God has willed" the United States, not "some Communist or neo-Fascist state" to have atomic bombs. To utilize the "breathing space" provided by these weapons, Churchill asked for "a fraternal association of the English-speaking peoples" operating under the principles of the United Nations, but not inside that organization, to reorder the world. This unilateral policy must be undertaken because "from Stettin in the Baltic to Trieste in the Adriatic, an iron curtain has descended across the Continent" allowing "police government" to rule Eastern Europe. The Soviets, he emphasized, did not want war: "What they desire is the fruits of war and the indefinite expansion of their power and doctrines."[17]

The "iron curtain" phrase made the speech famous. But, as Churchill himself observed, the "crux" of the message lay in the proposal that the Anglo-Americans, outside the United Nations and with the support of atomic weaponry (the title of the address was "The Sinews of Peace"), create "a unity in Europe from which no nation should be permanently outcast." The Soviets perceived this as a di-

---

[15]J. V. Stalin, *Speech Delivered by J. V. Stalin at a Meeting of Voters of the Stalin Electoral Area of Moscow, February 9, 1946* (Washington, Embassy of the U.S.S.R., March 1946).
[16]*Forrestal Diaries*, pp. 134–135; *New York Times*, February 10, 1946, p. 1.
[17]Text in *The New York Times*, March 6, 1946, p. 4.

rect challenge to their power in Eastern Europe. Within a week Stalin attacked Churchill and his "friends" in America, whom he claimed resembled Hitler by holding a "racial theory" that those who spoke the English language "should rule over the remaining nations of the world." This, Stalin warned, is "a set-up for war, a call to war with the Soviet Union."[18]

Within a short period after the Churchill speech, Stalin launched a series of policies which, in retrospect, marks the spring and summer of 1946 as a milestone in the Cold War. During these weeks the Soviets, after having worked for a loan during the previous fifteen months, finally concluded that Washington had no interest in loaning them $1 billion, or any other amount. They refused to become a member of the World Bank and the International Monetary Fund. These rejections ended the American hope to use the lure of the dollar to make the Soviets retreat in Eastern Europe and join the capitalist-controlled bank and IMF. Actually there had never been reason to hope. Control of their border areas was worth more to the Russians than $1 billion, or even $10 billion. Moreover, as early as September 1944 an American intelligence report had indirectly warned against trying to use financial pressure. It observed that with internal sacrifices Russia "could carry through this reconstruction with its domestic resources, without foreign loans or reparations." The State Department agreed with this conclusion in April 1946 when Byrnes told the Cabinet that "the only place where money has not influenced national interest is Russia." (The secretary of state notably added that "we are in this thing all over the world to an extent that few people realize.")[19] Thus the attempt to buy off the Soviets had worked no better than Washington's vague hope that the atomic bomb might somehow make them more "manageable."

At home Stalin announced a new five-year plan, then initiated an intense ideological effort to eliminate Western influences, purify and propagate Stalinist dogma, and deify the dictator himself. The name of Andrei Zhdanov soon became synonymous with this campaign. One close observer described this supposed "intellectual" of the politburo as "short, with a brownish clipped mustache, high forehead,

---

[18]Interview in *Pravda*, reprinted in *The New York Times*, March 14, 1946.
[19]Memorandum for Baruch from Sam Lubell," March 1945, Papers of Bernard Baruch, Princeton University Library, Princeton, N.J.; "Cabinet Meeting, April 19, 1946," Notes on Cabinet Meetings, 1945–1946, White House File, Truman Library.

pointed nose, and sickly red face," who had "some knowledge of everything," but did not know a single field thoroughly, "a typical intellectual who became acquainted with and picked up knowledge of other fields through Marxist literature." Zhdanov prophesied that Marxism-Leninism had a messianic destiny, "the right to teach others a new general human morality."[20]

The Stalinist and Churchillian declarations of Cold War appeared by the summer of 1946 to have a dramatic effect on the two touchstones of world politics, Germany and the control of atomic weapons. In Germany reparations were the central issue. Secretary of State Byrnes attempted to meet Russian fears of a remilitarized Germany by proposing that the Big Four powers sign a treaty unifying the country and guaranteeing its demilitarization. Molotov rejected this because of a key Russian policy change on reparations. Sometime during the spring the Soviets stopped removing machinery from eastern Germany and determined instead to produce goods in their zone, where labor and resources were more readily available, then ship the products to Russia. While Molotov was rejecting Byrnes's overture, General Lucius Clay informed Russian commanders in Germany in May that no more reparations would be removed from the Western zones. These areas, Clay feared, were becoming bankrupt. Unless reparations were stopped and the zones rebuilt, he was convinced, the population had little chance for survival. Molotov's and Clay's moves were decisive moments in the Cold War, for they terminated any real hope of useful negotiations on Germany. Each power had now set out to develop its own zone.

Byrnes analyzed this growing rigidity in a highly publicized speech at Stuttgart, Germany, on September 6. The secretary of state announced that Germany must develop exports in order to be "self-sustaining," refused to recognize the Oder-Neisse boundary for eastern Germany, specified that Germans should be given primary responsibility for running their own affairs (this was particularly frightening to the Russians and the French), and emphasized that the

---

[20]Milovan Djilas, *Conversations with Stalin* (New York, 1961), pp. 149–150; Frederick C. Barghoorn, "Great Russian Messianism in Postwar Soviet Ideology." In Ernest J. Simmons, ed., *Continuity and Change in Russian and Soviet Thought* (Cambridge, Mass., 1955), pp. 545–546.

American presence in Central Europe would not be withdrawn. This was the first time a high American official had said such things publicly. The speech, however, was historic, not prophetic; it only summarized events of the previous eighteen months.

A second occurrence in the summer of 1946 intensified the Cold War. Since Hiroshima the horror of atomic energy had overhung every diplomatic exchange. In March 1946 the United States released a plan for the control of the atom, the so-called Acheson-Lilienthal proposal. This report suggested a series of stages through which the world could pass to international control of atomic weapons. Throughout the transition period the United States, possessing the only atomic bombs, would remain in a favored position while other nations agreed to be inspected by international agencies. A month later Truman named Bernard Baruch as the first American delegate to a new UN Atomic Energy Commission. American policy soon began to change. Deeply suspicious by nature, Baruch distrusted the Acheson-Lilienthal report, partly because he had not sat on the committee and partly because it said nothing about the Russian veto in the Security Council.

Baruch determined to eliminate any Soviet power to veto inspections or sanctions. The Acheson-Lilienthal report, on the other hand, planned to obtain Russian agreement to general principles and then discuss the veto problem. Baruch became increasingly bitter about Under Secretary of State Acheson (whom he mistakenly accused of recording their telephone conversations) and those "One Worlders" like columnist Walter Lippmann "whom I can't understand any more." All the "One Worlders" criticized Baruch's belief that he could force the Soviets to surrender their veto power.[21] But he finally triumphed by convincing Truman that it was better to be tough with Russia sooner rather than later. After recalling the dismantling of the American Navy in the 1920s, the President agreed: "We should not under any circumstances throw away our gun until we are sure the rest of the world can't arm against us."[22] Military and political advisers bolstered this view by avowing that Russia could not build

---

[21]Acheson file, Atomic Energy, Baruch Papers, especially telephone conversation between Baruch and Acheson, November 26, 1946.
[22]"BMB [Bernard M. Baruch] Memorandum of Meeting on June 7, 1946, with the President and J.F. Byrnes," Truman File, Atomic Energy, Baruch Papers.

atomic bombs for at least five to fifteen years. Only a few scientists warned that the period might be considerably shorter.

In a dramatic speech at the United Nations in June, Baruch presented his plan: atomic energy would be controlled through international management of the necessary raw materials and inspection by international agencies. No vetoes of these controls and inspections would be allowed, and majority vote would rule. In the realm of peaceful uses of atomic energy, an Atomic Development Authority, again free of the veto, would establish atomic plants not according to need (as in underdeveloped areas or in large stretches of Russia) but according to strategic and geographic criteria. By controlling a majority within the authority, the United States could thus control the development of the industrial uses of nuclear energy *within* the Soviet Union.

This was totally unacceptable to the Russians. They countered by demanding destruction of all atomic bombs, the cessation of their production, agreement of all powers not to use these weapons, and then a discussion of controls. When they offered to bargain, Baruch retorted that they must accept the entire American plan or there would be no plan. So there was no plan. Instead, Congress established a U.S. Atomic Energy Commission under the Atomic Energy Act of 1946. Under strong military pressure, the act prohibited an exchange of information on the use of atomic energy with any nation until Congress should decide by joint resolution that "effective" international controls were in force. That, obviously, would be a long time off.

So, a year after Japan's surrender, the Pandora's box of atomic power remained open, Byrnes's speech illustrated the deadlock over Germany, and Russian-American loan discussions had collapsed. Stalin and Churchill had issued world-shaking statements. But—significantly—Harry Truman had not. He and other Americans even reacted coldly to Churchill's suggestion of an Anglo-American partnership that would tie the United States to a declining, nearly bankrupt England. The President publicly offered no alternative to Churchill's. Throughout 1946, even during the Iranian and Turkish crises, Truman never publicly condemned Soviet policy.

No one doubted that the Western world would be shaped by Truman's decisions. On the train ride to Fulton, Missouri, Churchill delighted his hosts when he recited by memory long portions of John Greenleaf Whittier's poetry. Truman meanwhile walked up to the engine. While the Britisher quoted American authors, the President drove the train. It was all appropriate. Throughout 1945–1946 Truman had confronted the Russians, but he had not formulated a coherent policy or a consensus at home to support such a comprehensive policy. The question was in which direction, and how rapidly, Truman would drive the train of the Western nations.

By autumn the President's task was, oddly, made more difficult as the Soviets became quiet. Truman's problem was no longer centered on the threat of immediate Russian expansion, as in Iran or Turkey. It rapidly became the infinitely more complex chore of rebuilding war-devastated Western Europe as it entered perhaps the harshest winter in living memory. Great Britain was so deeply discouraged that a radical swing to the left seemed politically possible. Parts of Central Europe faced starvation. France was chaotic. Truman had so feared a French Communist party seizure of power from within that in May he secretly ordered the U.S. Army in Germany to prepare for a march into France.[23] The West was threatened not by the Red Army, but by internal collapse. Truman's closest advisers urged him to use massive economic and military aid "to build up a world of our own" before the Soviets won by default.[24]

But for the President this advice seemed only a pipe dream. Congress and the American people would respond to a Soviet attack; spending billions of the taxpayers' dollars in Europe, however, was different. Americans recalled with bitterness how ungrateful Europeans appeared for help given during World War I. Nor would it be popular to enrich England and France, whose trade practices and imperial policies had long angered the United States. Moreover, Americans had sacrificed during the war. Now they wanted to spend on themselves. This was not easy, for a rush of inflation, labor strikes, and meat shortages in late 1946 wounded both the economy and Truman's popularity. Many Americans believed that if the President wanted to help someone he should help them by cutting taxes. Truman's difficulties came into the open during the autumn of 1946, when he was attacked by liberals for being too militaristic and by conservatives for his economic policies.

The liberal attack was led by Henry Agard Wallace, a great sec-

---

[23]*FRUS, 1946, Europe*, V: 435–438.
[24]The best discussion of this approach is Richard M. Freeland, *The Truman Doctrine and McCarthyism* (New York, 1972), pp. 56–57; see also John Lewis Gaddis, *The United States and the Origins of the Cold War* (New York, 1972), pp. 321–322.

retary of agriculture during the early New Deal, Vice President from 1941–1945, maneuvered out of the vice-presidential nomination in 1944 so that Harry Truman could be FDR's running mate, and finally secretary of commerce in 1945. Here he devoted himself to the cause of what he liked to call the "Common Man," by extending increased loans to small businessmen and, above all, enlarging the economic pie by increasing foreign trade. Wallace soon discovered that Truman threatened to clog the trade channels to Russia, Eastern Europe, perhaps even China, with his militant attitude toward the Soviets.

At a political rally in New York on September 12, 1946, Wallace delivered a speech, cleared personally, and too rapidly, by Truman. The address focused on the necessity of a political understanding with Russia. This, Wallace declared, would require guaranteeing Soviet security in Eastern Europe. He hoped the capitalist and communist systems could compete "on a friendly basis" and "gradually become more alike." Wallace, however, added one proviso for his happy ending: in this competition "we must insist on an open door for trade throughout the world. . . . We cannot permit the door to be closed against our trade in Eastern Europe any more than we can in China."[25] At that moment Byrnes and Vandenberg were in Paris, painfully and unsuccessfully trying to negotiate peace treaties with Molotov. They immediately demanded Wallace's resignation. On September 20 Truman complied.

The vigor of their reaction to Wallace's speech measured the distance American policy had moved since the close of World War II. Wallace was essentially pleading for a renewal of the administration's invitation of 1945 to the war-decimated Soviet economy to join a friendly game of economic competition with the American industrial mammoth and to play the game according to American rules.[26] By mid-1946 Truman and Byrnes had moved far beyond this. They now assumed that Stalin would not accept such rules but would cooperate only when directly faced with the threat of superior force. Given this background and the ringing declaration of a worldwide open door, little wonder that the Communist party newspaper *Daily Worker* in New York at first attacked Wallace's speech as a cover for

---

[25]Henry Wallace, "The Way to Peace," *Vital Speeches*, October 1, 1946, pp. 738–741.
[26]Ronald Radosh, "The Economic and Political Thought of Henry Wallace," unpublished master's thesis, State University of Iowa, 1960, pp. 46–50, 130–134.

"American imperialism." Only after Byrnes and Truman had landed on Wallace did the *Worker* discover virtue in his ideas.

Wallace nevertheless voiced the concerns of many New Dealers. In late September a group of labor leaders met with Harold Ickes and Henry Morgenthau, Jr., two stalwarts of the Roosevelt years, to proclaim support for Wallace's views and to issue a plea to end tests of atomic bombs. Truman was meanwhile convinced that Wallace was a "pacifist," more dangerous than the pro-Nazi groups in the country during World War II, and part of "a sabotage front for Uncle Joe Stalin."[27]

This splitting of the New Deal coalition badly wounded Truman's political fortunes, but worse lay ahead. The President had become so unpopular that only 32 percent of those polled thought he provided adequate leadership. His fellow Democrats did not even ask him for support in the 1946 congressional campaign. They preferred to broadcast recordings of Roosevelt's speeches. The election was a disaster for the administration. Republicans gained solid control of both Senate and House for the first time since 1928. The Republican "Class of 1946," moreover, included such notable conservatives as Joseph McCarthy of Wisconsin, John Bricker of Ohio, George Malone of Nevada, and William Knowland of California. The new legislators had stressed their anticommunism during the campaign but had also called for deep tax cuts. There seemed little chance they would support any large-scale economic and military program to help Europe, particularly if Stalin remained quiet.[28] Several leading Americans, including Senator J. William Fulbright (Democrat of Arkansas) and columnist Walter Lippmann, suggested that Truman could best serve his country by resigning.

During the last days of 1946, the counterattack began. A group of liberals prepared to meet in Washington to form the Americans for Democratic Action. This organization, in contrast to Wallace's, pledged to continue working within the Democratic party and to fight communism both at home and abroad. Chairing the founding session was Reinhold Niebuhr, theologian, philosopher, historian, and perhaps the most important contemporary influence on American thought. Not since Jonathan Edwards's day of the 1740s had an

---

[27]Margaret Truman, *Harry S Truman* (New York, 1973), pp. 346–347.
[28]Susan M. Hartmann, *Truman and the 80th Congress* (New York, 1971), p. 49.

American theologian so affected his society. Like Edwards, Niebuhr emphasized the importance of sin and sinful power in that society. He disavowed the "sentimental optimism" that had shaped American thought during the 1900–1930 era and which again was appearing in the post-1945 world under the guise of "positive thinking."

In a remarkable series of books and lectures, Niebuhr developed his central theme that, because of avarice, finiteness, and inability to realize the limits of their own power, humans were overwhelmed with anxieties and unable to use freedom constructively. This anxiety led to a will-to-power and this, in turn, to conflict. Given such "egoistic corruption in all human virtue,"[29] Niebuhr warned that reason, and particularly faith in science, could not be wholly trusted, for both reason and science often refused to use the religious and historical insights required to solve secular problems.

As the Cold War heightened, Niebuhr stood ready with an explanation and a solution. Communism was at once the worst and most aggressive of societies because its faithful believed they could find a perfect union among the sinful simply by changing economic relationships. Private property, he warned, "is not the cause but the instrument of human egotism."[30] Niebuhr charged that communists overlooked what was more important and ineradicable, the will-to-power. Worse, communism historically had sought to achieve the better society by centralizing power in one or several leaders rather than working out a balance of power within that society. By employing science and so-called scientific rationales, moreover, communism had proved once again to Niebuhr that science is highly serviceable to and easily maneuvered by a totalitarian society.

Since "all life is an expression of power," he believed that the West could preserve its freedoms only by creating the best possible balance-of-power situations. He thought New Deal capitalism offered the most promise inside the United States. Abroad, no trust could be placed in world government. He supported instead the Baruch Plan for atomic energy and wrote article after article in 1946 and 1947 pleading for a revitalized Europe to offset the communist threat.[31]

After a visit to Europe in 1946, Niebuhr fixed upon the German

---

[29]Reinhold Niebuhr, "The Foreign Policy of American Conservatism and Liberalism." In *Christian Realism and Political Problems* (New York, 1953), p. 66.
[30]*The Nation,* March 6, 1948, p. 268.
[31]*Christianity and Crisis,* July 8, 1946, p. 2.

problem. Here again he became an important symbol, and a strong influence, in American foreign policy. Niebuhr was one of the earliest to spell out in detail the spiritual, political, and economic unity of the Atlantic community and the pivotal role that Germany must play if Europe was to be saved from communism. "Russian truculence cannot be mitigated by further concessions," he wrote in October 1946. "Russia hopes to conquer the whole of Europe strategically or ideologically." Then came a thrust at Wallace: "It has been the unfortunate weakness of both liberalism and liberal Christianity that they have easily degenerated into sentimentality by refusing to contemplate the tragic aspects of human existence honestly."[32] In applauding the rapid development of the German steel industry in 1947, Niebuhr accepted the "explicit division between East and West which has taken place. . . . Only God can bring order out of this kind of mixture of good and evil. We must, meanwhile, keep our powder dry."[33]

Niebuhr's work thus provided points of departure for criticizing Wallace, condemning communism, formulating a Europe-first policy, and rebuilding Germany. Most important, he provided a historical basis and rationale for the tone, the outlook, and the unsaid, and often unconscious, assumptions of these years.

But transforming Niebuhr's views into policy would require time. Given the slide of Western Europe and the Republican hold on Congress, Harry Truman did not appear to have enough time or support. Knowledgeable Americans who were usually calm began to sound shrill and desperate. For example, exactly one year after Henry Stimson had advised reasoning with the Soviets, Secretary of the Navy James Forrestal counseled with the retired statesman. "He said," Forrestal recorded in his diary that night, "the way things had now developed he thought we should not delay in going forward with the manufacture of all the atomic missiles we could make."[34] Others agreed with Stimson's suggestion, but it would not prevent the economic collapse of Europe no matter how many missiles were built.

Truman, unlike Churchill and Stalin, had not yet publicly joined the Cold War. The direction and speed of the Western train remained to be determined. Meanwhile the President's winter promised to be nearly as bleak as Europe's.

[32]*Life*, October 21, 1946, pp. 65–72.
[33]*Christianity and Crisis*, August 4, 1947, p. 2.
[34]*Forrestal Diaries*, p. 200.

CHAPTER 3

Two Halves of the Same Walnut (1947–1948)

On March 12, 1947, President Truman finally issued his own declaration of Cold War. Dramatically presenting the Truman Doctrine to Congress, he asked Americans to join in a global commitment against communism. The nation responded. A quarter of a century later, Senator J. William Fulbright declared, "More by far than any other factor the anti-communism of the Truman Doctrine has been the guiding spirit of American foreign policy since World War II."[1]

An odd circumstance, however, must be explained if the Truman Doctrine is to be understood. The Soviet Union had been less aggressive in the months before the President's pronouncement than at any time in the postwar period. Stalin consolidated his hold over Rumania and Poland through manipulated elections, and at home Soviet propagandists encouraged Western socialists and other "proletarians" to follow pro-Russian policies. But throughout the winter of 1946–1947, the Soviets acted cautiously. State Department officials privately believed that "the USSR is undergoing serious economic difficulties" which have led to "the less aggressive international attitude taken by Soviet authorities in recent weeks." This policy was only "a temporary retreat." Nonetheless, the problems seemed so great that the Russians gave military discharges to "hundreds of thousands of young men [who] will now become available for labor force in industry, agriculture and construction."[2] Stalin reduced his 12 million military men of 1945 to between 3 and 4 million in 1947. (American forces dropped from 10 million to 1.4 million, but Americans enjoyed a monopoly of atomic weapons.) Russian military levels would go no

---

[1]J. William Fulbright, *The Crippled Giant* (New York, 1972), pp. 6–24.
[2]Daily Staff Summary, January 3, January 15, February 24, February 10, 1947, Lot File, NA, RG 59.

lower, for the Red Army was Stalin's counter to Truman's atomic bomb. Poised in Eastern Europe, the troops threatened to take the continent hostage in case of atomic attack on Russia. Stalin had no navy capable of long-range offensive strikes. The fleet depended on 300 submarines geared for defensive purposes.[3]

Truman's immediate problem was not the threat of a Russian invasion. As Dean Acheson privately remarked, the Russians would not make war with the United States "unless they are absolutely out of their minds." The greater danger was that Stalin might be proved correct when he indicated that the communists could bide their time since a "general crisis" was becoming so "acute" in the West that it would sweep away "atom-dollar" diplomacy. Communist party power rose steeply in Europe, particularly in France where the first cabinet of the new Fourth Republic contained four communists, including the minister of defense. Chaotic conditions in former colonial areas also opened exceptional opportunities to revolutionaries. The two gems of the British Crown, India and Egypt, shattered the empire with drives for independence. They were soon joined by Pakistan, Burma, Ceylon, and Nepal. France began a long, futile, eight-year war to regain Indochina. The Dutch faced full-scale revolution in Indonesia. The Middle East was in turmoil over the determination of a half-dozen countries to be totally independent, as well as over the influx of 100,000 Jews who hoped to establish a homeland in Palestine.

In late 1946 and early 1947, American officials gave increasing attention to these newly emerging areas. Europe could not be fully stabilized until England, France, and the Netherlands settled their colonial problems. The State Department also assumed that the American economy, as well as the economy of the Western community, which depended upon American prosperity, demanded a proper settlement of these conflicts. In a speech in November 1946, Will Clayton explained that the expansion in the domestic economy and the "depletion of our natural resources" would make the United States much more dependent on the importation of raw materials and minerals. Many of these came from the newly emerging areas. "No nation in modern times," the assistant secretary of state warned, "can long expect to enjoy a rising standard of living without increased for-

---

[3]Thomas Wolfe, *Soviet Power and Europe, 1945–1970* (Baltimore, 1970), pp. 10–11, 33, 45–46.

eign trade." Adolf Berle, economist, adviser to Roosevelt and Truman, and State Department official, declared in late 1946 that the Soviets and the United States had begun a battle for the allegiance of the less industrialized nations. "Within four years the world [will] be faced with an apparent surplus in production beyond any previously known," Berle explained. If American surpluses were used to "take the lead in material reconstruction" of the newly emerging countries, the United States could level off those "cycles of 'boom and bust' which disfigured our prewar economy."[4]

"Boom and bust" already threatened. The American economy sagged, and unemployment rose in early 1946 before some expansion began. State Department experts worried that the improvement was temporary, for it rested on a $15-billion American export trade, nearly four times the level of the 1930s. Most of these exports were rebuilding Western Europe, but the Europeans were rapidly running out of dollars to pay for the goods. When its remaining dollars and gold were spent, Europe would stagnate, then perhaps grasp at socialism to save itself. Americans would face the loss of their most vital market and probably the return of the 1930s state of affairs with all the attendant political consequences. Truman understood this by early 1947, but a tax-cutting Republican Congress and his own low popularity seemed to block any action.

The turn came on February 21, 1947, when a British embassy official drove to the State Department building. He informed Acheson that because of its own economic crisis (more than half its industry was quiet), England could not provide the $250 million of military and economic support needed by Greece and Turkey. As Secretary of State George Marshall later observed, "It was tantamount to British abdication from the Middle East with obvious implications as to their successor."[5]

American officials were not taken by surprise. From 1944 until early 1947 they had closely watched the British attempt to regain control of Greece become bogged down in a Greek civil war. On one side was a conservative-monarchical group supported by London. On the other was the National Liberation Front (NLF), with communist leadership, which had gained popularity and power by leading resis-

[4]R. Dennett, ed., *Documents on American Foreign Relations*, VIII (Princeton, 1951): 607–608.
[5]James Forrestal, *The Forrestal Diaries*, Walter Millis, ed. (New York, 1951), p. 245.

tance efforts against the Nazis. By 1947 the NLF received support from Yugoslav communist leader Josip Broz (Marshal Tito). The Yugoslav was not motivated by affection for his fellow communists in Greece. Rather, he hoped to annex parts of Greece to a large Yugoslav federation. Stalin was not directly involved and indeed developed a strong dislike for Tito's ambitions.

But as NLF strength grew, the United States did become involved. Throughout 1946 it sent special missions, poured in $260 million of aid, and sided with the British. Drawing on this experience, the State Department was able to work out a detailed proposal for assistance within a week after Acheson received the British message. After only nineteen days Truman could appear before Congress with a complete program. Clearly, the President's request on March 12 for $400 million in Greek and Turkish aid (the Truman Doctrine speech) was not a sudden, drastic departure in American foreign policy.

The reasoning in Truman's speech, however, was radically new. That reasoning was worked out by American officials who had long been waiting for this opportunity. As they developed the speech, "they found release from the professional frustrations of years," as one later declared. "It seemed to those present that a new chapter in world history had opened and they were the most privileged of men."[6] Those words help explain why the officials made certain choices. For example, they could have determined simply that Greece was in a civil war and therefore the United States had no business intervening. Or they could have quietly asked Congress to continue aid to Greece and Turkey while transferring to those nations weapons left from the war. The administration, however, rejected those alternatives, choosing instead to appear dramatically before Congress to request support for a global battle against communism. A White House adviser remarked that the message would be "the opening gun in a campaign to bring people up to [the] realization that the war isn't over by any means."

As State Department officials prepared drafts of the speech, Truman, Secretary of State Marshall, and Acheson met with congressional leaders. It was not a warm audience. The Republicans were busily cutting taxes 20 percent and chopping $6 billion from Truman's already-tight budget. The legislators remained unmoved until Acheson swung into the argument that the threat was not a Greek civil

[6]Joseph M. Jones, *The Fifteen Weeks* (New York, 1955), pp. 146–147.

war but Russian communism; its aim was the control of the Middle East, South Asia, and Africa; and this control was part of a communist plan to encircle and capture the ultimate objective, Germany and Europe. It was a struggle between liberty and dictatorship. By defending Greece and Turkey, therefore, Americans were defending their own freedoms. "The Soviet Union was playing one of the greatest gambles in history at minimal cost," Acheson concluded. "We and we alone are in a position to break up the play."[7]

The congressmen were stunned. Silence followed until Arthur Vandenberg (now the chair of the Senate Foreign Relations Committee) told Truman that the message must include Acheson's explanation. As the senator advised, the President "scared hell" out of the American people. Insofar as public opinion was concerned, this tactic worked well for Truman (at least until three years later when Senator Joseph McCarthy and others turned the argument around and accused the administration of handling such a horrible danger too gently). The President also won over Congress with assurances that the United States would not only control every penny of America's aid to Greece but run the Greek economy by controlling foreign exchange, budget, taxes, currency, and credit.

Inside the State Department, however, Acheson ran into opposition. George Kennan, the top expert on Soviet affairs, objected bitterly to sending military assistance to nations such as Turkey that had no internal communist problems and bordered the Soviet Union. Unlike economic help, military aid could be provocative. Acheson rejected the argument. The opportunity to build Turkey's military strength was too good to miss. Thus in the words of one official, "Turkey was slipped into the oven with Greece because that seemed the surest way to cook a tough bird." Kennan also protested against the harsh ideological tone and open-ended American commitment in the speech drafts. He was joined by Secretary of State Marshall and Charles Bohlen, another expert on Russia, who told Acheson that "there was a little too much flamboyant anticommunism in the speech." Acheson stood his ground. Marshall was informed that Truman believed the Senate would not approve the doctrine "without the emphasis on the Communist danger."[8]

---

[7]Dean Acheson, *Present at the Creation* (New York, 1969), pp. 292–293.
[8]George Kennan, *Memoirs, 1925–1950* (Boston, 1967), pp. 315–322; Charles E. Bohlen, *Witness to History, 1929–1969* (New York, 1973), p. 261.

Acheson, however, carefully kept the central economic factors out of the speech. He and Truman wanted a simple ideological call to action that all could understand, not a message that might trigger arguments over American oil holdings in the Middle East. The economic interests were nevertheless crucial. As State Department official Joseph Jones noted, if Greece and similar key areas "spiral downwards into economic anarchy, then at best they will drop out of the United States orbit and try an independent nationalistic policy; at worst they will swing into the Russian orbit," and the result would be a depression worse than that of the 1930s.[9]

Jones's insight was incorporated into a major speech made by Truman at Baylor University on March 6. The address provided the economic dimension to the Truman Doctrine pronounced six days later. The President frankly declared that if the expansion of state-controlled economies (such as the communists') was not stopped, and an open world marketplace restored for private business, a depression would occur and the government would have to intervene massively in the society. Americans could then bid farewell to both their traditional economic and personal freedoms. "Freedom of worship—freedom of speech—freedom of enterprise," Truman observed. "It must be true that the first two of these freedoms are related to the third." For "Peace, freedom and world trade are indivisible." He concluded, "We must not go through the thirties again."[10] The President had given the economic reasons for pronouncing the Truman Doctrine. The Baylor speech (written by Acheson and Will Clayton) explained why Americans, if they hoped to preserve their personal freedom, had to rebuild the areas west of the Iron Curtain before these lands collapsed into anarchy, radical governments, or even communism.

The Truman Doctrine speech itself laid out the ideological and political reasons for the commitment. The President requested $400 million for military and economic aid, but he also asked for something else. Truman warned Congress that the world must now "choose between alternative ways of life." He urged Americans to commit themselves to helping "free peoples" and to opposing "totalitarian regimes." This request, plus Truman's failure to place any geographic

[9]Barton J. Bernstein, ed., *Politics and Policies of the Truman Administration* (Chicago, 1970), p. 57.
[10]*Public Papers of the Presidents . . . Truman . . . 1947* (Washington, 1963), pp. 167–172.

limits on where Americans must commit themselves (Africa as well as Germany? Southeast Asia as well as Western Europe?), raised criticism.

Robert Taft of Ohio, the Senate's Republican leader, accused Truman of dividing the world into communist and anticommunist zones, then said flatly, "I do not want war with Russia." On the left, Henry Wallace, traveling in Europe, accused Truman of "reckless adventury" that would cost the world "a century of fear." Senator Vandenberg rushed to the President's defense by calling Wallace an "itinerant saboteur." But such fear was not only on Taft's and Wallace's minds. Shortly before the speech, Acheson told J. Robert Oppenheimer, a leading scientist in the atomic weapons field, "We are entering an adversary relationship with the Soviet," and "we should bear that in mind" while making atomic plans.[11]

Congress wriggled uncomfortably. As Senator Vandenberg began closed-door hearings on what he called "the most fundamental thing that has been presented to Congress in my time," Acheson hedged on whether the Truman Doctrine had any limitations. "If there are situations where we can do something effective, then I think we must certainly do it." But he was clear on one issue: "I think it is a mistake to believe that you can, at any time, sit down with the Russians and solve questions." Only when the West built unbeatable bastions of strength would Stalin listen to American terms. Acheson assumed Russia was primarily responsible for the Greek revolution. After all, said Lincoln MacVeagh, U.S. ambassador to Greece, "Any empire that bases itself on revolution always has expansionist tendencies." (The ambassador was alluding to the revolution of 1917, not 1776.) This view of Soviet involvement was wrong. The Greek problem was caused by internal forces and fueled by Tito for his own purposes. But this point made little difference. The administration asked for a commitment against communism anywhere, not just against the Soviets.

That caused a special problem in Greece, for as MacVeagh admitted, "the best men" in Greece "are the heads of the Communist movement. . . . That is the sad part of it." But Americans had to keep on "trying to make bricks without straw . . . or you are going to lose

[11]Jones, *Fifteen Weeks,* pp. 175–178; Lloyd Gardner, *Architects of Illusion* (Chicago, 1970), p. 201.

the country." The Greek government became so brutal that the State Department privately warned that it must stop torturing its political prisoners or "the President's program" would be damaged. When criticized for helping the Greek and Turkish right-wing parties, however, Truman could simply ask Americans whether they preferred "totalitarianism" or "imperfect democracies." This settled that question.[12]

The President and Acheson mousetrapped those in Congress who wanted to be both anticommunist and penny-pinchers. As a leading Democrat chuckled privately, of course the Republicans "didn't want to be smoked out. . . . They don't like Communism but still they don't want to do anything to stop it. But they are all put on the spot now and they all have to come clean." The President, moreover, had moved so quickly that Congress had no choice but to give him increased powers. "Here we sit," mourned Vandenberg, "not as free agents," but dealing with something "almost like a Presidential request for a declaration of war." "There is precious little we can do," the senator concluded, "except say 'yes.' "[13] Vandenberg was correct. Congress's acceptance of Truman's definition of the crisis marked the point in the Cold War when power in foreign-policy formulation began shifting rapidly from Capitol Hill to the White House.

Nine days after his speech Truman helped ensure his victory by announcing a loyalty program to ferret out security risks in government. The first such peacetime program in American history, it was so vaguely defined that political ideas and long-past associations were suddenly made suspect. Most ominously, the accused would not have the right to confront the accuser.[14] Truman thus strikingly dramatized the communist issue, exerting new pressure on Congress to support his doctrine. By mid-May Congress had passed his request by large margins.

The Truman Doctrine was a milestone in American history for at least four reasons. First, it marked the point at which Truman used

[12]Material in the preceding two paragraphs is from U.S. Senate, Committee on Foreign Relations, 80th Cong., 1st Sess., *Legislative Origins of the Truman Doctrine: Hearings . . .* (Washington, 1973), pp. 5, 17, 95, 46, 45; *FRUS, 1947*, V: 142–143.

[13]Phone conversation between Carl Vinson and Forrestal, Speech to Congress on Greece file, March 13, 1947, Box 28, Papers of Clark Clifford, Truman Library; Senate, *Legislative Origins*, p. 128.

[14]Richard Freeland, *The Truman Doctrine and the Origins of McCarthyism* (New York, 1972), pp. 208–211.

the American fear of communism both at home and abroad to convince Americans they must embark upon a Cold War foreign policy. This consensus would not break apart for a quarter of a century. Second, as Vandenberg knew, Congress was giving the President great powers to wage this Cold War as he saw fit. Truman's personal popularity began spiraling upward after his speech. Third, for the first time in the postwar era, Americans massively intervened in another nation's civil war. Intervention was justified on the basis of anticommunism. In the future, Americans would intervene in similar wars for supposedly the same reason and with less happy results. Even Greek affairs went badly at first, so badly that in late 1947 Washington officials discussed sending as many as two divisions of Americans to save the situation. That proved unnecessary, for when Yugoslavia left the communist bloc in early 1948, Tito turned inward and stopped aiding the rebels. Deprived of aid, the Greek left wing quickly lost ground. But it had been close, and Americans were nearly involved massively in a civil war two decades before their Vietnam involvement. As it was, the success in Greece seemed to prove that Americans could, if they wished, control such conflicts by defining the problem as "communist" and helping conservatives remain in power.[15]

Finally, and perhaps most important, Truman used the doctrine to justify a gigantic aid program to prevent a collapse of the European and American economies. Later such programs were expanded globally. The President's arguments about anticommunism were confusing, for the Western economies would have been in grave difficulties whether or not communism existed. The complicated problems of reconstruction and U.S. dependence on world trade were not well understood by Americans, but they easily comprehended anticommunism. So Americans embarked upon the Cold War for the good reasons given in the Truman Doctrine, which they understood, and for real reasons, which they did not understand. Thus, as Truman and Acheson intended, the doctrine became an ideological shield behind which the United States marched to rebuild the Western political-economic system and counter the radical left. From 1947 on, therefore, any threats to that Western system could be easily explained as

---

[15]*FRUS, 1947*, V: 466–469; Thomas Paterson, *Soviet-American Confrontation* (Baltimore, 1973), p. 205. An interesting State Department view on how American opinion was changed is in H. Schuyler Foster, "American Public Opinion and U.S. Foreign Policy," *Department of State Bulletin*, XLI (November 30, 1959).

communist-inspired, not as problems which arose from difficulties within the system itself. That was the most lasting and tragic result of the Truman Doctrine.

The President's program evolved naturally into the Marshall Plan. Although the speech did not limit American effort, Secretary of State Marshall did by concentrating the administration's attention on Europe. Returning badly shaken from a Foreign Ministers conference in Moscow, the secretary of state insisted in a nationwide broadcast that Western Europe required immediate help. "The patient is sinking," he declared, "while the doctors deliberate." Personal conversations with Stalin had convinced Marshall that the Russians believed Europe would collapse. Assuming that the United States must lead in restoring Europe, Marshall appointed a policy-planning staff under the direction of George Kennan to draw up policies.

Kennan later explained the basic assumption that underlay the Marshall Plan and, indeed, the entire range of America's postwar policies between 1947 and the mid-1950s. Excluding the United States, Kennan observed,

> . . . there are only four aggregations which are major ones from the standpoint of strategic realities [that is, military and industrial potential] in the world. Two of those lie off the shores of the Eurasian land mass. Those are Japan and England, and two of them lie on the Eurasian land mass. One is the Soviet Union and the other is that of central Europe. . . .
>
> Viewed in absolute terms, I think the greatest danger that could confront the United States security would be a combination and working together for purposes hostile to us of the central European and the Russian military-industrial potentials. They would really create an entity . . . which could overshadow in a strategic sense even our own power. It is not anything, I think, which would be as easy of achievement as people often portray it as being here. I am not sure the Russians have the genius for holding all that together. . . . Still, they have the tendency of political thought, of Communist political expansion.[16]

---

[16]U.S. Senate, Subcommittee to Investigate the Administration of the International Security Act . . . of the Committee on the Judiciary, 82nd Cong., 1st Sess., *The Institute of Pacific Relations* (Washington, 1951), pp. 1557–1558. (Hereafter cited as *I.P.R. Hearings*.)

Building on this premise, round-the-clock conferences in May 1947 began to fashion the main features of the Marshall Plan. Kennan insisted that any aid, particularly military supplies, be limited and not given to just any area where communists seemed to be enjoying some success. The all-important question then became how to handle the Russians. Ostensibly, Marshall accepted Kennan's advice to "play it straight" by inviting the Soviet bloc. In reality the State Department made Russian acceptance improbable by demanding that economic records of each nation be open for scrutiny. For good measure Kennan also suggested that the Soviets' devastated economy, weakened by war and at that moment suffering from drought and famine, participate in the plan by shipping Soviet goods to Europe. Apparently no one in the State Department wanted the Soviets included. Russian participation would vastly multiply the costs of the program and eliminate any hope of its acceptance by a purse-watching Republican Congress, now increasingly convinced by Truman that communists had to be fought, not fed.

Acheson's speech at Cleveland, Mississippi, in early May and Marshall's address at Harvard on June 5 revealed the motives and substance of the plan. In preparing for the earlier speech, Acheson's advisers concluded that American exports were rapidly approaching the $16-billion mark. Imports, however, amounted to only half that amount, and Europe did not have sufficient dollars to pay the difference. Either the United States would have to give credits to Europeans or they would be unable to buy American goods. The President's Council of Economic Advisers predicted a slight business recession, and if, in addition, exports dropped in any substantial amount, "the effect in the United States," as one official wrote, "might be most serious."[17] Acheson underlined these facts in his Mississippi speech.

At Harvard, Marshall urged Europeans to create a long-term program that would "provide a cure rather than a mere palliative." On June 13 British Foreign Minister Ernest Bevin accepted Marshall's suggestion that Europeans take the initiative. Bevin traveled to Paris to talk with French Foreign Minister Georges Bidault. The question of Russian participation became uppermost in their discussions. *Pravda* had labeled Marshall's speech as a Truman Doctrine with dollars, a useless attempt to save the American economy by dominating

---

[17]Jones, *Fifteen Weeks*, p. 207.

European markets. Bidault ignored this; pressured by the powerful French Communist party and fearful that Russia's absence might compel France to join the Anglo-Saxons in a divided Europe dominated by a resurrected Germany,[18] he decided to invite Molotov. The Russian line immediately moderated.

On June 26 Molotov arrived in Paris with eighty-nine economic experts and clerks, then spent much of the next three days conferring over the telephone with Moscow officials. The Russians were giving the plan serious consideration. They had even ordered their East European satellites to be prepared to join the plan. Molotov finally proposed that each nation individually establish its own recovery program. The French and British proposed instead that Europe as a whole create the proposal for American consideration. They also watered down his demands that new controls be clamped on Germany. Molotov angrily quit the conference, warning that the plan would undermine national sovereignty, revive Germany, allow Americans to control Europe, and, most ominously, divide "Europe into two groups of states . . . creating new difficulties in the relations between them."[19] Within a week after his return to Moscow, the Soviets set their own "Molotov Plan" in motion. The Poles and the Czechs, who had expressed interest in Marshall's proposal, now informed the Paris conference that they could not attend because it "might be construed as an action against the Soviet Union."

As the remaining sixteen European nations hammered out a program for Marshall to consider, the United States moved on another front: it determined to revive Germany quickly. In late 1946 the Americans and British had overridden French opposition to merge economically the U.S. and British zones in Germany. Administrative duties were given to Germans. By mid-July 1947 Washington officials so rapidly rebuilt German industry that Bidault finally pleaded with Marshall to slow down or else the French government would never survive to carry through the economic recovery program. The United

---

[18]For example, *The New York Times*, June 19, 1947, p. 1.
[19]Text in *The New York Times*, July 3, 1947, p. 3; Scott D. Parrish and Mikhail M. Narinsky, *New Evidence on the Soviet Rejection of the Marshall Plan: Two Reports*. Cold War International History Project, Woodrow Wilson International Center (Washington, D.C., 1994), pp. 4–29.

States nevertheless continued to rebuild German nonmilitary industry to the point where the country would be both self-sufficient and able to aid the remainder of Western Europe. On September 22 the Paris meeting completed its work, pledging increased production, tariff reductions, and currency convertibility in return for American aid. The State Department could view its successes in Germany during the summer as icing on the cake.

The European request for a four-year program of $17 billion of American aid now had to run the gauntlet of a Republican Congress, which was dividing its attention between slashing the budget and attacking Truman, both in anticipation of the presidential election only a year away. In committee hearings in late 1947 and early 1948, the executive presented its case. Only large amounts of government money which could restore basic facilities, provide convertibility of local currency into dollars, and end the dollar shortage would stimulate private investors to rebuild Europe, administration witnesses argued. Then a rejuvenated Europe could offer many advantages to the United States: eradicate the threat of continued nationalization and socialism by releasing and stimulating the investment of private capital; maintain demand for American exports; encourage Europeans to produce strategic goods, which the United States could buy and stockpile; preserve European and American control over Middle Eastern oil supplies from militant nationalism, which might endanger the weakened European holdings; and free Europeans from economic problems so that they could help the United States militarily. It would all be like magic.

George Kennan summarized the central problem in a note to Acheson. "Communist activities" were not "the root of the difficulties of Western Europe" but rather "the disruptive effects of the war on the economic, political, and social structure of Europe." So in the final plan Italy, with Europe's largest Communist party, received less aid than other, more economically important nations. In this sense the plan revolved around a rebuilt and autonomous Germany. As Secretary of State Marshall told Congress, "The restoration of Europe involved the restoration of Germany. Without a revival of German production there can be no revival of Europe's economy. But we must be very careful to see that a revived Germany cannot again threaten the European community." The Marshall Plan offered a way to circumvent Allied restrictions on German development, for it tied the Germans to a general European program and then offered vast sums to such nations as France which might otherwise be reluctant to support reconstructing Germany.[20]

The Marshall Plan served as an all-purpose weapon for Truman's foreign policy. It charmed those who feared a slump in American exports and who believed, communist threat or no communist threat, that American and world prosperity rested on a vigorous export trade. A spokesman for the National Association of Manufacturers, for example, appeared considerably more moderate toward communism than some government officials when he argued that Europe suffered not from "this so-called communistic surge," but from a "production problem" which only the Marshall Plan could solve.[21] Appropriately, Truman named as administrator of the plan Paul Hoffman, a proven entrepreneur who, as Acheson once observed, preached a "doctrine of salvation by exports with all the passion of an economic Savonarola."[22] The plan also attracted a group, including Reinhold Niebuhr, which placed more emphasis upon the containment of communism. The plan offered all things to all people. Or almost all, for Henry Wallace decided to oppose it in late 1947 on the grounds that only by channeling aid through the United Nations could calamitous relations between the United States and the Soviet Union be avoided.

The Marshall Plan now appears to have signaled not the beginning but the end of an era. It marked the last phase in the administration's use of economic tactics as the primary means of tying together the Western world. The plan's approach, that peaceful and positive approach which Niebuhr applauded, soon evolved into military alliances. Truman proved to be correct in saying that the Truman Doctrine and the Marshall Plan "are two halves of the same walnut." Americans willingly acquiesced as the military aspects of the doctrine developed into quite the larger part.

[20]*FRUS, 1947,* III: 225–229; U.S. House of Representatives, Foreign Affairs Committee, 80th Cong., 1st and 2nd Sess., *United States Foreign Policy for a Post-War Recovery Program . . .* I (Washington, 1948): 354–359.

[21]U.S. House of Representatives, *U.S. Foreign Policy for a Post-War Recovery Program,* I: 680–681.

[22]Dean Acheson, *Sketches from Life of Men I Have Known* (New York, 1959), p. 19.

Why such programs could so easily be transformed into military commitments was explained by George Kennan in a well-timed article appearing in July 1947 under the mysterious pseudonym Mr. "X." Washington's most respected expert on Soviet affairs, Kennan (who once called Niebuhr "the father of us all") had warned throughout the early 1940s against any hope of close postwar cooperation with Stalin. In early 1946 he sent a long dispatch to Washington from Moscow suggesting that at the "bottom of the Kremlin's neurotic view of world affairs is the traditional and instinctive Russian sense of insecurity." In post-1917 Russia this became highly explosive when mixed with communist ideology and "Oriental secretiveness and conspiracy."[23] This dispatch brought Kennan to the attention of Secretary of the Navy James Forrestal, who helped bring the diplomat back to Washington and then strongly influenced Kennan's decision to publish the "X" article.

The article gave the administration's view of what made the Russians act like communists. The analysis began not by emphasizing "the traditional Russian sense of insecurity" but by assuming that Stalin's policy was shaped by a combination of Marxist-Leninist ideology, which advocated revolution to defeat the capitalist forces in the outside world, and the dictator's determination to use "capitalist encirclement" as a rationale to regiment the Soviet masses so that he could consolidate his own political power. Kennan belittled such supposed "encirclement," although he recognized Nazi-Japanese hatred of the Soviets during the 1930s. (He omitted mentioning specifically the American and Japanese intervention in Russia between 1918 and 1920 and the U.S. attempt to isolate the Soviets politically through the 1920s.) Mr. "X" believed that Stalin would not moderate communist determination to overthrow the Western governments. Any softening of the Russian line would be a diversionary tactic designed to lull the West. For in the final analysis Soviet diplomacy "moves along the prescribed path, like a persistent toy automobile wound up and headed in a given direction, stopping only when it meets some unanswerable force." Endemic Soviet aggression could thus be "contained by the adroit and vigilant application of counterforce at a series of con-

[23]Barton J. Bernstein and Allen J. Matusow, *The Truman Administration: A Documentary History* (New York, 1966), pp. 198–212; *Forrestal Diaries*, pp. 135–140. Kennan's view of Niebuhr was confirmed in Kennan's remark to the author at Cornell University in 1966.

stantly shifting geographical and political points." The United States would have to undertake this containment alone and unilaterally, but if it could do so without weakening its prosperity and political stability, the Soviet party structure would undergo a period of immense strain climaxing in "either the break-up or the gradual mellowing of Soviet power."[24]

The publication of this article triggered one of the more interesting debates of the Cold War. Walter Lippmann was the dean of American journalists and one of those who did not accept the "two halves of the same walnut" argument. He condemned the military aspects of the Truman Doctrine while applauding the Marshall Plan because he disagreed with Kennan's assessment of Soviet motivation. And that, of course, was a crucial point in any argument over American policy. In a series of newspaper articles later collected in a book entitled *The Cold War*,[25] Lippmann argued that Soviet policy was molded more by traditional Russian expansion than by communist ideology: "Stalin is not only the heir of Marx and of Lenin but of Peter the Great, and the Czars of all the Russias." Because of the victorious sweep of the Red Army into Central Europe in 1945, Stalin could accomplish what the czars for centuries had only hoped to obtain. This approach enabled Lippmann to view the Soviet advance as a traditional quest for national security and, in turn, allowed him to argue that Russia would be amenable to an offer of withdrawal of both Russian and American power from Central Europe. The fuses would thus be pulled from that explosive area.

Lippmann outlined the grave consequences of the alternative, the Mr. "X"–Truman Doctrine policy: "unending intervention in all the countries that are supposed to 'contain' the Soviet Union"; futile and costly efforts to make "Jeffersonian democrats" out of Eastern European peasants and Middle Eastern and Asian warlords; either the destruction of the United Nations or its transformation into a useless anti-Soviet coalition; and such a tremendous strain on the American people that their economy would have to be increasingly regimented and their men sent to fight on the perimeter of the Soviet bloc. The

---

[24]"The Sources of Soviet Conduct," *Foreign Affairs*, XXV (July 1947): 566–582. Kennan much later believed that the essay had been misinterpreted; see George Kennan, *Memoirs, 1925–1950* (Boston, 1967), pp. 364–367. But also see Gardner, *Architects of Illusion*, pp. 270–300.

[25]Walter Lippmann, *The Cold War: A Study in U.S. Foreign Policy* (New York, 1947).

columnist warned that if Mr. "X" succeeded in applying counterforce to the "constantly shifting geographical and political points," the Soviets would perforce be allowed to take the initiative in the Cold War by choosing the grounds and weapons for combat. Finally, Lippmann, like the administration, emphasized Germany's importance, but he differed by observing that Russia, which controlled eastern Germany, could, at its leisure, outmaneuver the West and repeat the 1939 Nazi-Soviet pact of offering the ultimate reward of reunification for German cooperation. "The idea that we can foster the sentiment of German unity, and make a truncated Germany economically strong," Lippmann wrote, "can keep her disarmed, and can use her in the anti-Soviet coalition is like trying to square the circle."

Lippmann was profound, but he had no chance of being persuasive. By the end of August 1947, the State Department rejected Lippmann's proposals for disengagement in Germany. American officials instead assumed that the "one world" of the United Nations was "no longer valid and that we are in political fact facing a division into two worlds."[26] The "X" article also indicated that the administration was operating on another assumption: economic development could not occur until "security" was established. This increasing concern with things military became evident in late 1947 when Kennan suggested that the United States change its long-standing hostility to Franco's government in Spain in order to cast proper military security over the Mediterranean area. A year earlier the United States had joined with Britain and France in asking the Spanish people to overthrow Franco by political means because his government was pro-Nazi and totalitarian. Kennan's suggestion marked the turn in Spanish-American relations, which ended in close military cooperation after 1950.[27]

The quest for military security also transformed U.S. policy in Asia. With Chiang Kai-shek's decline the State Department searched for a new partner who could help stabilize the Far East. The obvious candidate was Japan, which from the 1890s until 1931 had worked closely with Washington. It was also the potential industrial powerhouse of the area, the Germany of the Orient. Since 1945 the United

[26]*Forrestal Diaries*, p. 307.
[27]*Forrestal Diaries*, p. 328.

States had single-handedly controlled Japan. The Soviets had been carefully excluded. Even Australia was allowed to send occupation forces only after promising not to interfere with the authority of General Douglas MacArthur, head of the American government in Japan. MacArthur instituted a new constitution (in which Japan renounced war for all time), then conducted elections which allowed him to claim that the Japanese had overwhelmingly repudiated communism. To the general, as to Washington officials, this was fundamental. In 1946 MacArthur privately compared America in its fight against communism to the agony of Christ at Gethsemane, for "Christ, even though crucified, nevertheless prevailed."[28]

He added that Japan was becoming "the western [*sic*] outpost of our defenses." In 1947–1948 Japan received the "two halves of the same walnut" treatment. The State Department reversed its post-1945 policy and decided to rebuild Japanese industry and develop a sound export economy. At the same time, American bases on the islands were to be expanded and maintained until, in one official's words, "the at present disarmed soldiers of Japan are provided with arms and training to qualify them to preserve the peace."[29] As in Europe, economic development and security moved hand in hand as Americans buttressed the Pacific portion of their system.

The new security policy underwent a trial run in that longtime laboratory of U.S. policies, Latin America. After several postponements, the American nations convened at Rio de Janeiro in late summer of 1947. The U.S. delegation candidly laid out the rules for the conference. There would be no discussion of economic aid, Secretary Marshall explained, because European recovery took precedence over Latin American development. The conference must instead initiate steps toward a collective security arrangement. In doing so, the United States expected each nation to take some action against future aggressors, whether that action be military or otherwise. No nation, the American delegation argued, could remain truly neutral.

On September 2 the delegates signed the Rio Treaty providing for collective self-defense for the hemisphere, the first such treaty formulated under Articles 51 and 52 of the UN Charter. The treaty provided that an attack against one American nation would be consid-

[28]*Forrestal Diaries*, pp. 177–178.
[29]Leahy Diaries, Box 6, September 22, 1948, Leahy Papers.

ered as an attack upon all, and that when two-thirds of the hemispheric nations agreed to resist such an attack, all states must cooperate by contributing either troops or supplies.[30] Nine months earlier Vandenberg had lamented that a "Communistic upsurge" in Latin America was dividing the hemisphere, although he provided no evidence of this "upsurge."[31] After the signing of the Rio Treaty, Vandenberg rested more easily: "This is sunlight in a dark world," he informed his Senate colleagues.

The following March, the Ninth Inter-American Conference convened at Bogotá, Colombia, to provide yet more sunlight for depressed Washington officials. Again, the United States refused to make any economic commitments. At the most, Marshall hoped that he could use the occasion to create the proper atmosphere so that Latin American laws, particularly those relating to oil resources, might be made more attractive to U.S. investors. Out of this approach came the Charter of the Organization of American States, which established administrative machinery for hemispheric consultation and an Advisory Defense Committee for military strategy. This much the United States welcomed. The Latin Americans, however, stubbornly insisted on adding a statement of the principles and standards that would govern hemispheric relations. Despite U.S. objections, the motion passed. Articles 15 and 16 were incorporated in the charter. The first stated: "No State or group of States has the right to intervene, directly or indirectly, for any reason whatever, in the internal or external affairs of any other State." Article 16 was more specific: "No State may use or encourage the use of coercive measures of an economic or political character in order to force the sovereign will of another State and obtain from it advantages of any kind."[32] The U.S. Senate ratified the charter, but this was the last major inter-American conference held during Truman's presidency. The administration had obtained the desired military arrangements and, perhaps, too many political obligations.

[30]Raymond Dennett and Robert K. Turner, eds., *Documents on American Foreign Relations,* IX (1947) (Princeton, N.J., 1948): 531–543.

[31]Arthur H. Vandenberg, Jr., ed., *The Private Papers of Senator Vandenberg* (Boston, 1952), p. 335.

[32]Raymond Dennett and Robert K. Turner, eds., *Documents on American Foreign Relations,* X (1948) (Princeton, N.J., 1950): 484–502.

Of special importance to Truman's "security" effort, the President transformed what he termed "the antiquated defense setup of the United States" by passing the National Security Act through Congress in July 1947. This bill provided for a single Department of Defense to replace the three independently run services, statutory establishment of the Joint Chiefs of Staff, a National Security Council to advise the President, and a Central Intelligence Agency to correlate and evaluate intelligence activities. James Forrestal, the stepfather of Mr. "X" and the leading advocate among presidential advisers of a tough military approach to Cold War problems, became the first secretary of defense. Forrestal remained until he resigned in early spring 1949. Two months later on the night of May 22, Forrestal, suffering from mental and physical illness, jumped or accidentally fell to his death from the twelfth floor of the Bethesda Naval Hospital.

The military and personal costs of the Truman Doctrine–Mr. "X" policy were higher than expected. And the cost became more apparent as Truman and J. Edgar Hoover (director of the Federal Bureau of Investigation) carried out the President's Security Loyalty program. Their search for subversives accelerated after Canadians uncovered a Soviet spy ring. During hearings in the Senate on the appointment of David E. Lilienthal as chairman of the Atomic Energy Commission, the first major charges of "soft on communism" were hurled by Robert Taft because of Lilienthal's New Deal background and his opposition to the Baruch position on the veto in 1946. (See page 42.)

Taft's action sickened Vandenberg, who compared it to "the 'Lynch law,' " but such charges were just beginning. The House Un-American Activities Committee began to intimate that Truman was certainly correct in his assessment of communism's evil nature but lax in destroying it. In March 1948 the committee demanded the loyalty records gathered by the FBI. Truman handled the situation badly. Unable to exploit the committee's distorted view of the internal communist threat, he accused it of trying to cover up the bad record of the Republican Congress. He refused to surrender the records, ostensibly because they were in the exclusive domain of the executive, more probably because of his fear that if the Republicans saw the FBI reports, which accused some federal employees of disloyalty on the basis of hearsay, unproven allegations, and personal vendettas, November might be an unfortunate month for Truman's political aspirations.[33] Unable to discredit the loyalty program he had set in motion, trapped by his own indiscriminating anticommunist rhetoric designed to "scare hell" out of the country, Truman stood paralyzed as the ground was carefully plowed around him for the weeds of McCarthyism.

Since the Iranian and Turkish crises of 1946, the Soviets had not been active in world affairs. But Molotov's departure from the Marshall Plan conference in Paris during July 1947 marked the turn. Russian attention was riveted on Germany. Documents opened in the 1990s confirmed that the politburo interpreted the Marshall Plan to mean that Americans intended "to restore the economy of Germany and Japan on the old basis [of pre-1941] provided it is subordinated to interests of American capital." Rebuilding Europe through the plan and tying it closer to American economic power threatened Stalin's hope of influencing Western European policies. Incomparably worse, however, was linking that Europe to a restored western Germany. This not only undercut Soviet determination to keep this ancient enemy weak, as well as divided, but vastly increased the potential of that enemy, tied it to the forces of "capitalist encirclement," and revived the memories of two world wars. Finally, Stalin believed—correctly—that the Marshall Plan aimed to break up Soviet control of Eastern Europe by tying that region into a general multilateral capitalist reconstruction of all Europe. The Soviet dictator sharply reacted. The Cold War itself drastically changed.[34]

Molotov quickly initiated a series of moves to tighten Soviet control of the bloc. A program of bilateral trade agreements, the so-called Molotov Plan, began to link the bloc countries and Russia in July 1947. The final step came in January 1949, when the Council for Mutual Economic Assistance (COMECON) provided the Soviet answer to the Marshall Plan by creating a centralized agency for stimulating

[33]A useful analysis is Athan Theoharis, *Seeds of Repression: Harry S Truman and the Origins of McCarthyism* (New York, 1971).
[34]The quote is in a telegram from the Moscow Embassy to Secretary of State Marshall, May 26, 1947, Papers of Joseph Jones, Truman Library; newly available documents are analyzed in Parrish and Narinsky, *New Evidence on the Soviet Rejection of the Marshall Plan*, pp. 1–51.

and controlling bloc development. As a result of these moves, Soviet trade with the East European bloc, which had declined in 1947 to $380 million, doubled in 1948, quadrupled by 1950, and exceeded $2½ billion in 1952. Seventy percent of East European trade was carried on with either the Soviet Union or elsewhere within the bloc.[35]

Four days after his return from Paris, Molotov announced the establishment of the Communist Information Bureau (Cominform). Including communists from Russia, Yugoslavia, France, Italy, Poland, Bulgaria, Czechoslovakia, Hungary, and Rumania, the Cominform provided another instrument for increasing Stalin's control. This was his answer to the Czech and Polish interest in joining the Marshall Plan. In late August, a month before the first Cominform meeting, Soviet actions in Hungary indicated the line that would be followed. After a purge of left-wing anticommunist political leaders, the Soviets directly intervened by rigging elections. All anticommunist opposition disappeared. Three weeks later at the Cominform meeting in Warsaw, Zhdanov formally announced new Soviet policies in a speech that ranks next to Stalin's February 9, 1946, address as a Russian call to Cold War.

Zhdanov's analysis of recent international developments climaxed with the announcement that American economic power, fattened by the war, was organizing Western Europe and "countries politically and economically dependent on the United States, such as the Near-Eastern and South-American countries and China" into an anticommunist bloc. The Russians and the "new democracies" in Eastern Europe, Finland, Indonesia, and Vietnam meanwhile formed another bloc which "has the sympathy of India, Egypt and Syria." In this way Zhdanov again announced the rebirth of the "two-camp" view of the world, an attitude that had dominated Russian policy between 1927 and 1934 when Stalin bitterly attacked the West, and a central theme in the dictator's speech of February 1946. In some respects Zhdanov's announcement resembled the "two-world" attitude in the United States. The mirror image was especially striking when Zhdanov admonished the socialist camp not to lower its guard. "Just as in the past the Munich policy united the hands of the Nazi aggressors, so today concessions to the new course of the United States and

[35]Stanley J. Zyzniewski, "Soviet Foreign Economic Policy," *Political Science Quarterly*, LXXIII (June 1958): 216–219.

the imperialist camp may encourage its inspirers to be even more insolent and aggressive."[36]

Following Zhdanov's call to action the Cominform delegates sharply criticized French and Italian communists, who seemed to want a more pacific approach, and, once again following the disastrous practices of the 1927–1934 era, ordered all members to foment the necessary strikes and internal disorder for the elimination of independent socialist, labor, and peasant parties in their countries. The meeting was the high-water mark of the tough Zhdanov line in Soviet foreign policy. Its effect was soon felt not only in bloc and Western European countries but inside Russia as well. Stalin cleansed Soviet economic thinking by discrediting and removing from public view Eugene Varga, a leading Russian economist who had angered the politburo by warning that Marxists were wrong in thinking that the Western economies would soon collapse.

American officials fully understood why the Soviets were trying these new policies. As Secretary of State Marshall told Truman's cabinet in November 1947, "The advance of Communism has been stemmed and the Russians have been compelled to make a reevaluation of their position."[37] America was winning its eight-month Cold War. But the Soviets' difficulties provided an excuse for Congress, which was not anxious to send billions of dollars of Marshall Plan aid to Europe if the Russians posed no threat. Congress dawdled as the plan came under increased criticism. Taft urged that good money not be poured into a "European TVA." On the other side of the political spectrum, Henry Wallace labeled it a "Martial Plan." In speeches around the country Marshall tried to sell the program for its long-term economic and political benefits. His arguments fell on deaf ears. The American economy seemed to be doing well. Just weeks before the 1948 presidential campaign was to begin, Truman faced a major political and diplomatic defeat.

And then came the fall of Czechoslovakia. The Czechs had uneasily coexisted with Russia by trying not to offend the Soviets while keeping doors open to the West. This policy had started in late 1943, when Czech leaders signed a treaty with Stalin that, in the view of most observers, obligated Czechoslovakia to become a part of the

---

[36]Andrei Zhdanov, "The International Situation," reprinted in *The Strategy and Tactics of World Communism,* Supplement I (Washington, 1948): 212–230.
[37]*Forrestal Diaries,* pp. 340–341.

Russian bloc. President Edvard Beneš and Foreign Minister Jan Masaryk, one of the foremost diplomatic figures in Europe, had nevertheless successfully resisted complete communist control. Nor had Stalin moved to consolidate his power in 1946 after the Czech Communist party emerged from the parliamentary elections with 38 percent of the vote, the largest total of any party. By late 1947 the lure of Western aid and internal political changes began to pull the Czech government away from the Soviets. At this point Stalin, who like Truman recalled the pivotal role of Czechoslovakia in 1938, decided to put the 1943 treaty into effect. Klement Gottwald, the Czech Communist party leader, demanded the elimination of independent parties. In mid-February 1948 Soviet armies camped on the border as Gottwald ordered the formation of a wholly new government. A Soviet mission of top officials flew to Prague to demand Beneš's surrender. The communists assumed full control on February 25. Two weeks later Masaryk either committed suicide, or, as Truman believed, was the victim of "foul play."

Truman correctly observed that the coup "sent a shock throughout the civilized world." He privately believed, "We are faced with exactly the same situation with which Britain and France was faced in 1938–9 with Hitler."[38] In late 1947 Hungary had been the victim of a similar if less dramatic squeeze. Within two months new opportunities would beckon to the Cominform when the Italian election was held. On March 5 a telegram arrived from General Clay in Germany. Although "I have felt and held that war was unlikely for at least ten years," Clay began, "within the last few weeks, I have felt a subtle change in Soviet attitude which . . . gives me a feeling that it may come with dramatic suddenness." For ten days government intelligence worked furiously investigating Clay's warnings and on March 16 gave Truman the grim assurance that war was not probable within sixty days.[39] Two days before, on March 14, the Senate had endorsed the Marshall Plan by a vote of 69 to 17. As it went to the House for consideration, Truman, fearing the "grave events in Europe [which] were moving so swiftly," decided to appear before Congress.

In a speech remarkable for its repeated emphasis on the "in-

---

[38]Margaret Truman, *Harry S Truman* (New York, 1973), p. 392; for the Czech-U.S.S.R. background, see Vojtech Mastny, *Russia's Road to the Cold War* (New York, 1979), pp. 133–142, 281–282.
[39]*Forrestal Diaries*, pp. 387, 395.

creasing threat" to the very "survival of freedom," the President proclaimed the Marshall Plan "not enough." Europe must have "some measure of protection against internal and external aggression." He asked for Universal Military Training, the resumption of Selective Service (which he had allowed to lapse a year earlier), and speedy passage of the Marshall Plan.[40] Within twelve days the House approved authorization of the plan's money.

With perfect timing and somber rhetoric, Truman's March 17 speech not only galvanized passage of the plan but accelerated a change in American foreign policy that had been heralded the previous summer. Congress stamped its approval on this new military emphasis by passing a Selective Service bill. Although Universal Military Training, one of Forrestal's pet projects, found little favor, a supposedly penny-proud Congress replaced it with funds to begin a seventy-group air force, 25 percent larger than even Forrestal had requested.

Perhaps the most crucial effect of the new policy, however, appeared in the administration's determination to create great systems that would not only encourage military development but also compel the Western world to accept political realignments. The first of these efforts had been the Rio Pact and the new policies toward Japan. The next, somewhat different, and vastly more important effort would be the North Atlantic Treaty Organization (NATO).

Some 45 years later documents came to light revealing that much of the March 1948 crisis had been invented. The fall of Czechoslovakia was certainly real, although its causes and implications were more complex and ambiguous than Truman announced in 1948. Less complex and ambiguous were the other causes of the war scare. It is now clear that U.S. officials, especially Forrestal and his Pentagon advisers, concocted the scare (including General Clay's remarkable telegram) to terrify Congress into passing bills for a major military buildup (especially in the air force, where U.S. aircraft manufacturers lobbied for more money) and Universal Military Training. The scare was also designed to push neutral-minded Europeans into seeking the protection of a U.S.-dominated military alliance. Except for the Universal Training, the scare tactics worked to a remarkable degree. Domestic needs, at least as some officials and interests defined those needs, again determined foreign policy.[41]

---

[40]*Documents on American Foreign Relations*, X (1948): 5–9.
[41]Frank Kofsky, *Harry S Truman and the War Scare of 1948* (New York, 1995), especially "Foreword" to 1995 edition.

CHAPTER 4

The "Different World" of NSC-68 (1948–1950)

During the spring of 1948 a united administration, enjoying strong support on foreign policy from a Republican Congress, set off with exemplary single-mindedness to destroy the communist threat that loomed over Europe. Within two years this threat had been scotched, but the officials who created the policy had split, the Congress that ratified the policy had turned against the executive, the administration had fought off charges that it had been infiltrated by communists, and the United States found itself fighting a bloody war not in Europe but in Asia. These embarrassments did not suddenly emerge in 1950 but developed gradually from the policies of 1948–1949.

During March 1948, as Congress approved the Marshall Plan, the British, the French, and the Benelux signed the Brussels Treaty. In this defense arrangement each signatory promised to aid the other parties in the event of attack with all military and other aid "in their power." Truman applauded the treaty, and soon Senator Vandenberg and Robert Lovett, Acheson's successor as under secretary of state, were spending long evenings in Vandenberg's Wardman Park Hotel suite drawing up a congressional resolution to pave the way for American entry into the new European association. Presented to the Senate on May 19, the Vandenberg Resolution genuflected briefly before the UN Charter, then passed on to the more vital business of requesting a regional arrangement, under Vandenberg's pet Article 51, in which the United States would participate militarily. This breezed through the Senate on June 11 by a 64 to 4 vote, and Lovett began a three-month-long series of conferences with European leaders to draft a final treaty. These discussions had barely begun when they were shaken by two events. In Europe the Berlin blockade severely tested Western unity. In the United States a foreign-policy debate erupted during the presidential campaign.

The Berlin blockade had its beginnings in those moments of 1945 and 1946 when the breakdown of the Four Power Allied Control Council made impossible the reunification of Germany. The Soviets continued to hope they could create a unified but demilitarized Germany under their own aegis, or, as Molotov told Byrnes in 1946, a united Germany which could be neutralized after Russia received adequate industrial reparations. As Americans stressed, however, the prosperity of Western Europe depended on German industrial recovery. If it could not reunify Germany, the West could develop the western, industrial portions controlled by France, Great Britain, and the United States and integrate the areas into a new European community. These three powers plus the Benelux reached agreement on this approach during intermittent meetings in London from February into June. As outlined in a communiqué of March 6, 1948, the London Conference determined to bring Germany within the "economic reconstruction of western Europe." The basis for an independent Germany with a "federal form of government" would also be shaped through a fusion of the three Western zones. The Ruhr's great resources were to be brought under joint control of the Western powers.[1] By late June the conference began a currency reform to repair the inflation and widespread black market activities caused in Germany and West Berlin by the weak reichsmark.

For the Soviets the crisis was at hand. The Western moves were obviously designed to accept and exploit the status quo in Germany. The Soviets, however, predicated their European policy on a weakened non-Western Central Europe, and with the passage of the Marshall Plan and the rebuilding of West Germany they now faced the imminent defeat of that policy. Worse, Stalin confronted the prospect of a revitalized West Berlin deep inside the Soviet zone. Then, suddenly, the dictator's authority was challenged from within the bloc itself.

Tito was quite unlike Stalin's other followers in Eastern Europe. As a guerrilla leader he had successfully resisted the Nazis, and in doing so had created a mass basis of support at a time when Stalin and other communist leaders increasingly rested their power on elite groups. His country, unlike Czechoslovakia, did not border on the Soviet Union and enjoyed access to the Mediterranean area. Tito's be-

---

[1]U.S. Senate, Committee on Foreign Relations, 87th Cong., 1st Sess., Documents on Germany, 1944–1961 (Washington, 1961), pp. 87–88.

lief in communism had never been in question. He was the only bloc leader who fully supported Stalin's and Zhdanov's creation of the Cominform. Tito's nationalism, however, had never been questioned either. When Stalin began to demand full Yugoslav adherence to the new economic and mutual assistance pacts, Tito balked. Enraged, Stalin claimed, "I will shake my little finger—and there will be no more Tito."[2]

The Yugoslav's secret police, however, proved superior to Stalin's, and after the Soviet dictator tried in vain to overthrow Tito with an internal coup, Stalin called a special Cominform meeting in June 1948 to expel Yugoslavia from the bloc for "taking the route of nationalism." Tito not only successfully challenged Stalin's power but disproved Stalin's key assumption that the world was divided into "two camps," with any so-called third force only a cover for capitalism. Having shaken both Stalin's power and theory, Tito's example threatened Soviet control throughout Eastern Europe. At that moment in mid-June when Stalin was preparing to bring Tito's many sins into the open, the Allies challenged Soviet policies in Germany. Stalin's first reaction was the ordering of bloody purges in Eastern Europe to exterminate nascent Titos. During the next two years probably one of every four communist members in the bloc fell from grace.

He next attempted to sever the West from the 2.4 million West Berliners. On June 24 the Soviets stopped all surface traffic between Berlin and the Western zones. The Western powers had never negotiated a pact guaranteeing these rights. The Soviets now rejected arguments that occupation rights in Berlin and the use of the routes during the previous three years had given the West legal claim to unrestricted use of the highways and railroads. On June 28 came the American response. Without consulting anyone but a few cabinet members, Truman decided, as Forrestal recalled the President's words, "We [are] going to stay period." Secretary of State Marshall later placed this decision within a context that bore an eerie resemblance to Stalin's policy framework: "We had the alternative of following a firm policy in Berlin or accepting the consequences of failure of the rest of our European policy."[3] The domino theory could

---

[2]Nikita S. Khrushchev, *The Crimes of the Stalin Era. Special Report to the 20th Congress of the Communist Party of the Soviet Union,* annotated by Boris I. Nicolaevsky (New York, 1956), p. 48. This copy from *The New Leader* is well annotated.

[3]James Forrestal, *The Forrestal Diaries,* Walter Millis, ed. (New York, 1951), pp. 454–455.

work, apparently, on both sides of the Iron Curtain, and Germany had become the first domino.

The United States began a massive airlift, ultimately lasting 324 days, which soon delivered 13,000 tons of supplies a day. Stalin was playing for high stakes, but so was Truman. In July he transferred to England two groups of B-29 bombers, the planes designated to carry atomic bombs. Truman's action indicated how the monopoly of these bombs allowed the administration to balance the budget and cut back conventional army forces, yet not diminish its capacity or willingness to brandish military force. The President assured Forrestal and Marshall that, although he prayed the bomb would not have to be used, "if it became necessary, no one need have a misgiving but what he would do so." The evening after Truman made this remark, a meeting of leading newspaper publishers agreed that if war occurred over Berlin, the American people would expect the bomb to be dropped. Taking these words at face value, the Pentagon requested that control of the bomb be transferred from the President to the military so that preparations could be made for its use. Here Truman drew the line: he did not intend "to have some dashing lieutenant colonel decide when would be the proper time to drop one." This decision became more significant when Lovett brought word back to Washington that General Clay, the American commander in Berlin, "was now drawn as tight as a steel spring."[4]

In mid-May 1948 Truman gave further evidence of his presidential power, although this occurred less in the context of possible atomic war against the Soviets than inevitable political war against Republicans. Shortly after 6:00 P.M. on May 14, the President recognized the state of Israel just minutes after the Israelis had proclaimed the existence of their new nation. Truman did this after rejecting the advice of both his military and diplomatic advisers. For months Forrestal had warned that recognizing the Israelis, who were fighting a bloody war against the Arabs for possession of Palestine, would lead to the loss of vital Middle Eastern oil resources in the Arab states. Truman, however, had supported large-scale Jewish immigration into Palestine. In 1947 he hoped Palestine could be partitioned so that a separate Jewish state could be created. Not illogically, therefore, he agreed with his political rather than his diplomatic advisers. The Jew-

---

[4]*Forrestal Diaries*, pp. 487–489, 460–461, 480–481.

ish vote could be decisive in such key states as Ohio, New York, and California. Although the President sincerely sympathized with the Israeli effort in Palestine, British Prime Minister Clement Attlee was also correct when he observed that Truman overrode his diplomatic advisers because "there's no Arab vote in America but there's a very heavy Jewish vote and the Americans are always having elections."[5]

In the decisions on Berlin and Israel, Truman enjoyed such strong congressional support (although Congress had not been formally consulted in either instance) that foreign policy never became a major issue between Truman and the Republican nominee, Thomas E. Dewey of New York, during the 1948 presidential campaign. Reinhold Niebuhr summarized the basic viewpoint of most Republicans and Democrats when he wrote in *Life* magazine in September 1948, "For peace we must risk war." The Soviets were weaker and would not fight, Niebuhr declared. "We cannot afford any more compromises. We will have to stand at every point in our far-flung lines."[6] These views underlay the foreign-policy planks of both parties, although the platforms did not agree in every particular. In contrast to the Democrats, the Republicans emphasized the need to save China, lauded bipartisanship, placed heavier emphasis on building the military, and accused the President of not comprehending the real nature of the Russian peril. The Democrats answered the last charge by inserting a plank (which had no counterpart in the Republican platform) condemning communism "overseas and at home," and pledging strong enforcement of antisubversive laws.

The Cold War entered the campaign, but the clash occurred between the Democrats and Henry Wallace's Progressive party. As the Progressives cried that the "old parties" did not want a settlement with Russia, Wallace, along with many of his noncommunist supporters, became fair game to those Americans committed to fighting the Cold War with no holds barred. Apparently because of his political views, one Wallace supporter was stabbed to death in Charleston, South Carolina. At Evansville College, Bradley University, Northwestern, the University of Georgia, the University of Miami, and the University of New Hampshire, Progressive party adherents were either fired or made to suffer in other ways for their political convic-

---

[5]Clement Attlee, *Twilight of Empire* (New York, 1961), p. 181.
[6]Reinhold Niebuhr, "For Peace We Must Risk War," *Life*, XXV (September 20, 1948): 38–39.

tions. The Americans for Democratic Action, afraid that Wallace might split the liberal vote and hand the victory to Dewey, tried to use guilt-by-association tactics by printing in major urban newspapers the names of the Progressive party's principal contributors and then listing the organizations on the attorney general's list of subversive groups to which these contributors belonged—or had belonged long before.[7]

The growing tension over Berlin and Truman's shift to the left on domestic issues killed any hopes the Progressives nursed of determining the election. Clark Clifford, Truman's closest political adviser, was prophetic, for a year before he had told the President: "There is considerable political advantage to the Administration in its battle with the Kremlin. . . . The worse matters get, up to a fairly certain point—real danger of imminent war—the more there is a sense of crisis. In times of crisis the American citizen tends to back up his President."[8] Wallace received only 1,157,326 votes; half came from New York. Overcoming handicaps imposed by defections to the Wallacite left and the Dixiecrat right, and by public opinion polls which showed him trailing Dewey, Truman lustily enjoyed scoring the greatest upset in twentieth-century American politics. The Progressive party rapidly declined, Wallace finally quitting in 1950 when he supported Truman's actions in Korea. In Europe negotiations resumed on the NATO treaty.

These negotiations for a military alliance moved to the front of American diplomatic activity. In his Inaugural Address of January 20, 1949, Truman made a slight effort to restore some balance when, in outlining the four major points of his foreign policy, he suggested as the so-called Point Four "a bold new program" to spread scientific and industrial knowledge to the newly emerging areas. The President and Congress moved slowly in implementing this glamorous concept. The business community, on which Truman depended for the passage and implementation of any large aid program, attacked the probability of more governmental interference in the less industrialized countries, asking instead that Truman negotiate with these nations treaties assuring fair and equitable treatment of private investment and personnel. For a year and a half, Truman could obtain no Point

---

[7]Karl M. Schmidt, *Henry A. Wallace: Quixotic Crusade, 1948* (Syracuse, 1960), pp. 86–88, 159, 252.

[8]Allan Yarnell, *Democrats and Progressives* (Berkeley, 1974), chapter III, especially p. 37.

Four legislation. In the summer of 1950 Congress finally passed a token appropriation of $27 million to begin a technical aid program in conjunction with the United Nations. Even the method was attacked by Senator Tom Connally, Democratic chairman of the Foreign Relations Committee: "I don't see why in the world we need to turn this over and let . . . the United Nations run it and . . . mess it all up."[9] Senator Connally's feeling ran somewhat contrary to Point One of Truman's Inaugural Address—full support of the United Nations.

The other two points of the address—the encouragement of European recovery and the pledging of aid to help nations defend themselves—were more plausible. Here Truman dealt with the familiar cultures and policies of Europe. He also worked with a new secretary of state who knew Europe intimately. The most important American policymaker in the post-World War II era, Dean Acheson founded his foreign policy on those Atlantic ties which statesmen in Europe traditionally considered the last hope of Western civilization. As a young, brilliant lawyer whom Roosevelt had plucked out of Washington's most august law firm, Acheson had resigned from the early New Deal because he considered Roosevelt's monetary policies rather weird. The approach of war, however, drew Acheson back into government, and between 1941 and 1947 he devoted himself to the European policies which climaxed with the Marshall Plan.

As a good conservative, Acheson gave his allegiance to the Western partnership, in which he correctly viewed the United States to be senior partner. This allegiance overcame his few qualms about the later New or Fair Deals. His fear of the Soviet menace satisfied even Vandenberg: Acheson "is so totally anti-Soviet and is going to be so *completely* tough," the Michigan senator wrote from a Foreign Ministers conference in May 1949, "that I really doubt whether there is any *chance at all*" for an agreement.[10]

Nor did Acheson allow the wishes of the multitude to disturb his outlook. The growing popularity of public opinion polls, he remarked in 1946, signifies that "we have become of a somewhat hypochondriac type, and ascertain our state of health by this mass temperature taking. Fortunately this was not one of the hardships of Valley Forge."

[9]Quoted in Richard P. Stebbins, *United States in World Affairs, 1950* (New York, 1951), p. 98.
[10]Arthur H. Vandenberg, Jr., ed., *The Private Papers of Senator Vandenberg* (Boston, 1952), p. 485.

As for the United Nations, "in the Arab proverb, the ass that went to Mecca remained an ass, and a policy has little added to it by its place of utterance." Congress did not escape his wrath. Its function in foreign policy, he later observed, "is the function of people who don't know and don't care and are obstructive, and they are just generally raising hell around." As for individuals, "the question of sincerity of a United States Senator is beyond me. . . . He is an honest man, he is an intense fellow, he gets all worked up, the blood rushes to his head, he takes on kind of a wild, stary look at you, and I just do not think his mind works in a normal way when he gets excited."[11]

Acheson preferred to place his confidence in power manipulated by an elite. In certain respects he sounded much like Niebuhr. After World War II, Acheson declared, Americans "learned how wrong the prophets of the Enlightenment had been about what moved peoples. These prophets overestimated the influence of wisdom, virtue, and understanding of experience, and underestimated prejudice, passion and dogma." And there was power: "Power politics had no place in our Celestial City; but a substantial place in the twentieth century." So there they were, sin and power. His war against communism, his trust in power (especially military power) to contain sin, and the veneration he had for traditional Europe admirably suited Acheson for the new era to be opened by the NATO pact.[12]

The world in which NATO was to be born was undergoing rapid change. Nowhere was this more evident than in the Soviet Union. The Allied response to the Berlin blockade and Tito's defiance of the Cominform forced Stalin to question Zhdanov's fanaticism. By the end of July 1948, Zhdanov was dead, perhaps poisoned, more likely the victim of a heart attack after violent arguments with Stalin. Zhdanov's supporters disappeared in a mass purge, and Georgy Malenkov and Nikita Khrushchev, both of whom wanted Stalin to devote more attention to internal economic problems, moved up the rungs of power.

During April 1949 the Soviets began lifting the Berlin blockade. In Western Europe, which NATO was to undergird, Italian and French communists lost considerable ground. Despite a recession

[11]Princeton Seminar, October 10–11, July 22–23, 1953, Acheson Papers, Truman Library.
[12]Dean Acheson, *Pattern of Responsibility; Edited by McGeorge Bundy from the Record of Secretary of State Dean Acheson* (Boston, 1952), pp. 17, 21; Dean Acheson, "The Truman Years," *Foreign Service Journal,* XLII (August 1965): 23.

caused by an American economic downturn, overall production in Western Europe exceeded the 1938 level by 15 percent. As Truman's chief diplomatic troubleshooter W. Averell Harriman testified, fear in Europe "no longer exists as it existed 18 months ago."[13]

In this changing, quieter international environment, the Senate opened hearings on the NATO pact. Twelve nations had signed it: the United States, Canada, Denmark, France, Iceland, Italy, Portugal, Norway, Great Britain, and the Benelux. They pledged to use force only in self-defense and to develop "free institutions," particularly through the encouragement of "economic collaboration between any or all" of the parties. Article 5 was central:

> The Parties agree that an armed attack against one or more of them in Europe or North America shall be considered an attack against them all; and consequently they agree that, if such an armed attack occurs, each of them . . . will assist the Party or Parties so attacked by taking forthwith, individually and in concert with the other Parties, such action as it deems necessary, including the use of armed force.

Article 11 modified this commitment by adding that the pact's provisions shall be carried out in accordance with each nation's "constitutional processes." Vandenberg and Connally had inserted this clause in an attempt to curb executive powers. Article 9 established a council to implement defense policies. Articles 12 and 13 provided for a review in ten years; after twenty years any member could quit after giving one-year's notice.

At first the hearings went well. Acheson calmed some fears by emphasizing that no one "at the present time" contemplated following NATO with "a Mediterranean pact, and then a Pacific pact, and so forth." Everyone present agreed that European defense could not be entrusted to the United Nations. A consensus formed on the proposition that NATO "is to create not merely a balance of power, but a preponderance of power." This fitted into Truman's and Acheson's policies of dealing with the Russians from "positions of strength." The West, however, already enjoyed such a "preponderance" because of its possession of the atomic bomb. NATO promised to add little more. This led to questions which soon revealed that even administration spokesmen had difficulty discovering the pact's military importance.

[13]U.S. Senate, Committee on Foreign Relations, 81st Cong., 1st Sess., *Hearings . . . on . . . The North Atlantic Treaty* (Washington, 1949), p. 203.

At the time, the West's dozen underequipped divisions faced twenty-five fully armed Russian divisions in Central Europe. When asked whether the administration planned to send "substantial" numbers of U.S. troops to shore up the European defenses, Acheson and General Omar Bradley, Chairman of the Joint Chiefs of Staff, assured the Senate, in Acheson's words, "The answer to that question, Senator, is a clear and absolute 'no.' " Continuing their search for the manpower that would fill NATO, Acheson was asked whether he contemplated putting Germans back into uniform. "We are very clear," he replied, "that the disarmament and demilitarization of Germany must be complete and absolute."[14]

The questioning necessarily took another line. Perhaps NATO was then aimed at preventing internal subversion in Western Europe? Acheson called the possibility of successful subversion "remote" and thought the American reaction to a coup would be the less-than-drastic response of allowing the victim to leave the NATO alliance. Clearly the treaty's military significance was not overwhelming.[15]

The key to the American view of the treaty emerged when Harriman remarked that if NATO was not carried through "there would be a reorientation" in Europe climaxing in "a restrengthening of those that believe in appeasement and neutrality." In a similar vein, Acheson commented a year later, "Unity in Europe requires the continuing association and support of the United States. Without it free Europe would split apart." Now that the Marshall Plan was reviving Europe economically, the United States, in the full splendor of its postwar power, was attempting to strengthen its political ties with, and influence over, Europe through the creation of common military institutions. Senator Connally succinctly phrased this in the Senate debate: "The Atlantic Pact is but the logical extension of the principle of the Monroe Doctrine."[16]

The Senate ratified the treaty 82 to 13. On the day he added his

---

[14]Committee on Foreign Relations, *Hearings on* [NATO], pp. 54, 57, 47, 183, 144.
[15]Committee on Foreign Relations, *Hearings on* [NATO], pp. 25, 310, 317.
[16]Committee on Foreign Relations, *Hearings on* [NATO], p. 231; Acheson, *Pattern of Responsibility*, p. 55; Tom Connally, *My Name Is Tom Connally* (New York, 1954), p. 231. This political (rather than military) importance of NATO is also emphasized in U.S. Senate, Committee on Foreign Relations, 81st Cong., 1st and 2nd Sess., *Review of the World Situation, 1949-1950* [Executive hearings of 1949-1950 made public in 1974] (Washington, 1974), pp. 6, 12-13.

signature in mid-July 1949, Truman sent Congress a one-year Mutual Defense Assistance (MDA) bill providing for $1 ½ billion for European military aid. This was the immediate financial price for the NATO commitment. A memorandum circulating through the executive outlined the purpose of MDA: "to build up our own military industry," to "create a common defense frontier in Western Europe" by having the Allies pool "their industrial and manpower resources," and particularly, to subordinate "nationalistic tendencies."[17] In the House, however, the bill encountered tough opposition from budget-cutting congressmen. On September 22 President Truman announced that Russia had exploded an atomic bomb. Within six days the NATO appropriations raced through the House and went to the President for approval.

Although publicly playing down the significance of the Russian test, the administration painfully realized that, in Vandenberg's words, "This is now a different world." Few American officials had expected the Soviet test this early. Because it was simultaneous with the fall of China, the American diplomatic attitude further stiffened. As Leo Szilard, one of the foremost scientists in the development of the American bomb, explained, "The Russians can affect the political attitude of Western Europeans just by threatening to bomb them."[18] For American policymakers the struggle for Europe had reopened. Truman took a first step in the new battle by ordering that development of the hydrogen bomb be accelerated. The second step occurred when American military authorities determined to build a large conventional European army which would include German military units. In August the first elections in West Germany for a national parliament had given Konrad Adenauer's Christian Democratic Union a plurality of 31 percent of the votes. A vigorous seventy-three years of age, Adenauer had spent his early political life in Cologne city government and then, from 1933–1945, in Nazi prisons. His rise to power in 1949 resulted more from ruthless political infighting than from charisma. He personally enjoyed little national support, but he had a

---

[17]"Effect of the MAP on U.S. Security," draft from Foreign Assistance Coordinating Committee, June 22, 1949, Papers of David D. Lloyd, Truman Library.
[18]Leo Szilard, "A Personal History of the Bomb." In "The Atlantic Community Faces the Bomb," *University of Chicago Roundtable,* September 25, 1949, p. 4.

clear vision: a restored, independent Germany could develop only through close cooperation with the United States. Adenauer dedicated the last two decades of his life to realizing this vision. American officials appreciated Adenauer's obvious statesmanship but disagreed over tactics. A U.S. Army planning unit outlined a program for German rearmament and launched a campaign to procure NATO's acceptance. The State Department, however, demurred, arguing that building a German army could create political reaction at home, unpleasant responses from Poland and Russia, and strong hostility in France.[19] The French probably knew little about this Washington infighting, but they fully comprehended the threat that overpowering American influence in NATO, and a possibly rearmed Germany, posed to their own independence. As it had in the past and would in the future, France retaliated by trying to increase its power on the continent at the expense of the Americans.

French Foreign Minister Robert Schuman proposed in early 1950 that "Little Europe" (France, Germany, Italy, and the Benelux) combine their heavy iron, coal, and steel industry. Like the American military's plans for German rearmament, the "Schuman Plan" would have political repercussions. Germany's basic industry would be integrated into Western Europe; the Ruhr would essentially be internationalized, thus (the French hoped) destroying Germany's military capacity while giving France entry to the area's rich coal deposits; the combining of basic industries would shortly force transport and agriculture to follow in a movement of spectacular European integration. Last, but not least, exclusion of England and the United States from the plan would increase the ability of France to influence all of Western Europe.

The French hoped to tie down Germany and shape Western Europe through economic means. Americans planned to influence Germany and Western Europe through NATO. These two approaches, in full view by early 1950, posed the alternatives for European development through the next half century. They also made understandable the growing competition and bitterness between the United States and France. In 1949–1950 George Kennan offered a third alternative. He concluded that Russia could be contained, yet Cold War

---

[19]Laurence W. Martin, "The American Decision to Rearm Germany." In Harold Stein, ed., *American Civil-Military Decisions: A Book of Case Studies* (Birmingham, Ala., 1963), pp. 646–651.

tensions eased, through some kind of neutralization plan for Central Europe. Kennan considered NATO an obstacle to such neutralization, since the new alliance permanently divided and threatened to rearm Germany.[20]

When Kennan made such arguments within the State Department, he encountered vigorous opposition from Acheson.[21] The secretary of state preferred the old to the new Mr. "X." But the Russian atomic bomb explosion deepened Kennan's convictions. In early 1950 he announced he was leaving the State Department for a year of study at Princeton. So ended another "disengagement" debate within the State Department.

Kennan's departure did not free Acheson from criticism. As a Europe-first advocate, and as secretary of state during the months when Chiang Kai-shek finally gave up China, Acheson became the target for a growing body of Chiang's supporters known as the China Lobby. The lobby had begun in the Chinese embassy during World War II, coordinating pro-Chiang propaganda in the United States and paying its expenses by illegally smuggling narcotics into the country. Until 1948 the China Lobby was not significant but then became transformed into a highly effective pressure group. First, it gained the adherence of wealthy, conservative Americans who believed Truman was selling out China and the free enterprise system to communists. Second, many Americans could not understand why the greatest power in the world stood helplessly by while Mao Zedong's communist forces conquered China. Such frustration and their incredible ignorance of China (and of the limits of American power) led to the easy conclusion that communist sympathizers hidden in the bowels of the State Department must be doing the dirty work. The wealth, the political attractiveness of these reasons for China's fall, and, in some cases, their own personal experience in Asia, attracted political support from key congressmen. These included Walter Judd, William Knowland (later Senate majority leader for the Republicans), and Senator Kenneth Wherry (who had uttered, "With God's help we

[20]George Kennan, *Memoirs, 1925–1950* (Boston, 1967), pp. 446–449.
[21]*U.S. News and World Report*, XLIV (January 17, 1958): 63.

will lift Shanghai up and up, ever up, until it is just like Kansas City."[22]).

When the China enthusiasts argued that more American aid could save Chiang, Acheson correctly responded that lack of supplies was not causing the Nationalists' headlong retreat. The chief of the American advisory group in China reported in late 1948 that these "military debacles in my opinion can all be attributed to the world's worst leadership and many other morale destroying factors that lead to a complete loss of will to fight."[23] By February 1949 the Nationalists had lost nearly half their troops, mostly by defection. Eighty percent of the American equipment given Chiang had fallen into communist hands. In April, as Mao's troops successfully crossed the Yangtze and began to sweep across southern China, Truman finally moved to terminate aid. This aroused the full fury of the China bloc, but the critics could only attack the administration, for they had no useful alternatives to offer. As Knowland candidly admitted, no responsible opponent of the Truman policy had ever proposed sending an American army to fight in China.

In August 1949 Acheson tried for the knockout blow by releasing the so-called White Paper, a 1054-page compilation of documents to support the administration's thesis that, as Acheson wrote in a long introduction, "The unfortunate but inescapable fact is that the ominous result of the civil war in China was beyond the control of the government of the United States. . . . It was the product of internal Chinese forces, forces which this country tried to influence but could not." The only alternative policy would have been a "full-scale intervention" of American troops, which "would have been resented by the mass of the Chinese people, would have diametrically reversed our historic policy, and would have been condemned by the American people." He looked forward to the time when the Chinese would throw off the "foreign yoke" of communism, but Acheson warned that if China lent "itself to the aims of Soviet Russian imperialism," the United States would consider this a violation of the UN Charter and, he implied, move to stop any aggression. The China Lobby retaliated by terming the White Paper a "whitewash of a wishful, do-

---

[22]Quoted in Eric Goldman, *The Crucial Decade and After, 1945–1961* (New York, 1960), p. 116; Ross Koen, *The China Lobby* (New York, 1960).
[23]Tang Tsou, *America's Failure in China* (Chicago, 1963), pp. 482–483.

nothing policy which has succeeded only in placing Asia in danger of Soviet conquest."[24]

Despite the China Lobby, Truman and Acheson almost took a historic step during midsummer 1949: they nearly gave their approval when the American ambassador to China, J. Leighton Stuart, asked if he could talk with Mao. The initiative had come from the communists, who clearly hoped to have some kind of diplomatic relationship with the United States. State Department officials urged that Stuart be sent to the new government. After hurried meetings at the White House, however, Acheson told Stuart that a decision "at the highest level" forbade him from talking with Mao. It was a turning point of history, but Truman and Acheson refused to turn. They believed that Mao had pledged himself to follow Stalin, and that Truman would pay a bitter political price at home if he reached out to Mao. Acheson made the decision final by announcing on October 12 that the new Chinese regime could not be recognized by the United States. Americans were particularly angered when Mao's government seized American consular property and later jailed American Consul Angus Ward.

Chiang Kai-shek fled to Formosa (now Taiwan) to establish a rival Chinese government. This presented another set of problems to Washington. In late December the Joint Chiefs and Acheson agreed that since Mao would probably conquer Formosa sometime in 1950, the United States should not give military aid to the Nationalists.[25] Chiang's supporters again organized for battle in Congress, forcing the administration to compromise when they threatened to cut off aid to Korea if some assistance was not immediately sent to Formosa. The battle was bitter, and Vandenberg, seriously ill in Michigan, could not heal the wounds suffered by bipartisanship. This fight, waged just five months before the outbreak of the Korean War, left bipartisanship a shattered ideal and no longer a practice.

Truman and Acheson determined to move slowly in the revolutionary Asian situation. American experts were not certain whether

---

[24]Dean Acheson, "Letter of Transmittal, July 30." In *United States Relations with China* . . . *1944–1949* (Washington, 1949), pp. xiv–xvii. Quoted in H. B. Westerfield, *Foreign Policies and Party Politics: Pearl Harbor to Korea* (New Haven, 1955), p. 356.
[25]U.S. Senate, Committee on Armed Services and Committee on Foreign Relations, 82nd Cong., 1st Sess., *Hearings to Conduct an Inquiry into the Military Situation in the Far East* . . . (Washington, 1951), pp. 1770–1771; cited hereafter as *Military Situation in the Far East.*

a common allegiance to Marxism-Leninism would suffice to link China and Russia in a friendly partnership. Stalin remembered the debacle of his China policies during the 1920s. The Chinese communists recalled how Stalin had cooperated with Roosevelt in recognizing Chiang's government and had kept a Soviet ambassador with the Nationalists in 1949 after most Western governments had deserted Chiang. Soviet and Chinese documents made public in the 1990s revealed that a suspicious and fearful Stalin had urged Mao not to launch the revolution in 1945, and—stunningly—apparently tried to keep China divided between Mao and Chiang as late as 1949. (Fearful of growing crises with the United States in Europe, Stalin wanted no confrontation in Asia.) Perhaps common ideology would blot out such unhappy memories of the Stalin-Mao relationship. The more fundamental question soon arose, however, of who would define that ideology. In a widely publicized interview in 1946, Liu Shao-ch'i, Mao's chief theoretician, announced that Mao had given Marxism "a new development. He has created a Chinese or Asiatic form of Marxism. . . . There are similar conditions in other lands of southeast Asia. The courses chosen by China will influence them all." In November 1949, just days before Mao left for Moscow to negotiate with Stalin, the Chinese revived Liu's 1946 interview.[26] Within the politburo itself, Stalin's policies were also being questioned.

A debate evidently erupted among top Soviet officials over whether the possession of the atomic bomb and the victory of the Chinese communists had so weakened the threat of "capitalist encirclement" that internal discipline could be eased and domestic consumer production increased. On November 6 Georgy Malenkov, one of Stalin's closest associates since the early 1930s, delivered a speech which subtly advanced the thesis that "capitalist encirclement" was crumbling. He stressed the unity of the Russian peoples and the security of Soviet borders. Boasting that the five-year plan was ahead of schedule, Malenkov challenged the West to "peaceful competition

---

[26]Quoted in Donald S. Zagoria, The Sino-Soviet Conflict, 1956–1961 (Princeton, 1962), pp. 14–15. This paragraph is also based on Brian Murray, Stalin, the Cold War, and the Division of China. . . . Cold War International History Project, Woodrow Wilson Center (Washington, D.C., 1995), pp. 1–17.

with socialism."[27] Old-line Stalinists lashed back in a speech made to the Cominform in late November. Mikhail A. Suslov, chief of the Department of Agitation and Propaganda, took Malenkov's premises and neatly turned them around to the opposite conclusion: the rising successes of Soviet power increased the immediate danger of armed conflict. Suslov argued that because the Soviets had scored such great economic and political victories, the United States had created NATO and begun work on the hydrogen bomb. Such "war-mongering" attempts to change the balance of power, now tipping slowly in favor of the Soviets, could, Suslov warned, lead to Western attacks on Eastern Europe, Communist China, and North Korea.[28]

Stalin himself reacted more indirectly. Five days before the Korean War began, he countered growing arguments that Russia was now prepared (as Malenkov indicated) for a sudden, explosive break that would force the withering away of the socialistic, that is, Stalinist, state and give birth to the long-promised utopia of communism. Explaining in an article on linguistics that language develops gradually, not through "explosions," Stalin suddenly turned on "comrades who are engrossed in explosion," informing them that neither was the theory of sudden transition "always applicable to other social phenomena."[29] Textbooks were to be rewritten to construct a state-controlled educational system which would mold the New Soviet Man and, more important, keep him under control. For Stalin wanted control, not revolution. Although brandishing the vocabulary of Marx and Lenin, he had become not only conservative, but reactionary, in an attempt to secure himself against the challenges of Malenkov and Mao Ze-dong.

The challenge from the East became apparent in discussions between Chinese and Russian leaders which began in December. More than two months of hard bargaining ensued. Stalin gained economic advantages in Sinkiang and restricted credit arrangements to China for the purchase of Soviet exports to the value of $300 million spread over five years. The Soviets later cut the value of the loan about one-fifth by devaluing the ruble. China did succeed in making the treaty

[27]*Current Digest of the Soviet Press*, I (November 22, 1949): 3–10.
[28]Marshall D. Shulman, *Stalin's Foreign Policy Reappraised* (Cambridge, Mass., 1963), pp. 118–119.
[29]Robert C. Tucker, *The Soviet Political Mind: Studies in Stalinism and Post-Stalin Change* (New York, 1963), pp. 24–25, 100–114.

one of "mutual assistance"; Russia would consult with China in the event that Japan "or any other state that should unite" with Japan threatened aggression against China. Perhaps of most importance to Mao, the Soviets promised to surrender their special rights in Manchurian ports and the Manchurian railway system. While these points were argued, Stalin moved unsuccessfully back of the scene to loosen the allegiances of Manchuria and Inner Mongolia to Peking. The "fraternal alliance" was enduring an uncommon amount of horse trading and attempted backstabbing.

George Kennan privately explained the State Department's view of the talks. He believed that the Soviets "will be extremely cautious" in spreading Marxism around Asia "because they are very, very well aware of the fact that if you cannot overshadow a country militarily, ideology is in itself an untrustworthy means with which to hold them." He recalled "Stalin one time snorting rather contemptuously and vigorously because one of our people asked them what they were going to give to China when [the war] was over and [Stalin] said in effect, 'What the hell do you think we can give to China.' He said, 'We have a hundred cities of our own to build in the Soviet Far East. If anybody is going to give anything to the Far East, I think it's you.' And I think," Kennan concluded, "he was speaking quite sincerely."[30]

On January 12, 1950, as the Mao-Stalin talks edged along, Acheson developed Kennan's basic points before the National Press Club in Washington. He viewed the Soviet attempt to control Outer and Inner Mongolia, Manchuria, and Sinkiang as "the single most significant, most important fact" in Asia. Such attempts would prove to Mao that the Soviets wished not to help but to dominate. Acheson stressed that nationalism, not communism, had become the dominant fact in postwar Asia and that consequently the United States, not Russia, would prove to be the best friend of those Chinese who want "their own national independence." In this context Acheson issued his famous declaration that the Pacific "defensive perimeter" of the United States ran from the Aleutians to Japan, the Ryukyus, and down to the Philippines. (This was not a newly announced policy. In March 1949 General MacArthur defined the perimeter as encompassing exactly the same area.[31]) Acheson doubted that the Far East was threatened as much by military aggression as by "subversion and

[30]*I.P.R. Hearings*, pp. 1558–1563.
[31]*The New York Times*, March 2, 1949, p. 22.

penetration." The secretary of state, however, carefully made two exceptions to these general policies: first, in both Japan and Korea, the United States had special economic responsibilities; second, if attack occurred west of the defense perimeter (for example, in Korea), the "entire civilized world under the Charter of the United Nations" would aid "people who are determined to protect their independence."[32]

Acheson had issued a fascinating document, acute in its view of Asian nationalism, accurate in its pinpointing of a Sino-Soviet split, precise in its sorting out of Japan and Korea as of paramount importance to American policy, but wrong in its assumption that military aggression in the area was not imminent. He had left many options open for policy maneuvers. Within a month these options were severely cut. On January 13 Yakov Malik, the Soviet delegate to the Security Council, walked out of the United Nations after his proposal to unseat Chiang's regime in favor of Mao's lost 6 to 3. The next day the Chinese communists raided American consulate grounds in Peking. The U.S. view toughened. A month later the Sino-Soviet treaty became public. Acheson interpreted the agreement as Mao's selling out the Chinese people to Stalin.[33]

The Sino-Soviet pact, the explosion of the Russian bomb, the divisive arguments over NATO, and the whimpering end of bipartisanship added up to an unpleasant winter for the Truman administration. Peace would not be found soon. Indeed, it was not to be found at all. Americans, who, like other peoples, prefer their wars short and triumphant, wondered why.

One answer had already been suggested on July 30, 1948, as the nation felt the reverberations of the Czech coup and the Berlin blockade. Elizabeth Bentley and Whittaker Chambers, a self-confessed former Communist party member, claimed before the House Un-American Activities Committee that communists had infiltrated the State Department a decade before. Chambers specifically accused Alger Hiss of being a party agent. Hiss had worked in several exec-

---

[32]Dean Acheson, "Crisis in Asia," *Department of State Bulletin*, XXII (January 23, 1950): 111–117.
[33]Dean Acheson, "United States Policy Toward Asia," *Department of State Bulletin*, XXII (March 27, 1950): 4–8.

utive departments after 1933, including the State Department, where in 1944 he helped lay the groundwork for the United Nations. His friends included Dean Acheson and John Foster Dulles. Hiss replied to Chambers with a $75,000 libel suit. Chambers then took federal agents to his Maryland farm and picked from a hollowed-out pumpkin microfilms of State Department documents which Chambers claimed Hiss had passed to him in 1938. The typing irregularities on the microfilms, so the FBI claimed, seemed to match those of one of Hiss's old typewriters. Acheson supported the former Harvard Law School graduate in the strongest terms. But a newly arrived congressman from California, Richard Nixon, determined to pursue the case until Chambers was vindicated. After one hung jury Hiss was finally convicted of perjury on January 21, 1950. Many Americans now believed they understood why the Cold War was not ending quickly and happily.

Hiss's fall carried with it much of the reputation of the Eastern liberal-intellectual group which had become identified with the reforms of the New Deal. Wallace's defection and resounding defeat, Truman's failure to pass much of his Fair Deal domestic program, and Hiss's conviction illustrated how Roosevelt's remark during World War II that "Dr. Win-the-War" had replaced "Dr. New Deal" remained relevant far into the Cold War era. The American mood by 1949 was not founded on reform but conservativism and consensus.

Perhaps nowhere was this more noticeable and explicit than in the writing of American history. In 1948 Charles Beard, the greatest of those historians who between 1910 and 1940 had emphasized and applauded reform and class and political divisions in American history, published *President Roosevelt and the Coming of the War*. Charging that FDR had knowingly broken the constitutional boundaries imposed on the executive branch so that he could take the nation into war, Beard warned that this tragedy could be repeated in any new campaign undertaken by Americans to bring peace to "the whole world." Such a campaign would undermine the Constitution, Beard argued, for the President would possess "limitless authority publicly to misrepresent and secretly to control foreign policy, foreign affairs, and the war power." As he had throughout his life, Beard used James Madison and *The Federalist* as his primary references.

Such dissent from waging the Cold War was not the fashion in 1948 and 1949, and most American historians wanted to be fashionable. Samuel Eliot Morison, Boston Brahmin, rear admiral (appointed by Roosevelt), and president of the American Historical Association, attacked Beard's legacy in an article subtitled, "History Through a Beard." The year after Morison's article appeared, Arthur Schlesinger, Jr., whose intellectual debt to Niebuhr was great, published a primer for the new liberals, which viewed their role not to the left, where Beard had wanted it, but in *The Vital Center*. Schlesinger attacked American businessmen ("capitalists") who, since they were "incapable of physical combat," developed "a legal system which penalized the use of force and an ethic which glorifies pacifism." War had been useful, particularly when it closed domestic "rifts" between Americans, as in 1917 and 1941.[34] Like the historians, President Truman took pride in his ability to search the past for present policies, but he looked elsewhere as well. "We are on the right track, and we will win," he announced in early 1950, "because God is with us in that enterprise."[35]

The Antichrist nevertheless seemed to be everywhere, even in an age that venerated consensus. On January 14 the Chinese communists attacked the American consulate offices, a week later Hiss was convicted, and on January 31 the White House announced orders to make a hydrogen bomb. "Annihilation of any life on earth has been brought within the range of technical possibilities," Albert Einstein reported over national television. On February 3 London announced that a British spy ring headed by German-born, British-naturalized Klaus Fuchs had been discovered relaying atomic secrets to Soviet agents. (Russian scientists claimed in the 1990s that Fuchs's information enabled them to explode a bomb two years earlier than they had planned. After serving a prison term, Fuchs died in East Germany in 1988.) At Wheeling, West Virginia, the junior senator from Wisconsin, Joseph McCarthy (Republican), announced on February 9 that he held in his hand proof that the Department of State was riddled with communists. The paper he waved could prove nothing even faintly related to his charges, but no matter. The timing was perfect.

The senator had not previously been known for such ideological zeal, but for an uncommon amount of political savvy. In 1946 he over-

---

[34]Samuel Eliot Morison, "Did Roosevelt Start the War: History Through a Beard," *Atlantic Monthly*, CXLII (August 1948): 91–97; Arthur Schlesinger, Jr., *The Vital Center* (Boston, 1949, 1962), especially pp. 13–14, 173.

[35]U.S. Government, *Public Papers of the Presidents of the United States . . . Truman . . . 1950* (Washington, 1965), p. 344.

came a reputation as one of the worst circuit court judges in Wisconsin history to win the Senate seat from the popular Robert M. La Follette, Jr. McCarthy accomplished this in part by running on the slogan, "Congress needs a tail-gunner," which he had never been, and by apparently destroying the legal records that reflected unfavorably on his judiciary abilities. In early 1950, with another election fight in Wisconsin only two years away, he searched for an issue. During a conversation with advisers McCarthy first dismissed the St. Lawrence Seaway project as a possibility; then, with the Hiss case in the headlines, he eagerly seized on the communist issue. After the Wheeling speech he became the center of some of the wildest scenes in Senate history. As his fellow legislators tried to pinpoint what he had charged, McCarthy's figures whirled from the 205 communists, at Wheeling, to 57 the following night, 81 on February 20, and when brought before a special Senate committee headed by the highly respected Millard Tydings, Democrat of Maryland, his figures changed again to 10, then to 116, and finally to 1. The one was Owen Lattimore, a specialist on Far Eastern studies at Johns Hopkins University. On Lattimore's conviction, McCarthy said, he would "stand or fall." When pressed for evidence the senator responded in part by reverting to Truman's refusal to allow Congress to examine the loyalty files. The executive, McCarthy claimed, was keeping the evidence locked up. The Tydings committee dismissed McCarthy as a fraud and exonerated Lattimore, but the Wisconsin senator had only begun.[36]

Mao, Malenkov, the China Lobby, McCarthy, Stalin and Truman had learned that forming consensus on the Cold War was not free of complications. A grim President, pressed by domestic critics and the new Soviet bomb, demanded a wide-ranging reevaluation of American Cold War policies. In early 1950 the National Security Council began work on a highly secret document (declassified only a quarter of a century later, and then through an accident) that would soon be known as NSC-68. Truman examined the study in April, and it was ready for implementation when Korea burst into war.

NSC-68 proved to be the American blueprint for waging the Cold War. It began with two assumptions that governed the rest of the document. First, the global balance of power had been "fundamentally

[36]Richard N. Rovere, *Senator Joe McCarthy* (New York, 1959), pp. 6, 54, 39–100, 120–122, 130, 140–160; for Fuchs's importance, see *The New York Times*, January 14, 1993, p. A12.

altered" since the nineteenth century so that the Americans and Russians now dominated the world: "What is new, what makes the continuing crisis, is the polarization of power which inescapably confronts the slave society with the free." It was us against them. Second, "the Soviet Union, unlike previous aspirants to hegemony, is animated by a new fanatic faith, antithetical to our own, and seeks to impose its absolute authority," initially in "the Soviet Union and second in the areas now under [its] control." Then the crucial sentence: "In the minds of the Soviet leaders, however, achievement of this design requires the dynamic extension of their authority and the ultimate elimination of any effective opposition to their authority. . . . To that end Soviet efforts are now directed toward the domination of the Eurasian land mass."[37]

The two top State Department experts on Russia, George Kennan and Charles Bohlen, fought against using these phrases. They believed that Stalin had no grand design for world conquest, that his attention was focused almost entirely within the Soviet bloc, and that as a conservative he actually feared overextending Russian power. Kennan went further, arguing that NSC-68 should not be drawn up at all, for it could make American policies too rigid, simple, and militaristic. Acheson overruled Kennan and Bohlen.[38] The secretary of state determined to launch a global offensive to reclaim the initiative in the Cold War and to shut up critics at home. To do this he needed a justification. The justification would be his own view of the Soviet menace. That view undergirded NSC-68.

Given Acheson's outlook, the document moved to the inevitable conclusion: the United States "must lead in building a successfully functioning political and economic system in the free world," for "the absence of order among nations is becoming less and less tolerable." To impose "order" around the globe was a rather large task, but the United States was up to it. The key would be military power that could deter "an attack upon us" while Americans went about arranging the world so that "our free society can flourish." But the administration's confidence in the use of military power went beyond

---

[37]"NSC-68. A Report to the National Security Council by the Executive Secretary on United States Objectives and Programs for National Security, April 14, 1950, Washington," pp. 4, 8, 6, 34. (Hereafter cited "NSC-68.")

[38]Paul Y. Hammond, "NSC-68: Prologue to Rearmament." In Warner P. Schilling et al., eds., *Strategy, Politics and Defense Budgets* (New York, 1962), pp. 308–311.

mere deterrence: limited wars could be fought "to compel the acceptance of terms consistent with our objectives." To wage this kind of
war, the country had to mobilize its own and its allies' economies for
a vast military effort. ("Foreign economic policy is a major instrument
in the conduct of United States foreign relations" and "peculiarly appropriate to the Cold War.") This military rebuilding was immediately required, particularly since the Western economies were going
to decline "within a period of a few years at most . . . unless more positive governmental programs are developed." The crisis was at hand.

In conclusion, therefore, NSC-68 recommended (1) against negotiations with Russia since conditions were not yet sufficient to force
the Kremlin to "change its policies drastically"; (2) development of
hydrogen bombs to offset possible Soviet possession of an effective
atomic arsenal by 1954; (3) rapid building of conventional military
forces to preserve American interests without having to wage atomic
war; (4) a large increase in taxes to pay for this new, highly expensive
military establishment; (5) mobilization of American society, including a government-created "consensus" on the necessity of "sacrifice"
and "unity" by Americans; (6) a strong alliance system directed by
the United States; (7) and—as the topper—undermining the "Soviet
totalitariat" from within by making "the Russian people our allies in
this enterprise." How this was to be done was necessarily vague. But
no matter. The assumptions and recommendations of NSC-68 were
not overburdened with modesty. Truman and Acheson were no
longer satisfied with containment. They wanted Soviet withdrawal
and an absolute victory.[39]

But, as in early 1947 before Truman "scared hell" out of them, the
American people were by no means prepared to pay such costs for
victory. Republicans and many Democrats demanded lower taxes.
Even Secretary of Defense Louis Johnson fought against NSC-68, arguing that Acheson's policies could bankrupt the country. The secretary of state finally brought the military around to accept the civilian call for larger defense budgets. The Soviet Union meanwhile
appeared quiet and contained. The political circumstances threatened to destroy Acheson's hopes that NSC-68 could be used to build

---

[39] "NSC-68," pp. 9, 12, 25–26, 28, 31, 45, 57, 23, 65, 24, 10. See also the various perspectives on this document in Ernest R. May, ed., *American Cold War Strategy: Interpreting
NSC-68* (Boston, 1993).

global "positions of strength." Only he, the President, and a few others seemed to have a clear idea of what had to be done. NSC-68 was a policy in search of an opportunity. That opportunity arrived on June 25, 1950, when, as Acheson and his aides later agreed, "Korea came along and saved us."[40]

[40]Princeton Seminar, July 8–9, 1953, Acheson Papers, Truman Library.

CHAPTER 5

Korea: The War for
Both Asia and Europe
(1950–1951)

In June 1950 Korea was a Cold War–wracked country which lacked nearly everything except authoritarian rulers, illiteracy, cholera epidemics, and poverty. For nearly a century it had been a pawn in Far Eastern power plays. In 1905 Japan, after using force to stop a Russian thrust, had established a protectorate over Korea and in 1910 annexed that country. In 1945 Japanese armies, according to Soviet-American agreement, were disarmed north of the 38th parallel by Russia and south of the line by the United States. Lengthy conferences failed to unify the nation, for neither the Soviets nor the Americans wanted to chance the possibility that a unified Korea would move into the opposing camp.

Both superpowers, however, found themselves trapped in a bloody civil conflict, Korean killing Korean, which astonishingly claimed 100,000 lives after 1946 and *before* the formal beginning in June 1950 of what Americans call the "Korean War." New scholarship reveals that the main struggle was not the United States versus the Soviet Union but left-wing Koreans (including both communists and noncommunists) against right-wing Koreans.[1] The United States worked desperately to keep the rightist groups in power. These groups were led by the venerable Syngman Rhee, who had spent long years of exile in the United States. Meanwhile middle-of-the-road factions moved increasingly to the left, for the leftists espoused an ar-

---

[1]The best accounts are Bruce Cumings's prize-winning *The Origins of the Korean War. Volume I* (Princeton, 1981); and the essays by Cumings, Mark Paul, Stephen Pelz, John Merrill, and James I. Matray in *Child of Conflict; The Korean-American Relationship, 1943–1953*, Bruce Cumings, ed. (Seattle, 1983).

dent nationalism aimed at uniting the divided nation, while Rhee appeared to be dependent on the United States for survival and was willing to accept elections only in South Korea. Vicious guerrilla war erupted between left and right in 1946. As it continued over the next two years, several crack South Korean military units defected to leftist forces.

Harry Truman never wavered in his determination to keep South Korea in the West's camp, but the growing bloodshed and Rhee's authoritarian methods (including press censorship and mass arrests of political opponents) embarrassed Truman. In 1948 he moved to pull out the remaining U.S. troops and turn the headache of pacifying the area over to the United Nations. Soviet troops also retreated from the North, but they left behind the communist regime of Kim Il Sung and Red Army advisers to whip the North's army into shape. By 1949, with North and South Korea independent nations, the fighting escalated into conventional battles. Many of these were launched by Rhee to show that he was serious about reuniting the country by force. In early 1950 the fighting died down, but the pause lasted only until Kim believed he had amassed the forces to overthrow Rhee and unite Korea under his own control.

When, therefore, Harry Truman decided in late June to commit U.S. men and machines to war, he was involving Americans not in a conflict against Stalin but in a Korean civil war that had long been waged between Rhee and Kim. Three causes probably triggered the invasion from the North on June 24, 1950. The first was Kim's belief that Rhee was highly vulnerable. The State Department had even issued public protests against Rhee's crackdown on his own people. In a May 1950 election the South Korean leader lost control of his legislature, despite arrests of leading political opponents before the balloting. As he grew less secure at home, Rhee became more belligerent toward the North. Kim might well have struck not only because Rhee was wobbling but before the South Korean president could launch his own invasion of the North.

Second, since 1946 Kim had been closely tied to Mao's Chinese communists, indeed too closely for a Korean who was a nationalist as well as a communist. He had gained a measure of independence by moving closer to the Soviet military in 1949. In early 1950 Kim traveled to Moscow several times to ask Stalin for help in conquering the South. The Russian dictator finally gave the green light and promises of supplies, but he made clear that neither Soviet forces nor prestige would be involved. If Kim's grand plans collapsed, the cautious Stalin was going to be standing clear of the debris. If Kim succeeded, however, he would break free of Mao and unite Korea. It was worth the risk.

Third, Kim's plans fitted with a general strategy which Stalin was designing to counter two threats. In mid-May Truman announced that discussions on a Japanese peace treaty would receive high priority. The negotiations would particularly consider Japanese independence and the establishment of American military bases on Japan's soil under long-term agreements. The talks, American officials said, were not to be burdened with Russian representation. For Stalin this announcement opened the unhappy prospect of unity between the two greatest industrial nations in the Pacific, perhaps even the extension of a NATO-like organization to the Asian periphery of the Soviet Union. The Sino-Soviet pact in February had singled out Japan as a potential threat to Asian communism, and this had been followed by the Soviet press's accusing Truman of attempting to "draw the Asiatic and Pacific countries into aggressive military blocs, to entangle those countries in the chains of some 'little' Marshall Plan for Asia."[2] If North Korea could unify the country, peacefully or otherwise, the threat of a militarized, Western-oriented Japan would be blunted, perhaps neutralized.

Another threat might well have caused Stalin even more concern. Mao's success had not created but probably encouraged revolutions throughout Asia, particularly in Indochina, the Philippines, and Indonesia. The possibility that some of these revolutions might triumph, perhaps following the pattern set by Mao, could weaken Stalin's two-camp premise and loosen his direction over the world communist bloc. Stalin's view of world matters had become so rigid that he could not accept the nationalist content of these revolts without wrecking his own doctrines and tempering his grip on Soviet and satellite affairs. A short and successful war by a Russian-controlled North Korea could intimidate Japan and check the expansive aims and reputation of Mao. Thus, as a new study based on formerly secret Russian documents concludes, "It was Soviet weakness that drove Stalin to support the attack on South Korea, not the unre-

---

[2]*Current Digest of the Soviet Press*, II (April 22, 1950): 19; Nikita Khrushchev, *Khrushchev Remembers*, Strobe Talbott, trans. and ed. (Boston, 1970), pp. 367–370.

strained [Russian] expansionism imagined by the authors of NSC-68."[3]

Attending to family business in Independence, Missouri, when the attack occurred, Truman immediately returned to Washington. He and Acheson assumed the invasion was Russian-directed, perhaps the beginning of an extensive Sino-Soviet thrust. Their initial reaction, however, was carefully measured. They ordered MacArthur in Tokyo to dispatch supplies to the South Korean troops. Then, moving to contain the action, Truman ordered the American Seventh Fleet to sail between China and Formosa, and sent additional assistance to counterrevolutionary forces in the Philippines and Indochina. In a hurriedly called session of the UN Security Council, an American resolution branding the North Koreans as aggressors, demanding a cessation of hostilities, and requesting a withdrawal behind the 38th parallel, passed 9 to 0, with Yugoslavia abstaining. The Soviet Union was not represented, for Yakov Malik continued his boycott to protest the exclusion of Red China. Two days later, as the military situation worsened, Truman ordered American air and naval units into action. That same day, June 27, the United Nations passed a resolution recommending that its members aid South Korea in restoring peace. This passed 7 to 1, with Yugoslavia opposing and Egypt and India abstaining. Malik still had not appeared; the rapidity and extent of Truman's reaction had taken the Soviets by surprise.

The day after American units had been committed, the President conferred with congressional leaders for the first time to inform them of his action. The only strong objection was voiced by Senator Taft, who approved of Truman's action but disliked sending Americans to war without consulting Congress. Neither then nor later did the President discuss Taft's objection with the full Congress. On June 30 Truman made the final commitment. The South Korean army of 65,000 men had suffered heavy losses in the first week of fighting. The President decided that only American ground units could stop the southward flood. In sending these troops Truman emphasized that the United States aimed only "to restore peace there and . . . restore the border." Supporting air attacks were similarly to be limited to the area around the 38th parallel.

---

[3]Kathryn Weathersby, *Soviet Aims in Korea and the Origins of the Korean War.* Working Paper No. 8, Cold War International History Project, Woodrow Wilson International Center (Washington, D.C., 1993), p. 32.

CONFLICT IN KOREA, 1950–1953

Throughout the first week of the war, the President carefully refrained from publicly linking the Russians to the attack. He hoped thereby to enable them to stop the aggression without loss of public face. Truman also used his questionable grasp of history to warn that Korea might be only a diversion. "We must be careful not to cause a general war," he told a top adviser on June 30. "Russia is figuring on an attack in the Black Sea and toward the Persian Gulf. Both are prizes Moscow has wanted since Ivan the Terrible [the sixteenth-century Russian czar] who is now their hero along with Stalin and Lenin." On June 27 Truman dispatched a note to Moscow assuring Stalin that American objectives were limited; the President expressed the hope that the Soviets would help in quickly restoring the *status quo ante bellum.* The Soviets initially responded to Truman's overtures by accusing South Korean forces of invading North Korea. Within ten days this view underwent considerable change. The war was a "civil war among the Koreans," Deputy Minister of Foreign Affairs Andrei Gromyko claimed on July 4. Under these circumstances, Gromyko concluded, the Soviet Union could take no action.[4]

Privately in June and publicly during the late summer, the Truman administration became less restrained in defining the Soviet role. "In Korea the Russians presented a check which was drawn on the bank account of collective security," Acheson claimed. "The Russians thought the check would bounce. . . . But to their great surprise, the teller paid it."[5] The terms "collective security" and "UN action" became the catchwords which supposedly explained and justified Truman's decision in late June. Both terms were misleading. The United States had no collective security pact in the Pacific in 1950. As Acheson used the term "collective security," it meant the United States would both define the extent of the "collective" and unilaterally, if necessary, furnish the "security." Nor is there any indication that the President consulted his European or Asian allies before committing American air and naval units on June 27.[6] This was not the first nor would it be the last time the United States would take unilateral action in an explosive situation without consulting its Western European partners.

As for the sudden American concern to bolster the United Nations, this had not been apparent when the United States acted unilaterally or with some Western powers to establish the Truman Doctrine, the Rio Pact, the Marshall Plan, and NATO. American actions in Korea were consistent with this history, for the United States used the resolution of June 27 to establish a military command in Korea that took orders not from the United Nations but from Washington. "The entire control of my command and everything I did came from our own Chiefs of Staff," MacArthur later recalled. "Even the reports which were normally made by me to the United Nations were subject to censorship by our State and Defense Departments. I had no direct connection with the United Nations whatsoever."[7] Sixteen nations

---

[4]"June 30, 1950—Friday," Subject File, Box 71, Papers of George Elsey, Truman Library; Harry S Truman, *Memoirs*, II (Garden City, N.Y., 1955–1956): 341, 346; Max Beloff, *Soviet Policy in the Far East, 1944–1951* (London, 1953), p. 186.
[5]Dean Acheson, *Pattern of Responsibility*, McGeorge Bundy, ed. (Boston, 1952), p. 254.
[6]For example, Truman, *Memoirs*, II: 330–340.
[7]U.S. Senate, Committee on Foreign Relations and Committee on Armed Services, *Hearings: Military Situation in the Far East* (Washington, 1951), p. 10.

finally contributed to "UN" forces, but the United States provided 50 percent of the ground forces (with South Korea providing most of the remainder), 86 percent of the naval power, and 93 percent of the air power. In October, during the Truman-MacArthur conference at Wake Island, a dozen American officials prepared plans for the reconstruction of *all* Korea without consulting anyone, not even the United Nations or Syngman Rhee. The United States suffered 142,000 casualties in Korea, not for the sake of "collective security" or the United Nations, but because the executive branch of the government decided that the invasion signaled a direct threat to American interests in both Asia and Europe.

Indeed, although the war was limited to Korea, Truman and Acheson used the war as the opportunity to develop new American policies around the globe. Because of these American initiatives, the six months between June and December 1950 rank among the most important of the Cold War era.

Truman and Acheson moved to the offensive globally for two particular reasons: the Korean War gave them an opportunity to shut up their critics at home and to take advantage of new openings abroad. Within the United States Acheson was in trouble because he had happened to be in office when China fell to Mao. He compounded this problem by courageously reaffirming his faith in Alger Hiss while Hiss was convicted for perjury. Of perhaps equal importance, Acheson's impeccable mustache and attire, his sarcastic and brilliant arguments, and his Ivy League background did not endear him to people who disliked so-called eggheads who made the world seem more complicated than did down-home folks like Joseph McCarthy. In his memoirs he termed the onslaught "The Attack of the Primitives," and he viewed some critics as "animals."[8] But his January remarks implying that Korea was outside the primary area of American military responsibility left him open for those who had been waiting for just such a mistake. Never again would he make that error. Instead of defining defense perimeters, he would take the offensive and undercut the "primitives."

The offensive would also allow the administration to put plans

[8]Dean Acheson, *Present at the Creation* (New York, 1969), chapter 39.

into motion that had been on drawing boards up to a year or more. These included the NSC-68 blueprint and the revitalization of American military alliances around the world. So began the spectacular summer of 1950 in which Truman and Acheson transformed the United Nations, committed the United States to Formosa and Indochina, began rearming Germany, nearly tripled American defense spending, and—in the climactic act—invaded North Korea to show opponents at home and abroad that the United States was no longer content with mere "containment" but now aimed for liberation.

The secretary of state first went to the United Nations, which had given its support to the American commitment in Korea. It had done so, however, only because the absence of the Soviet delegation had prevented a Russian veto of the UN resolution. The United States could not trust to such luck in the next crisis. During the autumn Acheson pushed through the General Assembly a "Uniting for Peace" proposal giving the assembly the right to make recommendations to members for collective security measures, including the use of force, if the use of the veto stopped the Security Council from acting. This resolution transfigured the United Nations. It no longer rested on agreements among the great powers, without which neither the United Nations nor the world peace could be viable. Instead power was thrown into the General Assembly, where Costa Rica had voting power equal to that of the United States or the Soviet Union. Weakening the Russian veto, the United States also weakened its own. Assuming, however, that it could control the General Assembly, the administration had taken a calculated risk. It had, to paraphrase Acheson, issued a blank check on the future. After a decade of increased neutralist feelings among the multiplying nations in Africa and Asia, that check would appear increasingly rubberized by the 1980s.

A second part of the diplomatic offensive involved Formosa. During early 1950 Truman and his military advisers expected Communist China to conquer the island. When North Korea attacked, however, the President placed the American Seventh Fleet between the mainland and Formosa to stop any possible conflict in the area. The next step occurred in August when MacArthur's recommendations that American advisers and assistance be sent to Chiang were accepted by Truman. The early 1950 policy had been reversed. The United States had bedded down with Chiang Kai-shek and had placed itself on his side in the intra-Chinese dispute over Formosa.

Mao Ze-dong was shocked at the sudden U.S. move into China's civil war. Truman's protection of Formosa was one reason why Mao was ready to fight the Americans in Korea months later.[9]

A similar turn occurred in American policy toward Indochina. The French had been the dominant colonial power in Southeast Asia since the late nineteenth century. The area's riches made it a formidable prize: Burma, Thailand, and Indochina provided rice for much of Asia. Southeast Asia produced nearly 90 percent of the world's natural rubber, 60 percent of the world's tin, and the bulk of Asia's oil. During World War II Franklin D. Roosevelt became convinced the French could not control this strategic area (particularly after the Japanese had humiliated the white colonial rulers in warfare during 1940–1941) and tried to ease the French out so that Indochina could become a UN trusteeship, with actual control in Chinese and American hands. In the weeks before his death, however, Roosevelt changed his mind. Chiang could no longer be trusted, and the United States had major problems elsewhere. His alternatives were clear: either allow the French to reenter, or part of the area would be controlled by the revolutionary nationalism of the Vietnamese communist leader Ho Chi Minh. Ho's forces made overtures to the United States throughout 1945, but neither Roosevelt nor Truman was in any mood to allow Ho to control such a vital area. First FDR and then Truman encouraged the French to reclaim their colonies. By late 1946 France and Ho's forces were locked in war, a war that would not end for Vietnam until nearly thirty years later.

The Soviets also refused to recognize Ho's Republic of Vietnam. By 1948 Ho was turning to Communist China for aid. He had not easily reached this decision, for the Indochinese had feared and fought against their giant neighbor for 1000 years. (In 1946, when he tried to negotiate with the French, Ho quieted his Vietnamese critics by declaring, "It is better to sniff the French dung for a while than eat China's all our lives."[10]) In January 1950 China recognized Ho's government. The Soviets followed within two weeks. After an intensive policy review the United States fully committed itself to the French cause in early February, four and one-half months before the Korean War began. Financial aid began to flow from Washington to the

---

[9]This is an important theme in Thomas J. Christensen, "A 'Lost Chance' for What?" *Journal of American–East Asian Relations,* IV (Fall 1995): 250–276.

[10]Jean Lacouture, *Ho Chi Minh* (New York, 1968), p. 119.

French in May. But not until after the Korean War began did American personnel become involved. On July 27, in the same announcement giving American support to South Korea, Truman revealed that he was dispatching a military mission to Vietnam.

The commitment had been made, as a State Department pamphlet noted in 1951, because the United States had such vital interests as the "much-needed rice, rubber, and tin" in Southeast Asia. The pamphlet added, "perhaps even more important would be the psychological effect of the fall of Indochina. It would be taken by many as a sign that the force of communism is irresistible and would lead to an attitude of defeatism." Without American aid, "it is doubtful whether [the French] could hold their ground against the Communists." John Foster Dulles was more specific at a private dinner of Asian experts in October. Japan, Dulles warned, could move in only one of two directions if it hoped to become prosperous and stable: either toward its traditional markets in China, now communist, and thus deal with Mao's government, or else find markets in Southeast Asia.[11] Because Japan was the key to the entire American position in the Pacific, Southeast Asia had to remain open for Japanese exploitation.

At the same time new American commitments were forged in Asia, Acheson concentrated on Europe, the area he and Truman considered of most importance. The secretary of state moved quickly to tighten the American military alliance with Western Europe, but he did not do so solely for military objectives. Acheson never believed that the military, political, or economic aspects of a problem could, in his words, "be separated in the intellectual equivalent of a cream separator."[12] Acheson knew that intelligence reports interpreted the Korean invasion as a "local affair" which did not apparently foreshadow a communist attack in Europe.[13] He nevertheless believed that future European political problems, particularly those which threatened American interests, could be solved through the use of military alliances. It was in this context, not in that of an imminent Russian in-

[11]U.S. Department of State, *Indochina: The War in Southeast Asia* (Washington, 1951), pp. 1–7; Dean Rusk, *The Underlying Principles of Far Eastern Policy* (Washington, 1951), p. 8222; Council of Foreign Relations Study Group Reports, October 23, 1950, Conference Dossiers, Draft of Japanese Peace Treaty, Dulles Papers, Princeton.

[12]Dean Acheson, *Sketches from Life of Men I Have Known* (New York, 1961), p. 103.

[13]Richard J. Barnet and Marcus Raskin, *After 20 Years* (New York, 1965), p. 29.

vasion which few expected, that Acheson proposed to horrified British and French officials that Germany be rearmed.

The Joint Chiefs had approved a German rearmament plan as early as April 1950. After the Korean outbreak State Department officials restudied the problem. During long and bitter discussions the State and Defense Departments worked out a package deal in September. Germany would be rearmed and Western European qualms quieted with three devices: more American money to aid Europe with its financial problems, four to six divisions of American troops to assure Europe of American aid in case of future Russian—or German—aggression, and an integrated military command headed by an American general. Agreement was reached just before British Foreign Minister Bevin and French Foreign Minister Robert Schuman sailed from Europe to meet Acheson at the Waldorf-Astoria Hotel in New York City for the September NATO Council meetings.[14]

On September 12 Acheson dropped, as one official called it, "the bomb at the Waldorf." To the unbelieving British and French, he proposed the creation of ten German divisions. Bevin finally went along, believing that the French would never accept the plan anyway.

In December the NATO foreign ministers discussed a compromise: German troops at the regimental level would be incorporated into the NATO establishment but would not constitute more than 20 percent of its strength. Despite strong last-minute Soviet protests, which some officials believed threatened war if Germany were rearmed, the foreign ministers finally accepted in principle German participation, but they could not agree on details. The ministers did approve an integrated force under a supreme commander. President Truman appointed General Dwight D. Eisenhower to this post on December 19.

Truman and Acheson next sent four divisions of American soldiers to Europe in September. This immersed the administration in deep political trouble. During congressional hearings in April 1949, Acheson had assured touchy senators that he expected no large numbers of American troops would be sent to the NATO command. In early 1950, however, NSC-68 had proposed rapid and costly rebuilding of Western defenses. The Korean conflict provided the op-

[14]Laurence W. Martin, "The American Decision to Rearm Germany." In Harold Stein, ed., *American Civil-Military Decisions: A Book of Case Studies* (Birmingham, Ala., 1963), pp. 653–659.

portunity to move ahead. Congress cooperated with Truman's request in July for an additional $4 billion of defense funds and a rapid buildup of the army. The President announced on September 9 that this buildup would be followed by "substantial increases" in the number of American troops in Europe. To have the administration that had "lost" China send troops to Europe while war was raging in Asia was too much for Republican and some Democratic politicans.

On January 5, 1951, Taft accused Acheson of misleading the American people with his April 1949 statement. Taft's timing was excellent; Chinese intervention had turned Korea into a nightmare for American officials, and just the month before, the French and British had proved most obstinate in cooperating with the U.S. plans for NATO. Truman hurriedly told the rebellious congressmen that the serious European situation demanded four divisions but no more. After hearings in which Acheson described the troops as serving political as well as military objectives, the Senate on April 4 approved by a 69 to 21 vote a resolution that endorsed the administration's proposals for NATO, including the integrated command; urged the military utilization of Germany, Italy, and Spain in order to protect Europe; and approved the sending of the four divisions but asked the President to send no more without consulting Congress. The administration had successfully used the Korean War to create the framework within which European and general East-West problems would be discussed during the next decade.

This debate over the commitment to NATO did not occur in an atmosphere of congenial executive-legislative relations. The junior senator from Wisconsin had just launched a new onslaught against "communists," especially those in the State Department. As Cold War passions rise, rational public debate correspondingly sinks, and as the Korean War intensified, McCarthyism received a second life. "Today American boys lie dead in the mud of Korean valleys. Some have their hands tied behind their back, their faces shot away by Communist machine guns," the senator wrote the President in mid-July 1950. These horrors occurred, McCarthy charged, because the congressional program for Korea "was sabotaged."[15] He was not clear

---

[15]Joseph R. McCarthy to President Truman, July 12, 1950, Office File 20, Truman Papers, Truman Library.

on the substance of that program, but during the following months he did not hesitate in condemning the man he believed to be the chief saboteur. George Catlett Marshall, former army chief of staff, architect of military victory over Germany and Japan, secretary of state, now secretary of defense, was, McCarthy claimed, part of a "conspiracy so immense and an infamy so black as to dwarf any previous such venture in the history of man." Because Henry Stimson, a man with impeccable credentials as an anticommunist and a conservative, had ranked Marshall only with George Washington, McCarthy felt compelled to have his aides document his accusations with a book on Marshall. The senator himself probably never read the book through; if he did, he found no evidence to substantiate his charges.

Truman also considered Marshall one of the greatest Americans who ever lived, and the President began replying to McCarthy's charges by calling the senator, among other things, the Kremlin's greatest asset. In the ensuing war of slanderous personal abuse, Truman did not stand a chance. McCarthy's use of the "multiple lie" (an accusation so long and containing so many untruths that no one could ever pin down all the lies at one time), and his repeated emphasis on so-called facts and documents in a society which easily accepts the superficial appearance of truth for the truth itself, made McCarthy invulnerable to Truman's retaliation.[16] Nor had Truman helped his cause by advancing his own conspiratorial view of Soviet activity and creating a noxious loyalty program. In 1949 and 1950 Attorney General J. Howard McGrath crossed the country protesting against professors of dubious political beliefs who infected student minds, pressed the need to bring increased numbers of anticommunist speakers and literature to campuses, and warned that the "many Communists in America" were "everywhere—in factories, offices, butcher stores, on street corners." With such tactics, the President and the attorney general played into the hands of the spreading McCarthyism.

Soon few were free of suspicion. A McCarthyite line properly applied could end any controversy. "It seems that the only argument some persons can present is to holler about Alger Hiss and then refer to Yalta," Senator Tom Connally complained. "Every time something

---

[16]Richard Rovere, *Senator Joe McCarthy* (New York, 1959), pp. 110, 167–170. The book on Marshall is *America's Retreat From Victory: The Story of George Catlett Marshall* [n.p.], 1952.

comes up, they get out a Communist and chase him around."[17] In too many cases this sufficed. Even the Americans for Democratic Action, that staunch defender against the Progressives in 1948, fell under suspicion because its 1950 convention urged the abolition of the House Un-American Activities Committee and suggested ties "sooner or later" with "the Chinese people." As soon as the Korean War erupted, the Americans for Democratic Action dropped all references to the House committee and continued to do so until 1959; it also modified its enthusiasm for the Chinese.[18]

Congress demonstrated its patriotism in September by passing the McCarran Internal Security bill. A measure so confused that its supporters could not explain parts of it, the act required communist organizations and their members to register with the attorney general. It did not call such membership a crime, but this was covered by the Smith Act of 1940, which prohibited membership in any group advocating violent overthrow of the government. If the Supreme Court declared the Communist party to be such a group, those registering under the McCarran Act would automatically incriminate themselves. With such conditions, skeptics doubted that registrars would be overwhelmed by people insisting on labeling themselves criminals. The bill also allowed the deportation of aliens who had been communists, no matter when, and in time of war allowed detention of persons whether they were communist or not. This legislation passed the House 354 to 20 and the Senate 70 to 7. Many congressmen who hated it in private voted for it in public. Their political lives were at stake. Truman gave the bill a ringing veto on September 20, arguing that the act could not work properly and so would result in an even more repressive act in the future. The House took one hour to pass the act over the President's veto. The Senate did so after a handful of liberals led by Hubert Humphrey and Paul Douglas tried to hold back the inevitable with a twenty-two-hour filibuster. The political facts were plain for all to see, and any doubters were soon convinced by the results of the November congressional election. The Republicans picked up twenty-eight seats in the House. In the Senate they won five more seats, and in three of those contests (John Marshall Butler's victory over McCarthy nemesis Millard Tydings in Maryland, Everett Dirksen's defeat of Senate Majority Leader Scott Lucas in Illinois, and

[17]Tom Connally, *My Name is Tom Connally* (New York, 1954), pp. 351–352.
[18]Clifton Brock, *Americans for Democratic Action* (Washington, 1962), pp. 143–144.

Richard Nixon's triumph over Helen Gahagan Douglas in California), McCarthy happily accepted credit for helping the winners.

The election occurred when American forces were advancing to greater victories in Korea. What uplifting effects some battle losses would have on Republican power and McCarthyism, Democrats did not wish to contemplate. Truman and Acheson, however, believed they had removed that danger—indeed, had cut the ground out from under the "primitives"—by deciding to cross the 38th parallel and liberate North Korea. This decision can be fully understood only when placed with the administration's initiatives in Korea, the United Nations, Formosa, Indochina, and Germany. Together these commitments provided Acheson with new and exceptionally strong "situations of strength" from which he could deal with communists and domestic critics.

The origins of the decision to cross the 38th apparently date from mid-July. MacArthur had finally halted the North Korean advance. Rumors circulated in the State Department that plans were being made to advance beyond the 38th. George Kennan considered such a move highly dangerous. He did not want MacArthur to go to "the gates of Vladivostok [the giant Soviet naval base bordering North Korea]. The Russians would never under any circumstances agree to this." Kennan had intense arguments with Dulles and Assistant Secretary of State for the Far East Dean Rusk, both of whom apparently supported Acheson's hope that the United States could forcefully unite the Koreas.

The decision was finally based upon an evaluation of possible Soviet reaction. By August Stalin had defined Russia out of Korea's "civil war." Moreover, Secretary of Defense Louis Johnson privately told the Senate Foreign Relations Committee that the Soviets would not attack in either Asia or Europe "because Russia was probably aware of the fact that at the present time we had a greater supply of atomic bombs than she had."[19] China was of less concern, partly be-

---

[19]Kennan's views are in George Kennan, *Memoirs, 1925–1950* (Boston, 1967), p. 488; Johnson's, in "Memorandum of Executive Meeting of the Foreign Relations Committee," August 23, 1950, Foreign Relations, 1950, Secretary Louis Johnson, Box 101, Papers of H. Alexander Smith, Princeton. The decision to cross the 38th is discussed at length, and with more extensive bibliographical references, in W. LaFeber, "The Cold War in Microcosm." In Ronald Pruessen and Lynn Miller, eds., *Reflections on the Cold War* (Philadelphia, 1974). See also William Stueck, "The March to the Yalu." In Bruce Cumings, ed., *Child of Conflict* (Seattle, 1983), pp. 195–238.

cause Acheson believed Stalin controlled Chinese movements and also because Mao's army, after the long civil war, did not seem capable of effectively fighting the United States.

On September 1 the directive allowing MacArthur to drive beyond the 38th was completed by the National Security Council. Truman signed it on September 11. Four days later MacArthur made a brilliant landing at Inchon, back of North Korean lines, cut off large numbers of enemy troops, and began a rapid northward drive. With the general's triumph, Truman instructed him on September 27 to move through North Korea if he did not encounter Chinese or Russian resistance and if he was certain of success in the field. Given MacArthur's self-confidence, if not arrogance, that was an invitation for him to drive to the Yalu. On October 7 the United Nations followed obediently, endorsing Truman's order by a lopsided vote.

All eyes now turned to China. In late August American officials had asked for the open door "within all parts of Korea." At that point Foreign Minister Jou En-lai reminded the world that "Korea is China's neighbor" and asked for negotiations so that the affair could be settled "peacefully." In late September China warned India, which had become China's main link with the Western world, that it would not "sit back with folded hands and let the Americans come to the border." Jou formally told India in a dramatic midnight meeting that China would attack if UN troops moved into North Korea. The United States discounted the threat. MacArthur, never one to pass up the opportunity for the grand if empty gesture, responded by demanding North Korea's total surrender. The Americans were ignorant of two vital facts: the Chinese were willing to die to keep a U.S. force away from their borders, and they were being egged on to fight by Stalin.[20]

Soviet and Chinese documents opened in the 1990s revealed that Stalin told Chinese leader Mao Ze-dong on October 5–7, 1950, that if China sent in "at least five or six divisions," the United States could be beaten. But if Mao waited, Stalin warned, the Americans and their rebuilt Japanese allies would become all-powerful in Asia. The Soviet dictator had many motives for giving this advice, including the hope that China would drive back the Americans without the need to shed

---

[20]The account in this and the following paragraph follows in most respects that of Allen Whiting, *China Crosses the Yalu* (New York, 1960); *Washington Post,* December 20, 1995, p. A27; Chen Jian, *The Sino-Soviet Alliance and China's Entry into the Korean War.* Cold War International History Project, Woodrow Wilson Center (Washington, D.C., 1991).

any Russian blood. Of special importance, Stalin wanted China and the United States to sink into a full conventional war with each other—a conflict that would make the already war-ravaged Chinese more dependent on the Soviets, while weakening and distracting the Americans. Stalin assured China that the Soviet Union "stands [behind] its ally." He apparently meant far behind. For when China moved toward war in mid-October, Stalin suddenly refused to honor his promise to provide at least air support for Mao's exposed troops. The Soviet dictator did send China large amounts of arms and planes, but he wanted no part of any direct Russian confrontation with the Americans. Knowing Stalin's deviousness, Mao first hesitated; he had no desire for war with the United States either. But under Soviet pressure and the relentless U.S. advance toward China, Mao decided to throw the dice. His decision was also shaped by Truman's earlier move in June to use the U.S. Navy to protect Chiang's exiled regime on Taiwan, a move a surprised Mao had seen as direct American intervention in China's civil war. Mao nevertheless apparently paced the floor some 60 hours before he decided to fight the world's strongest power. On October 16 the first Chinese "volunteers" moved across the Yalu into North Korea.

Americans and Chinese were now headed for a conflict that was to poison and misshape their relationship, and indeed the entire global arena, for nearly the next quarter century. But neither would back down. On September 10, 1950, Acheson commented on national television, "I should think it would be sheer madness for the Chinese to intervene." On October 9 the danger reached a new high when two American F-80 jets strafed a Soviet airfield only a few miles from Vladivostok. After the Soviets protested, the United States apologized. Vexed that the crisis arose, and angered that he had to back down before the Soviets just a month before national elections, Truman canceled a trip to Independence and flew to Wake Island to check on MacArthur. In the heavily censored text of the meeting, the general assured the President, "We are no longer fearful of [Chinese] intervention. We no longer stand hat in hand." China might move 60,000 men across the Yalu, but if these troops tried to move farther south without air cover (and the Chinese had no air force), "there would be the greatest slaughter."[21]

[21]U.S. Senate, Committee on Armed Services and Committee on Foreign Relations, *Substance of Statements Made at Wake Island Conference on October 15, 1950,* compiled by General of the Army Omar N. Bradley (Washington, 1951), p. 5.

On October 26 the first Chinese prisoner was captured, "so that you began to know, at that point," Acheson later commented, "that something was happening." MacArthur nevertheless continued his drive toward the Yalu. On November 21 advance elements of American troops peered at Chinese sentries stationed across the river. Three days later MacArthur grandly announced the launching of the end-the-war offensive. On November 26 the Chinese moved across the Yalu in mass, trapping and destroying large numbers of UN troops, including 20,000 Americans and Koreans at the Chosin Reservoir. Three weeks later the retreating UN forces again fought below the 38th, and now it was Jou En-lai who proclaimed his nation's intention of reunifying Korea. "They really fooled us when it comes right down to it, didn't they?" a senator once asked Acheson. "Yes, sir," the secretary of state replied.[22]

On November 15 Acheson, usually so debonair in his public appearances, became nearly incoherent in explaining why the Chinese should not fear American forces on the Yalu. "Everything in the world" was being done to reassure the Chinese that their interests were not jeopardized, he declared, "and I should suppose that there is no country in the world which has been more outstanding in developing the theory of brotherly development of border waters than the United States."[23] Such an American "brotherly development" of the Yalu, of course, was precisely what the Chinese were determined to prevent. From a position on the Yalu, the United States could exert pressure on both Mao's internal and external policies. China's intense hatred for the West, reaching a peak after a century of Western exploitation of the country, and Mao's determination to restore Chinese power in Asia made impossible the acceptance of such an American presence.

The decision to cross the 38th proved exceptionally costly to the United States. Four-fifths of all American casualties in the war occurred after UN forces crossed the parallel. The war froze the United States into a Cold War posture for the next two decades, paralyzing particularly American-Chinese relations. As one observer noted, "700

[22]*Military Situation in the Far East*, pp. 1832–1835. Much in this section depends on two superb accounts by Thomas J. Christensen: "A 'Lost Chance' for What?" *Journal of American–East Asian Relations*, IV (Fall 1995): 249–278; and *Useful Adversaries . . . 1947–1958* (Princeton, 1996).
[23]*Department of State Bulletin*, XXIII (November 27, 1950): 855.

million potential customers had turned into the apparition of 700 million dangerous adversaries."[24] The United States began to look upon ferocious Chinese armies as a new and more dangerous form of the "Yellow Peril" that had long haunted Americans. The "Peril" became more dangerous in the 1950s and 1960s precisely because so few Americans knew anything about it.

Washington officials were frightened. Truman reiterated that the United States had no "aggressive intentions toward China." He believed that the Chinese people opposed this sending of troops by their leaders. This belief was in line with Truman's general theory that communism anywhere never had popular support. The aggression must be crushed, the President continued, or "we can expect it to spread throughout Asia and Europe to this hemisphere." Truman's views on the need to continue the war were shaped by yet another belief—a belief voiced especially by Acheson and his advisers who had written NSC-68. Acheson and now even the President had come to realize that the war with China allowed the passage of huge defense budgets through Congress. It was the opportunity to put the United States, finally, on full military footing to fight the larger Cold War. Truman, as one record revealed, told a secret meeting of the NSC in late November 1950, "If the Chinese threat evaporates, the President doubts that you could go ahead with a $45 billion program." (The prewar military "program" had been under $14 billion.) Thus domestic politics provided a key, if not *the* key, to understanding Truman's historic decisions to move above the 38th and then fight a war with China. For those decisions were shaped by the President's determination (1) to quiet Republican critics who wanted "Asia first," (2) to silence Senator Joseph McCarthy's screeching attacks, and (3) to push through the massive defense budgets envisioned by NSC-68—budgets that ushered in the high military spending of at least the next fifty years.[25]

Truman's public response, however, seemed more cautious at first. He countermanded MacArthur's order to bomb Chinese troops and supplies in Manchuria. Then, in a news conference of November

---

[24]A. T. Steele, *The American People and China* (New York, 1966), p. 60.

[25]U.S. Government, *Public Papers of the Presidents of the United States . . . Truman . . . 1950* (Washington, 1965), pp. 724–727; the interpretation linking the war to the new defense budgets is based on Christensen, "A 'Lost Chance' for What?" pp. 268–278, and the work in progress of Professor Frank Kofsky.

30, Truman showed signs of losing this restraint. He intimated that the United States would use all its power to contain the Chinese. He explicitly did not exclude using atomic bombs. This remark brought British Prime Minister Attlee flying to the United States on December 4.

Attlee was not without responsibility for the crisis; his government had participated in the decision to send UN troops to the Yalu. He now worried that in the newly expanded war Truman would not be able to control the military and particularly wondered at the spectacle of Truman's flying 5000 miles to Wake Island to meet MacArthur, who had flown 1900. ("I thought it a curious relationship between a Government and a general," Attlee commented later.) The prime minister received Truman's assurances that the United States was not planning to use the bomb. The two men then undertook a full, candid, and most revealing evaluation of the Asian tinderbox.

Both agreed that a general war must be averted and that the UN forces should not evacuate Korea unless forced out militarily. Then basic differences emerged. Attlee argued that China's admission to the United Nations could bring it into regular consultations leading to a cease-fire. Acheson doubted that in their present advantageous military position the Chinese would want a cease-fire; if they did and negotiations resulted, Mao would next demand a UN seat and concessions on Formosa. The United States had refused to discuss these two items before the intervention, and Acheson now was in no mood to reward aggressors. Attlee countered that a cease-fire would make explicit the divisions between China and Russia: "I want them [the Chinese] to become a counterpoise to Russia in the Far East," Attlee argued. If "we just treat the Chinese as Soviet satellites, we are playing the Russian game."

Truman now hardened his earlier view of the Chinese. They were "Russian satellites," and if they succeeded in Korea "it would be Indo-China, then Hong Kong, then Malaya." Acheson interposed that he did not think it mattered whether China was a satellite or not, for it would act like Russia anyway. He believed the invasion into Korea "had design," and, like Truman, he adopted the domino theory to warn that any compromise with the Chinese would have a "serious" effect on the Japanese and Philippine Islands. Acheson recalled a "saying among State Department officials that with communistic regimes you could not bank good will; they balanced their books every night." Therefore, he argued, the West must develop great military power to stop "this sort of thing from happening in the future." Acheson and Truman also reminded Attlee that the United States could not be "internationalist" in Europe and "isolationist" in Asia; domestic political pressures made that impossible. At that point Attlee questioned the basic American premise, the fundamental belief that underlay U.S. policy in Europe as well as Asia. He emphasized that the United Nations must be kept together even if this meant alienating important segments of American public opinion. Whatever the United States and Great Britain did would have to be done through the United Nations, Attlee argued, and this could not be accomplished by the efforts and votes of only the United States and the United Kingdom, "important as we are."[26] Truman and Acheson disagreed; they believed the two nations were "important" enough. The administration expected little help from the United Nations in thwarting Soviet drives. The most the United Nations could do was brand the Chinese as aggressors, which it did on February 1, 1951, by a vote of 44 to 7 with 9 abstentions.[27]

Although the military situation steadily eroded, not even the other nations in the Western Hemisphere would offer much assistance. The Latin Americans dutifully voted with the United States on resolutions in the United Nations and the Organization of American States, but in the early spring of 1951, when Truman personally appealed to Latin American foreign ministers to "establish the principle of sharing our burdens fairly," only Colombia responded with troops. Several other nations sent matériel, but Latin America as a whole failed to see the relevance of Korea to its own economic deprivation and political instability. Later in 1951 a shocked administration attempted to woo its southern neighbors by extending to them the Mutual Security Program of military aid. Eight nations took the money in 1952 to protect themselves against communist aggression; both giver and receiver interpreted this to mean preservation of the domestic status quo. No other Latin American nation, however, sent men to Korea.

The United States would have to depend primarily upon its own resources in defending what Niebuhr had called "our farflung lines." In December and January the President requested emergency powers to expedite war mobilization. Closely following the guidelines

---

[26]Truman, *Memoirs*, II: 396–411.
[27]See Truman, *Memoirs*, II: 420–421, for a relevant U.S. intelligence estimate.

suggested in NSC-68, he submitted a $50-billion defense budget; this contrasted with the 13\frac{1}{2}$-billion budget of six months before. The administration doubled the number of air groups to ninety-five and obtained new bases in Morocco, Libya, and Saudi Arabia. Army personnel increased 50 percent to 3$\frac{1}{2}$ million men.

In Asia the administration focused on tightening American military ties with Japan through a new peace treaty. John Foster Dulles assumed control of the negotiations and almost single-handedly drove the treaty through to a successful conclusion in September 1951. It was a bravura performance. The pact restored Japanese sovereignty over the home islands but not over the Ryukyus (which included the large American base at Okinawa). In an accompanying security agreement Japan allowed the stationing of American troops and planes on its soil but not those of any third power. Dulles simply excluded Russia from the early, decisive negotiations. When the Soviets were allowed to participate, Dulles interpreted their proposal as an attempt to dominate the area around Japan. As one participant recalled, Dulles demonstrated the effect of the Soviet plan on a map, "took this map dramatically and held it up like this . . . and then threw it on the floor with the utmost contempt. And that made a tremendous impression."[28]

Dulles also ran roughshod over demands from American allies and neutrals in Asia, who demanded reparations from Japan for its occupation during World War II. He warned that the United States would brook no "Carthaginian peace" which would "lead to bitter animosity and in the end drive Japan into the orbit of Russia." Some American allies wanted reparations to weaken Japanese potential for producing weapons. Dulles solved this problem by negotiating a series of mutual defense treaties to ensure the Philippines, Australia, and New Zealand against both reemerging Asian giants, Japan and China. Thirty months before, Acheson had assured the Senate that other than NATO the administration contemplated no further regional pacts. On September 1, 1951, the United States signed with Australia and New Zealand the so-called ANZUS Treaty, pledging the security of those two nations.

Because Australia and New Zealand belonged to the British Commonwealth, Great Britain was conspicuous by its absence from

---

[28]Interview with C. Stanton Babcock, in Dulles Oral History Project, Dulles Papers, Princeton.

ANZUS. As early as March 1914 Winston Churchill, then First Lord of the Admiralty, predicted that with British resources increasingly devoted to Europe, the "white men" in the Pacific would soon have to seek American protection. Thirty-seven years later the British were not so understanding. When Great Britain protested that the United States had not adequately consulted it on the Japanese or ANZUS pacts, Dulles granted the point, but countered that if Britain came in, the French and Dutch would also and thereby transform ANZUS in the eyes of suspicious Asians into a colonial alliance. This argument effectively reduced British influence in the Pacific. "All roads in the Commonwealth lead to Washington," a Canadian official observed.[29] The United States was single-handedly preparing Asia for the containment of China.

These negotiations determined the geographic extent of the American commitment in the Pacific. During the spring of 1951, with drama and flourishes seldom seen in American history, the military extent of that commitment was decided. In late January UN forces opened a successful drive back to the 38th parallel. As the battle stalemated along the former boundary line, State Department and Pentagon officials cautiously explored the possibility of negotiations with the Chinese on March 20. Three days later General MacArthur issued a personal statement urging that the Red military commanders "confer in the field" with him on surrender; if he could attack China's "coastal areas and interior bases," the general insisted, that nation would be "doomed" to military collapse. MacArthur had again undercut his superiors in Washington.

As early as July 1950 he had shown reluctance to accept Truman's decision that Chiang Kai-shek should be contained on Formosa rather than unleashed on the mainland or allowed to ship troops to Korea. A month later MacArthur sent a message to the annual convention of the Veterans of Foreign Wars, which the President viewed as an attack upon his policy toward Chiang. Truman angrily demanded that this message be recalled, and MacArthur complied although it had already been published. The Wake Island conference

---

[29]Interview with General Matthew Ridgway, in Dulles Oral History Project, Dulles Papers, Princeton; Churchill and the Canadian official are quoted in Geoffrey Barraclough, *An Introduction to Contemporary History* (New York, 1964), p. 67.

muted these differences, but the published minutes are embarrassing in their revelation of MacArthur's incredible condescension and Truman's tittering insecurity. Once the President was back in Washington, this insecurity disappeared. After MacArthur again recommended a naval blockade of China, air attacks to level Chinese military and industrial installations, and the use of 30,000 Formosan troops in Korea, Truman patiently explained on January 13 "the political factors" involved in the "world-wide threat" of the Soviet Union which made containment of the Korean War necessary.[30] When MacArthur issued his ultimatum of March 23, Truman's patience, never inexhaustible, evaporated.

Only the method and timing of relieving the general remained to be decided. On April 5 Joe Martin, the leading Republican in the House, read a letter from MacArthur which charged that "here we fight Europe's war with arms while the diplomats there still fight it with words." "We must win," the letter emphasized. "There is no substitute for victory." The Joint Chiefs of Staff agreed with Truman that MacArthur would have to be relieved immediately; reports from the field indicated that the general was losing the confidence of his men and had already lost confidence in himself.[31] On April 11 the President recalled MacArthur.

Truman knew the political dynamite in the decision. Less than two weeks earlier he had agreed with top advisers that an all-out speaking campaign would have to be undertaken by cabinet-level officers because the administration's " 'story' was not reaching the American public."[32] The American people preferred quick victory to containment. This preference was dramatically demonstrated when the general returned to the greatest popular reception in American history. Senator McCarthy expressed the feelings toward Truman of not a few Americans when, with characteristic restraint, he told a press conference, "The son of a bitch ought to be impeached." Congress warmly received MacArthur's speech before a joint session,

---

[30]*Military Situation in the Far East*, pp. 503–504.

[31]Cabell Philipps, *The Truman Presidency* (New York, 1966), pp. 337–347.

[32]"Memorandum for the President," from Joseph Short, Secretary to the President, April 2, 1951, Office File 386, Truman Papers, Truman Library. A superb analysis stressing the domestic politics-foreign policy relationship is Roger Dingman, "Politics in Peril: The Truman-MacArthur Controversy," a paper given at the Georgetown University conference, *The Korean War: An Assessment of the Historical Record*, July 24–25, 1995.

then in April and May settled down to investigate the case of the President versus the general.

In a battle of MacArthur versus Truman, the long-range issues tended to be overshadowed by the personalities involved. In MacArthur's case this was not an advantage. Having last set foot in the United States fourteen years before, the general seemed unable or unwilling to grasp the political and social as well as the diplomatic views of his country. Although he had repeatedly advocated policies which contained the most somber worldwide ramifications, he now admitted having only a "superficial knowledge" of NATO and European affairs.

His basic message was curiously close to Truman's and Niebuhr's in 1948: because communism posed a threat to all civilization, "you have got to hold every place." Or again, "What I advocate is that we defend every place, and I say that we have the capacity to do it. If you say that we haven't you admit defeat." Like Acheson, he insisted on not putting military power and politics into the intellectual equivalent of a cream separator. In time of war, however, MacArthur demanded the reversal of Acheson's priority: once involved in war, the general argued, the military commander must be supreme over all military and political affairs in his theater, "or otherwise you will have the system that the Soviets once employed of the political commissar, who would run the military as well as the politics of the country." Such a remark cut across the grain of traditional American policies of subordinating military to civilian officials even if the nation was involved in total war. When the embattled general heard the suggestion of Assistant Secretary of State Dean Rusk that war in Korea must not become a "general conflagration," MacArthur branded it "the concept of appeasement, the concept that when you use force, you can limit the force."

The general believed that by controlling the sea and air no one could "successfully launch an effort against us," but the United States could "largely neutralize China's capability to wage aggressive war and thus save Asia from the engulfment otherwise facing it." He expressed contempt for the Chinese communists. "Never, in our day, will atomic weapons be turned out of China. They cannot turn out the ordinary weapons." Nor was there a threat of Soviet intervention. Time, however, was short. If, as MacArthur once remarked, Europe was a "dying system," and the Pacific would "determine the course of history in the next ten thousand years," victory must be won immediately. The "dreadful slaughter" had to end, MacArthur pleaded; American blood as well as dust is settling in Korea, and the "blood, to some extent" rests "on me." But now, he concluded emotionally, "There is no policy—there is nothing, I tell you, no plan, or anything."[33]

The administration had a plan, and Acheson outlined it in his testimony after MacArthur finished. Korea must be viewed as part of a "collective security system," Acheson argued. When so viewed, two things readily became apparent. First, all-out war in Korea would suck in Russian force to aid Stalin's "largest and most important satellite." "I cannot accept the assumption that the Soviet Union will go its way regardless of what we do," the secretary of state declared. If Russia did intervene, there could be "explosive possibilities not only for the Far East, but for the rest of the world as well." Unlike MacArthur, Acheson insisted on keeping the European picture uppermost in dealing with Korea. (Truman once added a variant on this: expansion of the war would "destroy the unity of the free nations," the President declared. "We cannot go it alone in Asia and go it with company in Europe.") Second, if Europe and the prevention of Russian entry in force did compose the main objectives, American forces were not engaged in a "dreadful slaughter" or, as Acheson remarked, "a pointless and inconclusive struggle," but had "scored a powerful victory" by dealing "Communist imperialist aims in Asia a severe setback" in preventing the armed conquest of all Korea.[34]

U.S. policies in the Pacific between 1949 and 1952 were not shy. Indeed, as Dean Rusk recalled years later, "Our general attitude was . . . that it was important for the United States to have control of every wave in the Pacific Ocean."[35] The only argument was over the best strategy to control those waves, as well as the waves in the Atlantic. MacArthur lost the argument. He lost it so decisively, moreover, that, while negotiations to conclude a stalemated war fitfully began in Korea during the summer of 1951, Acheson accelerated the military buildup of Europe.

[33]*Military Situation in the Far East*, pp. 39, 45, 54, 66–68, 78, 81, 83, 86–87.
[34]*Military Situation in the Far East*, pp. 924–926.
[35]Ronald L. McGlothlen, *Controlling the Waves* (New York, 1993), p. 21.

CHAPTER 6

New Issues, New Faces
(1951–1953)

The MacArthur hearings epitomized a wide-ranging debate over American foreign policies during the twenty-four months before the 1952 presidential election. From the vantage point of twenty years later, the importance of this debate is not limited to those particular months, but has grown with time until historians can discover at that early point the turn of American thinking that led the nation into the involvements, particularly in Asia, of the next decade. One can also observe the beginnings of the dissent which would later divide American liberals and split intellectuals from policymakers. If the period is extended to 1953, it is equally important for Soviet policy, but with one difference: the internal debates arising out of the Party Congress of late 1952 and Stalin's death five months later marked an end to an epoch in Russian history.

By the time the de facto armistice was agreed upon in July 1953, the Korean War had made as much impact upon American aid to Europe as to Asia. The agreement in principle on German rearmament and the sending of additional American troops to Europe were major steps in this direction. American strategy in NATO during 1951 and 1952 rested first upon the "trip-wire" theory that any Soviet attack upon a NATO command containing American troops would automatically trip a nuclear attack from the United States. One European official stated this theory in elementary terms; when asked how many American soldiers must be stationed in Europe to protect the West, he replied one would be enough if that one was shot during the first wave of an attack. To further its nuclear capability, the United States conducted its first successful thermonuclear test at Eniwetok Island in the Pacific during March 1951. In mid-June 1952 the keel went down for the USS Nautilus, the first submarine to be powered by atomic energy. Truman proposed a $60-billion defense budget for

1952, 20 percent above that of 1951. If the wire was tripped, the United States was preparing to respond massively.

NATO strategy also rested upon the hope that the war could be contained east of the Elbe. For this, a large conventional force would be needed; Eisenhower wanted thirty-five to forty ready divisions and ninety-six more which could be brought up within a month. The present 300 aircraft would have to multiply ten times. These grandiose plans, Truman observed, "tripped over one hard, tough fact. This fact was the poverty of western Europe."[1] Three years after the launching of the Marshall Plan, the recipient nations were sinking back into an economic morass. Only Germany gained ground; it used the new concern over military power to rearm and end the Allied occupation of its territory.[2] The other Europeans discovered that jamming their meager resources into defense spending produced scanty results. They owned more conventional arms in a nuclear era and lost resources that they had hoped to invest in their own overseas empires.

Some nations attempted to bolster their economies with increased exports to the communist bloc. These shipments included goods that, many Americans feared, would greatly aid the Sino-Russian war machines. Congress retaliated by passing the Kem Amendment and the Battle Act, which in certain circumstances cut American aid going to those nations that exported strategic goods to communists. Another response was more positive. In 1951 Congress passed the Mutual Security Act (MSA), which coalesced the economic, military, and technical assistance programs. This allowed an injection of a stronger military emphasis than ever before. As Acheson remarked, the "whole impact" of MSA would be "to carry out the rearmament program," for, he somehow concluded, the Marshall Plan's "original task has been accomplished."[3]

NATO strategy, as well as Cold War politics, rested also on a third approach: that the basis of the alliance be expanded as far as possible. In May 1951 the United States proposed adding Greece and Turkey to the military pact to prevent those two nations from entertaining ideas of becoming politically neutral. Yugoslavia, although not wishing to enter NATO, began requesting military assistance in

---

[1]Harry S Truman, *Memoirs*, II (Garden City, N.Y., 1955–1956): 258.
[2]Charles Wolf, Jr., *Foreign Aid: Theory and Practice in Southern Asia* (Princeton, 1960), pp. 115–116.
[3]Wolf, *Foreign Aid*, pp. 114–116.

addition to the economic aid that it had already obtained from the West. In September 1951 the Western Foreign Ministers agreed to release Italy from restrictions imposed in 1945 upon its military. Most notable was the rapidly evolving American attitude toward Franco's Spain.

Kennan had observed in 1947 that the Truman Doctrine implied a new view of Franco. By 1949 a congressional–Defense Department axis had formed to force the issue. Senators Pat McCarran, Owen Brewster, and Robert Taft urged the administration, in Taft's words, to "shake loose from its communist-front philosophy" by working with Franco. One congressman, among the many who junketed to Madrid in 1949 and 1950, publicly called the Spanish dictator a "very, very lovely and loveable character." Lower-echelon naval and air force officers heartily cooperated; they wanted bases as widely dispersed, as close to the Soviet bloc, and as independent of British bases as possible. In several secret meetings in McCarran's Senate office, these Pentagon officers and congressmen charted political strategy. In March 1950 McCarran succeeded in securing a $62 $\frac{1}{2}$-million loan for Franco. For ideological reasons, Truman despised this and every other pro-Spanish move, but after June 1950 the logic of his own military policy forced him to recognize the Franco government late that year. The following summer the administration began negotiations to obtain Spanish military bases. On August 25, 1953, the Spanish ambassador to the United States pinned the special medal of the Grand Cross on McCarran for the senator's exceptional devotion to Spain. A month and one day later, the base treaty was completed. Franco had driven a hard bargain. The United States granted economic assistance and a quarter-billion dollars of military aid in return for the right to construct and use military bases which would remain under Spanish sovereignty.[4]

The Spanish base treaty augmented American military power in Europe but contributed less to Acheson's political objectives; most of Western Europe too vividly remembered Franco's cooperation with Hitler. The political aims rested instead on the success of the Pleven Plan and German rearmament. To the accompaniment of shrill Soviet protests, the Western Foreign Ministers worked on these issues throughout 1951, then gathered at Lisbon in February 1952 to ham-

---

[4]Theodore J. Lowi, "Bases in Spain." In Harold Stein, ed., *American Civil-Military Decisions: A Book of Case Studies* (Birmingham, Ala., 1963), pp. 667–697.

mer out final ground rules for the new Western alliance. Agreement did not come easily. The Big Four split down the middle on the form of German rearmament as well as on other problems. "More often than not, I found myself agreeing with . . . Adenauer," Acheson recalled, "and Eden [agreed] with Schuman."[5]

The French and British split, however, on the critical issue. The Pleven Plan had been transformed in earlier negotiations into a European Defense Community (EDC) comprising France, Germany, and the Benelux. The EDC would operate under separate European control but be linked with NATO so that Germany could directly participate in NATO defenses. Schuman and the Netherlands officials now insisted that Great Britain formally join the EDC. They did not want to be in the EDC virtually alone with German power and refused to consider the American and British presence in NATO sufficient to control the possibility of German domination of the new grouping. The newly elected government of Winston Churchill refused to commit itself so solidly to European affairs. Too many Anglo-American ties would be severed. Any British integration into European affairs would have to come "in doses rather than at a gulp," Eden later remarked.[6] Acheson could not settle this dispute by quieting the French fear. Several months after the Lisbon conference, President Vincent Auriol of France told the secretary of state "with considerable passion," as Acheson later recalled, "that our policy toward Germany was a great mistake. He knew Germany; he reviewed German history since Bismarck. We were wrong in thinking that the greater danger came from Russia. It came from Germany."[7]

Acheson finally obtained Schuman's consent to allow 500,000 Germans in twelve divisions to enter the EDC, but the French exacted a price. Adenauer agreed to allow Western forces to remain in Germany for internal security as well as military purposes, swore to deal with Russia only through the Allies, and allowed the West to continue governing Berlin. Acheson opened wide the American and German pocketbooks, promising to help France meet its defense expenditures in Vietnam and Europe. For this, Acheson even won an agreement to double NATO manpower to fifty divisions (including twelve French) by the end of 1952.

[5]Dean Acheson, *Sketches from Life of Men I Have Known* (New York, 1961), p. 47.
[6]Anthony Eden, *Full Circle: The Memoirs of Anthony Eden* (New York, 1960), p. 34.
[7]Acheson, *Sketches from Life*, p. 53.

There would never be fifty NATO divisions; there would never be an EDC. In the long run the Lisbon conference produced much ill will. Acheson's troubles began immediately after the conference adjourned. On March 10 the Soviets proposed to the three Western powers that discussions be held on a peace treaty which would declare Germany united and independent. Russia further suggested allowing Germany to have a national army with ties to neither the East nor the West, withdrawing all foreign troops, and admitting Germany to the United Nations. This breathtaking proposal came out of cold Russian fear of a rearmed, Western-oriented Germany. It might have been a propaganda ploy, a mere delaying tactic. Or it might have been an opportunity to neutralize Germany and drastically reduce the Cold War tensions infecting the Central European hothouse which had germinated so many hot wars in the past.

No one will ever know what the Soviets meant. Acheson refused to follow up on the proposal. At this point his diplomacy stood revealed not as the building of "positions of strength" to facilitate negotiations for the easing of East-West conflict but the building of strength so that such negotiations might be avoided. The West had to be kept together. This meant Germany had to be rearmed under Western guidance. The "peace offensive" out of Moscow was a " 'golden apple' tactic," Acheson announced in April. The Soviets resembled the Goddess of Discord who, angered that she had not been invited to a wedding party, threw a golden apple over the fence "hoping to cause a ruckus among the guests and break up the party."[8] The wall would be built higher to make such apple throwing more difficult, and so on May 26 and 27 Acheson, Eden, and Schuman signed the agreement ending the occupation of Germany. They then initialed the EDC treaty. Now the EDC had only to pass the various parliaments before coming into effect.

Even as Acheson threaded his way through the EDC negotiations of 1951 and 1952, Americans vigorously debated new policies which, by the middle-1950s, would set their foreign policies on new paths. In short, the debates of 1951–1952 thrashed out the premises which governed American foreign policy for at least the next decade and a

[8]Dean Acheson, "Progress Toward International Peace and Unity," *Department of State Bulletin,* XXVI (April 28, 1952): 648.

half. At the simplest level, the arguments pivoted on the question of whether Asia should enjoy equal priority with Europe in American policy. Overall the debate was far more complex. It became a prime example of how oversimplified (often unquestioned) premises of one historical era could, almost inevitably, develop into apparently unrelated but far-reaching policies affecting life and death in a later era. Chiang's defeat on mainland China, American involvement in Korea, and the sending of additional U.S. soldiers to Europe initiated the debate. The MacArthur hearings greatly intensified it. Then the arguments were systematically reformulated and can now be found in Senator Robert Taft's *A Foreign Policy for Americans*, Hans Morgenthau's *In Defense of the National Interest*, Reinhold Niebuhr's *The Irony of American History*, and, finally, the 1952 election campaign.[9]

Taft's and Morgenthau's books chalked in the boundaries of the debate. Like the majority of Americans, both men agreed on the need to contain Russia. They substantially differed on the means to accomplish this, and it was on the issue of these means that the argument was waged. Morgenthau was a distinguished professor of international relations at the University of Chicago and Taft was running for the 1952 Republican presidential nomination, but despite their different vantage points, the two men surprisingly agreed on a number of issues. Both considered the United Nations, particularly after the passage of the "Uniting for Peace" resolution, to be a fifth wheel in world diplomacy; both badly oversimplified their argument by tracing the origins of the Cold War back only to the 1945 Yalta and Potsdam conferences. More fundamentally, both feared that Truman and Acheson used insufficient restraint in employing American power. Morgenthau attacked Acheson for harping about "positions of strength" when "the supreme test of statesmanship," to Morgenthau's mind, was not building power blocs but discovering areas in which tensions could be reduced through negotiations. Morgenthau did not believe Acheson could stand up to that test.

On four basic points, however, the senator and the professor profoundly differed. Taft tended to see the Cold War as a crusade against the Antichrist, and he bolstered this view by emphasizing the purity of American intentions. Morgenthau realized the unique virtues of

[9]Robert A. Taft, *A Foreign Policy for Americans* (New York, 1951); Hans J. Morgenthau, *In Defense of the National Interest* (New York, 1951); Reinhold Niebuhr, *The Irony of American History* (New York, 1952).

American democracy, but he held no brief for the spotlessness of American morality or ideology. After all, he was not running for office. Nor in this particular did he share Taft's view of history, for Morgenthau believed that the new technological and political problems which appeared in 1945 marked "the definite and radical end of the . . . conditions under which the Western world lived for centuries." The professor drily observed that Russia's use of the "religious order" of communism to remake the world in its image was not unlike those Americans who "heed the noble words of Jefferson, Wilson, and Franklin D. Roosevelt, and . . . set out on a crusade to make the world safe for true democracy."

Taft would not entirely discard military power. He advocated the development of air and naval units but not the infantry. He believed that this policy would save manpower, cut military expenditures, and, in all, be politically attractive. Taft could also in this way slash the executive power to involve the United States in European problems through the commitment of American troops. Morgenthau would have none of this. He deplored the common tendency of both Taft and the Truman Doctrine to lay out "a world-embracing moral principle" that committed American power, of whatever nature, to such broad, undefined, and dangerous limits. The United States must realize, Morgenthau admonished, that military threats to its interests in Europe called for different solutions than did dangers posed by "genuine revolutions" in Asia. American policymakers must follow not the dictates of "moral principle" but the classic formula of spheres of interest. The United States could no longer wish for an open world. It would have to accommodate itself to the realities of power, and anyone who refused to believe in balances of power, Morgenthau added, resembled "a scientist not believing in the law of gravity."

The professor considered the spheres-of-interest approach feasible because the Soviet threat was fueled not by communist ideology but by traditional Russian national power. Unlike the religious passion of communism, Russian national power could effect compromises because it was subject to the same restraints and limitations as American power. Taft, on the other hand, viewed communist ideology as the principal threat. He cared little whether it was attached to Soviet national power, except that by being so attached, its power became immeasurably increased. The senator, therefore, refused to settle for the spheres-of-interest approach, for this would not neutralize communist ideology; instead, he advocated fighting communism everywhere, including inside the labyrinthine bureaucracy of the State Department. Here Morgenthau sharply scored Taft. Many "anticommunists," the professor observed, talk about protecting American security when they really mean protecting the "security of the status quo" at home and abroad.

These differences on the roles of morality, the place of power, and the nature of the Soviet threat inevitably led Taft and Morgenthau to opposite conclusions on the climactic question of Asia. The senator deplored past American policy which treated Western Europe like one big happy family while allowing Asia to go communist almost by default. Running close to the MacArthur line, Taft sought "only . . . the same policy in the Far East as in Europe." That is, he wanted the use of air and naval power as a deterrent in both Europe and Asia. In case of a conflict, his policy lessened the chances for limiting the war short of nuclear exchange. He left unanswered the question of how this naval and air power could deflect the considerably more subtle threat of communist ideology.

Morgenthau necessarily reversed Taft's priorities. Europe, particularly Germany, he argued, comprised such a technological, industrial, and cultural powerhouse that "he who controls all of Europe is well on his way toward controlling the whole world." Europe could not be left to chance, possibly to communism. A further point necessarily shaped American policy: the United States could understand and cooperate with Europe because of common backgrounds and values. Asia, however, was immeasurably different. Unlike the "phony" revolutions in Eastern Europe, those in Asia were "genuine." This meant that Russian imperialism and "genuine" revolution were by no means the same thing. To confuse the two could lead to an American involvement in Asia which would be calamitous. Asian revolutions, Morgenthau observed, were generated not by communism but, ironically, by the political, technological, and moral revolutions which the West transferred to the Orient. Once Asia mastered this technology, a "shift in the distribution of power" would result which, "in its importance for the history of the world, transcends all other factors. It might well mean the end of the bipolarity centered in Washington and Moscow." Given their different race and culture, Americans could not hope to control this momentous change, but only adjust to it. The United States had no real means of dealing with "genuine revolutions" in non-Western lands, according to Morgenthau.

In 1951 and 1952 Niebuhr neatly combined Taft's emphasis on ideology with Morgenthau's conclusions. Partly because of such feats, one observer called Niebuhr's views "part of the canon of a new generation of American liberals and the spiritual guide of those who are now revisiting conservatism."[10] More significant than his appeal to various shades of the political spectrum was Niebuhr's change of tone. Something had happened to the earlier advocate of a quickly revitalized Germany; now he acknowledged that the rearming of Germany "was too precipitate and too indifferent" to European feelings. The loud cry of 1948 to guard the far-flung battle lines became a quiet listing of the reasons why American policymakers must not become overly committed to battle lines in the newly emerging world, especially Asia. Niebuhr now lectured the wielders of the titanic American power that they too were subject to the sins of all humankind.

The Irony of American History argued that because of pride, presumed innocence, and lack of restraint, American power was walking the rim of the abyss. American idealism, which had been instrumental in developing immense national power, now ironically blinded the United States to the dangers of overusing that power. "American power in the service of American idealism," Niebuhr approvingly quoted a European official as saying, "could create a situation in which we would be too impotent to correct you when you are wrong and you would be too idealistic to correct yourself." In addition, not even extensive use of this power could solve fundamental American dilemmas. This provided a second irony: a century or two before, when their power was much less, Americans could solve their problems more easily.

To Niebuhr, communism remained as evil as it had been in 1947 and 1948, but the United States had become the victim of many of the same inconsistencies and delusions about human nature and the so-called virtues of science that had corrupted communism. In the past, Americans had been protected from themselves by the Constitution, whose authors knew more about human nature and the limitations of science than their twentieth-century descendants. They had been protected also by the good fortune that, in having blown hot and cold in their dedication to remake the world, Americans had been saved by their own historical inconsistencies. Niebuhr cited John Adams:

---

[10]Morton White in *New Republic*, May 5, 1952, pp. 18–19.

"Power always thinks it has a great soul and vast views beyond the comprehension of the weak; and that it is doing God's service when it is violating all His Laws." Niebuhr extended Adams's observation by adding that Americans believed they could solve problems simply "by the expansion of our economy." The frontier, Niebuhr intimated, had closed; expanding production "has created moral illusions about the ease with which the adjustment of interest to interest can be made in human society."

In the penultimate section of *Irony*, Niebuhr applied his views to the Asian situation. The United States, he echoed Morgenthau, had little in common with the Orient. Any attempt to use the present American Cold War weaponry to save Asia from communism would be, as he had mentioned earlier in the book, like the "spears of the knights when gunpowder challenged their reign." In phrases tinged with condescension, Niebuhr warned that Asia wanted Western technology but refused to accept the West's view of man, society, or history. He advised working with Japan and the Philippines to contain Asian communism by means of a militarized Pacific "island littoral." So contained, communism would repeat the history of Islam during the Middle Ages and be destroyed "not so much by its foes as by its own inner corruptions." But if it hoped to witness that collapse, the United States would have to remedy its own "inner corruptions" first.

Niebuhr's fear of extending the Cold War to the mainland of Asia partly explained the changed tone in his writings. Above all, Niebuhr feared that the new Republican administration of Dwight D. Eisenhower could commit the ultimate transgressions in foreign policy. A year earlier, in 1951, Niebuhr had looked with much concern on the rising influence of businessmen and Republicans on foreign-policy formulation. Eisenhower's victory transformed this influence into domination: "His victory was significantly engineered by eminent proconsuls of the budding American imperium, partly drawn from the Army and partly from business." Niebuhr feared the effect of this victory upon Washington's Asian policies, for "American conservatives" viewed communist gains in that area as resulting from State Department perfidy

> and as capable of rectification by rigorous military action on our part. This "illusion of American omnipotence," . . . is a natural mistake of a commercial community which knows that American hegemony is based upon our technical-economic power but does not un-

derstand the vast complexities of ethnic loyalties, of social forces in a decaying agrarian world, of the resentments which a mere display of military power creates among those who are not committed to us.[11]

Niebuhr's abhorrence of "the budding American imperium" did not noticeably brake the Eisenhower steamroller in 1952. The general won on a platform that committed the party to save Asia and with a campaign in which he refused to repudiate McCarthyism. Adlai Stevenson ran a more literate and less successful campaign for the Democrats but significantly patterned his appeal after Eisenhower's in two respects: Stevenson refused to embrace the record of the Truman administration with any enthusiasm (at one point asking privately that Acheson publicly announce his intention to resign after the election), and he once went further than Eisenhower in a specific commitment to save Asia.

On October 24 the Democratic nominee warned that to withdraw American troops from Korea and allow "Asians to fight Asians," as the general wanted, "we would risk a Munich in the Far East, with the probability of a third world war not far behind." Unlike Eisenhower, Stevenson did see indigenous nationalism, not international communism, at the root of the Asian upheavals, but, as the campaign progressed, Stevenson's dedication to Asia and his determination to apply military strength in the area seemed to increase as Eisenhower's declined. On September 4 the Republican candidate explained how the United States must protect "the far corners of the earth" which provided the nation with "materials essential to our industry and our defense." Yet on October 24, when he dramatically pledged, "I shall go to Korea," he advocated as a military backstop only the building up of the South Korean forces and shaping "our psychological warfare program into a weapon capable of cracking the Communist front." This was a less militant course than Stevenson was advocating in a speech that same day.[12]

Beneath the Eisenhower moderation, however, was the less restrained Republican platform. It contrasted "Russia's 'Asia-first' policy" with "the 'Asia-last' policy" of the Truman administration. "Containment is defensive," one plank read, "negative, futile and immoral

[11]Reinhold Niebuhr, "The Foreign Policy of American Conservatism and Liberalism." In *Christian Realism and Political Problems* (New York, 1953), pp. 58, 64.
[12]*The New York Times*, October 25, 1952, pp. 1, 8.

[in abandoning] countless human beings to a despotism and Godless terrorism." John Foster Dulles, who was largely responsible for these sections of the platform, later announced in a campaign speech at Buffalo, New York, that the new Republican administration would, if elected, use "all means to secure the liberation of Eastern Europe." When Eisenhower heard this, he immediately phoned Dulles to inform him that the phrase should have read "all peaceful means." "Yes," Dulles promptly replied, "it's just a complete oversight."[13] It was a strange oversight for a renowned international lawyer who had spent forty years honing words to great precision.

Behind Eisenhower also loomed the figure of Joseph McCarthy. We will "eliminate" from the federal government, the platform pledged, those "who share responsibility for the needless predicaments and perils in which we find ourselves." This was a rather loose definition of malfeasance, but the Republicans were not to be denied the profit of hammering the point at the voters. "There are no Communists in the Republican Party," began one long party plank.[14]

Eisenhower's speeches were not that blunt. He also refused to invite General Douglas MacArthur to participate in the campaign, although this would have appeased a large number of conservative Republicans. Eisenhower, however, never publicly repudiated McCarthy's activities. That would not have been sound politics. Sitting on the same stage with McCarthy in Milwaukee, Eisenhower held in his hands a speech paying loving tribute to General George Marshall, who had been a sponsor of Eisenhower's rise in the military but had been termed a traitor by McCarthy. At the last minute Eisenhower bowed to McCarthy's brand of Americanism and deleted the tribute.

Stevenson and many other Democrats seemed particularly open to the charge that, as one McCarthyite journal phrased it, "Chinese coolies and Harvard professors are the people . . . most susceptible to Red propaganda." At Wheeling, West Virginia, in 1950, McCarthy had declared that it was "not the less fortunate" Americans who "have been selling this nation out, but rather those who have had all the benefits." Those "bright young men" in the State Department who were "born with silver spoons in their mouths are the ones who

[13]Interview with Dwight Eisenhower, Dulles Oral History Project, Papers of John Foster Dulles, Princeton.
[14]Clarence W. Baier and Richard P. Stebbins, eds., *Documents of American Foreign Relations, 1952* (New York, 1953), pp. 80–85.

have been worse." Such attacks on the "Eastern intellectual establishment" paid dividends, especially when voters were reminded that Acheson and Stevenson had rushed to the defense of Alger Hiss. Many of the "less fortunate" supported McCarthy and the Republicans, and thus one more group left the New Deal coalition. Polls revealed that the most earnest supporters of the Wisconsin senator were the small businessmen, who felt squeezed between the big unions and big corporations, and manual laborers. Other support came from the new wealth groups (such as oil wildcatters and real estate manipulators), ethnic groups such as Irish and Germans determined to prove their "Americanism," and, paradoxically, some Eastern intellectuals who had prayed to the communist "God who failed" in the 1930s and now attempted to gain redemption by embracing either McCarthy's causes or effects, or both.[15] These groups endorsed the senator's definition of McCarthyism as "Americanism" with its sleeves rolled." No Republican politician without quixotic tendencies tried to buck that slogan in 1952.

Having won on issues that Republican Senator Karl Mundt neatly formulated as K_1C_2—Korea, Communism, and Corruption—the Eisenhower administration's foreign policy could not be impervious to McCarthy or the Cold War mentality which had spawned McCarthyism. Unlike 1948, foreign policy played a central role in the 1952 campaign,[16] and the campaign in turn left its mark on the foreign policy of the following months. In early 1953 the new chief counsel for McCarthy's committee, Roy M. Cohn, and a friend, David Schine, junketed throughout Europe upbraiding American diplomats supposedly soft on communism, attacking U.S. Information Service libraries for exhibiting the work of such "radicals" as Mark Twain and Theodore Dreiser, and provoking the wrath of the European press. Secretary of State Dulles did nothing to stop Cohn and Schine.

The test came when Dulles, without consulting McCarthy, suggested Soviet expert Charles Bohlen as ambassador to Russia. The senator immediately unleashed an attack that centered on Bohlen's role as Roosevelt's interpreter at Yalta. Bohlen correctly assured Dulles

---

[15]Seymour Lipset, *Political Man: The Social Bases of Politics* (New York, 1960), pp. 171–172; Daniel Bell, *The End of Ideology: On the Exhaustion of Political Ideas in the Fifties* (Glencoe, Ill., 1960), pp. 110–112; Richard Rovere, *Senator Joe McCarthy* (Cleveland, 1959), p. 13.
[16]Angus Campbell, Gerald Gurin, and Warren E. Miller, *The Voter Decides* (Evanston, Ill., 1954), pp. 46, 67, 119.

that there was nothing injurious in his past record. The secretary of state was glad to hear this, since, as he sighed, "I couldn't stand another Alger Hiss." Dulles, however, did little to aid Bohlen, refusing even to have pictures taken of them together. The appointment finally went through the Senate only after Eisenhower and Taft worked out a deal whereby Taft and Senator John Sparkman, Democrat of Alabama, closely examined Bohlen's record in confidential State Department files, and the President promised not to make any more major appointments to which McCarthy might object.

Within four months after taking office, the administration bragged that it had fired 1456 federal employees under its "security program." The program had not, however, uncovered one proven communist. So challenged, the Democrats replied that they had effectively fired even more "risks" under Truman's loyalty program.[17] In the midst of this frenzy, one distinguished American Foreign Service officer who had never been tainted by any McCarthyite accusation commented, "If I had a son, I would do everything in my power to suppress any desire he might have to enter the Foreign Service of the United States."[18] The McLeod-McCarthy group countered with the slogan, "An ounce of loyalty is worth a pound of brains." The price, however, would soon be paid for such slogans. As the McCarthyites threw many of the ablest people out of the State Department (and Dulles and Eisenhower uttered too little protest), experts, particularly in the areas of China and South Asia, left government. A decade later they would not be on hand to inform Presidents about the realities of China and Vietnam. The 1960s' generation paid in blood and treasure for the excesses of the early 1950s.

Dulles contented himself with his favorite biblical quotation: "All things work together for good to them that love God, to them who are called according to His purpose."[19] Like Truman, the new secretary of state was confident about whom the Creator was calling. Dulles nevertheless left little to chance. He built his power base within the administration with care. No cabinet officer in American history had a closer working relationship with a President than did Dulles.

[17]Rovere, *McCarthy,* pp. 17–18, 32–33.
[18]Emmet John Hughes, *The Ordeal of Power: A Political Memoir of the Eisenhower Years* (New York, 1963), p. 91.
[19]Dulles to John Nagel, January 21, 1952, Correspondence, Papers of John Foster Dulles, Princeton.

When competing power centers began to appear in the White House in the person of Harold Stassen or Nelson Rockefeller, the secretary of state moved ruthlessly. "He cut off Nelson at the ankles," was the way one official described the encounter. "We will make the most successful team in history," Dulles supposedly told Eisenhower.[20]

Few could challenge Dulles's grasp of world events. He had learned much about Europe as a young law student in Paris. As a senior partner in the powerful law firm of Sullivan and Cromwell of New York City, he operated regularly during the 1920s and 1930s out of the firm's Paris and Berlin offices. He had undertaken his first important diplomatic mission in 1919–1921 with his uncle, Robert Lansing, who was Woodrow Wilson's secretary of state. In cabinet meetings few took issue with him. "After all," one Eisenhower assistant remarked, "how are you going to argue with a man who has lived with a problem—for instance, in respect to Iran—for longer than most of us knew there was such a country?"[21]

But one person did have greater knowledge about, and experience with, world issues and leaders than Dulles—Eisenhower. The general from Abilene, Kansas, not only had commanded the greatest invasion force in history during World War II but had almost daily dealt successfully with some of the most complex giants of the twentieth century, including Roosevelt, Churchill, and French leader Charles de Gaulle. After he became President, Eisenhower seemed to do little but flash his famous grin and play many rounds of golf. The joke circulated that an Eisenhower doll was one that could be wound up and then do nothing for eight years. Fresh research and the opening of new documents from the 1950s, however, now reveal that Eisenhower's calm exterior hid a strong hand, which he wielded to control policy behind the scenes.[22] Nor was the exterior always calm. Privately he could explode and become what one friend called "a human Bessemer furnace." His Vice President, Richard Nixon, later observed that the avuncular Ike was "a far more complex and devi-

[20]Sherman Adams, *First-Hand Report* (New York, 1961), p. 89.
[21]Interview with Sherman Adams, Dulles Oral History Project, Princeton.
[22]Much of the following is based on the pioneering work of Fred I. Greenstein, *The Hidden-Hand Presidency: Eisenhower as Leader* (New York, 1982), especially pp. 9, 26, 57, 69, 91–92; and Richard Immerman, "Eisenhower and Dulles: Who Made the Decisions?" *Political Psychology*, I (Autumn 1979): 3–19.

ous man than most people realized." Eisenhower had early learned how to control those around him. "He's a great poker player," a chief military aide remarked, "and [an] extremely good bridge player. . . . He's a tremendous man for analyzing the other fellow's mind, what options are open to the other fellow, and what line he [Eisenhower] can best take to capitalize or exploit the possibilities." Truman, with his penchant for desk pounding, liked the phrase, "The buck stops here." On his desk Eisenhower had a plaque with a Latin phrase that translated, "Gently in manner, strong in deed." Part of the manner was delegating authority and allowing his subordinates, such as Dulles, to act as lightning rods for both public praise and criticism. Eisenhower once told his press secretary to take a certain action. The secretary objected that if he did that he "would get hell." Eisenhower patted him on the back and said, "My boy, better you than me."

A major reason why he had run for the presidency was his fear that the Republican party might fall into the hands of the Asia-first, "isolationist" faction that rallied around Senator Robert Taft. Eisenhower agreed with Taft on the need for smaller military budgets and on drastically slicing government spending, but he determined to make the party accept its global, not merely Asian, responsibilities. He once told a friend that Senator William Knowland (Republican of California), a leader of the pro-Chiang Kai-shek group, had "no foreign policy except to develop high blood pressure whenever he mentions the words 'Red China.' " With such views, Eisenhower became the transition figure that transformed the Republican party of Taft into the party of Ronald Reagan. While agreeing with Taft on spending cuts, Eisenhower anticipated Reagan (and before him, Senator Barry Goldwater's conservative campaign of 1964) by creating a strong presidency that was especially active in foreign policy; by showing a determination to exercise U.S. power globally; and by holding fast to the belief that the overriding threat to world stability was communism, not starvation, inequality, or other wants that led the have-nots to rebel against the haves. Eisenhower understood the demands of the have-nots and could eloquently articulate the policy problems they presented, but he believed they could be handled in the long run by private investment, while communism posed an immediate threat and had to be destroyed by various forms of military power. Eisenhower changed the more limited commitments of Taft Republicanism into the virtually unlimited commitments of Reagan Republicanism. And he did this by shaping a consensus at home that has been unmatched by any other President after 1945. In a 1955 Gallup Poll nearly two-thirds of those calling themselves liberals saw Eisenhower as liberal, and almost the same percentage considering themselves conservatives saw him as conservative.

Similar dramatic changes occurred in the Soviet Union. In August 1952 Stalin surprised the world by calling the Nineteenth Party Congress to convene on October 5. Thirteen years had passed since the eighteenth session of 1939. The Soviet dictator obviously had a task for the obedient members to perform.

Western officials doubted that Stalin aimed to ease tensions. Throughout 1951 and 1952 he had taken a tougher foreign-policy line than before and nearly doubled the Soviet Army to 4.9 million men while increasing defense expenditures by 50 percent. On October 2 Stalin published his *Economic Problems of Socialism,* a text enunciating the main line of Soviet domestic and foreign policies. This set the tone for the congress. The Soviet dictator announced not only that primary emphasis would continue to be placed on heavy industry but that state ownership must be extended over portions of the agricultural economy that had long remained in the hands of agricultural collectives.

Stalin then assaulted those who challenged his foreign policies. The West, he predicted, would soon be overwhelmed by economic catastrophe. Communist successes since 1945 had contracted the capitalists' market. This contraction had so aggravated the Western economic system that the capitalists would soon begin a death struggle among themselves. Because the United States had placed Western Europe, Germany, and Japan on a "dole," Stalin observed sarcastically, "some comrades" see only "the external appearances which glitter on the surface." "To think that these countries will not attempt to rise to their feet again, smash the U.S. 'regime' and break away on a path of independent development is to believe in miracles." (Malenkov dutifully repeated this section in his keynote address.) This development, Stalin concluded in a brief speech at the congress, indicated two courses for communists: the tightening of party control to prepare fully for the protection of the bloc against capitalist warfare, and cooperative efforts with nationalists everywhere, but especially those in

Germany, Japan, and France, in order to accelerate the revolt against American control.[23]

The theme of the congress was a renewed emphasis on the inevitability of war. This was only partly tempered by Stalin's and Malenkov's remarks upon the desirability of international peace movements, united fronts, and a German treaty. The strategy toughened while the means softened. A second, more implicit theme also became apparent. The congress emphasized through omission the Soviet domination of the communist world. Although Chinese officials attended and spoke, only insignificant references to China occurred in the hundreds of thousands of published words uttered by Russians at the congress.

Another outcome of the congress was the most significant. In an apparent attempt to cement his control over both the Malenkov and Khrushchev factions, Stalin announced at the congress the creation of a new politburo, to be named the Party Presidium, consisting of twenty-five instead of eleven members. The new additions would be fervent young Stalinists. This stroke cut the present and potential power of both Malenkov and Khrushchev while giving Stalin even greater authority. In January 1953 Stalin's power received further impetus from an important article which appeared in the party's leading theoretical journal, *Kommunist*. After elaborately developing the "capitalist encirclement" doctrine, the analysis concluded that, because of the growth of the Western economic crisis and the success of the international communist movement, not détente but "a fierce struggle against the enemy" must now be pursued.[24]

On January 13, 1953, concrete evidence dramatically appeared to support the "capitalist encirclement" thesis. A group of Kremlin doctors was suddenly arrested by Soviet security police for the killing of Andrei Zhdanov in 1948 and was accused of being in the hire of American and British espionage agents. Some observers believed that the episode indicated Stalin's firm belief that an East-West détente of

---

[23]J. V. Stalin, "Economic Problems of Socialism in the U.S.S.R." in *Current Soviet Policies: The Documentary Record of the 19th Communist Party Congress and the Reorganization After Stalin's Death*, edited and with an introduction by Leo Gruliow (New York, 1953), pp. 1–10, 235–236. This is an exceptionally useful compendium of primary documents which emerged from those events between October 1952 and April 1953.

[24]*Current Soviet Policies*, p. 105, has Malenkov's speech; the *Kommunist* article is analyzed in Robert C. Tucker, *The Soviet Political Mind* (New York, 1963), pp. 30–31.

any kind, including possible armistice in Korea, was impossible. Closer to the ruling circles of the Kremlin, the "Doctors Plot" had another meaning. As the plot unfolded, Stalin evidently made indirect threats to the lives of Central Committee members, including some as close to him as Molotov and Anastas Mikoyan. These threats, apparently, were the breaking point. On February 17 the chief of security in the Kremlin who had protected Stalin for thirty years suddenly was announced by the Soviet press to be dead. Within three weeks Stalin fell victim to what was officially termed "hemorrhage of the brain."

The truth, as usual, was more complex and interesting. Stalin's policies were failing abroad (especially in the key area of West German rearmament) and becoming yet more terrifying at home. He had seemed determined to eliminate even those closest to him in the Kremlin. Harrison E. Salisbury, correspondent of *The New York Times* in Moscow during those extraordinary days of 1953, later concluded that the cause of Stalin's death was suspect. On the night of Saturday, February 28, Georgi Malenkov, Lavrenti Beria, Nikolay Bulganin, and Nikita Khrushchev—the four leading contenders for Stalin's throne—had an all-night drinking bout with the dictator at his villa outside Moscow. The next day Stalin was found asleep on the floor. He reportedly had suffered a stroke. The four contenders were summoned for advice. But they did nothing for twenty-four hours. Salisbury surmised that the four men decided that "if they let him go a few more hours they might be rid of him for all time." A visitor to Stalin's home on the day of his death, March 5, believed that he "was speeded to his grave."[25]

Malenkov quickly took over Stalin's top jobs. He immediately cut back politburo membership to throw out the ardent young Stalinists whom the old dictator had just appointed. Malenkov also announced that new policies would arise from a "collective" rather than from the whims of one man. He issued amnesties for many political prisoners, including those locked up by Stalin for the alleged "Doctors Plot." The doctors' confessions, the Soviet press suddenly discovered, had been obtained "through the use of impermissible means of investigation which are strictly forbidden under Soviet law."[26]

---

[25]Harrison E. Salisbury, "The Days of Stalin's Death," *The New York Times Magazine*, April 17, 1983, pp. 38–48.
[26]*Current Soviet Policies*, pp. 249–251.

This final twist to the "Doctors Plot" indicated changes in Soviet foreign policies. Malenkov confirmed the changes in a speech before the Supreme Soviet: "At the present time there is no disputed or unresolved question that cannot be settled peacefully by mutual agreement of the interested countries," he announced. "This applies to our relations with all states, including the United States of America."[27] Soon the new Russian leaders allowed Soviet citizens married to foreigners to leave the country; reestablished diplomatic relations with Greece, Israel, and later Yugoslavia; renounced Soviet claims to Turkish territory; and, most important, agreed to an end to the Korean War.

Eisenhower and Dulles suddenly found themselves dealing with a new set of Soviet policies. A fresh set of issues, a different kind of Soviet challenge had dramatically appeared. The question became whether the new American leaders could become flexible enough to deal with the new faces in Moscow, particularly in the aftermath of the terrible war in Korea and amidst the plague of McCarthyism.

[27]*Current Soviet Policies*, pp. 256–260.

CHAPTER 7

A Different Cold War
(1953–1955)

Former Secretary of the Treasury George Humphrey recalled his impressions of Washington when the Eisenhower administration moved into power. "We were under war controls," Humphrey remembered, "and we were in war."[1] Entering office as the struggle continued in Korea, the President pledged that he would more efficiently and successfully wage the Cold War against Stalinist Russia. "Let's face it," one Republican adviser had remarked in early 1952. "The only excuse for Ike's candidacy is that he's the man best qualified to deal with Stalin."[2]

In early March 1953 Stalin died. The Cold War that began to confront Eisenhower and Dulles during their first months in power assumed new and puzzling traits. Georgi Malenkov assumed Stalin's place in the Soviet government, but he did not appropriate the departed leader's foreign policies. Malenkov instead began urging friendly negotiation in Europe and peace in Korea. Rapid changes in other parts of the world also began to confuse Americans. The Republicans had won with a platform promising more military firepower and a firming up of the containment policy, but new international crises increasingly revolved around rampaging nationalisms in the Middle East, Latin America, and Southeast Asia rather than around military problems in Europe or Korea. As Morgenthau and Niebuhr had foreseen, the Eisenhower administration was soon engaged in a new kind of Cold War.

Immediately after Stalin's death American intelligence informed the President that the new Soviet premier would have to consolidate

---

[1] Interview with George Humphrey and Herbert Hoover, Jr., Dulles Oral History Project, Princeton.
[2] Norman A. Graebner, *The New Isolationism* (New York, 1956), p. 98.

his internal control and consequently would not undertake new departures in foreign affairs.[3] Many Americans believed that Stalin's death would create a chaos which might permanently damage Soviet power, or at least force a long, painful, and unproductive transition period upon new leadership. This did not happen. The possibility of one-man rule by Malenkov apparently disappeared after a severe internal party struggle. He maintained his premiership but surrendered the key post of first party secretary to Nikita Khrushchev.

A precarious collective leadership emerged as Malenkov, with his power based on the technicians and government bureaucracy, and Khrushchev, with his strong support from the party, began a struggle for supreme power. The first important casualty in the battle was Lavrenti Beria. When Beria moved too fast and overtly in making the secret police his own political tool, the new rulers arrested and executed him in July. In stark contrast to Stalin's methods, however, Beria was probably the only victim of execution within the high party hierarchy. While conveniently blaming Beria for many of the excesses of previous years, Malenkov cautiously moved to liberalize the functioning of the party and demanded a reduction of investment in heavy industry so that Russians could enjoy more consumer goods.

This policy of relaxation soon stretched to foreign affairs. If the Western alliance was unable to agree upon such ventures as the European Defense Community in the present "tense international situation," Malenkov observed to the Supreme Soviet on August 8, 1953, "a lessening of this tension might lead to [the] disintegration" of that alliance. The premier, however, hedged his bet. In the same speech he announced that the Soviets had successfully tested a thermonuclear, or hydrogen, bomb. With the American thermonuclear monopoly broken, the Soviets stood ready to negotiate on European problems. To strengthen their position further, they dropped their emphasis on revolution by an international proletariat and attempted to influence Western policies by playing upon the peace hopes of the European middle classes.[4]

The American response to these Soviet changes was slow and unsure. The Washington bureaucracy was fearful and confused, partly because of its terror of the ubiquitous McCarthyism. Underneath this

---

[3]Dwight D. Eisenhower, *The White House Years: Mandate for Change, 1953–1956* (Garden City, N.Y., 1963), pp. 148–149.

[4]*Current Digest of the Soviet Press*, V (September 5, 1953): 3–12, 26.

confusion lay a deeper problem. Soviet communism, Dulles told the Senate Foreign Relations Committee in January, "believes that human beings are nothing more than somewhat superior animals . . . and that the best kind of a world is that world which is organized as a well-managed farm is organized, where certain animals are taken out to pasture, and they are fed and brought back and milked, and they are given a barn as shelter over their heads." Apparently the secretary of state had read George Orwell's *Animal Farm* literally. "I do not see how, as long as Soviet communism holds those views," Dulles concluded, ". . . there can be any permanent reconciliation. . . . This is an irreconcilable conflict."[5] By defining the conflict as so intensely ideological, Dulles severely limited the possibility of easing tensions through a flexible diplomacy.

On April 16, 1953, Eisenhower made the first formal response to Malenkov's new tactics. If the Soviets sincerely desired détente, the President remarked, there must be "free elections in a united Korea" the end of communist revolts in Malaya and Indochina; "United Nations control and inspection" of disarmament; "a free and united Germany, with a government based upon free and secret elections" the "free choice" of governments in Eastern Europe; and a treaty restoring Austria's independence.[6] The day following this address Dulles appeared before the Senate Foreign Relations Committee; his testimony was headlined by *The New York Times* as "Dulles Bids Soviet Cooperate or Face Vast West Arming."

Within a month, however, the American approach was questioned by the most eminent statesman within that alliance. Without previously informing either Eisenhower or his own Foreign Office, Winston Churchill announced on May 11 that the time had arrived for world leaders to confer "on the highest level" to see which problems might be solved. The prime minister indirectly attacked Eisenhower's demand that a multitude of questions would have to be settled at once. This was obviously impossible and, moreover, might unfortunately "impede any spontaneous and healthy evolution which may be taking place inside Russia." Churchill instead recommended

---

[5]U.S. Senate, Committee on Foreign Relations, 83rd Cong., 1st Sess., *Nomination of John Foster Dulles . . . , January 15, 1953* (Washington, 1953), pp. 10–11.
[6]Department of State, *American Foreign Policy, 1950–1955, Basic Documents*, 2 vols. I (Washington, 1957): 65–71.

a piecemeal approach, tackling solvable problems but assuming all the while that Russian security must be assured.[7]

Senate Majority Leader William Knowland responded by accusing Churchill of "urging a Far Eastern Munich." The official Washington response was characterized as "cool." Eisenhower explained why to a news conference. "The world happened to be round and it had no end and he [Eisenhower] didn't see how you could discuss the problem, the great basic problems of today, which were so largely philosophical in character, without thinking in global terms," or so reported the official text of the conference.[8]

The President was arguing that, because the Soviet menace was basically ideological, or "philosophical," it was also indivisible and thus posed a threat everywhere in the world. One implication followed: problems in Europe and those in Asia were linked and could be approached with similar strategies. A second implication was that the ideology posed a worldwide threat regardless of whether the Soviets possessed the military, economic, and political power to support that ideology globally. In a sense this seemed an accurate appraisal, for communism could become disruptive in areas closed to Soviet arms. But Eisenhower's approach quickly led to confusion.

In May 1952 and again in January 1953, Dulles had condemned "containment" as a "policy which is bound to fail because a purely defensive policy never wins against an aggressive policy." He advocated instead "liberation of these captive peoples" in Eastern Europe through such "processes short of war" as "political warfare, psychological warfare and propaganda." In late May 1953 the Soviets loosened political controls in East Germany but also demanded more production from workers for the same wages. Laborers protested with a march down East Berlin's Stalinallee on June 16. The next day began with a general strike and demonstrations which climaxed with the tearing down of communist flags and demands for free elections. The American radio in West Berlin broadcast encouragement to the workers and lauded the spreading of the strikes throughout East Germany. Then suddenly Soviet tanks appeared in Berlin, Dresden, Leipzig, Magdeburg, and Jena. As the armor smashed the demonstrations, Dulles made no move other than sending food ("Eisenhower packages") to try to win East Germans and undermine Com-

[7]*The New York Times,* May 12, 1953, pp. 8–9.
[8]*The New York Times,* May 15, 1953, p. 6.

munist control. "Liberation" had failed its first test and had done so in Germany, the European prize of the East-West struggle.[9]

Facing the problem of captive peoples in North Korea shortly after, the administration came up with a more satisfactory, if not exactly happy, solution by recognizing the limits of its military and political power. Eisenhower's trip to Korea in December 1952 buttressed his belief that the United States should not be entrapped in a conventional war on the Asian mainland. For his own reasons, Secretary of the Treasury Humphrey supported this view. One-third of the budget had to be cut to eliminate deficit spending, Humphrey told the President, and that means "you have to get Korea out of the way."

To get Korea "out of the way," the administration first employed what would later be called "brinksmanship." Returning from Korea on December 14, Eisenhower warned that, unless the war ended quickly, the United States might retaliate "under circumstances of our choosing." Six weeks later in his first State of the Union message, the President announced that the American Seventh Fleet would "no longer be employed to shield Communist China." He hurriedly added that this meant no intended aggression "on our part," but this so-called unleashing of Chiang Kai-shek so frightened England and France that Dulles flew to Europe to reassure the Allies. As tension mounted, Stalin conveniently died. The new Soviet leaders hinted their willingness to sponsor negotiations. On the crucial question of prisoner exchange (the UN forces reported that many North Korean and Chinese prisoners did not want to return home and should not be compelled to do so), the Chinese suggested on March 30 that prisoner repatriation be placed in the hands of international authorities. On April 23 armistice talks recommenced, but Dulles soon concluded that the Chinese were raising unnecessary barriers to a peace. On May 22 he hinted to Peking through Indian diplomats that if peace were not forthcoming the United States would bring in atomic weapons. The next day the State Department issued more moderate instructions on the prisoner-exchange problem.

Within eleven days the communists accepted the plan with minor changes. They held to the agreement even after President Syngman Rhee of South Korea tried to sabotage the negotiations by releasing

[9]Christian F. Ostermann, *The United States and the East German Uprising of 1953...*, Cold War International History Project, Woodrow Wilson International Center (Washington, D.C., 1994), pp. 2–3, 27, 43.

27,000 Chinese and North Korean prisoners on June 18. The seventy-eight-year-old Rhee was outraged that the American acceptance of a division roughly along the 38th parallel would prevent him from ever ruling a unified Korea. The final armistice was signed on July 27. Talks in 1953 and 1954 on reunification failed, and the United States proceeded to pour $6 billion of aid into South Korea over the next decade. Industrial production tripled, exports increased eight times to nearly $250 million, and the economy became increasingly self-sufficient. Rhee was not as fortunate politically. He fell from power after students rioted against his autocratic regime in April 1960 and was replaced by a military-controlled government. The North Korean government also endured political upheavals, although on lower levels, and rebuilt its air force with hundreds of modern Soviet fighter planes. The United States installed tactical guided missiles with atomic warheads pointing northward. Outside Panmunjom, where negotiators still gather to insult one another, grandstands and loud-speakers accommodated tourists who liked to witness the spectacle of international diplomacy and peer out over the desolate, bare hills where thousands of men died in a "limited" war.

Many lessons were to be learned from the Korean involvement. Dulles chose to apply most of them to both Europe and the rest of Asia. In his European policies, Dulles made Germany the pivot. As a lawyer in Germany between the wars, he had come to admire the German people; he prized Germany's location, industrial power, and military potential as a bulwark against Soviet expansion; and, by means of a steadily developing friendship, he enjoyed a similarity of views with Konrad Adenauer that he had with no other world leader.

In July 1953 Dulles made these views clear to everyone. Following the Churchill speech in May, Russia had proposed a coalition of East and West Germans to prepare a peace treaty which would neutralize Germany; then, and only then, Germany could have free elections. In July Dulles rejected this procedure. He proposed instead that free elections first be held throughout Germany and then a peace treaty be drawn. The Russians would have none of this, particularly after Dulles also insisted that the EDC could not be involved in the discussions; if a reunited Germany wanted to rearm and tie itself to the West through the EDC, Dulles thought it should be able to do so. He continued these strategies inherited from Acheson in the belief that any immediate détente was impossible, for, as he had told a distinguished assemblage of European statesmen, "The Soviet leaders are to a very large extent the prisoners of their own doctrine which is intensively held by their followers, who are fanatics."[10]

Accepting the status quo in Europe, or at least the status quo once the French formally endorsed the EDC, Dulles turned to ponder the problems of the newly emerging areas. These now required more and more attention. He hoped to build into those areas many of the same military and political institutions which had established the status quo in Europe. This policy moved from the assumption that disturbances anywhere outside the Iron Curtain usually worked against American interests sooner or later. Such a view had deep roots in U.S. history.

From the Declaration of Independence until the Civil War, Americans generally sympathized with revolutions abroad. In several respects, however, they dispensed their sympathy with care. They disliked revolutions that went beyond the political, social, and economic boundaries of their own. Americans also believed their own revolution superior to revolutions on the "right" (as John Quincy Adams viewed the Latin American upheavals) or on the "left." They best liked revolts on the North American continent, such as those in Florida, Texas, California, and Canada, which opened possible areas for annexation to the expanding Union.

In the middle of the nineteenth century, two events began to reshape American views toward revolutions: the continental conquest was completed, and Americans began emphasizing the commercial aspects of their foreign policy instead of landed expansion. These overseas commercial interests became especially important, for stability, peace, and confidence in the sanctity of contract were essential to any great trading venture. By 1900 the United States had burgeoned into a power which combined the interesting characteristics of being conservative ideologically and expansive economically. Such a combination would not be encouraging to revolution. Interventions against rebellions in Cuba and the Philippines were followed by Theodore Roosevelt's pronouncement that the United States would act as a policeman to prevent upheavals in the Caribbean area. A decade later Woodrow Wilson rationalized the use of economic and

[10]"Statement of Secretary Dulles at April 23 Session of North Atlantic Council Ministers' Meeting," Conference Dossiers, Dulles Papers, Princeton.

military force against Mexico with an ideological justification that employed the traditional American liberal rhetoric. The threat of revolution reached a crisis when, in 1917, Lenin joined the use of force to a doctrine worldwide in its ambitions and repugnant to most Americans.

The Eisenhower administration inherited this significant historical legacy. It became an heir to opposing revolutions at the point when European colonial rule and conservative monarchies crumbled before nationalist uprisings in the Middle East, Africa, Asia, and Latin America. The new spirit was captured by the highly corrupt King Farouk of Egypt. As nationalist army officers threw him out of Egypt, Farouk predicted that in a decade there would only "be five kings left: Hearts, Clubs, Diamonds, Spades, and England." He was not far wrong.

Eisenhower and Dulles understood and sympathized with much of the new nationalism. Their own people, after all, had won the first modern anticolonial struggle in 1776. Both men realized, moreover, that the worn-out British and French empires were breathing their last. They wanted the colonials quickly out of the way. When colonials remained, revolutionaries tended to move leftward in order to continue the struggle. Eisenhower preferred to attack that problem at the root by pushing out the Europeans. But Americans seldom seemed able to move fast enough. Revolutionaries in Iran, Indochina, and Guatemala gained ground. The President determined to stop them with force if necessary.

The problem thus became what kind of force Americans should use to control revolutions abroad. Eisenhower and Dulles, and indeed all later Americans, found themselves in a terrible bind. They did not want to fight conventional ground wars in Asia and Africa. Korea had vividly proved the dangers of such involvements. Using covert weapons employed by the Central Intelligence Agency could work in certain instances (and Eisenhower proved to be exceedingly skillful in employing the CIA), but in other cases the revolutionaries had gathered too much strength to be beaten by James Bond–like operations. Sometimes they even enjoyed direct Soviet or Chinese assistance.

Eisenhower devised a package of tactics for dealing with unwanted revolutionaries. First, he turned loose the CIA in such places as Iran and Guatemala, which were not yet out of control. Second, he sent U.S. military advisers to train native troops, as in Vietnam, where

Eisenhower began the so-called Vietnamization of the war against the communists a generation before "Vietnamization" became a catchword of Richard Nixon's policy in the early 1970s. Third, Eisenhower and Dulles engineered a series of military alliances to tie friends together in a common fight against the Soviets outside, and left-wing revolutionaries inside, various regions. The Baghdad Pact in the Middle East and the Southeast Asia Treaty Organization (SEATO) became two of the more famous examples of "pactomania," as Dulles's critics labeled the policy. Fourth, Eisenhower based his overall military policy on the use of huge hydrogen bombs as well as small tactical atomic weapons that planners believed could be deployed with almost surgical precision on battlefields. He especially threatened to use these weapons if Soviet or Chinese forces launched a direct invasion or became heavily involved with the revolutionaries (as, indeed, he had already threatened in Korea in mid-1953).

The President's growing reliance on nuclear bombs also grew out of his determination to cut back government spending. No President in the post-1945 years has been as fanatic in this regard as this famous military commander who dedicated himself to slashing military budgets. He preached repeatedly that the key to American power was its economic system and marvelous productivity, not its weapons. Military spending on the level of Truman's $50 billion annually, he feared, would set off a terrible inflation and ruin the economy. "We must not go broke," he reiterated. To Eisenhower, "broke" meant either a deficit in the federal budget, or an economy growing dependent on a "military-industrial complex," as he later termed it. "To Eisenhower," a close observer later remarked, "the United States economy was like the source of a mother's milk—tender and soft and not to be abused."[11]

At the same time, however, the President set out to stop left-wing revolutions and continue Truman's "containment" policy. These conclusions had been hammered out in a series of discussions during 1953 in "Operation Solarium" (named after the White House sun room in which they were held). If Eisenhower hoped to carry out Truman's policies without Truman's budget, his only solution was to rely on nuclear weapons that were cheaper than maintaining men in arms in a conventional force. In two years Eisenhower reduced Truman's

[11]Douglas Kinnard, *The Secretary of Defense* (Lexington, Ky., 1980), pp. 44–45.

military budget by nearly one-third to about $34 billion. His reliance on nuclear armaments to accomplish this reduction soon became evident as he allowed the development of the B41 bomb of over 20 megatons, or the equivalent of 400 Hiroshima-type bombs. (The B41 proved less usable than originally anticipated after tests revealed that if it were dropped close to Soviet coastlines, the radiation would pose greater dangers to U.S. forces and ships at sea than it would to large parts of Russia itself.) The size of the nation's nuclear stockpile doubled between 1953 and 1955, while new, huge B-52 bombers rolled off assembly lines to deliver the weapons. Eisenhower became the first President to consider atomic and nuclear bombs "conventional" weapons—to "be used exactly as you would use a bullet or anything else," as he remarked publicly in 1955. Eisenhower refused repeatedly to accept a nuclear test ban that would have stopped the deadly radioactive fallout from weapons tests that began to infect the world's food supplies. His refusal was based in part on the Soviets' refusal to agree to what he considered adequate inspections, in part on the belief that the development of his main weapons systems depended on such tests. Thus, Eisenhower was prepared to consider starting a nuclear war if necessary—not only if the Soviets invaded Europe but also if Cold War costs became so high that they were forcing "us to war— or into some form of dictatorial government."[12]

His strategy became known as "the new look," or "more bang for a buck." Dulles used the phrase "massive retaliation," by which he meant being "willing and able to respond vigorously at places and with means of [our] own choosing."[13] Eisenhower had a clear sense of when he might launch "massive retaliation," as noted above. But he also had an idea of the destruction that could result. In certain situations, no matter how tempting, war had to be avoided. For example, he made a remarkable response to Syngman Rhee in mid-1954

---

[12]Memorandum for the Secretary of State," September 8, 1953, Dulles Papers, Princeton. The discussion in this paragraph is also from Lawrence Freedman, *The Evolution of Nuclear Strategy* (New York, 1983), pp. 77–78, 81–83; David Alan Rosenberg, " 'A Smoking Radiating Ruin at the End of Two Hours,' " *International Security,* VI (Winter 1981–1982): 3–38; Robert A. Divine, *Blowing on the Wind: The Nuclear Test Ban Debate, 1954–1960* (New York, 1978), especially chapters 2, 3, 7; Samuel F. Wells, Jr., "The Origins of Massive Retaliation," *Political Science Quarterly,* XCVI (Spring 1981): 31–52; and *Washington Post,* December 27, 1983, p. A9.

[13]A standard version of Dulles's theory is his "Policy for Security and Peace," *Foreign Affairs,* XXXII (April 1954): especially 357–358.

when the South Korean leader tried to shame him into supporting a war to unify Korea. Eisenhower interrupted to say that he "regretted very much" the division of Korea, Germany, Austria, and Vietnam, "but . . . no one in this world will get America to go to war over these problems. . . . We cannot undertake any engagement that involves [the] deliberate intention of going to war with Iron Curtain countries."[14]

Eisenhower thereby defined the two extremes in which he would or would not go to war. But the extremes turned out not to be the problems. His dilemma involved the "gray areas"—as a young Harvard professor, Henry Kissinger, called them in 1955—the newly emerging areas where kings and colonials were giving way to nationalist revolutionary movements. In these areas Eisenhower faced the great challenge that has confronted all his successors: finding a way of successfully using U.S. power and—most important—understanding these movements. His first challenges arose in Iran, Guatemala, and Vietnam. The nation's response to these challenges was historic for it demonstrated the irrelevance of "massive retaliation" and unfortunately locked into place American beliefs about handling revolutionaries for the next twenty years.

In 1951 an Iranian nationalist movement headed by Mohammed Mossadegh had undercut the power of the shah and proceeded to nationalize the Anglo-Iranian Oil Company. The British government had received more taxes from the company than the Iranian government had received for its own natural resource. The company consequently provided a convenient target in an impoverished land where 500 of every 1000 newborns died. The British demanded payment for the confiscated holdings, a demand that the Iranians could not meet without binding themselves to foreign lenders. With oil exports at a standstill, the Iran economy began to sink, since income from oil provided 30 percent of its total income and 60 percent of its foreign exchange. When Eisenhower entered office, the United States, despite extensive efforts by Acheson, had not been successful in acting as a mediator.

After a three-week trip through the Middle East in May 1953, Dulles reached some disturbing conclusions. Western power had "deteriorated" in the area, he believed, and unless drastic action was

---

[14]"Korean-American Talks, July 27, 1954," Dwight D. Eisenhower Diary Series, Box 4, Dwight D. Eisenhower Library, Abilene, Kan.

taken, the Arab nations would become "outright" neutrals in "the East-West struggle." Israel and intra-Arab squabbles accounted for some of the problems, but Dulles also wondered about the British. "They interpret our policy as one which in fact hastens their loss of prestige in the area. To some extent," the secretary admitted, ". . . this may be true," but Great Britain's loss of power was also due to "altered world power relationships." Dulles decided that he would have to convince the Middle East that the United States had little to do with British and French colonialism.[15]

The opportunity came within the next two months when the State Department concluded that Mossadegh was moving into the Soviet orbit. Rumors of a Soviet loan to Iran began to circulate, and in August Mossadegh received 99.4 percent of the votes in a plebiscite, a percentage which Eisenhower later used as proof of increased communist influence.[16] Having earlier refused to help Mossadegh rebuild the Iranian economy, the United States now cut off all aid.

In August the shah staged a successful coup to regain power. The United States provided guns, trucks, armored cars, and radio communications for the shah's forces.[17] The new government quickly undertook discussions with representatives of the oil company, but the representatives were not those of the year before. Since the turn of the century, the United States had been trying to get into the Iranian oil fields only to be constantly repulsed by the British. Now the breakthrough occurred by the grace of the shah and under the guidance of State Department official Herbert Hoover, Jr., who had gained wide experience in the complexities of the international oil problem as a private businessman. A new international consortium was established giving the British 40 percent, five American firms (Gulf, Socony-Vacuum, Standard Oil of California, Standard Oil of New Jersey, and Texaco) 40 percent, and Dutch Shell and French Petroleum the remaining 20 percent of Iranian oil production. Profits would be divided equally between the consortium and Iran.[18] Iranian oil once more freely flowed into international markets, the shah's government was

---

[15]"Conclusions on Trip," May 9 to May 29, 1953, Conference Dossiers, Dulles Papers, Princeton.

[16]Eisenhower, *The White House Years*, pp. 160–166.

[17]Robert Engler, *The Politics of Oil* (New York, 1961), p. 206; Kermit Roosevelt, *Countercoup: The Struggle for the Control of Iran* (New York, 1979).

[18]Engler, *The Politics of Oil*, p. 207.

securely within the Western camp, and the British monopoly on the oil fields had been broken. For Dulles and Eisenhower it was one revolution with a happy ending. More accurately it was not a revolution at all.

Seven years before, American diplomats had hoped that similar problems would be avoided in Latin America by the formation of the Rio Pact and the Organization of American States (OAS). Dulles found to his frustration that Latin American governments too often moved outside the U.S. interpretation of these agreements. Dulles had phrased the problem dramatically in February 1953. Latin American conditions, he stressed, "are somewhat comparable to conditions as they were in China in the mid-thirties when the Communist movement was getting started. . . . Well, if we don't look out, we will wake up some morning and read in the newspapers that there happened in South America the same kind of thing that happened in China in 1949."[19] Despite this awareness Dulles never attempted to work out a comprehensive policy for encouraging Latin America to follow a path different from that which China trod in the 1930s. He instead approached the problem piecemeal. The first test for this approach came in Guatemala during the spring of 1954.

That country's population mainly comprises diverse groups of Indians who are poor, illiterate, and isolated. In an area roughly the size of Tennessee, only 10 percent of the land is tillable, yet 74 percent of the population is agrarian. Two percent of the landowners own 60 percent of the usable land. Until 1944 a succession of strongmen prevented any radical change in this society, but in that year student riots and unrest among professional classes brought in a new government, led by Juan José Arévelo, which supported land and labor reform. In 1951 Colonel Jacobo Arbenz Guzmán replaced Arévelo through proper constitutional procedures. Guatemalan politics polarized; the communists, who supported Arbenz, insisted, against strong conservative opposition, that further reforms were requisite. Arbenz's main objective became the United Fruit Company. For more than a half century that company had employed as many as 40,000 Guatemalans; monopolized shipping, communications, and railroads; and helped shape the country's politics.

In 1953 Arbenz confiscated 178,000 acres of company property.

[19]U.S. Senate, *Nomination of Dulles*, p. 31.

The State Department demanded proper payment, a demand Arbenz could not meet partly on nationalist grounds but also because it would require his country to tie itself economically to obligations which would prevent the financing of desperately needed internal reforms. When Arbenz refused to take the dispute to the Court of Arbitration at The Hague, Dulles moved to isolate Guatemala at the Tenth Inter-American Conference meeting at Caracas, Venezuela, in March 1954. He pushed through by a 17 to 1 vote a declaration that because "international communism . . . is incompatible with the concept of American freedom," the American states would "adopt within their respective territories the measures necessary to eradicate and prevent subversive activities."[20] Guatemala voted against, Mexico and Argentina refused to vote, and Costa Rica did not attend the meeting. Dulles interpreted the resolution as an application of the historic Monroe Doctrine. As Monroe's original message had been aimed at the political system of the Holy Alliance, now the doctrine sent a similar warning to international communism, a political threat "more dangerous than the open physical aggression."[21]

On May 15 Guatemala unloaded 1900 tons of arms from Czechoslovakia. The United States responded by airlifting arms to Nicaragua and Honduras, where the CIA trained Guatemalan exiles for an invasion of their homeland. The Eisenhower administration also secretly planned to erect a blockade around Guatemala and stop any "suspicious foreign-flag vessels" possibly carrying arms.[22] That decision could have led to a direct confrontation with Soviet ships. On June 18 Colonel Carlos Castillo Armas and his American-trained force of 150 men moved across the Honduran border into Guatemala. Armas did not distinguish himself in battle, but at the decisive moment several small planes, piloted by CIA operatives, bombed Guatemala City and key towns. U.S. aid was crucial, but, equally significant, Arbenz lost support from his army and the supposedly communist-controlled labor unions. By late June 1954 Castillo Armas ruled Guatemala.

---

[20]Department of State, *American Foreign Policy, 1950–1955, Basic Documents,* I: 1300–1302.
[21]U.S. Senate, Committee on Foreign Relations, 83rd Cong., 2nd Sess., *Statements of Secretary John Foster Dulles and Admiral Arthur Radford . . . , March 9 and April 14, 1954* (Washington, 1954), p. 18.
[22]"Memo for President for Leaders' Meeting, May 24/53," May 22, 1954, Meetings with the President, 1954 (3), White House Memoranda Series, Dulles Papers, Eisenhower Library, Abilene, Kan.

Eisenhower's overthrow of Arbenz marks a turning point in U.S. foreign policy for at least four reasons. First, Americans misunderstood the Guatemalan situation. Arbenz had been constitutionally elected and headed a reform—not communist—movement. A handful of communists sat in the national legislature and influenced the labor movement, but no one ever argued that they in any way shaped the country's most important institutions: the presidency, the army, and the Roman Catholic Church. Americans too easily confused nationalism with communism. Second, despite the confusion, the administration pulled off such a successful and covert operation that Dulles could deny that his brother Allen (director of the CIA) was involved with Arbenz's removal. The administration announced that the Guatemalan people themselves had deposed their president. Americans too quickly and mistakenly concluded that such an operation could easily be repeated elsewhere. Third, Arbenz finally fell when his military deserted. Future Latin American revolutionaries drew the appropriate lesson. Fidel Castro of Cuba and, in the 1980s, the Sandinista government of Nicaragua would make the army and the government parts of a single unit. Overthrowing such regimes would require a war, not simply a covert CIA operation. Finally, the United States won the battle but lost the longer war. In Guatemala (and later elsewhere) Americans failed to replace the deposed regime with an effective liberal reformer. Castillo Armas carried out large-scale executions that killed more Guatemalans after the invasion than had died during the conflict. Reactionary and ineffective, he was assassinated by members of his own regime three years later. The United States poured more aid into Guatemala between 1954 and 1965 than into any other Latin American nation, but the only results by the mid-1960s were a brutal military government and the growth of a revolutionary guerrilla movement more radical than any group in the country before 1954.

During the same hours that the Dulles brothers acted in Guatemala, Eisenhower made an equally fateful decision on the crisis in Southeast Asia. The United States was deeply involved in the conflict between the French colonial forces and the army of the nationalist communist leader, Ho Chi Minh. Between 1950 and 1954 Washington sent $1.2 billion for the French effort, and by 1954 it had paid for over 70 percent of the French military budget. Several hundred American military technicians were also helping. In early 1954 Eisenhower viewed the implications of such aid with some concern. "I cannot conceive of a greater tragedy for America," he told a press conference in February, "than to get heavily involved now in an all-out war in any of those regions, particularly with large units."[23] Then came Dien Bien Phu.

Ground down by the guerrilla tactics of Ho and the political instability in Paris, the dispirited French army decided to make its major stand at Dien Bien Phu. It was an odd choice. The town was located away from the coast, close to the Laotian and Chinese borders, and lay at the bottom of a valley easily commanded by the Viet Minh forces controlling the mountaintops. Wheeling up large artillery pieces, a feat the French refused to believe Ho's forces could accomplish, the Viet Minh lobbed a murderous bombardment upon the French garrison. On March 20 General Paul Fly, the French chief of staff, flew to Washington to request U.S. intervention. This set off a tumultuous six-week debate within Washington and among the Western Allies. Dulles and the chairman of the Joint Chiefs, Admiral Arthur W. Radford, urged an American air strike to save the French. Air Force Chief of Staff Nathan Twining agreed and later outlined his thoughts on how the crisis might have been handled:

> I still think it would have been a good idea [to have taken] three small tactical A-bombs—it's a fairly isolated area, Dien Bien Phu—no great town around there, only Communists and their supplies. You could take all day to drop a bomb, make sure you put it in the right place. No opposition. And clean those Commies out of there and the band could play the Marseillaise and the French would come marching out of Dien Bien Phu in fine shape. And those Commies would say, "Well, those guys might do this again to us. We'd better be careful." And we might not have had this problem we're facing in Vietnam now had we dropped those small "A" weapons.[24]

Dulles and Eisenhower disagreed with Twining on the use of atomic bombs, but the President began to waver on the question of American intervention in any form. On April 3 Dulles intimated to congressional leaders that the administration would appreciate a resolution allowing the commitment of U.S. forces. The congressmen and senators refused after questioning revealed that the Joint Chiefs were split on the problem (Army Chief Matthew Ridgway especially opposed any massive intervention) and that the Western Allies had not

---

[23]*Public Papers of the Presidents . . . , Eisenhower, 1954* (Washington, 1960), pp. 247–253.
[24]Interview with General Nathan Twining, Dulles Oral History Project, Princeton.

been consulted. The next day Eisenhower wrote Churchill that the threat in Vietnam compared with the dangers of "Hirohito, Mussolini and Hitler" and asked that the United States and Great Britain form a coalition to prevent a catastrophe.[25]

Three days later the President outlined what was at stake by presenting his "domino theory" to a news conference. The struggle was crucial, Eisenhower observed, because the area contained tin, tungsten, and rubber; if, moreover, France lost, "many human beings [would] pass under a dictatorship. . . . Finally you have . . . what you would call the 'falling domino' principle. You have a row of dominoes set up, you knock over the first one, and what will happen to the last one is the certainty that it will go over very quickly. So you could have a beginning of a disintegration that would have the most profound influences." He especially worried about the economic and political effects upon Japan, the key to the containment of Russia and China in the Far East.[26]

The administration next intensified the pressure on the British. At the height of the crisis, April 20–24, Dulles flew to London to ask for the go-ahead from Churchill so that the President could send Congress the intervention resolution. The prime minister never flashed the green light. He refused to commit his government to the lost French effort, particularly during the forty-eight hours before the interested powers were to meet in Geneva on April 26 to negotiate the Indochinese problem. Without British cooperation Senate and House leaders refused to support an intervention resolution. Within the White House General Ridgway was persuading Eisenhower not to follow any line that might lead to the landing of American conventional forces. Logistics, politics, and the memories of Korea, Ridgway argued, worked against such a commitment. On May 7 the decimated French garrison surrendered.

Despite the debacle at Dien Bien Phu, the diplomats made little progress in their negotiations at Geneva. Then in mid-June the government fell in Paris and was replaced by a Gaullist-radical coalition led by Pierre Mendès-France. The new premier promised either a peace in Indochina or his resignation by July 20. In the two pacts concluded on July 20–21, the Geneva Accords (or Final Declaration) and the Geneva Armistice Agreement, the parties agreed: first, that a truce

---

[25]Eisenhower, *The White House Years,* pp. 346–347.
[26]*Public Papers of the Presidents . . . , Eisenhower, 1954,* pp. 382–383.

would occur between Ho's forces and the French (not, it is important to note, any southern Vietnamese government); second, on a temporary partition at the 17th parallel with French troops withdrawing from north of that line; third, that North and South Vietnam would neither join military alliances nor allow foreign military bases on their territories; fourth, that national elections, supervised by a joint commission of India, Canada, and Poland, would be held within two years to unify the country, and—the parties understood—France would remain in the south to carry out those elections; fifth, that regrouping of pro-communist Pathet Lao forces would be allowed in Laos, and in that country and Cambodia general elections would be held (see map, p. 222).

Ho's armies controlled two-thirds of Vietnam, but by accepting these agreements he pulled his troops into the northern half of the nation. He so compromised because he apparently preferred to deal with Mendès-France rather than with another premier who might come in after the July 20 deadline, and because Ho further believed that the French would hold to their promise of conducting elections in 1956. In such an election the North Vietnamese leader would certainly win, for he was the best-known and most powerful nationalist in all Vietnam. (Eisenhower later estimated that Ho would have received possibly 80 percent of the vote if the elections had been held at that time.) The triumphant Vietnamese also needed time to solve their political and economic chaos in the north; this they set about accomplishing with important aid from the Soviets. In his careful analysis of the situation, Ho had overlooked just one possibility: the United States might replace the French in South Vietnam. If this occurred, the Geneva agreements would become devalued.

The American delegation had not been a party to the negotiations on the armistice and had refused to agree formally to the accords. Affixing an American signature to an agreement with communists that turned over half of Vietnam to Ho would not have enhanced the administration's popularity at home. The United States announced only that it would support "free elections supervised by the United Nations" and look on with "grave concern and as seriously threatening international peace and security" any renewal of "aggression in violation of the aforesaid agreements."[27]

---

[27]Department of State, *American Foreign Policy, 1950–1955, Basic Documents*, I: 750–788.

Within a year the United States replaced France as the Western power in South Vietnam. The process began at least as early as September–October 1954, when Dulles announced that henceforth American aid would go directly to the South Vietnamese and not through the French. As the secretary explained, this change would destroy the French "protected preferential market" and allow good friends like the Japanese to sell goods directly to the Vietnamese. Dulles denied any "desire" to "displace" French influence, but "a certain displacement is, I think, inevitable."[28] Military advisers under General J. Lawton Collins began training a South Vietnamese Army; they hoped it could defend its homeland without the aid of American troops. The effect of Korea upon American thinking was immense. Collins had been chief of staff during the Korean War and was a charter member of the "Never-Again Club," a group of American Army officers, including Matthew Ridgway, who swore they would never again commit American troops to Asia without having an ironclad promise from Washington that the troops would be supported by the bombing of such enemy cities and supply lines as sanctuaries in Manchuria and China. The Vietnamese Army now learned from its American advisers how to move in large units with heavy weapons from fortified points. The Vietnamese were being prepared to fight the Korean War all over again.[29]

This American aid carried political implications. For example, the revitalized Vietnamese Army soon was plotting against the government. That government had been placed in the hands of Ngo Dinh Diem over strenuous French objections. The United States had brought in Diem from his self-imposed exile at Maryknoll Seminary in Ossining, New York. Eisenhower pledged in a letter of October 1954 that the United States would support the Vietnamese government in the south with economic aid in order to enable Diem to resist subversion or aggression. The President made no offer of open-ended military aid, further hedging his pledge by asking Diem for economic and social reforms so that the aid could be beneficially used.

By July 1955 most of the French had evacuated Vietnam. Diem announced that the elections agreed to in the Geneva Accords would

---

[28]Press Conference in Manila, March 2, 1955, Conference Dossiers, Dulles Papers, Princeton.

[29]Joseph Kraft, *Profiles in Power* (New York, 1966), pp. 139–143.

not be held. Dulles fully supported the announcement with the argument that Diem's government had not signed the accords which promised the elections. More to the point, Dulles and Diem knew that the latter would have grave difficulties defeating Ho in a fair election, and American officials did not believe that the northern government had any intention of running a fair election. The secretary of state had set the stage for this announcement in May 1955, when he gave reporters a lesson in comparative history. The United States, he warned, would recognize an anti-Diem government in the south only if "it seems to be expressive of the real will of the people and if it is truly representative." The American Revolution, Dulles observed, deferred to what "is called a decent respect for the opinions of mankind," and, he continued, all "changes" should be undertaken soberly and "with a decent respect for the opinions of mankind."[30]

Despite such remarks Dulles no doubt realized that Asian revolutions bore a closer relationship to the ideas of Mao Ze-dong than to those of Thomas Jefferson. At least he acted upon such an assumption shortly after the Geneva Conference, when he led the drive to establish the Southeast Asia Treaty Organization. Such a military pact had long been discussed. Dulles brought the idea into reality in a treaty signed at Manila on September 8, 1954, by the United States, France, Great Britain, Australia, New Zealand, Thailand, Pakistan, and the Philippines. These nations agreed that any armed attack upon them "or against any State or territory which the Parties by unanimous agreement may hereafter designate" (which would include, through a separate protocol, Cambodia, Laos, and Vietnam) would endanger the "peace and safety" of each of the signatories.[31]

This agreement hid crucial differences among the signatories. Dulles realized that the treaty would have to run the gamut of the U.S. Senate, so he carefully provided for sending American forces only when "communist aggression" was evident, and only then after due "constitutional processes" were observed by Congress. Pakistan, however, did not like the "communist aggression" clause because it wanted help against possible trouble with India. (India refused to join because Prime Minister Pandit Nehru feared association with the

[30]Off the Record News Conference, May 7, 1955, in Paris, Conference Dossiers, Dulles Papers, Princeton.
[31]U.S. Senate, Committee on Foreign Relations, 83rd Cong., 2nd Sess., *Hearing . . . on the Southeast Asia Collective Defense Treaty . . .* (Washington, 1954), Part 1, pp. 4–5, 28.

Western colonial powers.) After an intense debate the defensive zone of SEATO was not extended to either Taiwan or Hong Kong but did include Cambodia, Laos, and South Vietnam. This left the treaty open to the charge that it was violating the Geneva Accords by implicitly bringing the former French colonies into an alliance system. Despite such potentially explosive issues the treaty sailed through the Senate by a vote of 82 to 1.

The Senate ratification is of major significance in American diplomatic history. As Republican Senator Alexander Wiley of Wisconsin observed, SEATO differed from NATO because the United States was now committed not only "to resist armed attack, but also to prevent and counter subversive activities directed from without."[32] Dulles acknowledged this and had earlier warned the cabinet of the inherent dangers in such an agreement: "If we take a position against a Communist faction within a foreign country, we have to act alone," he lamented. "We are confronted by an unfortunate fact—most of the countries of the world do not share our view that Communist control of any government anywhere is in itself a danger and a threat."[33] Dulles was nevertheless willing to commit the United States to such a view.

This carried another historic implication. The traditional "open-door" policy would no longer be followed in Asia. Instead of a policy of "fair field and no favor" to anyone, as Secretary of State John Hay had asked for at the turn of the century, Dulles announced that the Monroe Doctrine was being extended to Asia. As the doctrine had warned the Holy Alliance to keep "hands-off" Latin America in the nineteenth century, now the United States, in Dulles's words, "declared that an intrusion [in the Far East] would be dangerous to our peace and security."[34] Whether the United States could unilaterally enforce that doctrine in Asia remained to be seen.

A first challenge was successfully blunted in 1954 and 1955 when the Chinese communists threatened the offshore islands of Quemoy, Matsu, and the Tachens, which lay between the mainland and Taiwan. As the communists shelled the islands and then announced the imminent "liberation" of Taiwan, Eisenhower warned that such liberation forces would have to run over the American Seventh Fleet sta-

---

[32]U.S. Senate, *Hearing . . . on the Southeast Asia Collective Defense Treaty,* Part 1, p. 10.
[33]Sherman Adams, *First-Hand Report* (New York, 1961), p. 124.
[34]U.S. Senate, *Hearing . . . on the Southeast Asia Collective Defense Treaty,* Part 1, p. 21.

tioned in the Formosa Straits. Dulles flew to Taiwan in December and signed a mutual defense pact with Chiang Kai-shek, pledging the United States to defend Chiang in return for his promise not to try to invade the mainland without American approval. Nothing was said in the pact about the offshore islands. On January 18, 1955, the communists took the small northernmost island of the Tachen group. Eisenhower declared that, because this island had no relationship to the defense of Taiwan, the attack required no counteraction. Within five days, however, he asked Congress for authority to "assure the security of Formosa and the Pescadores [Matsu and the rest of the Tachen group]" and, if necessary, "closely related localities." Congress whipped through the resolution by a vote of 409 to 3 in the House and 85 to 3 in the Senate.

Some questioned the means involved. Perhaps the resolution was a dangerous precedent for less responsible Presidents who would demand open-ended authorizations from Congress to use force against communism. Herman Phleger, the legal adviser of the Department of State who helped Dulles draft the resolution, called it a "monumental" step, for "never before in our history had anything been done like that." The method, Phleger later observed, solved for future Presidents the problem that had brought down severe criticism upon Truman when he did not obtain congressional assent for the Korean intervention.[35] Anthony Eden, on the other hand, told Dulles of his concern about the objective of the resolution. Dulles vigorously defended protecting Chiang in this way, since, the secretary of state warned, the Chinese communists "have become more intemperate."[36]

Eden's questioning was a symptom of the strains working upon the Western alliance between 1953 and 1956. Many of the disputed points became clear when Dulles struggled to obtain French ratification of the EDC. The secretary of state had tried to force the hand of the French government in mid-December 1953, when he warned that France must ratify or face an "agonizing reappraisal" by Washington of American commitments to Europe. This implied a retreat to a "Fortress America" concept, which would leave Great Britain and

---

[35]Interview with Herman Phleger, Dulles Oral History Project, Princeton.
[36]"Copy of Paper Used in Conversation with Eden," February 24, 1955, Conference Dossiers, Dulles Papers, Princeton.

France alone to face once again a revitalized Germany. Dulles was playing a risky game, but he was deadly serious. Realizing that any French government which forced the passage of the EDC could well be committing political suicide, Dulles was willing to have one French coalition do this, for without the EDC Adenauer might well lose interest in his links with the West. The French also seemed expendable because Dulles wondered if they could ever again become a great power.[37]

The French had become the pawns in a climactic power struggle. They tried to stall the fateful vote by following a policy best described as *de conserver la cadavre dans le placard* ("keeping the corpse in the closet"). Three governments refused to bring the agreements to a vote. With the delay, French hostility grew. France, opponents argued, had an army that could lose its nationality in such a community; but West Germany had nothing to lose for it had no army. Anyway, why create a German army? France would also have to divide its armies between Europe and overseas possessions; any German military force could concentrate on Europe. And why do such things when Malenkov was attempting to ease tensions?

In a dramatic last-minute meeting in August 1954, Mendès-France told Western diplomats he would finally take the corpse from the closet, but only after conditions were attached to the EDC. But not even these modifications were enough. After a bitter debate on August 30 in which Mendès-France significantly refused to stake his government's life upon the outcome, the Assembly defeated the EDC 314 to 264 with 43 abstentions.

France had miscalculated. Not fully realizing how they were being acted upon rather than acting in the unfolding diplomacy, the French believed the defeat of the EDC had scotched, perhaps killed, German rearmament. Instead they had simply exchanged the EDC, which provided for controls upon that rearmament, for perhaps NATO, which had no such controls and would allow the development of a national German army. For Dulles insisted that West Germany must be rearmed. U.S. policy rested upon that imperative. As Dulles defined the aftermath of the French vote as "a crisis of almost terrifying proportions," Anthony Eden worked out a solution.

The British foreign secretary advocated enlarging the Western Eu-

---

[37]Anthony Eden, *Full Circle: The Memoirs of Anthony Eden* (Boston, 1960), pp. 64, 108.

ropean Union (WEU) of 1948 (which originally had been an anti-German tool) by including West Germany. The WEU would not allow complete supranational control, but it would give France what it had begged for during the EDC struggle, the commitment of four British divisions to mainland Europe. The French were doubly assured when Dulles pledged that American troops would remain in Europe if France accepted the WEU idea. Adenauer cooperated by promising that Germany would not manufacture long-range missiles, or atomic, bacteriologic, or chemical weapons, without the approval of the NATO commander and a two-thirds majority of the WEU Council. The other signatories pledged that West Germany would not "have recourse to force to achieve the reunification of Germany or the modification of the present boundaries" of Germany. These promises were written into the Paris Agreements of October 1954.[38] On Christmas Eve Mendès-France drove the pact through the French Assembly but only after overcoming strong opposition. West German armies entered NATO in 1955.

In Indochina and Europe, Paris officials had learned lessons in Cold War power politics which would reorient their foreign policies and make them less amenable to American pressure. By no means coincidentally, Mendès-France secretly initiated the independent development of a French atomic and nuclear power project in the midst of these crises. Dulles, on the other hand, believed that the Paris Agreements created a situation which was in the best interests of both Europe and the United States. With that status quo apparently ensured, the Eisenhower administration returned its attention to the newly emerging nations.

[38]Department of State, *American Foreign Policy, 1950–1955, Basic Documents*, I: 1476–1496.

CHAPTER 8

East and West of Suez
(1954–1957)

The mass of the newly emerging peoples had little interest in the ideological struggle between the Soviet Union and the United States. They wanted only political independence and release from grinding poverty. To obtain these, they were willing to borrow from both systems, and if Soviets and Americans would compete for their allegiance and resources, so much the better. That was indeed a compelling argument not to become too firmly aligned with either side but to remain in a "Third World." Neither Russians nor Americans, however, appreciated such views. When in April 1953 Dulles accused the Russians of looking "upon anybody who is not for them as against them," he was unfortunately also characterizing American attitudes. The secretary of state knew that, as he once phrased it, "to oppose nationalism is counter-productive," but as late as June 1956 his views of communism and an apparent confusion over the meaning of nationalism enabled Dulles to say that neutrality had "increasingly become an obsolete conception and, except under very exceptional circumstances, it is an immoral and short-sighted conception."

By the mid-1950s each superpower believed that the future vitality of its ideological, economic, and strategic systems depended upon "winning" the Third World. Each would have believed this even if the other superpower had not existed. The United States and Russia were expansive forces and had been so in many areas (as, for example, in Asia) since at least the nineteenth century. The Cold War sharpened these drives, allowing each side to intensify its dynamic, historic expansion with the defensive terms "anticommunism" or "anti-imperialism." As the nature of the Cold War changed between 1953 and 1956, pulling the attention of the United States and Russia away from Europe and toward longtime interests in the less developed world, this different Cold War required important adjustments in the Soviet and American societies.

In the Soviet Union a bitter internal party struggle obscured the meaning and extent of the Russian adjustment. Throughout 1953 and 1954 Malenkov attempted to brace his position by weakening the Communist party apparatus controlled by Khrushchev. In turn, Khrushchev began undercutting Malenkov by appealing to the military and stressing the need for investment in heavy industry. Khrushchev was following many of Stalin's tactics of the 1920s as he mobilized his power within the party. The question became whether the party would control the bureaucracy, or vice versa.

On New Year's Day 1955 Malenkov announced that the Russian possession of hydrogen bombs made peaceful coexistence "necessary and possible." Khrushchev immediately accused the premier of attempting to intimidate the proletariat revolution with atomic weapons.[1] This line of attack won the support of such military leaders as Defense Minister Nikolay Bulganin and World War II hero Georgi Zhukov, and brought old-time Stalinists like Molotov to Khrushchev's side. On February 8 Khrushchev demanded and obtained Malenkov's resignation. Bulganin became premier, but Khrushchev held the real power as first party secretary. With the simultaneous fall from power of some of Malenkov's more liberal associates in Russia and throughout the bloc (such as Imre Nagy as prime minister in Hungary), Russia appeared to be sinking back into Stalinist political, economic, and foreign policies.

Such appearances deceived. By the middle of 1955 Khrushchev turned against Molotov's policies and worked out a rapprochement with Yugoslavia and a peace treaty for Austria. Having used the questions of economic investments and foreign policy to oust Malenkov, Khrushchev now shrewdly adopted the former premier's policies. (The victor never thought much of his vanquished colleagues. Americans, Khrushchev once remarked, "are from a highly educated nation and they look upon us as being equally highly educated. They don't know that we [in Russia] are dominated by an unimaginative and unattractive bunch of scondrels.")[2] As early as

[1]Myron Rush, *Political Succession in the U.S.S.R.* (New York, 1965), pp. 48, 60; Arnold L. Horelick and Myron Rush, *Strategic Power and Soviet Foreign Policy* (Chicago, 1966), pp. 17–30.
[2]Quoted in Dino A. Brugioni, *Eyeball to Eyeball* (New York, 1990), p. 250.

1949 Malenkov had realized that Stalin's two-camp policy paralyzed Soviet attempts to influence the newly emerging nations. Khrushchev used this insight to work out a more subtle foreign policy, which attempted through the brandishing of military prowess, ideology, and economic aid to conciliate nationalist leaders.

Khrushchev structured this approach carefully. He safeguarded Soviet security both ideologically and militarily by developing the Warsaw Pact—a bloc military alliance, patterned after NATO, which could allow Soviet military control of Eastern Europe after the political controls were relaxed. On Aviation Day 1955 the Soviets flexed awesome military muscles by flying unit after unit of new jet planes over Moscow. (Only later did American intelligence learn that Khrushchev simply had a relatively few planes fly around in circles.) He also tried to deal with the challenges posed to Soviet authority by independently minded Yugoslavia and China. Khrushchev first announced that Russia was further along the road to communism than any other nation. This supposedly assured the Soviets of acting as the chief ideologist within the communist world. In 1954 he had magnanimously traveled to China and had personally returned to Mao the former Chinese possessions of Port Arthur and the Chinese Eastern Railway, long controlled by Russia. He also sought to bring China within the Soviet economic orbit by signing a new agreement to deliver large amounts of capital goods. A similar line was followed in Yugoslavia, despite Molotov's warning that easing relations with Tito would weaken Soviet control over the satellites. Khrushchev nevertheless went to Belgrade, blamed past Soviet-Yugoslav troubles on Stalin, and negotiated improved diplomatic and economic ties.

With the communist world supposedly reconsolidated, Khrushchev launched an aid program for the newly emerging nations which, as he candidly told a group of junketing American congressmen in 1955, he valued "least for economic reasons and most for political purposes." By the end of 1956 fourteen economic and military assistance agreements had been signed with nations in Asia and the Middle East. Khrushchev was highly selective in compiling the list. North Vietnam and Indonesia were favored in Southeast Asia. In the Middle East, Iran, Afghanistan, Turkey, and Egypt were targets of the Soviet economic offensive.

The Chinese provided the proper ideological accompaniment for this drive by attending the Bandung conference of nonaligned states in April 1955 and reaffirming the Five Principles of Peaceful Coexistence, which had been agreed upon between India and China the year before. These promised mutual respect for sovereignty and territorial integrity, noninterference in one another's domestic affairs, and peaceful coexistence. Soviet ideologists supported the Chinese proclamation by emphasizing that Stalin's old two-camp approach had been replaced with a confidence that communists and nationalists could work against Western imperialism and enter the promised land of socialism hand in hand. Never had the reputation of Communist China and Russia been higher among the newly emerging nations. Like the Eisenhower administration, Khrushchev was also thinking in global terms.

Dulles fully appreciated what communism was accomplishing. The secretary of state analyzed in detail the new world situation for the NATO Foreign Ministers during the May meetings of 1955 and 1956. Communism was on the move in Asia, Dulles warned. The Chinese brand posed a greater threat than the Russian, since it controlled a greater population mass and possessed a cultural prestige in Asia not enjoyed by Russia in either Europe or Asia. The secretary noted the major Chinese colonies which existed in many free Asian nations and feared that Mao could follow a rule of divide and conquer because the noncommunist countries were scattered geographically and divided politically, culturally, and economically. The West, Dulles declared, must never surrender those nations: "The stakes are too high." Japanese industrial power could not be allowed to combine with China; Indonesia and Malaya contained vast amounts of oil, rubber, tin, and iron ore, as well as held strategic positions. The Philippines "represent a symbol of how the West can create independence in Asia." There were 1.6 billion people in the underdeveloped areas now exposed to communist economic tactics. If those tactics prevailed, "the world ratio as between communist dominated peoples and free peoples would change from a ratio of two-to-one in favor of freedom to a ratio of one-to-three against freedom." "That," Dulles emphasized, "would be an almost intolerable ratio given the industrialized nature of the Atlantic Community and its dependence upon broad markets and access to raw materials."[3]

[3]"Far East Presentation," May 10, 1955, and "NATO Meeting, Etc.," Paris, May 1–7, 1956, Conference Dossiers, Dulles Papers, Princeton.

In understanding the differences between the Chinese and Russian expansion, as well as defining the economic-strategic importance of the Far East, Dulles was ahead of most Americans, particularly those within the Eisenhower cabinet. None of the President's advisers could contrive a coherent program that would appeal to the newly emerging nations while at the same time preserving American interests as Dulles defined them. Militarily, for example, the administration held fast to its determination to base security upon massive retaliation. Neither the Soviet development of a hydrogen bomb nor the evidence in Iran, Egypt, Guatemala, and Indochina that the threats to American interests did not come in open aggression by Red armies significantly changed that policy after it was adopted officially in 1954.

During the Dien Bien Phu crisis in Vietnam, one slight swing in American strategic thinking had begun to appear. Because NATO did not have manpower to match the communists, the secretary argued that the West should "use atomic weapons as conventional weapons against the military assets of the enemy whenever and wherever it would be of advantage to do so, taking account of all relevant factors."[4] When this tactic was employed in NATO war games in Europe, the results demonstrated that the type of limited war Dulles urged would incinerate most of Central Europe.

The only alternative seemed to be the development of American forces to fight wars which would stop short of nuclear exchanges. Scholars such as Bernard Brodie and Henry Kissinger began to advance this argument in late 1954. Within a year Army Chief of Staff General Maxwell D. Taylor split the Joint Chiefs by unsuccessfully demanding, against Admiral Arthur Radford's opposition, that the military response become more flexible. Taylor left the administration, as did Generals Matthew Ridgway and James M. Gavin. The new trend, which would become fully apparent in 1961, had set in and had done so as experts realized that massive retaliation was too inflexible for the demands of the changing Cold War. Whether, on the other hand, limited conventional war protected American interests in the less developed areas remained to be seen. Limited wars did not automatically exclude massive retaliation; what could not be limited might have to be destroyed. The problem would always be less a

---

[4]"Proposed 'Talking Paper,' " April 23, 1954, Conference Dossiers, Dulles Papers, Princeton.

proper choice of military means than a wise understanding of the objectives. In postwar American foreign policy the debate over the nature of the communist threat usually lagged behind the debate over which weapons to use against that threat.

Similar problems confronted the administration in the economic realm. Here Dulles recognized the importance of aid for the newly emerging nations but was powerless to do much about it, in part because of his own intellectual and political inhibitions. With the end of the demand generated by the Korean War, raw material prices slumped; economic depression struck underdeveloped areas that relied upon the export of such materials. No one in the administration had a solution. Eisenhower placed strong faith in productivity, "because it relieves pressures in the world that are favorable to Communism." He defined China as one huge claw reaching out for anyone who had five cents. Dulles's comment was dry and to the point: "In India today, the great peril of Communism comes from intellectual centers."[5] In his concern with productivity Eisenhower had overlooked the demand of the newly emerging peoples for a rapidly developing productivity regardless of the social and political costs.

Innovation was also wanting in the field of foreign aid. Eisenhower responded to the Soviet economic offensive by reorganizing the foreign aid administration, but this did not touch the real problem. In the newly emerging areas development had to occur literally from the ground up. This required internal stability and huge amounts of outside capital and technical aid. The Marshall Plan had worked because the Europeans had the technical know-how and capital resources to turn every dollar of American aid into six dollars of capital formation. This would obviously not be the case in Asia, Africa, or Latin America. Secretary of the Treasury George Humphrey warmly endorsed placing the burden on private capital, while allowing the World Bank (which depended upon the private money market) to make necessary long-term capital loans. The Export-Import Bank (operated by the government on money appropriated by Congress) would make only short-term loans to move American exports. Dulles attempted to show Humphrey that this approach would be insufficient, arguing that, because of the growing importance of the newly emerging nations, an agency must be formed "to make politi-

[5]Robert J. Donovan, *Eisenhower: The Inside Story* (New York, 1956), pp. 3, 9.

cal loans and 'soft' loans [that is, loans with low interest rates and payable in terms of local currencies] on a long term basis."

Dulles then proceeded to give Humphrey a lesson in political economy. In former days private capital could provide soft long-term loans because private persons ran the banks of issue and the governmental policies. "This," Dulles observed, "is all now changed." Governments everywhere make rules "for reasons quite unrelated to their effect upon investment." Private lenders consequently were no longer willing to make investments in unstable areas. Only governmental funds could promote such development in a meaningful way. Unless something was done quickly, Dulles warned, South America, for example, "might be lost" under Humphrey's policy: "It might be good banking to put South America through the wringer, but it will come out red."[6]

Dulles knew his history, but Humphrey essentially won the argument. Primary reliance was placed upon private capital. Humphrey then reduced the lending powers of the Export-Import Bank until outraged American exporters and congressmen forced him to issue more credit for American businessmen to use in their overseas trade. Despite such protests, Humphrey cut back so drastically that from fiscal 1955 to fiscal 1957 total loans repaid to the bank actually exceeded disbursements by $58 million. Only after Humphrey's departure from the cabinet was the bank allowed to become a "soft loan" agency in 1958.[7] Meanwhile private capital did not assume the task, for it favored more stable areas; between 1953 and 1956, for example, U.S. investments in Latin America increased $1.4 billion, or 19.2 percent, while in Western Europe and Canada they climbed $3.4 billion, or over 30 percent.[8]

Over all these debates hung the pall of McCarthyism. Wisconsin's junior senator, according to a public opinion poll, was regarded favorably by over half those polled in early 1954. His popularity had jumped sixteen points in six months, the same months he was encouraging the burning of supposedly "left-wing" books and accus-

---

[6]"Memorandum Re NAC Meeting," September 30, 1953, in file on NATO Meeting, December 8–15, 1956, Conference Dossiers, Dulles Papers, Princeton.

[7]Robert Reuben Dince, Jr., "The Lending Policy of the Export-Import Bank: A Study in Public Policy," unpublished doctoral dissertation, Cornell University, 1960.

[8]U.S. Bureau of the Census, *Historical Statistics of the U.S., Colonial Times to 1957* (Washington, 1960), p. 566.

ing the President of the United States of allowing the American allies to carry on a "blood trade" with China. One ramification of this feeling occurred early in 1954 when Senator John Bricker of Ohio proposed an amendment to the Constitution which aimed to eliminate the possibility of any more one-man "sellouts" similar, as some claimed, to that which Roosevelt accomplished at Yalta through executive agreements made between himself and Stalin or Churchill. The Bricker amendment, like McCarthyism, grew out of sentiment both anti-Democrat and antipresidential. "Since 1948," Bricker had charged in 1951, "the outstanding characteristic of the Truman administration has been its persistent effort to usurp legislative functions." The Republican senator warned that "the constitutional power of Congress to determine American foreign policy is at stake." (It is a major irony that twenty years later Bricker's major objective would be sought by liberal Democratic congressmen against a conservative Republican President; ironic, but understandable historically.)

Discussed since 1951, Bricker's proposal was softened until in 1954 the Senate voted on a version whose key section provided that an international agreement other than a treaty (for example, an executive agreement) could become internal law "only by an act of Congress." Eisenhower fought the measure, warning that foreign leaders would view such restraints upon presidential power as redolent of 1930's isolationism. The proposal nevertheless was supported by a majority, 60 to 31, although falling just one vote shy of the two-thirds needed for a constitutional amendment. The most fascinating result was that the debate produced the exact opposite of Bricker's intentions. In 1955 and 1958 during international crises, Eisenhower carefully asked Congress to authorize his actions (as Bricker wanted), but he did it so ingeniously that Congress gave the President a virtual blank check. Lyndon Johnson later used Eisenhower's tactics in obtaining congressional support for his intervention in Vietnam.

In 1953–1954 McCarthyism did not stop at the boundaries of politics. Although American scientists were increasingly needed for judgments and weapons in fighting the Cold War, the scientific community was not immune to attack. The anti-intellectualism which imbued McCarthyism, and the lack of ardor for the Cold War shown by some scientists, climaxed in the case of J. Robert Oppenheimer in 1954. Oppenheimer was perhaps the most distinguished physicist in the United States. He had directed the laboratory at Los Alamos, which produced the first atomic bomb in 1945. His downfall began when he questioned the building of the hydrogen bomb in 1949–1950. He was not alone. Many scientists, their political awareness made acute by their participation in the A-bomb project, had moved into Washington after 1946 to lobby long and earnestly for the imposition of strong controls upon the development and use of atomic energy. Probably a majority of American physicists opposed the decision to make the hydrogen bomb because they believed it strategically unsound and politically dangerous.[9]

Oppenheimer shared such sentiments, but unlike most of the other scientists, he had had close relations with Communist party members in the United States and had made personal enemies on the Atomic Energy Commission. A four-foot-six-inch-high FBI folder on Oppenheimer detailed his past but concluded that no evidence indicated that Oppenheimer had worked against the national interest. Eisenhower (who once defined an intellectual as "a man who takes more words than is necessary to say more than he knows") refused to take a public position. A special three-man board unanimously declared Oppenheimer to be "a loyal citizen" but nevertheless voted 2 to 1 against giving him continued access to classified information. This effectively removed Oppenheimer's voice from top governmental councils. The Atomic Energy Commission upheld this judgment 4 to 1 not on the basis of disloyalty but because of "fundamental defects in his 'character.'" No one ever proved that Oppenheimer was disloyal; the one AEC member who thought so in 1954, Thomas E. Murray, several years later admitted that his vote had been cast "within the exigencies of the moment." This was a euphemism for the McCarthyite influence, which discriminated against important members of the American scientific and intellectual community.

With the cabinet, the military, Congress, and intellectuals increasingly immobile, Dulles found himself torn between these political restraints on the one hand and, on the other, his recognition of the critical changes in international affairs. He had, for example, stalled off a summit meeting by arguing that the Soviets would have to show their sincerity in wanting negotiations by signing an Austrian peace treaty. As a part of their reorientation of policy, the Russians

[9]Urs Schwarz, *American Strategy: A New Perspective* (New York, 1966), pp. 77–79.

suddenly signed the treaty in mid-May 1955. As Eisenhower later related, "Well, suddenly the thing was signed one day and [Dulles] came in and he grinned rather ruefully and he said, 'Well, I think we've had it.' "[10] Dulles's interpretation of the break-through on the treaty revealed the American dilemma. He initially claimed that "liberation" had borne rich fruit: "an area of Europe is, in a very literal sense, liberated." At the same time, however, Dulles felt compelled to warn Americans that "the new set of dangers comes from the fact that the wolf has put on a new set of sheep's clothing, and while it is better to have a sheep's clothing on than a bear's clothing on, because sheep don't have claws, I think the policy remains the same."[11]

Dulles adopted that latter approach in preparing for the summit. He was concerned that the Soviets would use the conference to gain "moral and social equality" with the United States in order to encourage neutralism. The secretary consequently warned Eisenhower to maintain "an austere countenance on occasions where photographing together [with Russians] is inevitable" and to push hard publicly for "satellite liberation." The secretary then set up American demands that would be quite difficult to realize. His first goal was the unification of Germany "under conditions which will neither 'neutralize' nor 'demilitarize' united Germany, nor subtract it from NATO."[12] To this the Russians would not agree. Dulles effectively sealed this policy when West Germany formally regained its sovereignty, commenced rearming, and entered NATO in May, just weeks before the summit conference was to begin. On the eve of the meeting, Republican leader Senator William Knowland proposed the "Captive Nations" resolution; this expressed the Senate's hope that Soviet satellites "subjected to the captivity of alien despotisms shall again enjoy the right of self-determination."

Given this background, the summit could produce little more than a "spirit of Geneva." Eisenhower, Eden (who had succeeded Churchill as prime minister), Bulganin (who fronted for Khrushchev), and Edgar Faure of France opened the meetings on July 18 and im-

---

[10]Interview with Dwight D. Eisenhower, Dulles Oral History Project, Dulles Papers, Princeton.

[11]"Press and Radio News Conference . . . , May 15, 1955," Conference Dossiers, Dulles Papers, Princeton.

[12]"Estimate of Prospect of Soviet Union Achieving Its Goals," July 1, 1955, Conference Dossiers, Dulles Papers, Princeton.

mediately ran into a deadlock over Germany. A dead end was reached when Khrushchev overruled a wavering Bulganin by announcing that the Soviets would allow no elections in East Germany until West Germany was disarmed. The United States had successfully armed and tied West Germany to the Western alliance, at the same time pushing onto the Soviets the blame for blocking reunification through free elections.

The only major American initiative at Geneva was Eisenhower's "open skies" plan, proposing the exchange of plans of each nation's military facilities and allowing planes to photograph each nation's territory to ensure against surprise attacks. This plan emanated from a panel, headed by Nelson Rockefeller, which was concerned with quieting European fears over the stationing of American nuclear bombs in Europe.[13] The "open skies" proposal would quiet such fears while allowing the bombs to remain. Khrushchev predictably rejected the plan on the grounds that it would infringe on Soviet territorial sovereignty. (This proposal was Eisenhower's second move in the controlled-armaments field. In December 1953 he had proposed before the United Nations a plan to establish an international agency that would control the use of atomic materials for peaceful purposes. Although meeting initial resistance from the Russians and from the American Congress, the speech bore fruit three years later with the creation of the International Atomic Energy Agency.)

Geneva, and the profitless Foreign Ministers meeting that followed in October, reaffirmed the new Cold War themes. Having failed to gain their coveted European security pact, the Soviets made the best of a disadvantageous situation. They worked out formal diplomatic relations with the Adenauer government in mid-September 1955 and a week later gave East Germany full powers in foreign affairs; the latter move would force Adenauer theoretically to deal with affairs in East Germany directly through the East German communist regime instead of through the Russians. That was most repugnant to the West Germans and consequently reinsured the division of Germany. The split was widened in January 1956, when the East German People's Army entered the Warsaw Pact. Dulles's earlier hopes for reunification on Western terms now lost all foundation.

Dulles and Eisenhower also failed to imagine the extent to which

[13]Donovan, *Inside Story*, pp. 345–346.

Khrushchev would reorient the Kremlin. At the Twentieth Party Congress in February 1956, Khrushchev surprised his listeners, shocked the satellites, and astonished the West by detailing Stalin's crimes against the Communist party and (the same thing) Russian national interest.[14] But he exorcised the dictator's ghost with a scalpel, not a meat ax. Nothing was said about the particular purges in which Khrushchev himself had controlled the cattle cars slowly moving out of the Ukraine toward Siberia during the late 1930s; instead, he discussed the bloodlettings in which his present enemies on the Presidium had been more closely involved. Khrushchev further emphasized that Stalin and the "cult of the individual" had been at fault, not the communist system. He also carefully defended the party and the army against the Stalinist crimes, but not the masses or the intellectuals whom he himself would soon restrict and attack. Domestically Khrushchev was trying to increase his personal power, loosen Stalinist restrictions so that the Soviet economy could boom, and yet keep the society under absolute control without resorting to terrorist methods.

Foreign policy could not be walled off from this internal reorientation. The East European satellites were stunned. Khrushchev destroyed their supposedly unquestioning belief in Stalin and all acts of the Soviet Union. He thereby obliterated the frame of reference by which the satellites had been told since 1945 to measure their own policies. Khrushchev substituted the idea that several roads led to communism, emphasizing, nevertheless, that communism was the destiny toward which all were heading. The point was made most clearly in the apology for Stalin's tactics toward Tito. Khrushchev recalled Stalin saying that he would shake his little finger and Tito would fall; "we have," Khrushchev concluded, "dearly paid for this shaking of the little finger." In this and other speeches at the congress, the Soviet leadership announced that the two-camp approach, the belief that war was inevitable, and the fear of "capitalist encirclement" were all now unsound doctrines. The new policies were perhaps best illustrated in the destruction of Stalin's "capitalist encirclement" theme, for by questioning this, the "capitalist" and "neutralist" areas surrounding the communist bloc became not objects generating fear in the Soviet peoples but objects to be exploited by Soviet foreign policy. This turn in Russian thinking somewhat resembled the change in

[14]Nikita S. Khrushchev, *The Crimes of the Stalin Era. . . .* annotated by Boris I. Nicolaevsky (New York, 1956, 1962).

American thinking when the United States began to view the surrounding oceans not as barriers ensuring isolation, but as highways for internationalism. Within a general policy of détente with the Western world, the Soviets would tear down Stalinist-imposed barriers and move down adjoining highways into the third, uncommitted world. In keeping with this policy, Mikoyan, head of the Presidium, announced the dissolution of the Cominform on April 17, 1956.

After the Geneva conference of 1955, Dulles wondered whether the Soviet "maneuver" of easing tension "may in fact assume the force of an irreversible trend." Such seemed to be the case within weeks after Khrushchev's speech. In March 1956 riots erupted in Soviet Georgia, the home of the now degraded Stalin. In June mobs rioted against Communist party leaders in Poland and Hungary, demanding that more liberal officials assume authority. Khrushchev also came under attack from the other side when such old-line Stalinists as Lazar M. Kaganovich and Molotov demanded that he forcefully quiet the East Europeans before things got completely out of hand.

In a sense, the moment of "liberation" seemed to be approaching. At the crucial point where the prophecy needed a nudge, however, the prophet was looking the other way. Throughout the summer and autumn Dulles was caught in the maelstrom of Middle Eastern politics. A year and a half before, Israel had dramatically revealed the weakness of the Egyptian Army with a quick, overpowering raid into the disputed Gaza Strip. Egyptian leader Gamal Abdel Nasser soon opened negotiations with Western and communist powers for more modern military weapons. Declaring that American prices were not competitive, he discovered the communists anxious to do anything that would weaken the Baghdad Pact. In late September 1955 Nasser signed an agreement to buy arms from the Czechs.

Dulles suddenly became interested in helping Egypt finance the planned Aswân Dam, a huge project which Nasser hoped would harness the vast power of the lower Nile and serve as a symbol of how his regime was triumphantly taking Egypt into the twentieth century. In December 1955 the United States and Great Britain offered to help Nasser. As the United States realized, Egypt would have difficulty in paying for both the arms deal and the dam. To double-check this point, World Bank President Eugene Black traveled to Cairo to work out a deal whereby the World Bank, Great Britain, and the United States would supply the immediate funding for the $1.3-billion project. In February 1956 Black and Nasser reached agreement. The Egyptian leader then wrote to Washington regarding discussions on the proposal. Five months later he was still waiting for a reply.

Dulles had become trapped in Washington. Testifying before the Senate Foreign Relations Committee in February, the secretary argued that, although Egypt and Syria might receive communist arms, he should not have to bow before domestic political pressure and send arms to Israel. This could only lead to an all-out arms race in which Arabs would triumph because "thirty-odd million Arabs [have] far greater . . . absorptive capacity" than 1.7 million Israelis. Dulles was forced to admit, however, that the United States was sending tanks to another of Israel's enemies, Saudi Arabia, under terms of a mid-1951 agreement in which the latter country had allowed the United States to occupy Dhahran Airfield. Asked whether the arms buildup might cause Israel to launch a preventive war, Dulles admitted "there is some danger."[15] Having to take a stand on such questions in an election year was bad enough, but Dulles soon found his position worsening.

In April Egypt, Saudi Arabia, Syria, and Yemen formed a joint military alliance obviously aimed at Israel. These nations, along with Iraq, Lebanon, and Jordan, had refused to recognize the Israeli government. The Czech arms deal with Egypt now assumed a more ominous aspect. In May Nasser withdrew recognition from Chiang Kai-shek and recognized Communist China. This quickly mobilized the many American champions of Chiang to inform Dulles that they staunchly opposed any kind of deal with Nasser. On Capitol Hill this China Lobby found an easy alliance with southern congressmen, who demanded to know why the United States was offering to build a dam which would allow huge crops of Egyptian cotton to compete with American cotton. Above all, Egypt had not repudiated the arms deal. Dulles concluded that if he suddenly withdrew the offer, Nasser would suffer a disastrous political blow. The secretary also assumed that Khrushchev would not, in fact could not, replace American aid, an assumption with which Eugene Black concurred because of his belief that Nasser could not afford to become further involved with the

---

[15]U.S. Senate, Committee on Foreign Relations, 84th Cong., 2nd Sess., *Hearing . . . on the Situation in the Middle East, February 24, 1956* (Washington, 1956), pp. 43–46, 68.

communist bloc. Black nevertheless warned Dulles to go through with the deal or "hell might break loose."[16] Both of Dulles's assumptions were tragically wrong. He compounded the mistake by announcing the American decision in a cold, direct announcement on July 19, 1956, at the moment the Egyptian foreign minister was arriving to discuss the project and as Nasser himself sat in a widely publicized meeting with Tito and Nehru.

One week later Nasser seized the Suez Canal by nationalizing the British-controlled Universal Suez Canal Company. With a single stroke he recovered his lost prestige and gained the $25-million annual profit of the company for use in building the dam. The Egyptian leader also had his thumb on the jugular of the European economy; 67 million tons of oil had moved to Europe through Suez in 1955. As long as he compensated the shareholders of the company, Nasser was legally justified in seizing the canal. He promised, moreover, to keep the waterway open to all former users of the canal. This was not enough for Great Britain and France. Acutely aware of Western shipping interests and the possible disintegration of the Baghdad Pact, perhaps even of NATO, Dulles tried to ameliorate the crisis by establishing a users' association to manage the canal. This proved unacceptable; the British and French had no inclination to put their vital petroleum imports in the hands of Nasser, and the Egyptians refused to share control of the canal. As early as the end of July, British Foreign Secretary Harold Macmillan revealed to Dulles Britain's plans for military action if the problem was not quickly settled.[17] Dulles, however, refused to put excessive pressure on Nasser, did not take the British and French threats seriously, and of course was reluctant to be too closely associated with the former colonial powers.

These policy differences were compounded by the growing personal animosity between Eden and Dulles. Before the 1952 election Eden had dropped an unsubtle hint to Eisenhower that he preferred a secretary of state other than Dulles. The Eden-Dulles relationship never improved much beyond this point. Yet Anglo-American relations depended upon these two men in the autumn of 1956, for their ambassadors in Washington and London were relatively uninformed; the British ambassador actually left the United States on October 11 just as the crisis began to worsen. During the last two weeks of Oc-

---

[16]Interview with Eugene Black, Dulles Oral History Project, Dulles Papers, Princeton.
[17]Interview with Robert Murphy, Dulles Oral History Project, Dulles Papers, Princeton.

THE MIDDLE EAST AND THE SUEZ CRISIS, 1956

tober, communications between London and Washington almost completely broke down.

This was doubly tragic, for as the Middle Eastern situation deteriorated, rebellion erupted in Eastern Europe. The two events became closely related. Having unleashed unknown forces with his denunciation of Stalin, Khrushchev lost control of Poland's rapid de-Stalinization program headed by Władysław Gomułka. Khrushchev flew to Warsaw, moved Soviet military forces into striking position, and delivered a blistering speech against the Polish changes. Gomu ka responded by threatening to call out the Polish people. Khrushchev backed down. The news of Gomułka's success spread to Hungary. On October 23 students moved into the streets to demand that longtime Stalinist Ernö Gerö be replaced with Imre Nagy. When the secret police attempted to put down the protests, workers joined the students. One huge demonstration destroyed a gigantic statue of Stalin in central Budapest. The Soviets agreed to replace Gerö with Nagy, but that was no longer enough. The crowds demanded removal of Russian troops stationed in Hungary and the creation of a political party in opposition to the communists. On October 28 the Soviets began withdrawing the tanks that had moved to the outskirts of Budapest.

The next day the Israeli Army made a lightning attack that in hours nearly destroyed the Egyptian Army and conquered much of the Sinai peninsula. In close cooperation with Israel, England and France delivered ultimatums to Israel and Egypt on October 30, warning both nations to keep their forces away from the canal. When Nasser rejected the note, British and French planes began bombing Egyptian military targets. The next day, October 31, the Presidium reversed its policy toward Hungary. Nagy had announced the withdrawal of Hungary from the Warsaw Pact. This was going too far, much further, for example, than Gomułka was going in Poland.

The confrontation in the Middle East provided Khrushchev with the perfect opportunity for counteraction. As Anglo-French columns moved into the canal area on November 4 and 5, Russian tanks crushed the Hungarian uprising. The Soviets captured Nagy under false pretenses, shipped him off to Russia, and executed him sometime in 1957. The State Department watched all this helplessly. As one high official later remarked, Dulles, "like everybody else in the Department was terribly distressed," but "none of us had whatever imagination it took to discover another solution. We just were boxed."[18] At the height of the crisis on November 3, Dulles underwent emergency surgery on the cancer which would later kill him.

Having smashed the Hungarian rebellion, Khrushchev entered the Middle Eastern scene. He suggested to the State Department that a Russo-American settlement be imposed upon the area and warned Anglo-French forces that, unless they quickly withdrew, the Soviets would use force, perhaps long-range rockets, to squash their armies. On November 6, as Americans went to the polls in a presidential election, Eisenhower responded to Khrushchev's demands by placing American military forces on an emergency alert. He was not, however, primarily afraid of Soviet military action in the Middle East. The greater danger was that Khrushchev might inveigle his way into negotiating a settlement and thereby interject Soviet power in an area which for centuries Western Europe had fought to keep free of Russian influence.

Attempting to short-circuit the Soviet move, the State Department put tremendous pressure on London and Paris by passing a resolution through the General Assembly urging a truce, and then cutting off oil supplies from Latin America that England and France needed to replace their oil, which could not get through the clogged canal. Hours before they would have seized the canal area, the British and French agreed to a cease-fire and pullback. Throughout November Washington carefully rationed the oil flow to Europe. Not until the UN resolution was obeyed and the troops withdrawn did the oil flow freely. American officials argued that they could not afford to turn on the oil too quickly, for this would infuriate the Arab nations which held huge reservoirs of oil leased to Americans.[19]

By December 22 the armies had left, and a UN emergency force restored the canal area to Egyptian control. The Suez crisis was a graphic study of how the newly emerging peoples were reordering the power balance at the expense of the older and more powerful nations. These lessons were immediately taken to heart in Washington and Moscow.

The events in Poland and Suez occurred at the climax of the presidential campaign in the United States. Beginning at a time of rela-

---

[18]Interview with Robert Murphy, Dulles Oral History Project, Dulles Papers, Princeton.
[19]Robert Engler, *The Politics of Oil* (New York, 1961), pp. 261–263; "Memorandum of Conference with the President," November 20, 1956, White House Memoranda Series, Box 4, Dulles Papers, Eisenhower Library, Abilene, Kan.

tive quiet in foreign affairs, the early weeks of the campaign were marked by a discussion of farm issues and the possible effects of the heart attack suffered by Eisenhower a year before. Democratic nominee Adlai Stevenson tried to overcome this apathy, but he did so in a curiously paradoxical manner. At times he argued that disarmament must be placed at the heart of American policy, urged a restudy and possible discontinuance of the military draft, suggested the suspension of nuclear weapons tests, and accurately pinpointed "events in Eastern Europe and the Middle East" as "symptoms of a vast new upheaval in the balance of world power." At other times, however, Stevenson reaffirmed the Cold War clichés: half of Indochina had "become a new Communist satellite and . . . America emerged from that debacle looking like a 'paper tiger' "; NATO's decline threatened the entire Western world; and in his last speech, Stevenson detailed how Harry Truman had stood up to the Russians while Eisenhower rejected the "great opportunities to exploit weaknesses in the Communist ranks and advance the cause of peace."[20]

In playing such a political game with Eisenhower, Stevenson was outmatched. Republican spokesmen could detail the times Dulles had gotten "tough" with the Russians (or had "gone to the brink" of war, to use Dulles's phrase), while Eisenhower could pose as the military man who made peace in Korea and knew just when to step back from the brink. When the United States and Russia again approached the brink in the last hours before the election, most Americans had no doubt whom they would entrust with their lives and their Middle Eastern interests.

Eisenhower overwhelmed Stevenson partly because of the President's personal popularity; he received 57 percent of the vote, but the Democrats captured both Houses of Congress, the first time that such a split had occurred since 1848. Yet in judging the rhetoric of the campaign and the postelection analyses, the election clearly demonstrated something more than personal popularity. It marked a consensus of ideology. Voting analyses later revealed that a small majority of Americans preferred Democratic domestic policy, but a larger majority supported Republican foreign policy.[21] Since 1952 Eisenhower had brought nearly all sectors of the Republican party into the internationalist camp, adding numerous Democrats and independents by

---

[20] Adlai E. Stevenson, *The New America* (New York, 1957), pp. 27–34, 40–41.
[21] Angus Campbell et al., *The American Voter* (New York, 1960), pp. 198–200, 526–528.

combining appeals for peace with the history of brinksmanship. Henry Wallace, for example, could vote to have John Foster Dulles as secretary of state because Wallace believed that "Eisenhower . . . is the man most likely to preserve world peace." Reinhold Niebuhr, however, supported Stevenson because Eisenhower's foreign policies were "catastrophic" as a result of being based too much upon the peaceful "Geneva spirit." The United States, Niebuhr warned, had lost ground among the neutrals and (a fascinating if illogical conclusion on Niebuhr's part) had therefore made "former neutralist nations into virtual allies of Communism." "We are in greater peril than at any time since our victory over the Nazis," the theologian gravely concluded.[22]

Niebuhr's explanation revealed a basic agreement with Dulles's views. Accurately pinpointing the growing dilemma of American policy in Vietnam a year earlier, Niebuhr had warned against using military power when "it lacks a moral and political base." But he then applauded the "disinterested" Americans who were replacing the French as the Western power in South Vietnam.[23] Dulles, of course, had initiated this displacement and was trying to build the moral and political base which Niebuhr wanted. In these circumstances, Niebuhr's dislike and mistrust of Dulles became less significant, for both men agreed on a fundamental point: the United States could not keep its hands off politically unstable nations because such instability could turn "former neutralist nations into virtual allies of Communism," to use Niebuhr's phrase.

Eisenhower wove this consensus into policy just a few months after his reelection. The Suez crisis had seriously weakened the Baghdad Pact and had stimulated Nasser to attempt to increase his power in the Middle East. On January 5, 1957, Eisenhower tried to reverse those trends by replaying his performance of 1954–1955 in the Formosa Straits crisis. He asked Congress for authorization to extend economic and military cooperation and, if necessary, to employ American military forces in the Middle East if any nation in that area requested help against communist-instigated armed aggression. Dulles also secretly informed congressional leaders that the CIA was launching massive covert actions against pro-Soviet groups in the re-

[22]*Life*, May 14, 1956, p. 184; *New Republic*, October 29, 1956, p. 11.
[23]Reinhold Niebuhr, "The Limits of Military Power." In *The World Crisis* (New York, 1958), pp. 114–121.

gion. The Middle East Resolution, or the "Eisenhower Doctrine" as it came to be known, sailed through the House. The Senate, however, balked.

Senators attacked the resolution as being anti-Israeli, too vague, and injurious to the Western alliance. Dulles did not lessen this last criticism when he remarked that Anglo-French forces should remain in Europe, for "If I were an American boy . . . I'd rather not have a French and British soldier beside me, one on my right and one on my left." Such a remark was hardly tactful, but in a single sentence Dulles had given his view of how collective the security decision making should be in the Middle East.[24] With the help of Majority Leader Lyndon Johnson, the administration finally passed the resolution in March, 72 to 19. It did so despite little public support. Heavy congressional mail, in fact, ran 8 to 1 against the proposal in February. The passage of the Eisenhower Doctrine had interesting political overtones. A Democratic Congress formally surrendered some of its power, especially that of controlling the outbreak of war, to a Republican President.

If anyone doubted that Eisenhower would use this gift of power, they learned otherwise within a month after the Senate completed action. In April young King Hussein of Jordan came under attack from pro-Nasser elements within his country. Hussein asked for help because he was under attack from "international Communism and its followers." The Eisenhower Doctrine specifically and the general American ideological view of revolutions now faced a test: would the United States help Hussein defend the status quo against the Nasserite elements by brandishing the argument that Hussein was being saved from "international Communism"? Eisenhower responded by sending $10 million to Hussein and dispatching the Sixth Fleet to the Mediterranean area near Jordan. The CIA also apparently sprang into high gear. The official State Department announcement on the sending of this aid did not directly blame "international Communism"; instead it explained the action as safeguarding "the preser-

[24]U.S. Senate, Committee on Foreign Relations, 85th Cong., 1st Sess., *Hearings . . . to Authorize the President to Undertake Economic and Military Cooperation with Nations in the General Area of the Middle East* (Washington, 1957), Parts 1 and 2, especially pp. 4–41. This and the previous paragraph are also based on Douglas Little, "A Puppet in Search of a Puppeteer?" *International History Review*, XVII (August 1995): 516–525.

vation of the independence and integrity of the nations of the Middle East."[25] With such ease was a resolution giving the President military powers to war against international communism transformed into presidential power to intervene in any Middle Eastern situation which, by American definition, threatened the independence and integrity of any nation in the area. Anticommunism had become a rather strange phenomenon. It had also been integrated into a global Monroe Doctrine. The Eisenhower Doctrine was an extension of the dogmas of 1823 into the Middle East in the same sense that, as Dulles observed, SEATO extended the original doctrine into Southeast Asia.

In the early spring of 1957, the Eisenhower administration could believe that it had emerged from the winter crises with increased powers and prestige. Such was not the case with Nikita Khrushchev. Despite his triumphant proclamation that Dulles's failure to interfere in the Hungarian uprising had proved the hollowness of "liberation," the fiasco of Khrushchev's policies in Eastern Europe and his inability to take advantage of the power vacuum in the Middle East immersed him in deep political trouble in Moscow. He came under vigorous attack for having invited Chinese officials to fly to Warsaw at a critical moment to quiet the Poles. Having the Chinese play the role of mediator in Eastern Europe because of Khrushchev's mistakes at the Twentieth Congress gave Molotov, Malenkov, and Kaganovich their opening. Khrushchev soon counterattacked with his tactics of 1953–1955. "We are all Stalinists," he loudly announced at a New Year's Eve party, and then launched into a denunciation of "capitalist countries" who wanted "a feverish arms race." His talk became increasingly tough. For the first time since 1955 the Soviet press accused the United States of following, in the words of a joint Chinese-Soviet announcement, "a policy of aggression and preparation for war."[26]

During the summer of 1957 Khrushchev gained supreme power. His first target was the military. Having helped make him, Zhukov could perhaps help break him. Khrushchev's opportunity arose when the marshal began to issue pronouncements on sensitive political issues as well as on military strategy. Party leaders interpreted this as a direct and dangerous threat to the supremacy of the party over the

---

[25]Department of State, *American Foreign Policy: Current Documents, 1957* (Washington, 1961), p. 1024; Little, "Puppet in Search of a Puppeteer?" pp. 524–526.

[26]H. S. Dinerstein, *War and the Soviet Union*, revised edition (New York, 1959, 1962), pp. 154–163.

military. The danger was indeed even greater, for since Beria's execution four years before, the weakening of the secret police had allowed the military to gain a large measure of independence from party control. In late October Zhukov was stripped of his post as defense minister. When he apparently tried to fight back, he was also removed from the Presidium and the Central Committee.[27] Khrushchev next attempted to educate the Soviet intellectuals who had apparently misunderstood the de-Stalinization campaign to mean that more candid criticisms of Soviet society would be tolerated. At a garden party, Khrushchev made such a verbal assault upon the invited intellectuals that one woman fainted. That harangue climaxed with Khrushchev's shouting that Hungary would have remained orderly if several writers had been shot at the proper time; if such a threat ever faced the Soviet Union, he added, "My hand would not tremble."[28] The following year when the distinguished Russian author Boris Pasternak expressed some doubts about the results of the 1917 revolution in his novel *Dr. Zhivago,* the book was banned from mass circulation inside Russia, and Pasternak was prohibited from traveling to Stockholm to receive the Nobel Prize in literature. De-Stalinization had its limits, particularly if it threatened the power of the party and Khrushchev.

After a four-year struggle Khrushchev was supreme. In the United States Eisenhower began his second term in power. The world outside Moscow and Washington had greatly altered between 1953 and 1957. Having created an acceptable status quo in Europe, Washington shifted more and more of its energies to fighting the Cold War in the Third World. In the Soviet Union Khrushchev brought about changes that allowed his government to exploit opportunities within the newly emerging nations. Dwight Eisenhower provided the proper epitaph for the history of those years: "Somehow or other," he wrote Dulles in February 1955, "it seems not at all extraordinary that you should celebrate your birthday in Bangkok."[29]

[27]Raymond L. Garthoff, *Soviet Military Policy* (New York, 1966), pp. 52–54.
[28]Edward Crankshaw, *Khrushchev, A Career* (New York, 1966), pp. 253–255.
[29]The President to Secretary of State, February 15, 1955, Correspondence, Dulles Papers, Princeton.

CHAPTER 9

New Frontiers and Old Dilemmas (1957–1962)

On the morning of October 4, 1957, the Soviet Union successfully launched the world's first artificial satellite. Named "Sputnik," Russian for "traveling companion," the 184-pound satellite swirled above the earth at 18,000 miles per hour. More significant than the satellite was the powerful booster rocket that thrust Sputnik into orbit, for it indicated Soviet capability of sending a powerful weapon at very high speeds to targets within a 4000-mile radius. The launching also demonstrated the skill of Soviet missile science. Niebuhr's argument that scientists could be as efficiently exploited by a totalitarian as by a democratic society seemed true—and ominous.

Americans were extremely disturbed. Strategic air force units were dispersed and placed on alert, short-range Jupiter missiles were installed in Turkey and Italy to offset the long-range Soviet weapons, money was poured into missile and bomber programs, and "gaps" were suddenly discovered in everything from missile production to the teaching of arithmetic at the preschool level. Dulles attempted to play down the Soviet feat because he understood the impact it would have on world affairs. The newly emerging nations could view Russia as a people who in 1917 had been generations behind other industrialized nations but who, through harsh regimentation, had assumed first place in the race for control of outer space. They could also interpret the launching as a dramatic swing in the balance of military power toward Moscow. In August 1957 the Soviets had fired the world's first intercontinental ballistic missile (ICBM) and that same month had announced, "Co-existence is not only the absence of war between the two systems, but also peaceful economic competition between them, and concrete cooperation in economic, political and cultural areas."[1] Khru-

---

[1] "The Leninist Course of Peaceful Coexistence," *Kommunist*, No. 11, 1957, p. 5.

shchev could welcome such competition with the knowledge that the Soviet gross national product (the total amount of goods and services in the economy) had increased on the average of 7.1 percent annually between 1950 and 1958, nearly 50 percent greater than the American rate.

This economic growth was real, but the Soviet lead in ICBMs was not. The Soviets made a basic decision in 1957 not to build an elementary first-generation ICBM complex but to wait for the second- and third-generation models. This meant that for the next few years Russian foreign policy would attempt to exploit an imaginary lead. One interesting way Khrushchev did this was to have Russian radio and newspapers quote back to the West the West's own exaggerated views of Soviet missile capacity, thereby reinforcing the exaggerations.[2]

U.S. arms experts and politicians warned that Americans faced the grave danger of being on the wrong side of a "missile gap." Such warnings from John F. Kennedy and Lyndon Johnson grew more shrill as these Democrats opened early campaigns for the 1960 presidential election. In late 1957 their warnings received support from the Gaither Report. A top secret investigation of American military posture, it had been commissioned by Eisenhower's National Security Council. Named after its author, Rowland Gaither, the report updated NSC-68 of seven years before. The report ominously informed Eisenhower that unless US military spending increased 50 percent in the near future, the "expansionist" Soviet threat "may become critical in early 1959 or early 1960." Along with a massive arms buildup, the paper urged a $25-billion ("simple, even spartan") program of fallout shelters which would not only supposedly protect Americans from Soviet attack but permit "our own air defense to use nuclear warheads with greater freedom." Such vast spending would have few bad effects on the U.S. economy and could even "help to sustain production and employment."

Eisenhower (correctly, as it turned out) dismissed the Gaither Report as misguided. He ordered it pigeonholed, and it did not become public until 1973. The President knew from his intelligence sources that Soviet missile forces posed little threat to the United States. He blamed much of the post-Sputnik panic (again correctly)

[2]Arnold Horelick and Myron Rush, *Strategic Power and Soviet Foreign Policy* (Chicago, 1966), pp. 36–38.

on ambitious politicians such as Kennedy or Johnson, whose major priority was the 1960 election, or on longtime defense specialists— such as Paul Nitze, an author of both the Gaither Report and NSC-68, and later a top Reagan administration official—who could apparently not be satisfied no matter how large U.S. nuclear forces became. As one Republican senator recalled, "Ike took the heat, grinned, and kept his mouth shut."[3]

Eisenhower believed that current programs more than sufficed: between 1958 and 1960 the nation's nuclear stockpile stunningly tripled, from 6000 to 18,000 weapons. These included fourteen virtually untouchable Polaris nuclear submarines (each with sixteen missiles), the first of which went into service in 1960. Allies and new domestic pressure groups—such as SANE, or the National Committee for a Sane Nuclear Policy—meanwhile pushed Eisenhower to stop nuclear testing and to negotiate arms reduction. Testing temporarily stopped in late 1958 after a series of huge Soviet and American explosions released dangerous amounts of radioactive materials into the atmosphere and, ultimately, into rain and even milk. But Eisenhower and Khrushchev never took the second step to arms control, particularly given the pressures of the Gaither Report and Democratic rhetoric on the President, and of Soviet military officials on the premier.[4]

Despite those pressures Eisenhower refused to panic. He also refused to further skew the economy by dramatically increasing military spending. That refusal required some courage, because in 1957–1958 and again in 1959–1960 the economy suffered its second and third significant downturns of the decade. In retrospect the years between 1957 and 1960 marked a historic turn: in such key areas as Detroit's automobiles and Pittsburgh's steel, the U.S. economy became less competitive in world markets than Japan's and West Germany's. Unable to maintain large, favorable trade balances and forced

[3]This and the previous paragraph are based on Robert A. Divine, *The Sputnik Challenge* (New York, 1993), pp. 35–41; and the text available in Joint Committee on Defense Production, 94th Cong., 2nd Sess., *Deterrence and Survival in the Nuclear Age (The "Gaither Report" of 1957)* (Washington, 1976), especially pp. 12, 22–23, 30–31; on NSC-68, see pp. 95–98 of this book.
[4]Robert A. Divine, *Blowing on the Wind: The Nuclear Test Ban Debate, 1954–1960* (New York, 1978), especially chapters 9–11; David Alan Rosenberg, "The Origins of Overkill," *International Security*, VII (Spring 1983): 66; David Holloway, *The Soviet Union and the Arms Race* (New Haven, Conn., 1983), pp. 38–40.

to continue paying the costs of acting as a global policeman, Americans had to begin shipping abroad large amounts of gold to pay their bills—$2 billion of gold in 1958 alone. The dollar, the foundation of the West's economic and military system, wobbled. A top government official finally declared in 1960, "This is the first time in my lifetime that the credit of the United States has been questioned. A serious shadow lies over the American business picture."[5]

Eisenhower privately blamed the problem on greed and a lack of discipline in the United States which he believed threatened to undermine the capitalist system. In a cabinet meeting he also singled out the huge sums spent on weapons that were "just negative stuff adding nothing to the earning capability of the country." In 1960 he blasted the "almost hysterical fear among some elements of the country" that prevented slashes in military budgets.[6] This line of thinking climaxed in early 1961 with the President's famous farewell speech, which warned that a military-industrial complex threatened to distort the economy. At the same time, however, Eisenhower's own view of both the Soviet Union and revolutionary dangers in the Third World prevented him from trying to negotiate arms control agreements or even to educate his fellow Americans on the need to rethink foreign policy in the aftermath of the astonishing events of 1956–1959. Eisenhower understood the causes and costs of the Cold War better than most of the post-1945 Presidents. He also reigned when U.S. military superiority allowed him to negotiate on the causes and reduce the costs. Because of his anticommunism and caution, Eisenhower did neither. But he did manage to pigeon-hole (at least until John F. Kennedy moved into the White House) the Gaither Report's recommendations.

Eisenhower could thus afford to ignore Khrushchev's game of missile bluff, but for the rotund Russian leader the game turned out to be most costly. In months it contributed to a widening of the sur-

---

[5]Godfrey Hodgson, *America in Our Time* (New York, 1978), p. 7; Walt Whitman Rostow, *Diffusion of Power, 1958–1972* (New York, 1973), pp. 60–61.
[6]"Minutes of Cabinet Meeting, June 3, 1960," Cabinet Meetings of President Eisenhower, pp. 1–3, Dwight D. Eisenhower Library, Abilene, Kans. On Eisenhower and capitalism, see Robert Griffith, "Dwight D. Eisenhower and the Corporate Commonwealth," *American Historical Review*, LXXXVII (February 1982): especially 117–122.

prising split between the two communist giants. Khrushchev began by being properly cautious; he termed the ICBM the "ultimate weapon" and painted a picture of the horrible destruction that could result from a nuclear exchange. Mao Ze-dong, however, insisted in 1957 that "the international situation has now reached a new turning point. There are two winds in the world today; the East wind and the West wind. . . . I think the characteristic of the situation today is the East wind prevailing over the West wind."[7] Mao assumed, as a Chinese newspaper commented in February 1958, that the Soviet successes had created a "qualitative change in the distribution of world power [which] had . . . torn apart the paper tiger of American imperialism and shattered the tale of the 'position of strength.' "[8] The Chinese urged strong support for "wars of liberation" in the newly emerging nations, wars that could be safely fanned because the American strategic power had been neutralized. Khrushchev refused to cooperate in such recklessness. He knew that his ICBM program was considerably more of a "paper tiger" than the American long-range bombing force.

The break between China and Russia also became evident in other areas. The Soviets strongly disagreed with Mao's "Great Leap Forward" program in 1958, with its emphasis on forced collectivization. This disagreement pinpointed internal communist differences, for the Russians, as they had historically, insisted first upon industrial productivity and only secondarily upon infusing the masses with revolutionary ideology. Mao, however, was trying at best to balance the two and, in fact, actually to reverse the Soviet priorities in order to mobilize his tremendous manpower through mass revolutionary indoctrination. The Chinese became increasingly critical of Khrushchev's emphasis on consumer goods instead of military hardware and of the Soviet insistence on aiding "bourgeois" regimes in the underdeveloped world instead of fomenting revolution.

Dulles precisely and colorfully described the new Soviet attitude in May 1958. He no longer feared that the Soviets would pose a greater threat with their disavowal of force and "this policy of the smile." Dulles found hope in the belief "that a nation tends to become what it pretends to be. . . . I have seen lots of tough guys who have made

---

[7]William Zimmerman, "Russia and the International Order," *Survey*, 58 (January 1966): 209–213.
[8]Donald Zagoria, *The Sino-Soviet Conflict, 1956–1961* (Princeton, 1962), pp. 160–162.

their pile, who come to New York, wanted to get into society, and who have to behave differently."[9]

In these last months of his life, Dulles tried to influence the newly emerging areas by readjusting American economic aid. Nothing could be done through direct trade arrangements. The traditional reciprocal trade agreements program was in fact seriously injured when, in March 1959, Eisenhower imposed quota restrictions on foreign crude oil imports after two large oil companies refused to join in voluntary restraints. The restrictions were a body blow to Venezuelan and Middle Eastern oil producers and affected American foreign policy in those areas. The administration only slightly offset that misfortune by increasing foreign aid assistance. In fiscal 1957 Mutual Security Program funds were raised nearly 40 percent, and much of this went to Burma, Indonesia, and South Vietnam.

This increased emphasis upon Southeast Asia indicated the Eisenhower administration's growing concern over Mao's China. The President's policy became clear in late summer and autumn 1958, when the Chinese began to shell the offshore islands. Mao probably did not plan to invade the islands but hoped that, with the United States immersed in another Middle Eastern crisis, one of two results would occur: either the Quemoy garrison would surrender without being invaded, or the United States would strike back by bombing mainland China and thus bring the Soviets into the affair back of the Chinese. Neither occurred. The American Seventh Fleet escorted Nationalist troops and supplies into the islands, Dulles announced that Quemoy was "increasingly related" to Taiwan's safety, and American Marines moved into Quemoy eight-inch howitzers capable of firing atomic shells. Eisenhower's tough stand on the Chinese problem and his emphasis on tactical atomic weapons had merged into a concrete policy position. Khrushchev did little except assure Mao that Russia would help if China was actually attacked.

The Chinese calculations of the probable American response and the Soviet-American balance of power should have been more accurate, for Mao could have drawn the appropriate conclusions from the Middle Eastern crisis of July. In that episode the United States landed marines in Lebanon without any counterstroke from Moscow. Two months before the landings, Dulles had expressed the fear that the

[9]"Remarks to U.S. Ambassadors to Europe," Paris, May 9, 1958, NATO ministerial meeting, Conference Dossiers, Dulles Papers, Princeton.

growing power of Nasser and the United Arab Republic (formed by Egypt, Syria, and Yemen in early 1958) would endanger Jordan, Iraq, and Lebanon. On July 14 General Abdel Karim Kassim led a nationalist revolt which overthrew the Iraqi government and established a regime friendly to the UAR. The Baghdad Pact suddenly had a gaping hole. Repercussions were felt in Lebanon where pro-Nasser Moslems had been fighting Christians.

The news of the Kassim coup and the turmoil in Lebanon arrived in Washington early on the morning of July 14. Lebanese President Camille Chamoun, a Maronite Christian, urgently requested help from the United States. At 9:45 A.M. Dulles began explaining to congressional leaders "recent Soviet political activities" in the area. He declared that "it was time to bring a halt to the deterioration in our position in the Middle East." The administration wanted to land troops in Lebanon. There would be no military problem. General Nathan Twining of the Joint Chiefs assured Dulles, as General Twining later recalled, that the "Russians aren't going to jump us," and "if they do jump us, if they do come in, they couldn't pick a better time, because we've got them over the whing whang and they know it."[10]

The only problem was again the proper interpretation of the Eisenhower Doctrine (see p. 188). Some congressmen argued that, because any communist threat was only dimly apparent, Dulles was asking them to condone intervention in a Lebanese civil war. Logically, they continued, troops should also be sent into Iraq. But they placed no obstacles before Eisenhower, and at 2:30 P.M. the President issued the order. While British paratroopers landed in Jordan to help King Hussein once again stabilize his government, 14,000 American troops waded ashore around public bathers on Lebanon's beaches to quiet the threat of civil war. The size of the force warned both the new Iraqi government and Nasser that any threat to Western oil resources in the area would not be tolerated.

Kassim assured the West that its Iraqi interests were safe, and his government soon moved away from Nasser's influence. The Egyptian leader, so one top American official believed, received "one of the greatest lessons in world power politics that he ever had."[11] When

---

[10]Interview with General Nathan Twining, Dulles Oral History Project, Dulles Papers, Princeton.

[11]Interview with Robert Murphy, Dulles Oral History Project, Dulles Papers, Princeton; Burton I. Kaufman, *The Arab Middle East and the United States* (New York, 1995), pp. 26–29.

Nasser flew to Moscow during the crisis to request Soviet help, Khrushchev refused to make any significant response. As for the United States, Dulles informed the cabinet that again the free world had ruined Stalin's and Lenin's prophecies that communism would march through the newly emerging nations to conquer the capitalist West. In 1959 Kassim destroyed the shell of the Baghdad Pact by formally withdrawing Iraq. The United States then immediately signed new bilateral military aid treaties with Pakistan, Turkey, and Iran, while the remaining members of the pact formed the Central Treaty Organization (CENTO).

By the autumn of 1958 Eisenhower had turned Khrushchev's game of missile bluff into a string of real American victories. The Soviet leader suddenly moved to play for much higher stakes: the control of West Germany. Some of the Cold War's most tense moments followed in 1958–1959. Eisenhower had to respond to Khrushchev's challenge, moreover, amidst a bitter debate that threatened to divide the Western alliance.

The debate had been triggered in 1956 when West Germany dragged its feet on building conventional forces. Chancellor Adenauer instead ominously began to request missiles, artillery capable of firing nuclear shells, and fighter bombers that could haul nuclear bombs. The West soon delivered the artillery and bombers. This turn in German affairs set off speeches by European leaders, who proposed the neutralization and reunification of Germany before Central Europe entered a full-fledged arms race. In the United States the debate climaxed in an angry exchange between two architects of postwar policy, George Kennan and Dean Acheson. In words strikingly similar to those of Walter Lippmann's proposals of ten years before, Kennan proposed that before Germany received nuclear arms, the threat of such a possibility should be used to negotiate with the Soviets a neutralization of Central and Eastern Europe. Terms would include the withdrawal of both the Soviet and American armies.[12] This plan soon became known as "disengagement."

Acheson's response in January 1958 was acerbic. If the United States withdrew its troops from Germany and Western Europe, he declared, the Soviets would sooner or later exterminate "independent

---

[12]George F. Kennan, *Russia, the Atom and the West* (New York, 1957).

national life in Western Europe." Acheson particularly feared that Communist parties in Europe would gain the initiative. This indicated his belief that NATO shaped the internal political life of European countries as well as the overall military strategies. Withdrawal from and neutralization of Germany would be disastrous, Acheson warned, for, as he had once remarked, without American troops "to monitor the continued integration of Germany into the West, we should be continually haunted by the spectre of a sort of new [Nazi-Soviet] Agreement." As for Kennan, Acheson sarcastically observed that Mr. "X" had tried but had failed to convince any "responsible leader" of these ideas as early as 1949. "Mr. Kennan has never, in my judgment," Acheson commented, "grasped the realities of power relationships, but takes a rather mystical attitude toward them. To Mr. Kennan there is no Soviet military threat in Europe."[13]

This last sentence indicated a fundamental assumption on the part of Acheson and Dulles. During the six months following Acheson's outburst, however, a strange phenomenon occurred in Washington. Dulles apparently began to move away from Acheson and toward Kennan. The first indication of a change came in a little-noted speech by the director of the White House disarmament staff, Robert E. Matteson. He declared in February 1958 that "we may very well be at one of those great historical divides where a boldness in exploration of the relaxation-of-tension concept might pay greater dividends than we now suspect."[14] In May Dulles remarked that "disengagement" was such a "naughty word" that it "couldn't even be translated into a good language like French."[15]

On June 30, 1958, however, Dulles wrote a "My dear friend" letter to Adenauer. At the outset the secretary discounted any dismantling of existing military establishments, but he then observed that domestic and satellite demands were making the Soviets more open to negotiation. Dulles wondered if there could not be a "limitation of armament... through establishing significant zones of inspection which would greatly minimize the fear of massive surprise attack."[16] He disavowed any talk of paying a high political price, such as cutting the

[13]*U.S. News and World Report,* January 17, 1958, p. 63.
[14]Richard Rovere, "Letter from Washington," *New Yorker,* March 22, 1958, pp. 136–141.
[15]"Remarks to U.S. Ambassadors to Europe," Paris, May 9, 1958, NATO ministerial meeting, Conference Dossiers, Dulles Papers, Princeton.
[16]Dulles to Adenauer, June 30, 1958, Correspondence, Dulles Papers, Princeton.

power of the West German government through a reunification of Germany. The implication, however, was clear: negotiations with the Soviets could lead to the first hesitant steps toward a military neutralization of Central Europe. Within ten months Dulles would be dead. Where the secretary's thoughts of mid-1958 would have led is only speculation, but clearly he was taking into account those new international events that were reorienting East-West relations. The European status quo was further shaken in June 1958 (the month Dulles wrote Adenauer) when Charles de Gaulle returned to power in France. Franco-American relations had not improved since the Suez debacle. Dulles watched de Gaulle with some concern, for he appreciated how the general hoped to regain the *grandeur* of France through the reorientation of French foreign policy.[17] The reorientation would require considerable freedom of action, and that, Dulles believed quite accurately, would result in "neutralist" policies advanced by de Gaulle within the NATO alliance. At the same time that the communist bloc was dividing into Russian, Chinese, and Yugoslav factions, the Western alliance was also splitting apart.

The postwar world, like most thirteen-year-olds, was entering a new and uncertain stage. The widening split within NATO became more evident in late 1958 when France, West Germany, Italy, and the Benelux prepared for the formal initiation of the European Economic Community, or Common Market, on January 1, 1959. Following an accord first reached in March 1957, these nations agreed that within fifteen years they would form an economic union by eliminating tariffs and equalizing taxes within the community while creating a common tariff for outside goods. The immediate impact was political as well as economic, for in a stroke "the six" had decreased their economic dependence upon the United States, tied West Germany firmly to the rest of Western Europe, taken their first step toward possible political federation, and created a middle bloc between the United States and the Soviet Union.

In the last months of 1958, Great Britain attempted to enter the Common Market, but it failed after refusing to surrender its economic ties to the Commonwealth and to the United States. The British countered by forming, in November 1959, the Free Trade Association (or

---

[17]Alfred Grosser, *La Politique extérieure de la Ve République* (Paris, 1965), p. 44.

"Outer Seven") comprising themselves, Sweden, Switzerland, Portugal, Austria, Norway, and Denmark. The new grouping, however, failed to keep pace with the booming Common Market, and Washington watched as the British became increasingly isolated from Western Europe's economic upsurge.

Moscow feared these developments even more than Washington did. The success of the Common Market and, above all, West Germany's possession of artillery and aircraft that had nuclear capabilities, raised once again before the Soviets the specter of a militarized and economically aggressive Germany. After several days of publicizing his growing ICBM arsenal, Khrushchev began a series of moves on November 10, 1958. They climaxed in the demand that the United States, Great Britain, and France withdraw their 10,000 troops from West Berlin, make it a "free city," and negotiate with the East German government (which none of the Western powers recognized) for access into Berlin. If agreement was not reached within six months, Khrushchev threatened to turn the access routes over to East German control. With complete Western support, Dulles rejected Khrushchev's demands, refused to contemplate recognition of East Germany, and intimated that, if the East Germans did gain control of the access routes and refused to allow Western vehicles through, NATO would retaliate "if need be by military force." Khrushchev replied that this would mean World War III.

In focusing upon West Berlin, the Soviet leader had pinpointed the fulcrum that could change the balance of power within Europe. For American policymakers feared that, if the United States did evacuate West Berlin, the Adenauer government's confidence in NATO and the Common Market would be shaken and the basis laid for a West German–Russian deal. It soon became evident, nevertheless, that Khrushchev had concluded that the fulcrum was not worth a nuclear exchange. Denying that he had issued an ultimatum, he modified the six-month limit so that discussions could be held. Over strong Chinese protests the Soviet leader visited the United States in September 1959. Just before his arrival a Soviet "Lunik" (a rocket shot with a scientific payload) hit the moon. Khrushchev reminded the world of his nation's capabilities by presenting a replica of the Soviet pennant aboard the "Lunik" to the President. The visit produced few diplomatic results. Plans were made for a summit conference in Geneva the following spring, after which Eisenhower was to visit Russia.

By the end of April 1960, hopes for a settlement had shriveled before blistering announcements from Moscow and Washington. During trips to Indonesia and France in early spring, the Soviet premier again demanded a German settlement. On May 5, the eve of the summit conference, Khrushchev suddenly announced that the Soviets had shot down a U-2 American reconnaissance plane which had been violating Russian territorial sovereignty. The United States first denied that the aircraft had been on a spying mission but then became trapped when Khrushchev produced the pilot who had parachuted to safety. After some hesitation Eisenhower accepted full responsibility for the incident. He also finally announced that there would be no future overflights. The damage, however, had been done. This episode at Geneva did not ruin the conference. That had been accomplished by the growing intransigence over Berlin, the Sino-Soviet rift, and the decision (made by high American officials) to send a U-2 plane over Russian territory during highly critical hours in Russian-American diplomacy.

Khrushchev's major concern was not his relationship with Eisenhower; the President would shortly leave office anyway. More important was the embarrassing position in which the U-2 flights, which had been occurring over Russia for at least four years, placed his entire foreign policy, not least his relations with Mao. Khrushchev now recalled Stalin's snickering that "soon after my death, the arrogant Americans would wring your necks, like chickens."[18] There could be little doubt that on previous U-2 flights the United States had discovered the truth about Russian ICBM strength. This thought probably influenced Khrushchev to call off the Berlin crisis temporarily while intensifying his threats of how Russia would destroy any American ally allowing U-2 planes to leave from its territory. He particularly seized upon an issue in the summer of 1960 that somewhat appeased China and at the same time allowed him to wave his strategic power before the United States: Khrushchev welcomed Fidel Castro as a new force in Latin America and threatened to destroy the United States, "figuratively speaking," if it tried to attack Castro. The Monroe Doctrine, Khrushchev announced, was dead.

This incredible turn of events had begun on July 26, 1953, when the young middle-class lawyer, a species which the unbalanced Cuban society turned out in overabundance, led an armed assault on the regime of Fulgencio Batista. Castro was jailed, but he escaped to

---

[18]Anatoly Dobrynin, *In Confidence* (New York, 1995), p. 41.

Mexico, organized a small revolutionary band, and landed in Cuba in 1956. Batista's police were waiting, and Castro struggled into the mountains with only ten other survivors. American officials paid little attention, believing Batista's word that Castro was dead. In 1957 *The New York Times* correspondent Herbert Matthews found the rebel's hideaway and revealed to the world Castro's program and his astonishing success among the Cuban peasants. Matthews's reports had little positive effect on Washington, however.

The American failure to worry about or understand Castro was not the major mistake, for this was symptomatic of a Cuban policy that had left much to be desired ever since the United States had first taken de facto control in the summer of 1898. By 1956 Americans owned 80 percent of Cuba's utilities, 40 percent of its sugar, 90 percent of its mining wealth, and the island's key strategic location of Guantánamo Bay. The Cuban economy could be manipulated simply by changing the amount of Cuban sugar allowed into the American market. The United States had also landed marines three times after 1902 in efforts to stabilize Cuban politics. Washington had not intervened when Batista overthrew a constitutionally elected government in 1952 and began consolidating his power by following such diverse policies as allowing American advisers to train his military forces while inviting Cuban Communist party members to assume governmental positions. The communists were so close to Batista that they almost missed joining Castro's movement before Batista was driven from power. In Washington, officials did little until it was too late. They believed, as a U.S. intelligence officer phrased it, that "moderates" would replace Castro, or else "Cuba's economic dependence on the US" would force the revolutionaries to their senses. In 1960 the American ambassador to Cuba during Batista's last years, Earl E. T. Smith, more accurately summarized past Cuban-American relations and implicitly explained how disastrous the American colonial policy had been in Cuba for sixty-two years: "Senator, let me explain to you that the United States, until the advent of Castro, was so overwhelmingly influential in Cuba that . . . the American Ambassador was the second most important man in Cuba; sometimes even more important than the President. . . . Now, today, his importance is not very great."[19]

---

[19]The best account is Thomas Paterson, *Contesting Castro* (New York, 1994), especially pp. 250–256; Robert F. Smith, *What Happened in Cuba? A Documentary History* (New York, 1963), p. 273.

His importance declined because, upon grasping power on New Year's Day 1959, Castro determined to balance the Cuban economy and rectify the social injustices within the society. To accomplish this, a thoroughgoing revolution would be required. In the new ruler's mind this meant ending Cuba's dependence on Washington. Castro's trip to the United States in April almost inevitably produced no positive results. The following month he announced an agrarian reform program which met American resistance. By the summer Castro's personal power was unquestioned, but in his need for organized political support to carry out the revolution, he moved closer to the communists within his 26th of July movement. By the end of the year, the anticommunists within the movement were isolated and leaving Cuba. Confiscations of American property intensified, signaling increased anti-Americanism, as well as Castro's need for resources to finance socioeconomic changes. That need, moreover, prohibited him from paying for the confiscated property.

In February 1960 the Russians signed a trade agreement to exchange Cuban sugar for Soviet oil, machinery, and technicians. Ironically, as Cuban-Soviet bloc trade increased from 2 percent of the island's trade in 1960 to 80 percent by the end of 1961, Castro was forced to accept the position as a food and raw material producer which he had so strongly deprecated in past Cuban-American relations. In July 1960 the United States cut the Cuban sugar quota from the American market. In August Washington began to mobilize hemispheric opposition to Cuba, and three months later American naval forces moved to Central American waters to quell a rumored invasion from Cuba. At this time Eisenhower accepted a Central Intelligence Agency–State Department plan to train an anti-Castro army. Preparations began for an invasion in early 1961. In the first days of January 1961, U.S.-Cuban diplomatic relations were formally severed.

The attention of Americans now focused on this bearded jungle fighter who made four-hour-long speeches to entranced Cuban audiences and who had the gall to defy the world's greatest superpower just ninety miles away. But Castro was only an incredible symbol for a larger danger that confronted U.S. policy in its own hemisphere. In the late 1950s Latin America began passing through its most important change since it had obtained independence from Spain 140 years earlier.

Latin America is fundamentally different from most of the newly emerging areas in Asia or the Middle East. It is more highly developed and, in some areas, in an intermediate stage of economic growth that presents sophisticated economic and social problems. Large areas of Latin America were controlled by extremely conservative governments (the "oligarchs") that could not be removed from power as Africans and Asians removed European colonial rulers from their continents. In Vietnam, for example, the radical nationalists could fight an anticolonial war to send the "foreigners"—the French—back to Paris. But in El Salvador, Nicaragua, or Bolivia, the radical nationalists had to fight a revolution against oligarchs who were their own flesh and blood. The oligarchs, moreover, received strong support from the military elite and the United States, which had frowned on Latin American revolutions throughout the twentieth century.

The southern nations remained quiet between 1948 and 1958 as Latin America's economy grew at an impressive annual rate of 4.3 percent. But this growth occurred in a powder keg: the region's population grew 3 percent annually, an amount greater than that of any area of the world. By the year 2000 some 600 million people would live where 200 million lived in 1960. The economic growth also varied from country to country. Venezuela's oil and Mexico's viable political system gave those nations strong advantages. Elsewhere, poor resources and cementlike political systems contributed to internal pressures that threatened to explode in revolution. Outside democratic Costa Rica and Mexico, 2 percent of the population owned 75 percent of the agricultural land on a continent whose people had to live on their ability to scratch a living from the soil. Many of the poor moved out of the countryside to exist in some of the world's worst slums on the outskirts of major cities. Then in 1957–1958 economic recession in the United States dragged down an already stumbling Latin American economy. Since 1945 Washington officials had made no major effort to correct inequities in the economies of the southern nations—many of which were dependent for survival on American producers and consumers. Between 1945 and 1960 Washington had given three times more aid to Belgium, Luxembourg, and the Netherlands than to all twenty Latin American nations. Private American capital, meanwhile, had invested $1 billion in oil, $500 million in mining, and $750 million in manufacturing, thus increasing the imbalance of the Latin American economies.

After signing their first trade agreement with Argentina in 1953, the Soviets tried to take advantage of these conditions. By 1957 Soviet trade with Latin America amounted to only $200 million annu-

CENTRAL AND SOUTH AMERICA, 1954–1990

UNITED STATES

MEXICO
Threatened by $80 billion
foreign debt 1980s

Miami
Havana

BELIZE

Mexico City

GUATEMALA
Arbenz overthrown 1954
Castillo Armas assassinated 1957

EL SALVADOR

COSTA RICA
Arias peace plans, 1987–

Sandinistas overthrow Somoza 1979;
U.S. supports anti-Sandinista "contras" 1981–1990

PACIFIC OCEAN
Anti-Nixon riots 1958
Military coup 1962
Military coup 1968

Average annual per capita income 1978–1981

HONDURAS
U.S. naval and air bases 1981–

NICARAGUA
Canal Zone

PANAMA
Anti-U.S. riots 1959
U.S. returns canal zone to Panama by treaty 1978
Noriega seizes power 1983;
U.S. relations strained, 1987;
U.S. invades and overthrows Noriega, 1989

CUBA
Batista overthrown 1959
Attempted anti-Castro invasion 1961
Soviet military aid, U.S. quarantine 1962

BAHAMAS (Br.)

DOMINICAN REP.
U.S. broke diplomatic ties 1960
Trujillo assassinated 1961
Diplomatic ties restored 1962
U.S. and O.A.S. intervention 1965

JAMAICA

HAITI

PUERTO RICO

CARIBBEAN SEA

Caracas
VENEZUELA

Bogotá
COLOMBIA

Quito
ECUADOR

Lima
PERU

Pérez Jiménez overthrown 1958
Anti-Nixon riots 1958

BARBADOS

GRENADA Invaded by U.S. 1983

TRINIDAD AND TOBAGO

GUYANA

SURINAM (Neth.)
FR. GUIANA

U.S.-Colombian military attacks on drug cartels, 1988–1989

BRAZIL
Military seizes power 1964 and rules 1964.
Threatened by $90 billion foreign debt 1980s.

BOLIVIA
La Paz

Brasília

PARAGUAY
Asunción

Rio de Janeiro

Salvador Allende elected 1970
Overthrown by military and died 1973

CHILE
Santiago

Buenos Aires

URUGUAY
Montevideo

Punta del Este Conferences 1961, 1962

ARGENTINA
Threatened by $50 billion foreign debt 1980s
Returns to civilian government 1983

ATLANTIC OCEAN

Argentina	$2300
Barbados	3000
Bolivia	510
Brazil	1500
Chile	2000
Colombia	1100
Costa Rica	2200
Cuba	840
Dominican Rep.	1200
Ecuador	1050
El Salvador	640
Grenada	500
Guatemala	1080
Guyana	600
Haiti	260
Honduras	822
Jamaica	1340
Mexico	1800
Nicaragua	800
Panama	1100
Paraguay	1040
Peru	650
Trinidad & Tobago	4800
Uruguay	2800
Venezuela	3600
United States	10,600

ally. It increased to only $450 million by 1960. Nevertheless, it had doubled within three years (while the U.S. proportion of that trade had slipped), and it focused on a few select countries, such as Argentina, Brazil, and later Cuba.[20] During these same years anti-Yankeeism spread. Its intensity was not appreciated in Washington until April 1958 when Vice President Richard Nixon and his wife visited several Latin American nations. The North Americans were spat upon, had eggs and stones hurled at them, and in Caracas had their limousine attacked by mobs. Eisenhower rushed a thousand marines to U.S. bases in the Caribbean, but Nixon escaped and flew home before further outbreaks occurred.

President Juscelino Kubitschek of Brazil seized this opportunity to push for Eisenhower's acceptance of a proposed "Operation Pan America," in which the United States and Latin America would cooperate to promote long-term development. A pivotal part of the plan was an Inter-American Development Bank that would channel low-interest U.S. loans into the southern nations. Eisenhower had been cool toward this proposal in 1957—he wanted only private capitalists to handle development—but after Nixon's encounters and Castro's sudden appearance, Eisenhower's view changed. The bank was established in 1959 with $1 billion in capital. In 1960, with the Act of Bogotá, the hemispheric nations began working out details for a comprehensive program of economic development. These events marked the real beginnings of what John F. Kennedy would later popularize as the Alliance for Progress. But they appeared too late to prevent the rise of Fidel Castro and the stirring of revolutionaries in Central and South America.

Castroism and the rumbling problems in other newly emerging nations dominated the foreign-policy debates in the 1960 presidential campaign. The Democratic nominee, John F. Kennedy, charged the Republican nominee, Richard Nixon, with allowing a "missile gap" in the Soviets' favor. But Kennedy started a more significant debate when he suggested American support of "non-Batista democratic anti-Castro forces." Nixon appeared appalled at even the suggestion of American support for such intervention. He later explained

---

[20]Ronald James Clark, "Latin-American Economic Relations with the Soviet Bloc, 1954–1961," unpublished doctoral dissertation, Indiana University, 1963.

that, having access to the invasion plans already under way, he was forced to act surprised publicly at Kennedy's suggestion. Outside these exchanges the two nominees differed significantly on few other foreign-policy issues. The Eisenhower consensus, forged in 1956, was making its mark, and each candidate simply tried to exploit, not destroy it. In one of the closest presidential elections, Kennedy won by a margin of 114,000 votes out of 68.3 million cast. The electoral college vote went to the Democrats 303 to 219.

John F. Kennedy was a most sensitive and astute politician, and the narrow victory margin affected the development of his foreign policy. Presidential assistant Theodore Sorensen defined the problem: "President Kennedy is acutely aware of Jefferson's dictum: 'Great innovations should not be forced on slender majorities.' "[21] Kennedy tended to defer to military and intelligence experts and to those in Congress who preferred to fight the Cold War rather than risk negotiating its problems. His experiences abroad while his father, Joseph P. Kennedy, was ambassador to Great Britain in the late 1930s convinced him that democracies moved too slowly in reacting to totalitarian aggression, a view that permeated his widely read book, written while he was a Harvard senior, *Why England Slept.* His sensitivity to the political climate was also demonstrated during 1950–1954, when he was extremely reluctant to oppose Senator McCarthy. As a young senator from Massachusetts, Kennedy nevertheless realized that the growing importance of the newly emerging nations required changes in foreign policy. A 1957 speech was outspoken in support of Algeria's fight against France. In 1954 he warned against any American attempt to prop up the French regime in Indochina, but on this issue Kennedy equivocated, for in June 1956 he lauded Diem as an "offspring" of the American effort to keep Southeast Asia free. Aware of the challenge of the newly emerging peoples and fearful that the United States would not respond quickly or properly, Kennedy emphasized in a special message to Congress on May 25, 1961, "The great battleground for the defense and expansion of freedom today is . . . Asia, Latin America, Africa and the Middle East, the lands of the rising peoples."[22]

---

[21]Theodore C. Sorensen, *Decision-Making in the White House: The Olive Branch or the Arrows* (New York, 1963), pp. 44–48.
[22]U.S. Government Printing Office, *Public Papers of the Presidents, J. F. Kennedy, 1961* (Washington, 1962), p. 397.

In his first annual message on January 30, 1961, the President listed the priorities for waging the conflict between "Freedom and Communism," by noting "First, we must strengthen our military tools."[23] Upon entering office, the administration had discovered that the "missile gap," which Kennedy had heavily emphasized in the campaign, was only fictional. The Soviets and the Chinese also knew this, and, consequently, Kennedy and his advisers feared that the communists would place more emphasis on conventional, local wars. In 1961 the administration increased the defense budget 15 percent, doubling the number of combat-ready divisions in the army's strategic reserve, expanding the marines, adding seventy vessels to the active fleet, and giving a dozen more wings to the tactical air forces. General Maxwell Taylor returned to act as the President's military adviser.

Varying little in objective from Eisenhower's approach, this policy was a different kind of attempt to contain communism and revolutionary instability. The policy had been thought through and widely publicized by the reports of the Rockefeller brothers in the late 1950s and was the result of a logical progression of thought on the part of intellectuals such as Henry Kissinger. In this sense particularly, the Kennedy administration seized upon American intellectuals in a manner unmatched since 1933. The scholars responded.

Other parts of the society also responded. In his farewell address in January 1961, Eisenhower had warned the American people against the "conjunction of an immense military establishment and a large arms industry" which was "new in American experience," and whose "total influence . . . is felt in every city, every state house, every office in the federal government. . . . In the councils of government, we must guard against the acquisition of unwarranted influence, whether sought or unsought, by the military-industrial complex." The President declared, "The potential for the disastrous rise of misplaced power exists and will persist." For Eisenhower this was strong language. The Kennedy administration, however, took little heed of this speech. Determined to help noncommunist nations militarily, and worried over the outflow of American gold caused by an unfavorable balance in the nation's financial and trade exchanges with the rest of the world, the new President established in 1961 a special post in the Defense Department to sell American arms through private corpora-

[23]*Public Papers of the Presidents, Kennedy, 1961*, pp. 23–24.

tions to foreign nations. By 1965 American companies exported $1.9-billion worth of arms to Europe, Japan, Iran, Venezuela, and Saudi Arabia, among others. General Dynamics Corporation alone sold more than $1-billion worth of arms overseas between 1962 and 1965. Most of the goods were sophisticated and expensive electronic equipment. As one business periodical observed, in the 1930s such companies were known as " 'Merchants of Death.' . . . Times have changed."[24]

The drive for a unified but multimilitary response to foreign-policy problems was typified by Secretary of Defense Robert McNamara's management of the Pentagon. No more would individual services have wholly independent programs. McNamara instead brought the various services together under "program elements" in which the military units were coordinated for efficient war making on various levels. The professional soldiers lost some of their political power, but they gained greatly in military efficiency. By mobilizing resources in this way, the administration could massively retaliate on many military levels. The change under way since the days of Dulles had matured. Particular emphasis was placed upon preparing the United States for guerrilla wars. The Jungle Warfare School in the Canal Zone and another at Fort Bragg, North Carolina, brought U.S. Army Special Forces troops together with Latin American units. More than 600 Latin American policemen sharpened their talents in counterintelligence work and the handling of mobs by undergoing training in the Canal Zone school established by the Agency for International Development. At the end of 1966 anti-American guerrillas nevertheless operated in Venezuela, Bolivia, Colombia, Peru, Nicaragua, and Guatemala.

Kennedy picked Latin America for special attention. Besides the training of antiguerrilla forces and the establishment of the Peace Corps (young men and women trained to perform teaching and technical services in newly emerging nations), the President announced, on March 13, 1961, the Alliance for Progress. To the Eisenhower policies of 1959–1960, Kennedy added a ten-year commitment of $20 billion of American money and an appropriate image. The plan was worked out at the Punta del Este, Uruguay, conference in August. The U.S. aid, including $300 million annually from private capital, would

[24]*Forbes*, February 1, 1966, pp. 15–16.

quadruple the annual economic assistance given the area between 1946 and 1960. In return Latin America pledged $80 billion of investment over the ten-year period and, most important, land, tax, and other socioeconomic reforms. Kennedy hoped these efforts would result in a 5.5 percent increase in Latin America's growth rate, or a modest net increase of 2.5 percent over the population increase.

These ambitious plans quickly encountered major difficulties. The programs were undercut by bureaucratic infighting in Washington; the marked reluctance of such major Latin American nations as Brazil, Argentina, and Mexico to submit their development programs to hemispheric scrutiny; and particularly the inability or unwillingness of many governments to undertake the promised reforms. In some nations the requisite political stability could not be established; between 1961 and 1966 military forces overthrew nine Latin American governments. The Kennedy administration, trapped between the alternatives of intervening in the affairs of sovereign nations or watching the Alliance grow increasingly weaker, could not work out an effective response. By 1963 Alliance officials could claim that 35 million Latin Americans had benefited from the program, but only at the end of the first five years would the 5.5 percent growth rate be in sight, and not even then would there be evidence of the reforms which could ensure fair distribution of the benefits.

The Alliance was designed to create a stable and orderly Latin America without having the hemisphere endure a series of Castro-like revolutions. The Cuban ruler had become a primary concern of American officials, and they moved to eradicate him on April 17, 1961, when the administration supported an invasion at the Bay of Pigs by a group of Cuban exiles. This force had been trained for months in Guatemala by the Central Intelligence Agency. Although it was supposedly a secret operation, news of the preparations was widespread in American newspapers by April. President Kennedy was assured by the CIA, State, and military officials that the invasion could succeed if, under American-provided air cover, the anti-Castro units could establish a beachhead and then link up with other guerrillas in the mountains. Taking the word of his experts, Kennedy acquiesced, demanding only that no American troops be committed. Fifteen hundred Cubans waded ashore on the morning of April 17, only to find that one key air strike had been canceled because of clouds, that other naval and air supporting units had been immobilized by Castro's small air force, that the beachhead was indefensible, and that they had no hope of reaching the mountains. In the aftermath American Ambassador to the United Nations Adlai Stevenson was caught lying about U.S. support of the operation. Kennedy ordered an investigation of the CIA and removed some top officials. In Cuba Castro was ensconced more securely in power than ever before.

"All my life I've known better than to depend on the experts," the President wondered aloud shortly afterward. "How could I have been so stupid, to let them go ahead?"[25] The problem went deeper than that, however. Certainly the Guatemala operation of 1954 colored the view of both the CIA and the White House when they analyzed the Cuban project. The political-military philosophy of the invasion, moreover, was quite compatible with the new emphasis placed by the administration upon guerrilla-like warfare. The more fundamental problems were revealed by a State Department White Paper, written by White House aide and Harvard historian Arthur Schlesinger, Jr., which attempted to rationalize the invasion just days before the tragedy occurred. The paper condemned the Castro movement as communist and attempted to place the United States on the side of social and economic reform within the hemisphere. It was, however, an unfortunate example of how history was misconstrued to serve political ends. From the first, when the paper claimed that "the hemisphere rejoiced at the overthrow of the Batista tyranny" (a fact not overly obvious in Washington in January 1959), until the conclusion that the "inter-American system was incompatible with any form of totalitarianism" (which failed to show how Trujillo, Duvalier, Somoza, and even Batista, among others, had prospered within that system), the State Department paper was more propaganda than a sober recital of facts.[26] But the paper revealed the dilemma of American policy toward Latin America. The Bay of Pigs was a public confession by the United States that it had failed to understand or deal with the most significant political change in the hemisphere in fifty years. This conclusion would have been tenable whether the invasion had succeeded or failed.

The President publicly accepted complete responsibility for the Bay of Pigs, and it was in the weeks immediately following this debacle that he traveled to Europe to visit West European leaders and Premier Nikita Khrushchev. The meeting in Vienna on June 3 and 4

[25]Theodore C. Sorensen, *Kennedy* (New York, 1965), p. 309.
[26]Smith, *What Happened in Cuba?* p. 211.

with the Soviet leader resulted in an agreement to stop the growing conflict in Laos. Otherwise it only increased Kennedy's apprehension that the Soviets were determined to create dangerous tensions by supporting what Khrushchev called "wars of liberation," that is, support of nationalist and pro-communist elements in the newly emerging countries which were fighting Western political and economic influence. Worst of all, Khrushchev was militant about the necessity of eliminating Western power in West Berlin. The six-month notice was reimposed by the Soviet ruler, who became deeply angry at Kennedy's repeated warnings not to miscalculate American intentions. "I will tell you now," the President reported to the American people upon his return, "that it was a very sober two days."

Worried about the effects of the Bay of Pigs upon American credibility and disturbed at public reports that Khrushchev had browbeaten him at Vienna, Kennedy accepted Dean Acheson's argument that the Berlin issue was a "simple conflict of wills" and that no negotiations could be considered until the Soviets lifted their threat of turning over the access routes to East Germany. This argument refused to touch the Soviet premier's real problems: the growing military power of West Germany, its strengthened ties with the West, its attractiveness to technicians and other experts living in East Germany, the very weak position of the East German communist regime, the position of West Berlin as an espionage and propaganda center within the communist bloc, the growing fear of the Soviet peoples over West Germany's power, and, finally, Khrushchev's realization that with his ICBM braggadocio punctured as only myth, he needed a major strategic victory. Kennedy's reaction came in a national broadcast on July 25, 1961. He asked that National Reserve troops be placed on active duty and announced a dramatic increase of nearly 25 percent in American military strength. His premise was simple. The Berlin "outpost is not an isolated problem. The threat is worldwide," endangering Southeast Asia, "our own hemisphere," and "wherever else the freedom of human beings is at stake," as well as Berlin. That city and Saigon were, in this crucial sense, alike. Kennedy, like Eisenhower, defined the communist threat in global terms.

On August 13 the Soviets suddenly built the Berlin Wall. The flow of young and skilled labor from East Germany to the West stopped, and Khrushchev partly sealed the bloc from Western influences. The United States protested, but the wall stood, a final obstacle to hundreds of East Germans who were shot trying to escape to the West. It was mute and bloody testimony to the policy of both East and West which, since 1945, had preferred a divided rather than a neutralized and united Germany.

The wall had solved one of his problems, at least temporarily, but Khrushchev's supposed strategic power continued to come under attack in the West. In mid-1961 the Defense Department revealed that only a "handful" of Russian ICBMs were operational. Administration officials wondered aloud about Soviet credibility in the military realm. This no doubt made Khrushchev's political situation in Moscow uneasy, a situation already under attack because of the Sino-Soviet split. The division within the communist world had become irreparable by late 1960. Two weeks after the Berlin Wall appeared, Khrushchev broke the three-year Russian-American moratorium on the testing of nuclear bombs by beginning a series of tests which climaxed with the explosion in November of a 58-megaton weapon, 3000 times more powerful than the bomb that had obliterated Hiroshima.

Kennedy responded with underground testing in September 1961, but he remained fully confident that the United States held a wide lead in nuclear weapons capability. Indeed, his National Security Council decided that if it were necessary to break the Soviet "blockage to our access to Berlin," the United States would use "selective nuclear attacks" and, if necessary, escalate to "general nuclear war."[27] The President did attempt to reconvene the Geneva Disarmament Conference, which had been meeting intermittently since 1958. France refused to attend. Having exploded his first nuclear device in September 1960, de Gaulle did not want to be bound by any restraints at this early stage of his career as a nuclear power. The Soviets again refused Western demands for inspection and international control. On April 25, 1962, Kennedy ordered the first of some thirty American tests that occurred during the following year.

The President viewed his first eleven months in office as a period of continual international crisis, and it was in this context that he made two of his most fateful decisions. The first involved Laos. That former French colony was a key to Southeast Asia, for it rimmed

[27]National Security Action memorandum no. 109, October 23, 1961, in *Documents of the National Security Council,* 6th Supplement, reel 9 (University Microfilms of America, Bethesda, Md.)

China, both Vietnams, Cambodia, Thailand, and Burma. When Pathet Lao communist forces began major guerrilla action, the United States stepped up aid until, by April 1961, over 300 American military advisers were in Laos, and the country received $32 million in economic assistance, three times the annual rate of 1955–1959. An army coup and expanding communist control in eastern Laos worsened the situation until the Eisenhower administration had supported a right-wing coup in December 1960. Receiving large amounts of aid from Russia, the Pathet Lao responded by launching a major offensive which, by the Vienna meetings in June, had conquered the eastern half of Laos.

As China began building roads to the Laotian border for its own military power, the Soviets and Americans decided that the war must stop. With the support of Kennedy and Khrushchev, Great Britain and Russia reconvened the Geneva conference members of 1954. The sessions agreed on neutralizing Laos, but the U.S.-supported government of Boun Oum refused to surrender any of its power. The Pathet Lao revived their attacks. Kennedy responded by channeling in American supplies, mobilizing U.S. troops in Thailand after signing a sudden military aid treaty with that country, and, most important, causing Boun Oum's downfall simply by stopping American economic aid. This opened the way for a coalition government to be formed under neutralist Souvanna Phouma in June 1962. Nineteen nations, including China, promised to respect Laotian territorial integrity and sovereignty, and the SEATO powers explicitly excluded Laos from their area of control. It was a tenuous agreement, but a Soviet-American decision to enforce neutralization of a key area had moved Laos outside the torrid zones of the Cold War. "Thank God the Bay of Pigs happened when it did," Kennedy remarked privately. "Otherwise we'd be in Laos by now—and that would be a hundred times worse."[28]

The implications of that remark were not quite accurate, for meanwhile the President was making a pivotal commitment of American power to South Vietnam. The regime of Ngo Dinh Diem had become very unpopular by 1958, for it had stopped agrarian reforms begun by Ho in the countryside, canceled elections, arrested political opponents, and concentrated power in the hands of Diem, his brother, and his brother's wife, Madame Ngo Dinh Nhu. Anti-Diem guerrilla at-

[28]Sorensen, *Kennedy*, p. 644.

tacks stepped up in 1958. Two years later Ho's government in Hanoi acknowledged and encouraged the southern pro-communists by establishing the National Liberation Front (NLF). The American-trained South Vietnamese Army could not handle the guerrillas, but it also disliked Diem and tried unsuccessfully in November 1960 to overthrow the president. The Vietcong guerrillas meanwhile grew in number to nearly 10,000 in 1961, receiving support from the peasants and, for the first time, from Communist China.

With this civil war intensifying, President Kennedy sent Vice President Johnson on a fact-finding mission in May 1961 and followed this with a mission in October headed by General Maxwell Taylor and State Department official Walt Whitman Rostow, a fervent disciple of thwarting communism with guerrilla warfare. The Taylor-Rostow team recommended increasing the number of American military advisers and pledging complete support to Diem. Kennedy faced a momentous decision. Restraining him was the inability and unwillingness of the SEATO nations as a whole to make any major commitment, his knowledge that the Vietnamese situation was extremely complex and could not be divided into simple communist versus anticommunist groups, and his own doubts that the "domino theory" had any validity. He apparently believed that whenever Red China exploded a nuclear bomb, its influence would be dominant in Asia, regardless of what the United States did in Vietnam.[29] Military members of the "Never-Again Club" and some State Department officials, particularly those who gave first priority to European affairs, also warned against any large commitment.

Opposing these views were some of the President's highest advisers, including Vice President Johnson, who, during his trip to Vietnam, had called Diem the "Winston Churchill of Asia" (which Diem unfortunately believed). Johnson warned the President that the United States must make a "fundamental decision ... whether we are to attempt to meet the challenge of Communist expansion now in Southeast Asia ... or throw in the towel."[30] Others argued that this was the opportunity to contain China and that Vietnam's long coastline and apparently stable government provided optimum conditions. Most important, however, the President began to see Vietnam as part of the global communist menace. If the Vietcong were not

---

[29]Arthur Krock, in *The New York Times,* February 14, 1965, p. E9.
[30]Philip Geyelin, *Lyndon B. Johnson and the World* (New York, 1966), pp. 34–40.

SOUTHEAST ASIA, 1971

U.S.S.R.

MONGOLIA

NORTH KOREA

JAPAN

SOUTH KOREA

WEST PAKISTAN

KASHMIR

CHINA

NEPAL

BHUTAN

INDIA

EAST PAKISTAN

Mekong

BURMA

Dienbienphu

NORTH VIETNAM

TAIWAN

PACIFIC OCEAN

LAOS

Hanoi

SOUTH CHINA SEA

Rangoon

Vientiane

GULF OF TONKIN

17th parallel

PHILIPPINES

BAY OF BENGAL

THAILAND

Bangkok

CAMBODIA

Phnompenh

SOUTH VIETNAM

Saigon

Gulf of Thailand

Phnompenh

M A L A Y S I A

Equator

BORNEO

I N D O N E S I A

INDIAN OCEAN

AUSTRALIA

CHINA

NORTH VIETNAM

Hanoi

Dienbienphu

Plain of Jarres

Gulf of Tonkin

LAOS

Vientiane

17th parallel

Ho Chi Minh Trail

Mekong R.

Hue

THAILAND

Bangkok

CAMBODIA

Phnompenh

SOUTH VIETNAM

Saigon

Gulf of Thailand

x   Areas invaded by U.S. and South Vietnam in
    Cambodia, May 1970

▨   Areas invaded by South Vietnam and U.S. in
    Cambodia and Laos, Feb. 1971

stopped, the whole world balance might be upset.[31] Kennedy soon found himself no longer questioning the Eisenhower-Dulles policies he had inherited, including the "domino theory," but adopting them. Kennedy also had more motivation, since abroad (and at home) he was determined to blot out the image given his administration by the Bay of Pigs, the Vienna meetings, and the Berlin Wall. For an administration which prided itself on its "realism," its political pragmatism, and its determination to save the newly emerging nations, which were "the great battleground . . . of freedom," these arguments were irrefutable. The force was already present. The U.S. Pacific Command was a great military power with its 300,000 men, the largest mobile force on the globe (the Seventh Fleet), and logistics problems solved by bases in Okinawa, the Philippines, and Japan.

Within fifteen months following the Taylor-Rostow report, Kennedy expanded the American commitment from 500 to 10,000 men, allowed these "advisers" to engage in combat, ordered U.S. Air Force units to strike Vietminh strongholds in South Vietnam, and promised full support to Diem. The Vietnamese president interpreted this promise to mean that he could intensify his authoritarian methods without worrying about any questions, or a possible pullout, from the American side.[32] The American-Diem forces attempted to secure the countryside with a strategic hamlet program which uprooted and then concentrated peasants in fortified villages.

These decisions were signal and symbolic, for they, like many other policies adopted in 1961 to mid-1962, indicated that the Kennedy administration could not lessen but only intensify Cold War tensions. These policies differed in no important essential from the Eisenhower policies after 1954. The new administration was only much less restrained in carrying them out. When a reporter remarked in the autumn of 1961 that he wanted to write a book about the President's first year in office, Kennedy inquired, "Who would want to read a book about disasters?"[33]

---

[31]Arthur M. Schlesinger, Jr., *A Thousand Days: John F. Kennedy in the White House* (Boston, 1965), p. 548.

[32]David Halberstam, *The Making of a Quagmire* (New York, 1965), pp. 67–69.

[33]Told by Elie Abel, quoted by I. F. Stone in *The New York Review of Books*, April 14, 1966, p. 12.

CHAPTER 10

Southeast Asia—and Elsewhere (1962–1966)

What could have been the greatest of disasters nearly occurred one year later. The Cuban missile crisis, as President Kennedy remarked to Premier Khrushchev, at one moment approached the point "where events could have become unmanageable." This confrontation rechanneled the policies of the United States and the Soviet Union. It affected many facets of world affairs.

The roots of the crisis ran back to Khrushchev's ICBM-oriented foreign policies after 1957 and his intense concern with removing NATO power from West Berlin. By 1962 these policies were related, for the Soviets needed credible strategic force if they hoped to neutralize Western power in Germany. By the spring of 1962, however, high American officials had publicly expressed their skepticism of Soviet missile credibility. President Kennedy further observed in a widely publicized interview that under some circumstances the United States would strike first. In June Defense Secretary McNamara indicated that American missiles were so potent and precise that in a nuclear war they could spare cities and hit only military installations.[1]

Khrushchev and Marshal Rodion Malinovsky angrily responded that, contrary to McNamara's beliefs, cities would be the first victims in any nuclear war. The Soviet premier warned Kennedy against engaging "in sinister competition as to who will be the first to start a war." For the first time in five years, however, Khrushchev emphasized Soviet bomber strength instead of missiles. As for West Berlin,

---

[1]Stewart Alsop, "Kennedy's Grand Strategy," *Saturday Evening Post*, March 31, 1962, p. 14; Richard P. Stebbins, ed., *Documents on American Foreign Relations, 1962* (New York 1963), pp. 232–233.

the building of the wall and Kennedy's quick military buildup in 1961 had quieted Khrushchev's demands.

In the summer of 1962 Khrushchev moved to regain the initiative in the strategic realm. In late August an American U-2 reconnaissance plane flying fourteen miles above Cuba reported the first Soviet surface-to-air missile site (see map, p. 207). Forty-two Russian medium bombers were next observed on Castro's airstrips. On September 19, 1962, U.S. intelligence, in an official estimate, assured the President that the Soviets had not tried, and would not try, to install nuclear-headed missiles ninety miles from the American coast. As late as October 14, 1962, U.S. officials expressed disbelief publicly that the two communist leaders would emplace offensive ground-to-ground missiles—especially after Kennedy had expressly warned Moscow about this the month before. The disbelief was also based on Khrushchev's assurances that he would not jiggle East-West relations during the volatile U.S. election campaign of 1962.

The Soviet leader, however, was secretly moving not one, but two types of nuclear weapons into Cuba. According to later Soviet testimony Khrushchev risked nuclear war for several reasons. First, as he told his ambassador to Cuba, Aleksandr Alekseyev, the United States was planning to invade Cuba again, this time not with mercenaries, as at the Bay of Pigs, but "with its own armed forces." Second, "Since the Americans have already surrounded the Soviet Union with a ring of their military bases and various types of missile launchers, we must pay them back in their own coin . . . so they will know what it feels like to live in the sights of nuclear weapons." No opposition to Khrushchev's gamble appeared among his top advisers. In June 1962 Raul Castro, Fidel's brother and head of Cuba's armed forces, flew to Moscow and worked out details. Four months later, on October 16, Kennedy received the first photographs, taken by a U-2 plane, showing a launchpad under construction that could fire nuclear missiles 1000 miles. Several days later a site for weapons with a 2200-mile capability was photographed.[2]

The President was in a delicate political situation. For weeks some Republicans had warned of threatening Soviet moves in Cuba. These warnings, plus the frustrations which Castro was causing many

[2]Foreign Broadcast Information Service (FBIS), Daily Report Annex: Soviet Union, January 17, 1989, pp. 6–11; Dino A. Brugioni, *Eyeball to Eyeball* (New York, 1992) on the U-2, especially pp. 181–220, 276–277.

Americans, created in the early autumn what one acute observer called "a war party" which demanded military action against Cuba.[3] The elections were less than three weeks away. In this pressure tank a special committee (the EXCOM) of top administration officials began virtual round-the-clock meetings to consider a response to the Soviets. The alternatives narrowed down to a blockade or an air strike against the missile sites. Dean Acheson (especially invited back out of retirement by Kennedy) and General Maxwell Taylor, along with the Joint Chiefs of Staff, argued vigorously for the air strike, even though they knew that such an attack would probably kill Soviet technicians working on the sites. Other officials changed their minds several times in the course of five days of secret discussions, but Under Secretary of State George Ball slowly won support for a blockade. (As Ball later phrased it, he opposed a "surgical air strike" that the military proposed because he had closely studied U.S. bombing in the Second World War and was amazed at its inaccuracy. He "concluded from the record of Allied bombing in Europe that if the medical profession should ever adopt the air force definition of 'surgical,' anyone undergoing an operation for appendicitis might lose his kidneys and lungs yet find the appendix intact.") McNamara supported Ball with the argument that, if the blockade failed, the air strike could then be ordered. Acheson so strongly opposed the final decision merely to blockade that the crusty Cold Warrior resigned from EXCOM.[4]

At 7 P.M. on October 22, the President broke the well-kept secret to the American people. Because the Soviets were building bases in Cuba "to provide a nuclear strike capability against the Western Hemisphere," Kennedy announced, the United States was imposing "a strict quarantine on all offensive military equipment" being shipped into Cuba. American military forces, he added, were on full alert, and the United States would "regard any nuclear missile launched from Cuba against any nation in the Western Hemisphere as an attack by the Soviet Union on the United States, requiring a full retaliatory response upon the Soviet Union." He appealed to Khrushchev to remove the offensive weapons under UN supervision.

[3]Richard H. Rovere, "Letter From Washington," *New Yorker*, October 6, 1962, pp. 148–157.
[4]George Ball, "JFK's Big Moment," *New York Review of Books*, February 13, 1992, p. 18; Elie Abel, *The Missile Crisis* (Philadelphia, 1966), pp. 63–64, 70, 81, 88, 118–119.

A terrified world, as well as U.S. and Soviet nuclear forces, went on a full alert. Three days into the crisis, however, Russian ships headed for Cuba began to turn around. They were not going to challenge the blockade. Other Soviet vessels offered no opposition when U.S. warships stopped and searched them for missile parts. A break appeared on October 26 when Khrushchev, in a rambling letter, offered removal of the missiles in return for a U.S. pledge not to invade Cuba. The next day, however, the crisis again escalated when a Soviet officer in Cuba shot down a U-2 plane and killed its pilot. That same day (October 27) Khrushchev seemed to raise the stakes: he demanded the dismantling of American short-range Jupiter missiles in Turkey. EXCOM was now worn down by ten days of the most intense pressures. "I saw first-hand," Theodore Sorensen recalled, "how brutally physical and mental fatigue can numb the good sense as well as the senses of normally articulate men."[5] The EXCOM began to plan for a military strike the following week to destroy the missile sites before they became operational. Invasion preparations were also accelerated. But the President, at his brother's suggestion, first made the crucial decision to bypass the second Khrushchev letter and accept the more moderate first note. He also secretly dispatched his brother to tell a Soviet official in Washington that the order had gone out months earlier (as it had) to remove the outdated and unneeded Jupiters from Turkey. Khrushchev was receptive, not least because he had information that U.S. bombing of Cuba could begin in three to four days. On October 28, as U.S. officials prepared to strike the island on October 30, Khrushchev accepted Kennedy's offer.[6]

The crisis, however, was not over. Khrushchev made the decision to withdraw the missiles without consulting Castro. He knew that if he did, the Cuban leader would not agree and could delay a deal until it was too late to stop a military exchange. A furious Castro therefore refused to allow UN inspectors into his country to observe the missiles' dismantling, as Kennedy had required, and then refused to return Soviet long-range bombers. U.S. forces remained on highest alert until November 20, 1962, when Castro finally returned the bombers. Meanwhile Kennedy toughened his position. Contrary to what was believed then and for the next quarter century, the President did not

[5]Theodore Sorensen, *Decision-Making in the White House* (New York, 1963), p. 76.
[6]FBIS, January 17, 1989, pp. 8–10; *Documents on American Foreign Relations, 1962*, pp. 392–404.

give ironclad assurance that the United States would not invade Cuba. Instead, in a letter to Khrushchev on December 14, 1962, Kennedy wrote that his no-invasion pledge depended on two conditions: the final removal of "all offensive weapons" from Cuba, and the assurance "that Cuba itself commits no aggressive acts against any of the nations of the Western Hemisphere." The second part was a major loophole. It was not known publicly until the letter was declassified in 1992. Had it been known in the 1970s and 1980s when leftist revolutions erupted in Central America, there could have been loud demands heard in the United States to destroy Castro.[7]

The Soviets made an even more stunning revelation when they released information in 1991–1992. Kennedy's EXCOM had believed no nuclear warheads had been placed on the missiles in Cuba; they indeed had planned an air strike for October 30 before, they believed, such nuclear tips could be installed. Soviet officials later revealed, however, that forty-two intermediate-range missiles with warheads were in place during the crisis. Able to obliterate U.S. cities up to the Canadian border, they were guarded by 40,000 Soviet troops. Equally ominous, there were nine short-range nuclear missiles ready to be used against an American invasion. The EXCOM had known nothing about these warheads. A shaken Robert McNamara declared in 1992 after he learned this information, "This is horrifying. It meant that had a U.S. invasion been carried out . . . there was a 99 percent probability that nuclear war would have been initiated." McNamara added, "The actions of all three parties were shaped by misjudgment, miscalculations, and misinformation."[8]

The aftershocks of the near-tragedy rippled on. The possible horrors of nuclear war overhung the lifetime of the generation that lived through those days of October 1962. (Another generation was reliving them in the 1990s as new "horrifying"—to use McNamara's word—information emerged revealing the proliferation of nuclear weapons to unstable nations in the Middle East, such as Iraq, and South Asia.) Immediately after the crisis, Khrushchev began to try to prevent another such confrontation. Now that the "burning flames of thermonuclear war" had been "felt more tangibly," he told Kennedy, it was time to sign a nonaggression pact and prepare to break up the

---

[7]Anatoly Dobrynin, *In Confidence* (New York, 1995), p. 73; *Washington Post*, January 7, 1992, p. A12; *New York Times*, January 7, 1992, p. A5.
[8]*New York Times*, January 15, 1992, p. A11; *Washington Post*, January 14, 1992, p. A1.

U.S. and Soviet blocs. The President was not interested in moving that rapidly, but he responded more favorably in December when Khrushchev made the first offer in Russian history to have "2–3 inspections a year" of possible Soviet nuclear test sites.[9]

That offer opened the way to the historic nuclear test ban of 1963. In the summer of 1963 the United States and the Soviet Union negotiated and signed their first agreement to limit the arms race by prohibiting aboveground nuclear testing. These 1962–1963 events intensely angered the Chinese and widened the Sino-Russian split to the edge of a complete break. The Chinese called Khrushchev foolish for putting the missiles into Cuba and cowardly for removing them. They feared the growing cooperation between Moscow and Washington and ridiculed the less militant Soviet policy. The Chinese continued to believe that Americans were "paper tigers"; Khrushchev said such a characterization was "dung."

The crisis had not enhanced the Soviet leader's personal power within the communist bloc. His decline, combined with the Sino-Soviet breach and the warmer East-West relations, opened new opportunities for the satellites in Eastern Europe to regain more autonomy. Some competent observers believed that the fear of Germany, as much as Russian control, kept the Warsaw Pact nations together. Certainly no generalization could fit the spectrum of intellectual freedom which stretched from Poland's liberalism to Albania's Stalinism, the agricultural collectivization which was almost total in Russia but declining in Poland and Yugoslavia, the use of terror which was manifest in Czechoslovakia but little evidenced in Poland, or the ideological framework which was rigidly dogmatic in Albania but quite loose in Yugoslavia and Poland.[10] By 1963 anyone who talked about a monolithic communist threat was discussing a world that no longer existed.

In contrast to Khrushchev's decline, President Kennedy emerged from the missile crisis with new support and political charisma. His own conception of this power was exemplified at American University in Washington, D.C., on June 10, 1963. There Kennedy spoke of peace "as the necessary rational end of rational men" and dramati-

---

[9]*Washington Post,* January 7, 1992, p. A12.
[10]H. Gordon Skilling, "National Communism in Eastern Europe Since the 22nd Congress," *Canadian Journal of Economics and Political Science,* XXX (August 1964): 313–327; *New York Times,* January 22, 1992, p. A3.

cally appealed to the Soviets to seek a relaxation of tensions. This speech sped the negotiations of the nuclear test ban treaty, a pact which Kennedy then drove through the Senate over the strong opposition of American military officials and a few scientists led by Edward Teller of the University of California.[11]

The new warmth toward Russia did not improve the NATO alliance. De Gaulle and Adenauer had been angered when Kennedy offered to negotiate bilaterally with the Soviets over Berlin in August 1961, and when the United States twice rejected (in August 1961 and January 1962) de Gaulle's pleas for establishing a joint directorate for military strategy. These rejections reaffirmed the French determination to build an independent nuclear power. De Gaulle viewed the British application for admission to the Common Market in 1961–1962 as the stalking horse of American economic and political power. The French pondered Kennedy's July 4, 1962, speech, which urged Europe to join in a "declaration of interdependence," but which pointedly omitted any mention of possible nuclear sharing. This speech, together with American trade legislation that allowed large reciprocal cuts in tariffs, indicated that the United States sought increased economic leverage in Europe. De Gaulle's mistrust intensified during the missile crisis, when Acheson flew to Paris to "inform," not "consult" (the words were de Gaulle's) the French on the confrontation. The French president fully supported Kennedy, but the episode convinced Paris officials that the United States would involve them in a nuclear war without consulting them beforehand.

De Gaulle's views were confirmed at the conference between Kennedy and British Prime Minister Harold Macmillan at Nassau in December. The United States unilaterally canceled its development of the Skybolt missile on which the British had hoped to base their nuclear striking force. Instead Kennedy offered nuclear submarine and warhead information to Macmillan. The President pointedly did not make a similar offer to France. In January de Gaulle dramatically announced that he would veto the British entry into the Common Market. He explained that Great Britain had nitpicked for sixteen months of negotiations in an effort to bend the Common Market to British interests but had surrendered control of its own defense to the United States in a mere forty-eight hours at Nassau. De Gaulle, how-

[11]U.S. Senate, Committee on Foreign Relations, 88th Cong. 1st Sess., *Nuclear Test Ban Treaty* (Washington, 1963), pp. 422–423, 427.

ever, had made this decision for a more fundamental reason. He feared that if Great Britain entered the European Economic Community, "the end would be a colossal Atlantic Community dependent on America and directed by America, which would not take long to absorb this European Community." Shortly afterward a Franco-German friendship treaty was signed, which de Gaulle hoped would be the axis for an independent European diplomacy.

De Gaulle correctly believed that in the wake of the missile crisis East-West tensions would ease; in the long run a united Europe led by France would be able to influence international diplomacy if that Europe was free of both Russian and American control and if France had its own nuclear power. He also feared unchecked American military and economic power, believing that, because the United States would use the power unilaterally and irresponsibly, the French could suffer annihilation without representation.

The missile crisis did not advance Kennedy's "Grand Design" for Europe, but it tragically accelerated the American rush into Vietnam. Key Washington policymakers assumed that the one result of the October confrontation was a nuclear standoff between the two superpowers. Both had clearly indicated their reluctance to use nuclear force. The United States had won primarily because Khrushchev unwisely challenged Kennedy in the Caribbean, where American conventional naval power was decisive. Within months both sides were discussing the easing of Cold War tensions. If the assumption was correct that the two great powers mutually feared each other's nuclear arms, then, the Kennedy administration concluded, the leaders of the emerging nations might feel that they had considerable opportunity to play West versus East, or, as in Southeast Asia and Africa, to undertake revolutionary changes without fear that either the United States or Russia would be able to shape these changes. If nationalist leaders acted on these beliefs, the newly emerging world could become increasingly unmanageable, perhaps dangerously radical from Washington's point of view.[12] Such a view meshed perfectly with the other American fear that the communist policy line of support for (but

[12]The best analysis is Walt Whitman Rostow, "Domestic Determinants of U.S. Foreign Policy; The Tocqueville Oscillation," *Armed Forces Journal*, June 27, 1970, pp. 16D–16E; see also Rostow's *From the Seventh Floor* (New York, 1964).

not direct involvement in) "wars of liberation" had been established in 1960–1961 precisely to exploit the emerging nationalisms. The New Frontiersmen dedicated themselves to shattering "wars of liberation" within such nationalist movements. Vietnam would be used as the example.

The President also focused on Southeast Asia because he hoped to discipline what he believed to be the expansiveness of Communist China. In 1949–1950 Kennedy, then a member of the House of Representatives, had joined Republicans in denouncing the Truman administration for supposedly "losing" China. He softened these views during the 1950s, but in preparing to run for the presidency in 1960 he was reluctant to consider disavowing the use of nuclear weapons: "I wonder if we could expect to check the sweep south of the Chinese with their endless armies with conventional forces?"[13] After the missile crisis, Kennedy summarized his position in a conversation with André Malraux, French cultural affairs minister. Assistant Secretary of State for European Affairs William R. Tyler described this talk:

> [Kennedy] wanted to get a message to de Gaulle through Malraux . . . that really there was no reason why there should be differences between us and France in Europe, or between us and our European Allies, because there was no longer a likely Soviet military threat against Europe [since the Cuban missile crisis]. . . . But the area where we would have problems in the future . . . was China. He said it was so important that he and de Gaulle and other European leaders should think together about what they will do, what the situation will be when China becomes a nuclear power, what will happen then. . . . This was the great menace in the future to humanity, the free world, and freedom on earth. Relations with the Soviet Union could be contained within the framework of mutual awareness of the impossibility of achieving any gains through war. But in the case of China, this restraint would not be effective because the Chinese would be perfectly prepared, because of the lower value they attach to human life, to sacrifice hundreds of millions of their own lives, if this were necessary in order to carry out their militant and aggressive policies.[14]

---

[13]Kennedy to George Kennan, January 21, 1960, Oral History Interview with Mr. Kennan, March 23, 1964, Kennedy Library. Used by permission.
[14]Oral History Interview with William R. Tyler, March 7, 1964, Kennedy Library; and Mr. Tyler to author, December 10, 1971.

The missile crisis and the Berlin confrontation in 1961 also reinforced the administration's belief that it knew how to threaten to apply or, if necessary, actually apply conventional military power to obtain maximum results. White House officials joked that poor John Foster Dulles had never been able to find a suitable war for his "massive retaliation"; these pragmatic Kennedyites, however, had apparently solved the great riddle by perfectly matching power to crisis. One false premise ultimately wrecked this self-satisfaction: in Berlin and Cuba the Russians had backed down (Castro, noticeably, had been willing to fight to keep the missiles); in Vietnam the United States dealt with nationalist Vietnamese who, like Castro, had much to win by continuing to fight against apparently overwhelming American firepower.[15]

This fatal flaw did not clearly appear in 1962–1966. On the contrary, during the autumn of 1962 the President's policies seemed to be proved correct during the brief war between India and China. India provoked the war during a border dispute over territory more important to the Chinese than to the Indians. The Chinese attacked with devastating force, destroying both the myth of Indian power and the American hope that India could serve as a cornerstone in the containment of China. The Chinese carefully occupied only some of the disputed territory, voluntarily withdrawing from other conquered areas. On November 20 Prime Minister Nehru urgently asked Kennedy for aid. An American aircraft carrier moved across the southern Pacific toward India, but before it could become a factor, the crisis ended.[16] Some Washington policymakers nevertheless drew the false conclusion that the Chinese had backed down only after receiving warnings from the United States and, independently of the American move, from Russia.

Kennedy's advisers displayed similarly unwarranted confidence in their ability to control power in late 1962 when they decided to turn Laos into a pro-American bastion. They thereby helped destroy the Geneva Agreements which the United States had solemnly signed in midsummer 1962. Under the agreements, all foreign troops were to withdraw from Laos. The communist Pathet Lao were to join neu-

[15]David Halberstam, "The Programming of Robert McNamara," *Harper's*, February 1971, p. 68.
[16]Allen Whiting's review of Neville Maxwell's *India's China War* in *Washington Post*, May 25, 1971, p. B6.

tralist Souvanna Phouma's coalition government. American military advisers, indeed, began to leave, but the Central Intelligence Agency stepped up the supplying of the Meo tribesmen, an effective guerrilla army operating behind Pathet Lao lines.

In April 1964, however, a right-wing coup in Vientiane made Souvanna only a figurehead leader. The Pathet Lao retaliated with an offensive that threatened to conquer the entire Plain of Jarres. The United States then began initially small but systematic bombing raids on Laos, which Washington carefully tried to keep secret. To save a supposedly pivotal domino, the Kennedy-Johnson advisers confidently escalated their application of power.[17] The result, however, was that at the very time the United States escalated its commitment to South Vietnam, the key area of Laos became uncontrollable and formed an open channel for aid to the National Liberation Front in South Vietnam.

In 1962–1963 the assumptions that would govern American policies in Vietnam fell into place. First, Vietnam was vital to American interests because, in John F. Kennedy's words of 1956, "Vietnam represents the cornerstone of the Free World in Southeast Asia, the keystone to the arch, the finger in the dike. . . . Her economy is essential to the economy of all of Southeast Asia; and her political liberty is an inspiration to those seeking to obtain or maintain their liberty in all parts of Asia—and indeed the world."[18] As Kennedy emphasized in his May 25, 1961, address to Congress, the battle of "freedom versus tyranny" was being waged in newly emerging areas such as Vietnam. While belittling the foreign policies of the previous administration, the Kennedy advisers gulped down whole the Eisenhower "domino theory." More precisely, the Dulles and Eisenhower formulation of the 1950s remained valid because, without an open Southeast Asia for its raw materials and markets, Japan, essential to the entire American strategic policy in the western Pacific, would have to turn toward its traditional market of China.

Second, the Kennedy administration assumed that China was to be not only isolated but, as some thought it had been in India, militarily disciplined. Both the Chinese and the Russians were to be taught that "wars of liberation" were not possible in areas the United States

---

[17]D. Gareth Porter, "After Geneva: Subverting Laotian Neutrality." In Nina S. Adams and Alfred W. McCoy, eds., *Laos: War and Revolution* (New York, 1970), pp. 179–212.

[18]Quoted in Chester Cooper, *Lost Crusade* (New York, 1970), p. 168.

considered vital to its interests. Third, the missile crisis, the India-China conflict, and the emerging Laotian situation gave the administration confidence in its ability to escalate military power while keeping it under control. Because of McNamara's work, moreover, the military power was available. For the first time in their history, Americans entered war with a great army at the ready, a force created by self-styled "realists" who, in the tradition of Forrestal and Acheson, believed that they could ultimately shape world affairs with American firepower.

These assumptions—the validity of the "domino theory" (particularly its economic implications for Japan), the century-old American fear of the "Yellow Peril," and the belief held by American liberal spokesmen that, as children of Niebuhr, they knew the secrets of using military force effectively—these governed the Kennedy administration as it moved deeper into Vietnam.

In 1962 Secretary of Defense McNamara had observed, "Every quantitative measurement we have shows we're winning this war."[19] Some factors in Southeast Asia, however, could not be computed. Twelve thousand American military personnel were involved in the conflict, yet the Vietminh continued to gain ground. The strategic hamlet program, geared to secure the countryside, was failing despite, or perhaps because of, the determination of the Diem regime. The peasants disliked being forced to leave their homes and to resettle elsewhere, particularly by a government that had condemned any meaningful land reform program. "No wonder the [Vietminh] looked like Robin Hoods when they began to hit the hamlets," one civilian American official remarked.[20] Vietminh successes mounted despite their kidnapping and brutal murdering of village and hamlet officials.

Kennedy's hope of reversing the situation rested on the ability of Diem's government to wage a successful military campaign while stabilizing South Vietnam's political situation. Saigon's military capability was dramatically called into question on January 2, 1963, in the village of Ap Bac, approximately fifty miles from Saigon. A small Vietminh force was surrounded by a Vietnamese unit that was ten times larger, but despite the demands of American advisers to attack, the South Vietnamese refused. The Vietminh then methodically shot down five American helicopters, damaged nine more, killed three

[19]Arthur M. Schlesinger, Jr., *A Thousand Days* (Boston, 1965), p. 549.
[20]David Halberstam, *The Making of a Quagmire* (New York, 1965), pp. 186–187.

Americans, and disappeared. Apparently only U.S. soldiers had the will to fight in Vietnam, but Kennedy carefully pointed out after one firefight between Vietminh and American personnel that the U.S. forces in Vietnam were not "combat troops," and that if the situation changed, "I, of course, would go to Congress."[21] He was not prepared to do this in 1963. Nor was the White House even prepared to inform adequately the Congress and the public.

With an American presidential election little more than a year away, and his own belief that in 1964 his main challenge would come from the right wing of American politics, Kennedy carefully threw the best possible, even if misleading, light on Vietnamese affairs. American newspaper correspondents who candidly reported Diem's failures were rewarded either with Kennedy's unsuccessful attempt to give one critical correspondent a "vacation" from Vietnam, or with rejoinders to their questions like the one given by Admiral Harry Felt, commander of American forces in the Pacific: "Why don't you get on the team?"[22] In 1963 there was a widening abyss between the actual situation in Vietnam and the self-assurance of the Kennedy administration that it could manipulate military power to control nationalist revolutions.[23]

By late summer 1963 the abyss was so wide that it could no longer be covered. Throughout the early part of the year, Diem, with the assistance of his brother Nhu Dinh Diem and Madame Nhu, ruthlessly suppressed domestic opposition. When Washington protested the Nhus' activities, Diem and his brother openly objected to this pressure. The beginning of the end for Diem and Nhu occurred on May 8, when Diem's troops shot into a crowd of Buddhists who were celebrating Buddha's birthday by waving religious flags, thereby violating the regime's rule that forbade the exhibit of any banner but the government's. The firing climaxed years of bitterness between the Roman Catholic regime of Diem and the Buddhists, who comprised more than 80 percent of the country's population. Many Buddhist leaders wanted no part of the war, no part of any foreign intervention in their nation, and no part of the Diem regime. They represented a new, potentially radical nationalism that neither the Diem regime

---

[21]Cooper, *Lost Crusade,* pp. 193–194; also in U.S. Government, *Public Papers of the Presidents . . . Kennedy, 1962* (Washington, 1963), p. 228.
[22]Halberstam, *Making of a Quagmire,* p. 72.
[23]James Aronson, *The Press and the Cold War* (New York, 1970), pp. 182–183.

nor the American officials in Vietnam could understand, let alone cope with. In June Buddhist-led antigovernment riots spread through Saigon. Diem retaliated by raiding Buddhist pagodas. Several Buddhists burned themselves to death in public protest, an act that Madame Nhu sarcastically welcomed as a "barbecue show." Students in normally quiet schools and universities joined the Buddhists. Diem confronted a full-scale rebellion.

The Kennedy administration's confusion in dealing with the revolutionary situation became glaringly evident during the crisis.[24] While continuing to announce that the military program was going well, the White House attempted to push Diem into making necessary domestic reforms by cutting off relatively small amounts of military and economic aid. That move, however, was sufficient to encourage anti-Diem elements in the army. On November 1 and 2, with, at least, the knowledge and approval of the White House and the American ambassador in Saigon, Henry Cabot Lodge, a military junta captured Diem and his brother.[25] Within hours the two men were shot and the junta assumed power. Three weeks later President Kennedy was assassinated in Dallas, Texas.

President Lyndon B. Johnson inherited a set of badly decomposed foreign policies. In the last weeks of his life, Kennedy had said that the war was for the Vietnamese to win or lose. But the American consent given for Diem's overthrow, and the administration's full commitment to fighting what were intended to be limited wars with the conventional forces that Kennedy had so painstakingly devel-

[24]*The Pentagon Papers,* as published by *The New York Times* (New York, 1971), pp. 163–177, 191–196. *The Pentagon Papers* is a condensed version of a massive study of Defense Department documents on the involvement in Vietnam. Commissioned by Secretary McNamara as a secret analysis, the larger study was written and compiled by three dozen experts and finally covered 3000 pages of analyses and 4000 pages of supporting documents. The shorter *Pentagon Papers* is crucial and revealing, but it should be used carefully because it contains little from either State Department or presidential files. See especially, George Kahin, "*The Pentagon Papers:* A Critical Evaluation," *American Political Science Review,* LXIX (June 1975): 675–684.

[25]*The Pentagon Papers,* pp. 158–159, 215–232, especially Lodge to Bundy, October 30, 1963, No. 57, pp. 226–229. This interpretation is supported with evidence found later and collected in Anne E. Blair's analysis, *Lodge in Vietnam* (New Haven, Conn., 1995), pp. 63–75.

oped, indicated that the United States would, if necessary, become further involved in Southeast Asia. Certainly Kennedy would have done nothing to change radically the American involvement until after the 1964 elections. By then he might have been unable to throw four years of policy suddenly into reverse. In Europe the administration's "Grand Design" was coming apart piece by piece, allowing de Gaulle to assume the leadership in the Western European community. The Alliance for Progress was crumbling, the victim of the false assumption that enough money and bureaucratic technicians could tinker with and adjust the dynamic nationalisms of an economically unbalanced Latin America to the policy objectives of a prosperous, satisfied, and expanding United States.

As these policies encountered the inevitable obstacles, bitter infighting appeared among Washington officials. The White House staff blamed the State Department for not having sufficient imagination and initiative to solve important diplomatic problems. Two talented biographers of Kennedy who were on the White House staff, Theodore Sorensen and Arthur Schlesinger, Jr., wrote their histories from this point of view. Their interpretation was questionable, for it glossed over several points. For example, there was no indication that President Kennedy and Secretary of State Dean Rusk differed on fundamental points of policy. This is important, for Kennedy must have appointed, and kept, this key official in the full knowledge that Rusk, having served under Dean Acheson and Robert Lovett, accepted the military-oriented policies that those two officials had followed. Rusk had also been assistant secretary of state for Far Eastern affairs during the Korean conflict. It did not require Kennedy's acute perception to conclude that Rusk, like the President himself, might have an uncommon commitment to building positions of military strength around the periphery of China. Consequently, the Kennedy administration bequeathed to Lyndon Johnson not only deteriorating foreign policies along with the test ban but also, much to Johnson's discomfort, the over-powering image and somber rhetoric of the fallen President.

The new Chief Executive's first important diplomatic pronouncement explained that he would continue his predecessor's Vietnam policies. The policies that followed, as well as the style with which they were carried out, could be understood in terms of the President's own history and resulting world view. A sharp British official caught several of Johnson's important traits:

In view of the proximity of the Presidential election, and the urgency of the outstanding problems of Civil Rights and taxation, he will have to devote most of his time and energy to domestic affairs. In foreign affairs he is relatively inexperienced. . . . He speaks a language that Mr. Khrushchev understands, and his ability to hammer out a compromise may in time stand the West in good stead. Despite his desire for social reform, he has firm ideas about the pre-excellence of the American Way of Life, and tends to regard it as the only possible form of democracy.[26]

Lyndon Johnson's administration marked the point at which the historical legacies of Woodrow Wilson, Franklin D. Roosevelt, and the American frontier merged in the 1960s. Wilson believed that the American mission was to extend individual liberties throughout the world, but not out of altruism; it grew out of the belief that American liberties could not long exist at home unless the world was made safe for democracy. The basis of liberty at home was found in the economic system, for, as Wilson once observed, without "freedom of enterprise there can be no freedom whatsoever." Lyndon Johnson's own version was that "the very basis of a great nation is an educated mind, a healthy body, and a free enterprise system." With this established, the President could repeat time after time during the 1964 campaign, "Our cause has been the cause of all mankind." Whether the American system could work as well in the boiler houses of newly emerging nations as it had during its 300-year growth, and several mutations, in the United States was not discussed by the President. He simply moved to the conclusion: "Woodrow Wilson once said: 'I hope we shall never forget that we created this nation, not to serve ourselves, but to serve mankind.' "[27]

Emerging as a national political figure during the 1930s, and further developing the New Deal's domestic programs in the 1950s as the most powerful Senate leader in history, Johnson understood that even a well-functioning free enterprise system needed frequent governmental injections to provide balance and some economic justice. The New Deal, for example, had developed a previously poverty-stricken region of the United States through the Tennessee Valley

[26]F. O. Minute by J. L. N. O'Laughlin, December 2, 1963, FO371AU1012/5, Public Record Office; *The Pentagon Papers*, pp. 232–233.
[27]The Johnson quotes are cited from *The New York Times*, June 28, 1967, p. 24; and *Public Papers of the Presidents, 1964*, pp. 1242, 1103.

Authority's electrical-power system in the 1930s. "The over-riding rule which I want to affirm," the President remarked in Denver in 1966, "is that our foreign policy must always be an extension of our domestic policy. Our safest guide to what we do abroad is always what we do at home." This concern was easily translated to Vietnam: "I want to leave the footprints of America there. I want them to say, 'This is what the Americans left—schools and hospitals and dams....' We can turn the Mekong [River area] into a Tennessee Valley."[28] The role of the government, therefore, both in the United States and Vietnam, was first to clear away the obstacles (the unenlightened American businessman in the 1930s, the Vietnamese communist in the 1960s), build the infrastructure (the Tennessee Valley and the Great Society at home, the Mekong Valley projects in Vietnam), and then let free enterprise develop the resources, and therefore the freedoms, of the areas.

Johnson had an equally simple view of how this was to be accomplished, a view formed when he grew up in the frontierlike region of central Texas. His incredible ambition and energy exploited the opportunities of Texas and Washington, D.C., until he was privately wealthy and politically supreme. He had risen by making sharp distinctions between friends and enemies. "We are not a formal people," he observed in 1965. "We are not a people so much concerned with the way things are done as by the results that we achieve. Since the frontier really opened we have been this way." This remark, perilously close to an end-justifies-the-means point of view, could serve as a rationalization for both the Kennedy and Johnson conduct of the Vietnamese conflict. After all, as the President declared in 1965, "America wins the wars that she undertakes. Make no mistake about it." If the struggle became difficult, Johnson could again use the development of the American frontier as an example to reassure Americans that not they but a more inexorable power put them into Vietnam: "We had the good fortune to grow from a handful of isolated colonies to a position of great responsibility in the world. We did not deliberately seek this position; in a real sense the force of history

[28]This theme and its tragic implications are spelled out in the important study by Lloyd C. Gardner, *Pay Any Price: Lyndon Johnson and the Wars for Vietnam* (Chicago, 1995), especially chapters 1–3 and 9–11. *The New York Times,* August 27, 1966, p. 10; Interview with Henry Graff in *The New York Times Magazine,* March 20, 1966, p. 133.

shaped it for us."[29] History during the 1960s became a political tool to wield rather than a burden requiring understanding and humility.

Given this vision of American history, the President determined he must do nothing less than create a Great Society at home and wage the Cold War abroad. He demanded consensus for these objectives: "We cannot keep what we have and we cannot preserve the brightening flame of hope for others unless we are all—repeat *all* committed; all—repeat *all* willing to sacrifice and to serve wherever we can, whether it be in Vietnam, whether it be at home." Johnson justified using the widest possible presidential powers in foreign policy to shape this consensus. For there was the other side of the coin if Americans did not "sacrifice": "There are 3 billion people in the world and we have only 200 million of them. We are outnumbered 15 to 1. If might did make right they would sweep over the United States and take what we have. We have what they want."[30] Given such a world view, if discontent appeared at home the dissenters too quickly could be labeled "appeasers" of the "Munich variety"; national press and television could justifiably be manipulated; and policies could be acquitted by the latest poll, pulled from a coat pocket, which demonstrated through apparently incontrovertible quantitative data that "body count" indicated the war was being won in Vietnam and consensus reigned at home.

Johnson's policies in Vietnam were not aberrations but the culmination of nearly three-quarters of a century of American foreign policy. He only presented those policies—and their consequences—more starkly than had his predecessors. In this sense his continuation of Kennedy's approach to Vietnam was natural, but, like the New Frontier, the Great Society's hope for military-imposed stability in Southeast Asia soon vanished. Saigon politics were in chaos. Seven different governments rose to power in South Vietnam during 1964, three during the weeks of August 16 to September 3 alone. This was the struggle within the civil war.

Nor was the civil war itself abating. State Department Director of Intelligence Thomas Hughes remarked on June 8, 1964, that "by far the greater part of the Vietcong forces in South Vietnam are South Vietnamese, the preponderance of Vietcong weapons come not from

[29]*Public Papers of the Presidents, 1965,* pp. 770, 821; *Public Papers of the Presidents, 1966,* p. 984.
[30]*Public Papers of the Presidents, 1964,* p. 1640; *Public Papers of the Presidents, 1966,* p. 1287.

Communist countries but from capture, purchase, and local manufacture."[31] In such a civil war the United States could not find sufficient leverage to roll back the National Liberation Front. When Hanoi offered to negotiate in August 1964, the United States consequently rejected the proposal. U.S. officials argued fifteen months later, when the offer was finally revealed, that Ho Chi Minh was not serious about making an equitable settlement and that the military situation at the time gravely weakened the American negotiating position. The presidential campaign in the United States may also have been a factor. Johnson did not want to be open to the charge of appeasement, particularly when his Republican opponent, former Senator Barry Goldwater of Arizona, urged a "Let's Win" policy of total military victory.

The war entered a new phase on August 2, 1964, when North Vietnamese torpedo boats attacked the American destroyer *Maddox* in the Gulf of Tonkin. Bounded by North Vietnam and China, the gulf was a sensitive strategic area. Despite American warnings and the reinforcement of the fleet, the attack was apparently repeated on August 4. Hanoi claimed that the American ships had been participating in South Vietnamese raids on two North Vietnamese shore areas. *The New York Times* also reported that the destroyers had collaborated with South Vietnamese commando raids.[32] President Johnson, however, interpreted the attack as "open aggression on the high seas," adding in an ironic historical prophecy, "We Americans know, although others appear to forget, the risk of spreading conflict." He insisted that "the attacks were unprovoked."[33] Without consulting NATO or SEATO allies or the U.S. Congress, the President ordered the first American air attack on North Vietnamese ports in retaliation.

Four years later in congressional hearings, Secretary McNamara admitted that the American warships attacked in the gulf had been cooperating with South Vietnamese forays against North Vietnam. Since February 1964 the United States had developed a program of clandestine attacks on North Vietnam. Termed 34A, these operations included parachuting sabotage teams, commando raids, and the bombardment of coastal installations. As the Saigon political situation deteriorated, these raids were stepped up, although the administra

[31]Quoted in Philip L. Geyelin, *Lyndon B. Johnson and the World* (New York, 1966), p. 193.
[32]*The New York Times*, August 5, 1964, p. 4; and August 4, 1964, p. 2.
[33]*Public Papers of the Presidents, 1964*, p. 928.

tion concealed them from Congress. This evidence contradicted Mc-Namara's statement of August 6, 1964: "Our Navy played absolutely no part in, was not associated with, was not aware of, any South Vietnamese actions, if there were any."[34]

The truth, however, appeared much too late to prevent Congress from making one of its worst foreign-policy errors. The President requested a resolution supporting "all necessary measures" that the President may take to "repel any armed attack" against American forces. He demanded and received more, for Congress also gave advance consent that the President could "prevent further aggression" and take "all necessary steps" to protect any nation covered by SEATO which might request aid "in defense of its freedom." This Gulf of Tonkin Resolution sailed through the House of Representatives after forty minutes of debate by a vote of 416 to 0. In the Senate, however, Senator Gaylord Nelson, Democrat of Wisconsin, attempted to amend the resolution so that it would not justify a widening of the conflict. He was stopped by J. William Fulbright, Democrat of Arkansas and chairman of the Foreign Relations Committee, who argued that the President should be trusted and that an amendment would require further consideration by the House at a time when speed and the appearance of national unity were essential. The Senate then voted 88 to 2 (Democratic Senators Wayne Morse of Oregon and Ernest Gruening of Alaska dissenting) to give the President virtually unlimited powers in the Vietnamese conflict.

During the next four years Johnson waged war without an explicit declaration of war from Congress. He argued that the Gulf of Tonkin Resolution and the President's powers as commander in chief of the military gave him sufficient authority to send one-half million Americans into combat in Vietnam. The Senate finally repealed the resolution in 1970.

To examine the Vietnam War in isolation would be a grave historical error. The conflict was not an exception to the world view of American foreign policy–makers during the 1960s. Vietnam was only one of a number of revolutions in the newly emerging world with

[34]U.S. Senate, Committee on Foreign Relations, 90th Cong., 2nd Sess., *The Gulf of Tonkin, The 1964 Incidents* (Washington, 1968). *The Pentagon Papers*, pp. 234–242, 258–279, also analyzes the 34A operations and Gulf of Tonkin attack.

which Johnson had to deal during his first eighteen months in office. Since 1960 Africa had been the most chaotic area. In all of Africa in 1945, only Egypt, Ethiopia, Liberia, and South Africa could lay claim to independence. Otherwise the continent was under Belgian, British, French, Spanish, or Portuguese control. World War II destroyed the power of European colonialism; the Suez crisis and then the termination of British control of Ghana in 1957 (giving the first black African state its independence in the postwar era) set off a chain reaction. In 1960 sixteen new African states joined the United Nations. By 1970 fifty African nations were independent. Many of these states were national entities only in the sense that colonial authorities had formerly imposed central governments over the areas. Tribal ties often remained stronger, factionalizing the new nations, creating insoluble problems for nationalistic leaders, and thereby allowing army generals to use military force to consolidate their own as well as their nations' power. Nearly all new African nations, moreover, had been poorly prepared by the colonialists for independence. Necessary capital, technical skills, stable governmental institutions, and educated elites were in short supply. Both Washington and Moscow suffered serious reverses in attempting to come to terms with these changes.

The United States held a precarious position among black Africans because it refused to use sanctions to penalize the Republic of South Africa for its policy of apartheid, under which a small white minority of less than 20 percent of the population isolated and ruthlessly suppressed the black majority. That dilemma intensified in November 1965, when Southern Rhodesia, with a white population of 200,000 and a black population of nearly 4 million, broke away from the British Empire to establish another apartheid system. The United States publicized its dislike for these apartheid policies but refused to go further. Vast economic investments, strategic naval ports in South Africa, a reluctance to oppose military allies (such as Portugal) that still controlled colonial African territories, and a fear that such action would be a precedent for other nations to pass judgment on the American domestic racial situation—all these factors prevented the United States from effectively opposing apartheid.

Washington officials, however, did not hesitate to intervene in the Belgian Congo during the 1960s. This area, tragically unprepared by Belgium for independence, became a sovereign nation on June 30, 1960. Katanga Province, led by Moise Tshombe and bolstered by European and American copper and cobalt interests, attempted to secede from the Congo and become an independent state. In the ensuing two-year struggle the most popular nationalistic Congolese leader, Patrice Lumumba, was murdered by Katanga authorities. Order was restored only after the United Nations, with vast American support, helped the Congolese government capture Tshombe and reunite the country in January 1963. The United States had decided that removing Tshombe was less distasteful than allowing the continuation of a civil war that could become an open invitation to Soviet or Chinese intervention. The Soviets actually supported UN intervention, but not when the intervention was under US control.

Congolese stability proved short-lived. In the spring of 1964 left-wing nationalists attempted to overthrow the government. By this time the United States had replaced Belgium as the most powerful foreign element and had spent more than $6 million attempting to bolster the central government. As rebellion spread, the Central Intelligence Agency formed a mercenary army and air force, many of whose planes were piloted by exiled Cubans. The multilived Tshombe returned to head this central government. He recruited white mercenaries from southern Africa, Europe, and the United States. The rebels opened contact with Communist China, although communist influence in the movement was extremely small. The antigovernment forces tortured and executed perhaps 20,000 opponents. When they gathered 280 Belgians and 16 Americans as hostages, the United States organized a quick Belgian paratroop strike.[35] On November 24, 1964, the hostages were freed, and the rebels were dispersed. Shortly thereafter Tshombe was driven from power by a military regime led by General Joseph D. Mobutu. The political structure remained unstable, and Tshombe's use of white mercenaries enraged African nationalists. American influence continued to grow until by 1967 Belgians had to make appointments through the U.S. embassy to talk with Congolese governmental officials.[36] When rebellion again erupted in the summer of 1967, however, powerful senators, led by Richard Russell, Democrat of Georgia, so strenuously objected to further aid for Mobutu that the State Department acquiesced. Racial tensions at home as well as the rising combat fatalities in Vietnam were

---

[35]Richard J. Barnet, *Intervention and Revolution: The United States in the Third World* (New York, 1968), pp. 248–251.
[36]*The New York Times*, August 3, 1967, p. 2.

beginning to limit American initiatives in other newly emerging nations.

Africa ranked much lower on Washington's priority list than either Vietnam or Latin America. In the latter area, Johnson continued the downgrading of the Alliance for Progress. He placed control of policy under a new assistant secretary of state, Thomas C. Mann. A fellow Texan, Mann's top priorities were the stabilization of Latin American politics, protection of American private investments in the area, and a vigorous struggle against radicalism. He willingly accepted military governments in Latin America, particularly if these regimes replaced liberal reform governments that threatened to pass destabilizing economic measures. U.S. encouragement and acceptance of such a military coup d'état occurred first in Brazil in 1964. The new Brazilian military regime became one of the most stable— and repressive—governments in the hemisphere.

When President Johnson did attempt to increase investment in social enterprises such as education or health, his policies were attacked by the Treasury Department and its new secretary, Henry Fowler. The secretary's uppermost concern was not Latin American development but the correction of the worsening dollar deficit being incurred by the United States in international trade. Since the late 1950s Americans had spent more overseas than they had sold. The deficit was made up by shipping gold abroad. By the mid-1960s the U.S. gold supply had shrunk 40 percent since 1945, and the situation threatened to get out of hand as Vietnam costs spiraled upward in 1965–1966. One of the first victims of America's inability to balance its international budget was the Alliance for Progress.

Fowler and the Treasury insisted that support for American exports (the most important suction for drawing money back into the United States) receive preference over all overseas social investments. The department inserted an "additionality" clause in aid grants. Under this clause Latin American recipients of American aid promised to spend all of that money on American goods, even though those goods were more expensive than, say, similar British or French goods. "Additionality" drastically drove up the cost of development for the Latin Americans. The president of Colombia observed sardonically in 1968, "Colombia has received two program loans under the Alliance. I don't know if we can survive a third."[37] This intensi-

---

[37]Jerome Levinson and Juan de Onís, *The Alliance That Lost Its Way: A Critical Report on the Alliance for Progress* (Chicago, 1970), is the best analysis; see especially pp. 120–123.

fied attention to securing more exports also made the Johnson administration very sensitive to any unsettling factor that might threaten markets in Latin America. By 1966 the Alliance had failed to achieve its objectives. It had created rising expectations in Latin America, expectations that demanded more than American support for military regimes or the use of Latin America as a mere export market for U.S. goods. But worse was to come.

In the Dominican Republic on April 24, 1965, a civilian government headed by Donald Reid Cabral was attacked by liberal and radical followers of Juan Bosch (see map, p. 207). The nation's 3.3 million people were among the poorest in Latin America. Between 1916 and 1940 the government had been controlled by American Marines and customs officers, but the United States had withdrawn by 1940 in favor of Rafael Trujillo. The dictator, whom Franklin D. Roosevelt accurately characterized as "an s.o.b." but "our s.o.b.," brutally ruled and ruthlessly exploited his countrymen until he was gunned down by assassins in May 1961. When the dictator's relatives attempted to claim his power, President Kennedy deployed American naval units to safeguard the provisional government. In December 1962 the reform party led by Juan Bosch obtained 60 percent of the votes in a national election. Ten months later, Bosch fell to an army coup d'état that was supported by conservative businessmen, landholders, and church leaders. Neither the White House, whose staff had become dissatisfied with Bosch and viewed him as a mere "literary figure," nor the State Department protected Bosch's popularly elected government. The Reid Cabral junta which assumed power was soon deserted by both conservative and radical forces; it was deserted by everyone, apparently, except the United States. When Reid Cabral insisted on running for president in the June 1965 elections, and when Washington then extended a $5-million loan to his regime, pro-Bosch forces overthrew what was only the shell of a government.

Two days of fighting between the rebels and army forces followed. On Monday, April 26, the rebels began arming thousands of civilians. By April 28 the military seemed to have the upper hand, but Washington officials, acting on conclusions too hastily formed by the American embassy in Santo Domingo, concluded that marines would have to land to prevent a Castro-like revolution. Johnson and Mann had taken a tough line on Castro. Despite approaches from the Cuban government in the autumn of 1963 which hinted at its desire to have normal relations with the United States, Washington had replied very cautiously. When Castro then suggested an agenda for the talks, Johnson was President. Although he saw the Cuban memorandum, Johnson had refused to make any conciliatory move.[38] By late 1964 the United States, working through the Organization of American States (OAS), had successfully encouraged every Latin American nation except Mexico to break off diplomatic relations with Cuba. Faced with the Dominican revolt, the administration adopted a view that American policymakers had amplified from the Truman Doctrine to the Kennedy-Johnson interpretation of Vietnam: the revolt was part of a larger challenge, and a challenge in any area was thus a challenge to American security everywhere.

The initial public pretext for landing nearly 23,000 troops was the protection of Americans in strife-torn Santo Domingo. (This rationale was probably publicized in part because the U.S. action violated Articles 15 and 17 of the OAS Charter, which prohibited intervention "directly or indirectly, for any reason whatever, in the internal or external affairs of any other State.") On April 30, however, Johnson gave a different reason: "People trained outside the Dominican Republic are seeking to gain control." Unfortunately for the President, the CIA told him that no communists were involved. Furious, Johnson ordered the FBI to "Find me some Communists in the Dominican Republic." As a result the American embassy issued a poorly documented list of fifty-eight (or fifty-three) "identified and prominent Communist and Castroite leaders" in the rebel forces. American newspapermen on the scene considered the list propaganda, not fact, and agreed with Bosch's assessment that "this was a democratic revolution smashed by the leading democracy of the world."[39] In intervening unilaterally, the United States maneuvered a very reluctant vote of consent from the OAS, but Johnson's disdain for the organization's failure to be enthusiastic about the American Marines was unconcealed. "The OAS," the President remarked privately, "couldn't pour —— out of a boot if the instructions were written on the heel."[40]

The President went further. On May 2, 1965, he announced that the "American nations cannot, must not, and will not permit the establishment of another Communist government in the Western Hemi-

[38]Oral History Statement by William Attwood, November 8, 1965, Kennedy Library, Boston. Used by permission.
[39]*Newsweek,* May 17, 1965, p. 52; Randall B. Woods, *Fulbright* (New York, 1995), p. 382.
[40]Geyelin, *Lyndon B. Johnson and the World,* p. 254.

sphere." He warned that change "should come through peaceful process" and pledged that the United States would defend "every free country of this hemisphere." The importance of this "Johnson Doctrine," like both the Truman and Eisenhower doctrines, depended on how broadly the United States would define "communism" and how easily force would be committed to defend "every free country." The contradictions inherent in the administration's policies (in both Southeast Asia and Latin America) appeared on May 9 in an interview with Mann. Having just intervened with a large military force, the assistant secretary of state declared that the United States only wanted every nation to choose its "own government free of outside interference."[41]

In the spring of 1966 a conservative government led by Joaquin Balaguer assumed power through nationwide elections. Four years later Balaguer was reelected amidst increasing violence. Although the opposition refused to participate in what it considered to be a fixed election, more than 200 political murders occurred. During the first six months of 1971, political killings occurred at the rate of one every forty-eight hours. Balaguer's police evidently committed most of the crimes. "Even under Trujillo we had nothing like this," observed a veteran Dominican reporter. The effect of Johnson's intervention was incalculable among the Latin Americans themselves. But it also turned out to be incalculable at home. Johnson's good friend, J. William Fulbright, Democrat of Arkansas and powerful chair of the Senate Foreign Relations Committee, gave a speech in September 1965 carefully specifying how the administration had misled the American people about the danger of communism in the Dominican Republic. Fulbright never mentioned Johnson directly, but any attack on Johnson's policies, as the senator put it, meant "that's the end of you from his point of view." The President paid dearly for the break. For the next three years Fulbright used the Foreign Relations Committee as a launchpad for devastating attacks—largely from a conservative viewpoint—on Johnson's policies, above all those in the killing fields of Vietnam.[42]

The administration's policy thus came under severe attack at home. Most critics were concerned with the evolving pattern of Amer-

---

[41]*The New York Times*, May 9, 1965, p. E3.

[42]*Washington Post*, July 15, 1971, p. F7; Woods, *Fulbright*, pp. 390–484.

ican intervention around the globe and the resulting justifications issued by official sources. In this sense Santo Domingo was a microcosm of South Vietnam. During the 1964 presidential campaign Johnson had answered Goldwater's demands for bombing North Vietnam with the remark on September 25, "We're not going north and drop bombs at this stage of the game" because "I want to think about the consequences of getting American boys into a war with 700 million Chinese." The same day, however, William P. Bundy, assistant secretary of state for Far Eastern affairs, commented, "Expansion of the war outside South Vietnam . . . could be forced upon us by the increased pressures of the Communists." Bundy proved the more accurate prophet. At the time Johnson was campaigning, his closest advisers had decided that North Vietnam would have to be bombed. Target lists were drawn up, bombings were expected to begin at the outset of 1965, and only the President's permission, which his advisers now thought to be "inevitable," remained to be obtained. These counselors further understood that the bombing, once undertaken, would be only a stopgap measure to shore up the revolving South Vietnam regimes until American ground troops could be rushed into action.[43]

On February 8, 1965, the American bombing raids on North Vietnam began. The ostensible reason was a Vietminh attack on the American camp at Pleiku, killing seven Americans; this was one of a series of attacks against U.S. bases that had taken place since the autumn. In March the President began "Rolling Thunder," a systematic long-term bombing program against the North. Curtis LeMay, air force chief of staff, thought it time: "We are swatting flies when we should be going after the manure pile." By April, however, the bombing had only stiffened Hanoi's resistance. Johnson ordered more than 20,000 American troops into Vietnam, and now they were openly instructed to enter into combat. The inescapable logic of the commitment began to become apparent. Over 100,000 U.S. troops went to Vietnam in approximately four months. The escalation saved the tottering South Vietnamese government, but at an unimagined price.

"Rolling Thunder" aimed to cut off supplies being infiltrated from North Vietnam and to help stabilize South Vietnam politically. It accomplished neither objective. Hanoi, with aid from Russia and

---

[43]*Pentagon Papers*, pp. 307–342.

China, matched the American escalation step by step, sending 60,000 men into South Vietnam in 1966 (three times the number of 1965) and increasing daily tonnage of supplies by 150 percent. Bombing had little effect on the primitive supply route, which needed to provide only six tons of goods a day (an amount that could be carried by several hundred people) to keep the Vietminh refueled. Bombings north and south, moreover, probably killed a ratio of two civilians to one Vietminh, according to one estimate; American-Vietnamese search-and-destroy operations on the ground perhaps killed as many as six civilians for each Vietminh.[44] Ground fighting increased, with Americans assuming the burden. In April 1966, for the first time, more Americans than South Vietnamese were killed in action.

On the political side prospects only slightly improved. In June 1965 strongman Air Vice Marshal Nguyen Cao Ky came to power as premier. A North Vietnamese who had fought with the French against Vietnamese independence forces and later made a widely publicized remark praising Adolf Hitler, Ky was nevertheless welcomed by American officials because he promised to provide the necessary political stability. But desertions continued to rise dramatically in the South Vietnam Army. Inflation and corruption, appearing almost in proportion to the intensified American effort, decimated the Vietnamese economy. By February 1966 McNamara admitted that even if bombing destroyed all of North Vietnam's power systems, oil, harbors, and dams, "they could still carry on the infiltration of the men and equipment necessary to support some level of operations in the South."[45]

These disasters were visible in 1966 for any American who cared to see them. Too often the scene was blurred by statistics that poured out of Washington, most of them misleading. "Ah, *les statistiques!*" a Vietnamese general explained to an American, "Your Secretary of Defense loves statistics. We Vietnamese can give him all he wants. If you want them to go up, they will go up. If you want them to go down, they will go down."[46] The view was also distorted by various peace initiatives. In an April 7, 1965, speech at Johns Hopkins University, President Johnson offered what he termed "unconditional discussions" and proposed an internationally financed Asian Development

[44]Roger Hilsman, *To Move a Nation* (New York, 1965), p. 530.
[45]*The New York Times*, February 16, 1966, p. 1.
[46]Hilsman, *To Move a Nation*, p. 523.

Bank for peacetime reconstruction. Actually, peace discussions were impossible from the American view because of the deteriorating military situation. During his first months in office, moreover, President Johnson had ruled out any neutralization of South Vietnam. This undercut totally his professions for "unconditional discussions."[47]

For their part the North Vietnamese would settle for nothing less than a complete withdrawal of American power and the reunification of the country on their terms. They were not about to be betrayed as they felt they had been in the 1954 Geneva Conference. By 1965 the Vietnamese civil war could no more be compromised than the American Civil War could have been a century earlier.

The White House now aimed for military victory, for once a nation fell to "communism" (an elastic term applied to revolutionaries whether in China or Iraq, Cuba or Santo Domingo) or became unsteadily "neutralized," American liberty in the world was decreased and communism occupied a springboard for toppling other "dominoes." In this sense, the enemy of the 1960s was China. On the one hand, the Johnson administration believed that because of internal difficulties the Chinese would not intervene in Vietnam as long as the fighting remained away from their borders. On the other hand, "Over this war—and all Asia—is another reality: the deepening shadow of Communist China," as the President told the nation in his Johns Hopkins speech. "The contest in Vietnam is part of a wider pattern of aggressive purposes." During the same month McNamara explained most fully in a private conversation why the United States was in Vietnam.

The alternative to fighting, he observed, was not to negotiate a neutral noncommunist South Vietnam, for this was impossible. The real alternative was a Chinese-dominated Southeast Asia, which would mean a "Red Asia." If the United States withdrew, a complete shift would occur in the world balance of power. Asia would go Red, American allies would be shaken, and at home there would be a "bad effect on [the] economy and a disastrous political fight that could further freeze American political debate and even affect political freedom." Chinese attitudes might soften over the decades, but this would take longer than had the Russian change, for China "started from farther back than [the] Soviet Union in [the] industrializing process. The

---

[47]*Pentagon Papers*, pp. 285–286, especially cable from President to Lodge, March 20, 1964, Document No. 65.

Soviet Union was contained by a military alliance in an expansionist period. So [it is] possible to contain China in her expansionist phase by similar alliances." To stop China, the United States would not recognize "any sanctuary or any weapons restriction. But we would use nuclear weapons only after fully applying non-nuclear arsenal."[48]

The secretary of defense offered this explanation at a time when the Chinese were suffering a series of devastating foreign-policy setbacks that helped to cause a severe internal upheaval within China between 1966 and 1968. A domestically generated coup in Indonesia led by nationalist army elements, and having little to do with the American presence in Vietnam, destroyed pro-Peking communists in a bloodbath. Castro's Cuba, revolutionary Algeria, Egypt's Nasser, and a number of African nations publicly attacked Chinese policies, restricting or severing diplomatic ties. Despite China's explosion of an atomic bomb in 1964 and a thermonuclear device in May 1966, that nation's diplomatic leverage dissipated.

These failures influenced Mao to launch a "cultural revolution" within China, transforming foreign policy and enabling him to eliminate personal enemies within Peking. The turning point came in September 1965, when General Lin Piao, second in command to Mao, announced that China would encourage wars of liberation throughout the newly emerging nations. Lin Piao gave no hint that China would become directly involved in any of the revolutions. He warned other revolutionaries to help themselves as the Chinese had done.

In Washington, however, policymakers led by Secretary of State Dean Rusk immediately compared Lin Piao's statement to Hitler's *Mein Kampf*. The President announced that Lin Piao had confirmed that, if the domino of Vietnam fell, others would follow.[49] Nearly 200 scholars of Asian affairs urged a reevaluation of the policy toward China, but without success. They observed that, regardless of how the rhetoric was interpreted, Chinese capabilities and power could not and might never be able to achieve Lin Piao's objectives. Developments in Indonesia, Cuba, and Africa confirmed this view.

As usual, the greatest irony could be found in Vietnam. Following the Lin Piao statement, China pleaded with Hanoi to fight a pro-

---

[48]"Memorandum" of Background Session with Robert McNamara, April 22, 1965, Arthur Krock Papers, Princeton University Library.
[49]*Public Papers of the Presidents, 1966*, p. 936; see also *The New York Times*, August 31, 1966, p. 9.

tracted struggle that would tie down and bleed American power. Ho
Chi Minh disliked such advice. He saw no logic in an indefinite conflict that would benefit only China's objectives. He wanted to defeat
the United States rapidly. A long war would leave a weakened North
Vietnam more open to Chinese pressure.[50] Meanwhile, much to the
consternation of the Chinese, the Soviet Union replaced China as the
most important source of aid and support for Ho's regime. Worse, in
early 1966, clashes between Chinese and Russian troops occurred
along their long common border. The Chinese were being squeezed
from two directions by Russia: they were losing influence in Hanoi
as well as other key Third World capitals. And they were undergoing major political upheavals internally. At this point in 1965–1966,
the Johnson administration decided to send 400,000 American soldiers
to save Vietnam from China.

The Soviet Union was the primary, perhaps the only, nation that
benefited from American intervention. Documents opened in the
1990s show that Soviet officers secretly operated missile sites that
shot down U.S. planes. Thus the Soviets at once gained military experience, countered Chinese influence, and won favor with the North
Vietnamese. With U.S. attention and resources tied down in Southeast Asia, Russia made a dramatic recovery in world affairs between
1965 and 1971. After 1958 the Russian economy had grown at a considerably slower rate than previously, thus discouraging hopes of
challenging American economic supremacy. The decline also weakened Khrushchev's power within the Kremlin. Dissenting party leaders and some military officials combined to oust Khrushchev in October 1964. The victors divided his posts between two former protégés
of Stalin, Aleksey Kosygin, who became premier, and Leonid Brezhnev, the new first party secretary. This change occurred as the United
States stepped up its effort in Vietnam. Kosygin was actually visiting
Hanoi at that moment in February 1965 when, for reasons best known
to the State Department, the United States chose to begin the bombing. As Soviet influence grew in Hanoi, Moscow did nothing to mediate the war, partly because the two sides seemed irreconcilable but
also because the conflict—as long as it remained limited—drained the
United States and benefited the Soviet Union. The Soviets, moreover,

---

[50]David Mozingo, "China's Foreign Policy and the Cultural Revolution," Interim Report: Number 1, International Relations of East Asia Project, Cornell University, Ithaca,
N.Y., 1970.

had their own fear of China. Johnson continually hoped that Moscow would help him mediate a face-saving U.S. retreat from Vietnam, but as a top Soviet diplomat later noted, "Moscow had no intention of applying strong diplomatic pressure on Ho Chi Minh lest it drive him into the arms of the Chinese."[51]

The Russians further gained as the war helped divide the Western alliance. France, the former colonial power in Southeast Asia, now condemned the "foreign intervention" of the United States. (In the spring of 1966 American policies received a further blow when de Gaulle pulled France out of the NATO military organization.) The Western Europeans refused outright to send men for the American buildup in South Vietnam. Of the forty nations linked to the United States through treaties, only four (Australia, New Zealand, South Korea, and Thailand) committed combat troops. Korea and Thailand did so only after the United States promised to pay handsomely for their troops. Japan also grew critical of the escalation in the war.

No matter where he looked, Johnson had difficulty finding support for his policies. Soviet military and diplomatic leverage grew as unstable conditions spread in Africa and Latin America. The trouble with foreigners, the President lamented, "is that they're not like folks you were reared with." By mid-1966, however, the problems with the allies were rapidly becoming less important than the eruptions of the "folks" back home.

---

[51]Anatoly Dobrynin, *In Confidence* (New York, 1995), p. 115; I. V. Gaiduk, *The Soviet Union and the Vietnam War* (Chicago, 1996), traces Soviet involvement.

CHAPTER 11

A New Containment: The Rise and Fall of Détente (1966–1976)

Ironically, as the United States escalated the war in Vietnam to contain communism, the Johnson administration deescalated conflict with the Soviets. The seeds of détente, or lessening of international tension, were sown in 1967–1968, at the moment U.S. forces suffered setbacks in Vietnam, and blossomed in 1971–1972 as American bombers obliterated people and villages in large areas of Southeast Asia. Thus détente did not signal an American retreat from world affairs but was a new—and necessary—tactic for carrying on traditional containment policy. Overall the power of the U.S. economy and military (not to mention American culture, especially music, art, and McDonald's) remained dominant on the globe. But that power could no longer influence Soviet policy or the newly emerging areas as it had before the 1960s. A new world had appeared. For a decade (1966–1976) détente became both a safety valve for releasing tension in that world and a tactic for controlling the emergence of the Soviet Union as a global power. The collapse of détente in the mid-1970s tellingly revealed how both the United States and Russia had not yet been able to come to terms with the new world.

Johnson initially pursued détente in the hope that the Soviets, who were the largest suppliers of military goods to North Vietnam, might be able to pressure Ho Chi Minh to make peace. The Americans' hope was badly misplaced. On the battlefields the war dragged on, while at home the inflation rate doubled to 5 percent and antiwar protests intensified. Johnson's beloved Great Society program, created to erase domestic poverty and injustice, became a victim of a war 11,000 miles away. A top White House official elucidated the President's dilemma with the remark, "What the hell do you say? How do you half-lead a country into war?"[1]

Growing problems thus forced Johnson to approach the Soviets. Brezhnev and Kosygin were willing to talk, but not necessarily about Vietnam. Their influence in Southeast Asia increased each day the war dragged on. Unlike their late mentor, Stalin—whom Khrushchev once sarcastically described as thinking that "foreign policy meant keeping the antiaircraft units around Moscow on a twenty-four-hour alert"[2]—the new Russian leaders pushed their influence into such areas as the Middle East and South and Southeast Asia. Their military power was burgeoning. After the 1956 Suez crisis the Russians began a rapid buildup of conventional land and sea forces until by the late 1960s their fleet, once a subject of ridicule, began to appear regularly in the Mediterranean, Indian Ocean, and even Caribbean areas.[3] As for their nuclear forces, after the 1962 missile crisis a Soviet official warned an American that "you'll never be able to do that to us again," and by 1968 the Russians approached strategic parity with the once-supreme American arsenal.

The Vietnam morass and the new balance of power therefore also required that Johnson deal with the Soviets. Brezhnev and Kosygin were receptive, for although the Russians' military power had sharply increased, their economic growth rate had dropped drastically in the 1960s. They needed economic relief. The Soviets, moreover, have always delighted in bargaining as an equal with the United States, a nation they simultaneously fear, dislike, and try desperately to emulate. The time was ripe for a deal.

But the first deal on Vietnam was never struck. Rusk urged the Soviets to call off their North Vietnam ally because, he warned, if Russia was "backing the north to seize the south, then we [the United States and U.S.S.R.] were in trouble," for the United States would never allow it. The Soviets responded by threatening to give Ho new surface-to-surface missiles and flatly announcing that "since North

---

[1]Harry McPherson Oral History Interview, Tape #4, p. 20, Lyndon B. Johnson Library, Austin, Tex. (Hereafter cited as LBJ Library.)

[2]Nikita Khrushchev, *Khrushchev Remembers,* translated and edited by Strobe Talbott (Boston, 1970), pp. 392–393.

[3]J. M. McConnell and Bradford Dismukes, "Soviet Diplomacy of Force in the Third World," *Problems of Communism,* XXVIII (January–February 1979): 15–20.

Vietnam is a part of the Communist community, the Soviet Union must support and will assist it increasingly as the U.S. escalates its efforts."[4] Americans acted, moreover, as if the Soviets could actually force Ho to give up his struggle; that was a highly doubtful assumption.

Johnson was luckier in his attempts to slow the nuclear race. At a summit meeting with Kosygin at Glassboro, New Jersey, an impassioned warning by Defense Secretary McNamara about the suicidal arms race both nations were running helped lead to an announcement that a nonproliferation agreement had been reached. Each power pledged to halt the distribution of nuclear weapons. Ominously, China, France, and India, among others, refused to sign the pact.

Détente seemed to be moving ahead. And then it suffered two stunning setbacks. The first began in February 1968, when the North Vietnamese launched a surprise Tet (New Year) offensive that was not beaten back until they threatened even the grounds of the U.S. embassy in Saigon. Until that occurred, Johnson could claim that the war was going better and Americans could see "light at the end of the tunnel." Now the light seemed to be an onrushing freight train engineered by Ho. The North Vietnamese suffered heavy casualties during Tet, but they broke the illusion held by many Americans that the war could soon be won.[5]

Johnson consulted a group of elder statesmen, and the most famous "wise man," Dean Acheson, bluntly told the President that his advisers had led him "down the garden path." A month later Senator Eugene McCarthy, Democrat of Minnesota, ran on an antiwar platform and nearly defeated Johnson in the New Hampshire presidential primary. On March 31, 1968, the President dramatically announced on national television that he was pulling out of the race so that he could devote all his energies to making peace with Ho. Johnson turned down a military request for 206,000 more men to be added to the nearly 500,000 already in Vietnam, but he secretly allowed the

---

[4]Memorandum of Conversation between Rusk and Ambassador Anatoly F. Dobrynin, May 26, 1966, White House Confidential File (Asia), Box 7, LBJ Library; Thomas L. Hughes to Rusk, May 4, 1967, National Security File, Country File, U.S.S.R., LBJ Library; Memorandum of Conversation between Zbigniew Brzezinski and Yuri Zhukov, April 13, 1967, National Security File, Country File, U.S.S.R., LBJ Library.
[5]McPherson Oral History, Tape #9, p. 10, LBJ Library.

numbers to rise to 549,000. He planned to turn up the military pressure as he moved toward negotiations; if Ho refused to talk, then, as the State Department secretly informed U.S. ambassadors in Asia, it would "give us a clear field for whatever actions" were "required."[6] At home the United States seemed to be approaching a crisis. Between 1964 and 1968 ghetto riots claimed dozens of lives in Los Angeles, Detroit, and Newark. After Martin Luther King, Jr., was murdered in April 1968, even Washington erupted in flames, as army troops moved into the city and used the Capitol Hill lawn as a bivouac area. Three major political assassinations (John Kennedy in 1963, King and Robert Kennedy in 1968) shocked the world. When the Democratic National Convention met in Chicago during the summer of 1968, massive antiwar riots broke out. Six thousand troops were flown into the city, and Johnson could not attend his own party's meeting because of the danger. Amidst the chaos, Vice President Hubert Humphrey became the party's nominee. Maine's Senator Edmund Muskie (who fought against a proposed peace resolution at the convention) accepted the vice presidential nomination.

When Republicans met in Miami, three blacks died in a ghetto riot, but the media paid scant attention. Instead the nation watched Richard Nixon arise from the political grave. His 1962 defeat in the California gubernatorial race, one liberal columnist wrote at the time, had supposedly sent Nixon "to that small place in history which belongs to national disasters which did not happen." But Nixon refused to go. By 1968 he had become the most important Republican spokesman on foreign policy. With surprising ease he beat back the challenge of New York Governor Nelson Rockefeller (whose foreign-policy speeches were largely drafted by Harvard Professor Henry Kissinger) and won the Republican nomination. Maryland's governor, Spiro Agnew, who admitted his name was not "a household word," became Nixon's running mate. While Nixon pictured himself as a statesman during the campaign, Agnew took a lower road and accused Humphrey of being soft on communism.

These rapid political changes slowed the détente process, but it was knocked off its tracks in August 1968 by a second event: the Soviet invasion of Czechoslovakia. Since the mid-1960s the Soviets and their satellites had moved in different directions. Some Eastern Eu-

---

[6]*The Pentagon Papers,* as published by *The New York Times* (New York, 1971), pp. 622–623.

ropeans experimented with more liberal economic policies. The Czechs, during their so-called Prague Spring, even discussed a loosening of their one-party political system. The United States encouraged the process by opening trade channels. As one State Department official said, Western goods have "tended to open up more and more holes, shall we say, or windows, rather, in the Iron Curtain."[7]

The Brezhnev-Kosygin regime, meanwhile, stolidly and unimaginatively tightened its control within Russia. Stalin's image was refurbished, and a centralized planning system (tagged "Stalinism with computers") emphasized military and heavy industry investment. Intellectuals—especially Jews—were arrested, deported, or declared "insane" when they questioned governmental policies. Brezhnev, who survived an assassination attempt and became the most powerful figure in the politburo, warned that dissent could not be tolerated because "we are living in conditions of an unabating ideological war."[8] Détente meant a lessening of military and political tensions with the West, but ideological coexistence could not be allowed.

The Prague Spring strained this rigid ideological line to the limit. Soviet officials were divided over how to respond. Some Foreign Ministry officials, who did not want to endanger détente, were among those opposing intervention, but they were overbalanced not only by party leaders who feared ideological and economic contamination from Czech liberalism but also by some military and secret police officials who believed the Czech policies might infect the entire bloc. Brezhnev at first equivocated, but as the prointervention faction gained strength and threatened his own power, he joined it and ordered Soviet troops to smash the Czech regime.[9]

He did so at the moment Johnson prepared to meet the Soviet leaders at a summit conference. The President quickly canceled the meetings. Brezhnev's willingness to sacrifice détente indicated the extent of his fear of disorder and liberalization in the bloc, as well as his keen sense of how to survive cutthroat politburo politics. He capped the performance by issuing a "Brezhnev Doctrine" that justified So-

[7]Anthony Solomon Oral History Interview, LBJ Library.

[8]Wolfgang Leonhard, "The Domestic Politics of the New Soviet Foreign Policy," *Foreign Affairs*, LII (October 1973): 59–74; John Dornberg, *Brezhnev, The Masks of Power* (New York, 1974), chapters XV, XVI.

[9]Jiri Valenta, "The Bureaucratic Politics Paradigm and the Soviet Invasion of Czechoslovakia," *Political Science Quarterly*, XCIV (Spring 1979): 55–76.

viet intervention on the ground that a socialist nation had the right to save another from "world imperialism" and thus preserve the "indivisible" socialist system. Johnson did little in response, not only because of the military realities but perhaps also because the Brezhnev Doctrine for Eastern Europe was not unlike the Johnson Doctrine of 1965 for Latin America. Neither superpower would tolerate new ideological challenges in its own sphere.

As détente stalled, Nixon stumbled toward the White House. His 15-percentage-point lead in the polls during September dwindled to less than 1 percent in the November election. Nixon was the first newly elected President in the century who failed to give his party control over either house of Congress. Throughout the campaign he refused to take a clear stand on the war and said only that he had a mysterious "plan" to end it honorably. Privately he told aides, "I've come to the conclusion that there's no way to win the war. But we can't say that, of course." He preferred not to discuss concrete issues at all. ("You still have to put out a folder saying what you're for and against . . . ," he complained privately. "Women particularly like it. They don't have the slightest idea what it means."[10]) As usual, the election results were not a mandate on foreign policy. Despite the antiwar protests on the campuses, the prowar, third-party ticket of Alabama Governor George Wallace received more support from voters under the age of thirty than it did from the population as a whole. (Throughout 1965–1973, the war was most firmly opposed by older, not younger, Americans; by blacks who were doing a disproportionate share of the fighting and dying, rather than whites; by females rather than males; and by lower-class rather than middle-class Americans.[11]) As for the winner, Americans knew he stood for "law and order in the streets," but few knew his plans for Vietnam or détente.

Nixon, however, understood what had to be done, and he thought he knew how to do it. His plans became clearer when, surprisingly, he picked Henry Kissinger as national security adviser. Both men believed the 1970s would be shaped by developments that

[10]Richard J. Whalen, *Catch the Falling Flag* (Boston, 1972), pp. 137, 154.
[11]William L. Lunch and Peter W. Sperlich, "American Public Opinion and the War in Vietnam," *Western Political Quarterly,* XXXII (March 1979): 21–44; Richard M. Scammon and Ben J. Wattenberg, *The Real Majority* (New York, 1970), pp. 38–49, 92–93.

were sapping U.S. dominance in world affairs: the Soviet military buildup; the rising economic and political power of Western Europe and Japan, which threatened American markets and worked against Washington's policies in such areas as Vietnam and the Middle East; and the apparently bottomless pit of the Vietnam War.

Above all, as Kissinger liked to say, the greatest problem was how to "manage" the Soviets as they emerged as a global, instead of merely a regional, superpower. Containment was as important in the 1970s as in the late 1940s, but because of the new Russian strength, and the relative decline of American power, containment now had to be constructed differently than when Acheson or John Kennedy made policy. Nixon and Kissinger believed that the Soviets could be contained not by a massive arms race or increased U.S. global commitments (which neither the American public nor the economy could tolerate) but by making a deal: the Soviets could have sorely needed economic help if they cooperated in Vietnam and agreed to arms limitation.

In the new containment, Nixon also planned to open talks with China. For twenty years Mao had been the Asian villain to Americans, but since the late 1950s he had also become Russia's main concern. The realization that one communist power could be played against the other allowed Nixon to believe that an "era of confrontation" was ending and an era of negotiations beginning.[12] Once the relationship between the Americans and the Soviets was properly adjusted, Nixon and Kissinger concluded, the other problems—Vietnam and the Allies—could be resolved.

All this required time, order, and support at home. With various devices, both legal and criminal, Nixon gained time over the next five years. He also created—temporarily—order and support at home. For above all else, he and Kissinger sought order and control, both at home and abroad, with an awesome single-mindedness. When once asked whether he favored a revolution with justice or an orderly state that was unjust, Kissinger quoted Goethe: "If I had to choose between justice and disorder, on the one hand, and injustice and order on the other, I would always choose the latter."[13] At home this passion for

---

[12]For the new containment policies see especially Stanley Hoffman, "The Case of Dr. Kissinger," *The New York Review of Books,* December 6, 1979, p. 24; and I. F. Stone, "The Flowering of Henry Kissinger," *The New York Review of Books,* November 2, 1972, p. 26.
[13]John G. Stoessinger, *Henry Kissinger: The Anguish of Power* (New York, 1976), pp. 12–14.

order led Nixon to use criminal means in attempts to squelch antiwar protesters. Kissinger could not understand why college students refused to fight in Vietnam: "Conscientious objection is destructive of a society. The imperatives of the individual are always in conflict with the organization of society. Conscientious objection must be reserved for only the greatest moral issues, and Vietnam is not of this magnitude."[14] At that point more than a million people had been killed or wounded in Vietnam.

This determination to have order also led Nixon and Kissinger to control policymaking with an iron grip. Perhaps the President could have both directed policy and restored the public's shattered faith in government by structuring political coalitions in which his policies were debated and obtained support. In 1969 political analyst Richard Scammon thought such an opportunity existed. As ethnic and trade union voters became middle class and moved away from their loyalty to the Democrats, Scammon remarked, "There is a possibility that by following a centrist line—. . . moderately conservative—[Nixon] could build up a great new party of the center."[15] Other observers proclaimed the advent of an "emerging Republican majority." Nixon might well have been able to resolve one of the great problems in U.S. foreign policy: how to use American political institutions to gain support from Congress and the public, instead of resorting to an Imperial Presidency that acted without public debate and too often created support through lying.

Nixon never tried to create such political institutions. Instead, he planned all of his policies, including foreign relations, toward one supreme objective: his reelection in 1972. As early as mid-1970 one top aide said that Nixon was preparing to "gear everything to '72." He did so while believing mighty forces were intent on destroying him. Highly insecure personally, the President was "the most complete loner I've ever known," said Senator Barry Goldwater. "The man operates all by himself." Carrying the scars of too many political wars, the President preferred to circumvent a Democratic Congress. Nixon did not even trust the CIA: "It was staffed by Ivy League liberals" who had always opposed him politically. As for the State Department, he

---

[14]Quoted by Clayton Fritchey in *The New York Review of Books,* September 25, 1969, p. 26.
[15]William Whitworth, "Profiles," *The New Yorker,* September 20, 1969, p. 52.

believed that "no Secretary of State is really important. The President makes foreign policy."[16]

Nixon consequently named William Rogers, a New York lawyer and an old political ally in the Eisenhower years, as secretary of state to keep the department quiet while the White House made foreign policy. Kissinger ensured State's impotence by keeping information from Rogers (and other cabinet members), encouraging Nixon to believe that Rogers was not a loyal team player, courting reporters and congressmen who heard only Kissinger's side of a story, and conducting critical negotiations without informing the State Department. Nixon understood all this. He remarked privately, "Henry thinks Bill [Rogers] isn't very deep and Bill thinks that Henry is power crazy. In a sense they are both right."[17] It was the only time in American history that a secretary of state was appointed because of his ignorance of foreign policy. But then Kissinger often did not consult even his own staff. "Henry's chief lieutenants are like mushrooms," went the joke. "They're kept in the dark, get a lot of manure piled on them, and then get canned."[18]

Without assured congressional support, the trust of the State Department, or sometimes the confidence of Kissinger's staff, the President and his closest adviser had only each other. They considered this to be enough. When Kissinger was the ghost writer for Nixon's "State of the World" report in 1970, an observer thought it resembled a message from the Vatican, except that "the Pope quotes Scripture" while "Mr. Nixon quotes himself 31 times directly."[19] Kissinger meanwhile controlled the foreign policy–making process from the White House and, as the President's personal assistant, did not have to be accountable to Congress. Rogers, although knowing little about any policies, had to testify before committees in what one senator frostily called "a rather empty exercise." Instead of building political institutions, Nixon was systematically undermining them.

Despite his firm control over policy, Nixon enjoyed few early successes. He was reluctant to deal with the Soviets in the aftermath

---

[16]*Washington Post,* May 18, 1994, p. A6; Ibid., October 17, 1976, p. C4; Henry Kissinger, *White House Years* (Boston, 1979), p. 11; Whalen, *Catch the Falling Flag,* pp. 253–256.
[17]Leslie Gelb, "The Kissinger Legacy," *The New York Times Magazine,* October 31, 1976, pp. 78–79; William Shawcross, *Sideshow* (New York, 1979), p. 103.
[18]Bruce Mazlish, *Kissinger* (New York, 1976), p. 231.
[19]Hans Morgenthau, "Mr. Nixon's Foreign Policy," *New Republic,* March 21, 1970, p. 23.

of the Czech invasion. The President knew, moreover, that he could not negotiate with Brezhnev from a position of strength until the Vietnam War and the uproar at home were brought under control. He announced in 1969 that U.S. troops would leave Vietnam in a phased withdrawal. This policy promised to wind down the war and end the antiwar protests. Nixon, however, had no intention of following what he bitterly called "isolationism." The United States must retain its global obligations, but it had to uphold them with different policies than it had during the post-1945 years when it enjoyed overwhelming power.

In Vietnam Nixon pursued a policy of "Vietnamization," that is, building the South Vietnam Army so that it could replace the departing Americans. This approach actually resembled the failed policies of 1954–1965. As one U.S. official said, it simply meant "changing the color of the corpses." Elsewhere the President followed a "Nixon Doctrine." It provided that as the United States pulled back from some of its military commitments, Americans would help certain friends take up the burden of containment. In Asia the friend was to be Japan; in the Middle East, Iran; and in Africa, Zaire (the former Belgian Congo) and the white-dominated, but black majority, countries of Angola (a Portuguese colony) and South Africa.

Nixon and Kissinger sought containment-on-the-cheap. They even planned to make a profit. Overseas sales of American military arms amounted to $1 to $2 billion in the mid-1960s, but they surged toward $10 billion by the time Nixon left office. Iran alone bought $2½ billion of arms in 1972–1973. Nixon ordered that the shah could have the newest equipment, and all that His Majesty desired. The shah responded by ordering planes and other equipment "as if he was going through the Sears, Roebuck catalog," in the words of one official. In all, the Nixon Doctrine encouraged a dangerous military buildup in the Middle East and southern Africa; nearly bankrupted some nations and encouraged others, such as Iran, to raise oil prices rapidly to pay for the inflation-priced U.S. equipment; made these nations more likely to use force rather than negotiations to settle disputes; helped create dangerously strained relations with Japan when it refused to become an Asian policeman; and caused Nixon to become a political bedfellow of the shah and white supremacist regimes in Africa. The doctrine's only redeeming virtue was that it gave the President a rationale for pulling back from Vietnam.

But even that virtue was not immediately apparent. As Nixon

pulled out troops, he secretly escalated the bombing, particularly in Cambodia, which—although a neutral state—was used by the communists to funnel troops into South Vietnam. The bombings turned out to be a catastrophe. *The New York Times* published a story on the "secret" bombing in March 1969. Nixon set up a "Plumbers" unit to stop such leaks "whatever the cost." This decision led to a series of criminal acts by the Plumbers that climaxed in their attempt to break into Democratic party headquarters at Washington's Watergate Hotel in 1972.

The bombings meanwhile only drove the communist forces deeper into Cambodia and destabilized the country. In early 1970 the government of Prince Norodom Sihanouk, who miraculously had kept Cambodia out of the path of the war's destruction, was overthrown by a right-wing military officer, Lon Nol. The United States apparently was not directly involved in the overthrow, although the CIA certainly knew of Lon Nol's plans. But Nixon rushed to take advantage of the coup. On April 30, 1970, he announced in an emotional speech that the United States must not act as a "pitiful, helpless giant." American troops were therefore invading Cambodia to clean out the communist camps. In the name of winding down the war, Nixon expanded it[20] (see map, p. 218).

Both Cambodia and American campuses were soon devastated. Lon Nol proved to be an incompetent partner who watched helplessly as his own ally's planes, as well as communist armies, savaged his nation. By 1971 the communists controlled half the country. (By 1975 they had all of it. More than 250,000 persons had been killed, massive starvation began, and one of the world's most beautiful countries lay in ruins.) In the United States students at nearly 500 colleges went on strike to protest Nixon's invasion. At Kent State in Ohio and Jackson State in Mississippi, protesters were shot and killed. Thousands of antiwar Americans descended on Washington. Troops were stationed in the White House basement to repel a possible assault. Nixon, Kissinger feared, was on the edge of a nervous breakdown. The President would shout, "Let's go blow the hell out of them," as embarrassed aides looked on in stunned silence. But public opinion polls showed that 50 percent of the Americans surveyed supported Nixon's

---

[20]The standard account is Shawcross, *Sideshow*, especially pp. 102–121; Kissinger and Nixon quotes to be found in *The New York Times*, December 9, 1973, p. 76; *Washington Post*, February 19, 1974, pp. 1, 12–14.

invasion, although 53 percent did not believe his claim that the action would shorten the war. Congress loyally acted as a lightning rod, absorbing the antiwar protesters' fury but doing nothing until they left Washington and Nixon pulled the troops out of Cambodia. Congress followed the President, not the people in the street.[21]

The Cambodian tragedy was one in a series of disasters that marked 1970–1971 as a nadir in recent U.S. history. In 1971 Nixon authorized South Vietnamese troops to clean out communist sanctuaries in Laos. "Vietnamization" turned out to be a failure as American television showed South Vietnamese troops clinging desperately to departing American helicopters in order to escape communist gunfire. Nixon responded by stepping up the bombing of Laotian supply trails until Laos became the most heavily bombed country in history. By mid-1971 the communists were in a stronger position in Laos than at any time since 1962.

Vietnamization failed despite an enlarged war and the dropping of bombs at the rate of one ton for every minute Nixon was in office. Between 1969 and 1972, 20,000 Americans died in Vietnam, and over 300,000 Asians were killed while the war was supposedly winding down. In frustration one popular Saigon newspaper ran a daily contest in which readers submitted stories of such atrocities as rape or homicide committed by Americans. North Vietnam, that "raggedy-ass little fourth-rate country," as Lyndon Johnson once called it, was tormenting the United States. Americans tired of supporting a South Vietnamese regime that was corrupt and incapable. Many were also sickened by the slaughter dramatized during early 1971 when a military court-martial convicted Lieutenant William Calley, Jr., of killing at least twenty-one South Vietnamese civilians in 1968 at the village of Mylai. It was a war in which the enemy and the civilians were indistinguishable. Meanwhile, American soldiers, unwilling to be, perhaps, the last to die in such a war, used drugs in increasing amounts to avoid combat. Over 9000 were arrested for drug use in Vietnam during 1970, and their superior officers estimated that 65,000 U.S. troops had used drugs.[22]

[21]Shawcross, *Sideshow*, pp. 152–153; Marie Gottschalk, "Bring Us Together: Congressional Reaction to the Invasion of Cambodia, 1970," unpublished paper, 1980, pp. 54, 72–74 (in author's possession).
[22]Robert Shaplen, "Letter from Indo-China," *The New Yorker*, May 16, 1970, p. 125. On drug use, see *The New York Times*, January 11, 1971, p. 13.

And as Vietnamization failed, so too did the American economy. The gross national product (the sum of all services and goods produced) rose over the $1-trillion mark, but an apparently uncontrollable inflation accounted for half the increase in 1971. The nation's industries, moreover, were becoming so uncompetitive that, for the first time since 1894, Americans imported more merchandise than they sold abroad. As the economy weakened, so did the dollar—the foundation that had undergirded the remarkable post-1945 global trading system. In 1971 nearly $50 billion was held abroad, and more and more dollars were being printed in Washington, then pumped overseas, to pay for the nation's military expenditures and private investments. Overseas, dollars increased in number as they decreased in value. Europeans, watching helplessly as these dollars bought up their industries, grew angry and began to raise walls against the dollars and U.S. trade. "The rest of the world," French President Georges Pompidou announced, "cannot be expected to regulate its life by a clock [the dollar] that is always slow." The efficient Japanese economy sent streams of cars, steel, and electronic goods into American ports, and in 1969 had replaced the United States as Asia's leading trade partner. Nixon became furious when Japan refused to stop certain exports voluntarily until the United States regained its economic health. The Nixon Doctrine, indeed the entire alliance system, was in deep trouble.[23]

In 1970 Nixon promised he would never impose wage and price controls to stop the inflation that was making American goods more expensive than Japanese or West European products. But in midsummer 1971 the balance of payments suddenly showed the possibility of an unbelievable $48-billion annual deficit. The dollar, and hence the Western trading structure, threatened to collapse. In a Kansas City speech, the President discussed the "five great economic superpowers" (the United States, Russia, Japan, Western Europe, China), four of whom "challenge us on every front." "Because economic power will be the key to other kinds of power . . . in the last third of this century," he continued, and since domestic and foreign policies were so interlinked, Americans had to discipline themselves

---

[23]Lewis Beman, "How to Tell Where the U.S. Is Competitive," *Fortune,* LXXXVI (July 1972): 54–55; Seymour Melman, *The Permanent War Economy* (New York, 1974), pp. 112–114; *Washington Post,* May 27, 1971, p. A27.

and their economy before they groveled in the "decadence" that had toppled Ancient Greece and Rome.[24]

In August 1971 the President suddenly imposed a wage-price freeze to curb inflation. He also placed a surtax on foreign imports to stop the inflow of goods from Europe and Japan, a nation that—as a State Department briefing paper reportedly warned Nixon—must be viewed as a potential enemy. He and his secretary of the treasury, tough-talking Texan John Connally, put tremendous pressure on the Allies to revalue their currency while the United States devalued the dollar, thus making the dollar cheaper and more competitive in world markets. Finally, Nixon announced that the dollar would no longer be redeemable in gold. The French bitterly called this program "a Marshall Plan in reverse." Unfortunately it was not enough. In 1973 the economy and the dollar again began slipping after Nixon removed the wage-price freeze. The dollar again had to be devalued. As in 1807, 1893, and 1914, a failing economy forced the United States to change its foreign policies. The era of the all-powerful dollar temporarily ended, and with it went much of Washington's political power (and the good times abroad once cheaply enjoyed by American tourists).

A year before the 1972 presidential campaign began, Nixon was plagued with troubles. Then occurred a remarkable turnabout. The wage-price controls temporarily halted inflation. The economic picture brightened, albeit at the expense of the Allies. The military draft was cut back and student antiwar protests disappeared as if by magic. But most dramatically, in July 1971 Nixon seized the diplomatic initiative with the startling announcement that he would be the first President to visit China.

Since 1969 the two nations had sent subtle signals encouraging a new relationship. Nixon and Mao hoped to use the other to check Soviet power. China's fear of the Russians jumped in 1969–1970, when nearly 1 million Soviet soldiers encamped in a broad area along the Sino-Soviet border. Clashes occurred with Chinese troops. Nixon also hoped to develop a China market so that American businessmen could find economic relief—and enter China before the Japanese locked up the most promising trading ventures. Mao was receptive.

[24]*Public Papers of the Presidents . . . Richard Nixon . . . 1971* (Washington, 1972), pp. 806–812.

The President's major problem might have occurred at home, where for thirty years an anticommunist China Lobby had worked, often with Nixon's help, to make Americans believe that Chiang Kai-shek's government on Taiwan, not Mao's, was the real China. Opposition did develop, particularly from the American Federation of Labor, but the President enjoyed wide maneuvering room. A mid-1960s poll showed that about 25 percent of Americans were unaware that China even had a communist government.[25] Nixon, moreover, could not be charged with being soft on communism. He had made his political reputation with such remarks as calling the 1952 Democratic presidential nominee, Adlai Stevenson, "the appeaser . . . who got a Ph.D. from Dean Acheson's College of Cowardly Communist Containment." In 1971 Nixon was not threatened by politicians resembling the earlier Nixon.

His 1972 journey to China was a huge success. A friendship treaty was signed, trade opened up, the Soviets were made fearful of a possible Sino-American alliance, and within months the Chinese entered the United Nations while Chiang's delegation was expelled. (Chiang died in 1975, the last survivor of World War II's Big Four. U.S. officials increasingly considered Taiwan as an internal Chinese problem, and by 1980 China and Taiwan were cooperating on some economic policies.)

The China trip and the slowing of the Vietnam War placed Nixon in a position to travel to Moscow. He became the first President to visit the Soviet capital. Before his scheduled trip was due to begin in mid-1972, however, the North Vietnamese launched surprise attacks that threatened to overturn the South Vietnam government. Nixon, already called the "biggest bomber in world history," responded with intensified air attacks. In a dramatic departure called "Operation Linebacker" (the President was a devoted football fan), American planes bombed and sowed mines in the vital North Vietnam ports. Lyndon Johnson had refused to mine the ports; he feared that Russian and Chinese ships would be hit and the war escalated to a big-power crisis.

Nixon, however, believed he had to show American toughness as American troops left Vietnam and the presidential campaign approached. "Look," Kissinger later explained, "it wasn't just a matter

[25]Barry B. Hughes, *The Domestic Context of American Foreign Policy* (San Francisco, 1978), p. 57.

of this summit—his political ass was on the line." Kissinger talked tough with the Soviets. Although the war destroyed Johnson, he informed them, "Nixon will not permit three Presidents in a row to leave office under abnormal circumstances."[26] Then he tossed in the bait. Politics and economics had always been closely related in Russian-American relations, Kissinger noted. If the Soviets wanted economic help, they must cooperate politically. This "linkage" was a key to the summit's success.

Nixon calculated correctly. Regardless of events in Vietnam, the Soviets wanted to negotiate. Their readiness had been announced at the Twenty-fourth Party Congress in 1971 when Brezhnev presented a "peace program" that shaped Soviet views, especially détente policy, through the 1970s. Brezhnev's 1971 program rested on four legs, but only one of these was strong.

The strong leg was the military. In his era Khrushchev had tried to expand Soviet influence primarily through Russian economic successes and taking advantage of revolutionary situations in newly emerging areas. The plodding Brezhnev held no such illusions; the economy was in trouble and most revolutionaries mistrusted heavy-handed Russians. Brezhnev, a civilian who loved to parade around in a military uniform, placed his faith in a large buildup of military power. He increased defense budgets at a steady 3 percent annually (while the United States cut its post-Vietnam military) and drafted every able male at the age of seventeen for two-year active service and reserve service until the age of fifty. A force of 5 million stood at the ready. Brezhnev planned to wield it as a diplomatic weapon to obtain political dividends, especially in negotiations with the United States. Americans now had to deal with him as an equal superpower. For his part, he badly needed their help to prop up the other three, weaker, legs.[27]

One was Eastern Europe. Despite the Czech tragedy of 1968, the satellite states, particularly Rumania and Poland, slowly evolved national policies that did not fit the Russian model. The area was in a greater state of flux, and being more drawn to the booming Western economies, than Moscow desired. In a crisis the bloc could be con-

---

[26]William Safire, *Before the Fall* (Garden City, N.Y., 1975), pp. 434–436, 452.
[27]Helmut Sonnenfeldt and William G. Hyland, *Soviet Perspectives on Security* (London, 1979), pp. 16–18; Robin Edmunds, *Soviet Foreign Policy, 1962–1973* (London, 1975), chapters 8, 9.

trolled by force; that was one reason for the Russian military buildup. But the army could not resolve the deeper problems. In 1971 Brezhnev therefore made a deal in which the West Germans finally recognized the Eastern European boundaries imposed by the Red Army in 1945; in return, he settled the long-festering Berlin question by guaranteeing Western access to the city. He now wanted Nixon to agree to that arrangement and thereby further stabilize the weak leg.

The second wobbly leg was Sino-Soviet relations. This problem was indeed so dangerous that it provided a central reason for the military's expansion. The fear of "encirclement" that had haunted earlier Soviet leaders now reappeared, especially after the Chinese opened talks with Japan and the United States. Brezhnev designed his détente policy in part to ensure that it would remain in Nixon's interest to deal with him instead of moving closer to Mao.

The leg that needed the most support was the Soviet economy. The five-year plan of 1966–1970 had failed to reach its objectives. Despite, or because of, decades of coercion, Russian farm workers were only one-sixth as productive as the Americans. This economic decline, moreover, was part of a larger breakdown that was producing not only famous dissenters such as physicist Andrei Sakharov, and author Aleksandr Solzhenitsyn but also a growing underground anti-Soviet literature among educated classes. Brezhnev wanted U.S. technology and agricultural products. A mammoth wheat deal, part of a larger trade agreement worked out at the summit, nearly doubled Soviet-American trade. Unfortunately, the Russian negotiators outfoxed their capitalist counterparts, bought the wheat at bargain-basement prices, and helped create a grain shortage in the United States that worsened inflation. To Nixon and Kissinger, however, the "Great Grain Robbery" was a cheap price to pay. They opened new markets for American farmers while reaping diplomatic benefits.

Given, therefore, the economic problems of both nations, and their need to bring spreading military commitments under some control, Brezhnev as well as Nixon designed a détente policy. The two leaders signed a Strategic Arms Limitation Treaty (SALT I). The pact ended the race to develop a defensive antiballistic missile system (ABMs) that promised to be enormously expensive and highly ineffective. SALT I also froze the number of nuclear missiles so that the Soviets had no more than 1600 and the United States 1054. Those numbers, however, deceived. For the United States had developed a new monster weapon, the MIRV (multiple independently targeted reen-

A 1980s SOVIET VIEW

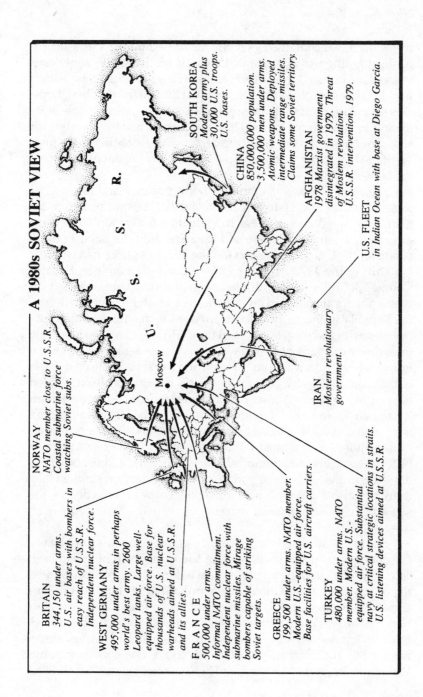

BRITAIN
344,150 under arms. U.S. air bases with bombers in easy reach of U.S.S.R. Independent nuclear force.

WEST GERMANY
495,000 under arms in perhaps world's best army. 2600 Leopard tanks. Large well-equipped air force. Base for thousands of U.S. nuclear warheads aimed at U.S.S.R. and its allies.

F R A N C E
500,000 under arms. Informal NATO commitment. Independent nuclear force with submarine missiles. Mirage bombers capable of striking Soviet targets.

GREECE
199,500 under arms. NATO member. Modern U.S.-equipped air force. Base facilities for U.S. aircraft carriers.

TURKEY
480,000 under arms. NATO member. Modern U.S.-equipped air force. Substantial navy at critical strategic locations in straits. U.S. listening devices aimed at U.S.S.R.

NORWAY
NATO member close to U.S.S.R. Coastal submarine force watching Soviet subs.

SOUTH KOREA
Modern army plus 30,000 U.S. troops. U.S. bases.

CHINA
850,000,000 population. 3,500,000 men under arms. Atomic weapons. Deployed intermediate range missiles. Claims some Soviet territory.

AFGHANISTAN
1978 Marxist government disintegrated in 1979. Threat of Moslem revolution. U.S.S.R. intervention, 1979.

U.S. FLEET
in Indian Ocean with base at Diego Garcia.

IRAN
Moslem revolutionary government.

269

try vehicle) that contained—on one missile—multiple warheads capable of hitting widely separated areas. With the MIRV, Americans enjoyed a 2 to 1 lead in deliverable warheads—another good reason why Brezhnev wanted an agreement that limited the number of missiles. One American submarine possessing MIRVs was capable of inflicting 160 Hiroshima blasts. The United States had over thirty such subs. The Soviets moved rapidly to deploy their first MIRV in the mid-1970s. SALT I therefore only placed a few limits on, but did not stop, the arms race.

The summit was a triumph for both Brezhnev and Nixon. The Russian leader successfully carried out his détente program announced at the Party Congress. In Vietnam the communist offensive ground to a halt; the Chinese and Russians did little publicly to retaliate for the U.S. bombing and mining. Nixon's policy had worked.

During the 1972 campaign the Democratic nominee, Senator George McGovern of South Dakota, had little chance. His left-of-center politics alienated many Americans and left him open to the unfair Republican charge that McGovern was the champion of "amnesty [for men who had illegally avoided the draft], acid, and abortion." He presented a carefully prepared foreign-policy program that urged an immediate withdrawal from Vietnam and a sharply reduced defense budget. But McGovern could not stir up a debate. As Nixon isolated himself in the White House, Republicans accused McGovern of following an "isolationist" foreign policy. When the Democratic nominee pointed to the Watergate break-in and claimed that the Nixon administration was the most politically corrupt regime in American history, the voters were unmoved. Playwright Arthur Miller observed that Americans tend to respond to calls for righteousness when they think it is also a call for lunch. The President won reelection by the second largest electoral vote margin in twentieth-century American history.

Kissinger enhanced the margin by announcing just days before the voting that "peace is at hand" in Vietnam. The timing had been carefully calculated. Nearly two years before, Kissinger had wanted the war to drag on, and then have "a pullout right at the fall of '72 so that if any bad results follow, they will be too late to affect the election," (as he was quoted by a top Nixon aide). The celebration in October 1972, however, proved premature. Kissinger had reached agreement with the communists, but he could not convince South Vietnam's President Nguyen Van Thieu to accept terms that allowed large numbers of communist troops to remain in South Vietnam. The deal collapsed. After the election Nixon began the most devastating bombing attack yet launched on North Vietnam. Parts of the country were carpet bombed. Congress watched, nearly 60 percent of Americans polled supported this "Christmas bombing," and no one stopped the President. As one journalist recorded Nixon's private conversation, he "did not care if the whole world thought he was crazy for resuming the bombing," for "the Russians and Chinese might think they were dealing with a madman and so better force North Vietnam into a settlement before the world was consumed in a larger war."[28]

Tragically, however, it was South Vietnam that held up a peace treaty. Nixon finally won Thieu's agreement with huge amounts of supplies and a secret letter assuring Thieu that if he would "go with us, you have my assurance of continued assistance in the post-settlement period and that we will respond with full force should the settlement be violated by North Vietnam."[29] So assured, Thieu agreed. The treaty was signed in February 1973. American prisoners of war returned home. The United States had terminated its longest conflict.

Nixon stood unchallenged at the peak of his power. Free of the Vietnam quicksands, and with the Russians apparently better "managed" by détente and linkage, the President turned to other foreign-policy problems. Kissinger grandly announced that 1973 was to be the "year of Europe"—that is, the United States would now deal with the increasingly bitter Western European allies to whom it had paid little attention while making momentous deals with China and Russia. Critics, who believed the Western alliance was beyond repair, remarked that Kissinger's phrase resembled the words of a long unfaithful husband who grandly announced this was to be the "year of the wife."

In the Western Hemisphere, Nixon dealt with the Chilean government of Salvador Allende, a devoted nationalist and sometime Marxist who, since his election to the presidency in 1970, had moved

[28]*Washington Post,* May 18, 1994, p. A6; Thomas L. Hughes, "Foreign Policy: Men or Measures?" *Atlantic Monthly,* CCXXXIV (October 1974): 56; Seymour Hersh, *The Price of Power* (New York, 1983), chapter 39.
[29]*The New York Times,* May 1, 1975, p. 16.

to break Chile free from its dependence on large landowners and American multinational corporations (see map, p. 207). Allende nationalized nearly $1 billion of American investment. At least one multinational, International Telephone and Telegraph (ITT), urged Nixon to get tough. The President did so, but not primarily because of ITT. He and Kissinger viewed Allende's Chile as a potential Soviet satellite, a second Cuba, whose infection could spread through the hemisphere and demonstrate that Nixon was too weak to secure his own backyard. With the help of the CIA and close ties between the U.S. and Chilean military, Kissinger systematically undermined the Chilean government. Allende lost control of his nation's economy. "We set the limits of diversity," Kissinger bragged, and in September 1973 Allende died as Chile's army seized power. The military established a brutally repressive regime. When the U.S. ambassador protested the torture methods, Kissinger ordered him "to cut out the political science lectures."[30]

Nixon also moved to control, or intimidate, key parts of the federal government. He gained some of this power through illegal wiretapping, breaking and entering, and misusing campaign funds. Kissinger passed all this off with the joking comment, "The illegal we do immediately; the unconstitutional takes a little longer." But a fundamental question remained: could American foreign policy be drastically changed, and a public consensus built to support new policies, without an Imperial Presidency that distorted the truth and manipulated the people? The Nixon presidency did not provide a happy answer to that fundamental question. Even Kissinger was apparently not safe. The daring diplomat, winner of a Nobel Peace Prize for his role in ending the Vietnam War, the man with the German accent and gravylike voice—"Superkraut" as he was happy to be called—was popular and powerful. Rumors spread in Washington that a jealous President was prepared to fire Kissinger. Then in mid-1973 Congress began hearings on the Watergate break-in of 1972. Nixon's political career and American foreign policy suddenly changed. A new era was about to begin.

The most dramatic event in this new era occurred when Richard Nixon became the first American President to resign from office. That historic turn had begun when he tried to cover up the break-in by his

---

[30]Roger Morris, *Uncertain Greatness* (New York, 1977), p. 241; *The New York Times*, March 6, 1975, p. C37.

Plumbers unit at the Watergate hotel complex in 1972. But his foreign policy also hastened his exit. In 1973 Congress and public opinion so turned against his brutal bombing of Southeast Asia that the House and Senate finally ordered an end to the attacks.[31] Resembling other Presidents, before and after, who found themselves becoming mired in political trouble at home, Nixon tried to save himself with foreign-policy spectaculars. Instead of firing the popular Kissinger as he had planned, the President named him secretary of state in the autumn of 1973. The two men then flew to Moscow for another highly publicized summit meeting. But it was too late; the House prepared impeachment articles, Nixon grew increasingly unstable and, since his finger remained on the nuclear button, increasingly dangerous. In August 1974 his aides and several Republican leaders convinced him to resign.

The Imperial Presidency had collapsed. In its place arose what some worried observers called an Imperial Congress. The legislature had repealed the Gulf of Tonkin Resolution in 1971, and by 1974 it had passed measures preventing American troops from reentering Vietnam. The House and Senate similarly outlawed military involvement in parts of Africa without their explicit consent. In 1974–1975 the Senate struck at the heart of Kissinger's détente policy by attaching conditions to the Soviet-American trade treaty that made the pact unacceptable to the Soviets. (These conditions included the widely discussed Jackson-Vanik amendment demanding that Moscow allow more Jewish dissidents to leave Russia if they wished, and—more important from the Soviet view—a Stevenson amendment sharply limiting the amount of money the stumbling Russian economy could borrow from the United States.)

Apart from these riflelike limitations, Congress used a political shotgun in its attack on presidential powers. The War Powers Act of 1973 required that "in every possible instance" the President must consult with Congress before sending troops into hostilities; when the President commits the forces, he must send a full explanation to Congress within two days and he must withdraw the forces within sixty days unless Congress expressly gives him permission to keep them in battle. The act, in reality, gives the President the power to wage war for sixty days without congressional approval, a power that the

---

[31]McGeorge Bundy, "Vietnam, Watergate and Presidential Powers," *Foreign Affairs*, LXVIII (Winter 1979–1980): 397–404.

founders wisely did not give the chief executive in 1787. Congress hoped, however, that the law could prevent future Vietnams.

Kissinger was furious. He warned that perhaps Congress could deal with domestic issues but, because of its supersensitivity to public opinion and interest groups, it was not designed to carry out long-term foreign policies. When his plans for Vietnam and Africa failed during 1975–1976, the secretary of state blamed Congress and the effects of Watergate. He apparently did not understand that his and Nixon's foreign policies in Southeast Asia between 1969 and 1973 had caused congressional anger and the Watergate scandal (see p. 262). He also failed to understand that by the mid-1970s congressional authority grew precisely because of legislative power in domestic affairs, for domestic and foreign policies were becoming one.

That intimate relationship became dramatically clear in 1973–1974 when Americans found themselves short of gasoline at home because of a war in the Middle East. An Arab-Israeli clash was, as usual, the eye of the conflict. After the Suez crisis of 1956, the Soviets had rebuilt the Egyptian Army while the United States helped make Israel the most powerful military force in the area. In 1967 the Egyptians threatened the Gulf of Aqaba, the entranceway to Israel's key southern port of Elat. On June 5 Israel suddenly struck. In a six-day war the Israelis drove the Egyptians back across the Suez, the Jordanian Army across the Jordan River, and the Syrians away from the strategic Golan Heights. Israel seized the old city of Jerusalem.

The United States and Russia did not intervene, but within months each helped replace its ally's stores. To block the Soviets and leftist Arab nationalists, Lyndon Johnson placed U.S. policy on the so-called Three Pillars: Israeli power, Iran's oil and military, and Saudi Arabia's massive oil reserves and strategic bases.[32] As the Soviets established port bases in Egypt, a confrontation loomed between the two superpowers. The new Egyptian president, Anwar el-Sadat, proposed negotiations, but only after Israel withdrew from lands taken in 1967. The Israelis, after having paid a heavy toll for their withdrawal from the Sinai peninsula following the 1956 war, refused Sadat's conditions and rejected U.S. pressure to withdraw from all occupied territories. In October 1973, on Yom Kippur, the holiest day

---

[32]Douglas Little, "Choosing Sides." In Robert A. Divine, ed., *The Johnson Years, Volume 3* (Lawrence, Kan., 1994), pp. 151, 169, 183.

THE MIDDLE EAST, 1967, 1979

U.N. partition of Palestine, 1947 (Jewish State)

Added to Israel after war of 1948–1949

Area controlled by Israel after Six Day War, 1967

Israeli-occupied area after October War, 1973

Israeli withdrawal after negotiations, 1979

in the Jewish calendar, the Egyptians and Syrians launched a sudden attack that drove the Israeli Army back in a surprising show of strength. The shocked Israelis counterattacked, surrounded the Egyptian Army in the Sinai, and threatened to open all of Egypt to invasion. Sadat appealed to Brezhnev. The Soviet leader threatened to act alone to enforce a cease-fire if the Americans would not cooperate with his policy.

Kissinger and Nixon warned Brezhnev to stay out of the area. They emphasized their warning by putting the nation's nuclear strike forces on alert. But the Americans also offered the olive branch. They demanded an Israeli cease-fire and the supplying of the surrounded Egyptian forces. Kissinger held back military supplies needed by Israel until it agreed with his demands. With fresh support from Sadat, who had expelled all Soviet military advisers from Egypt when they seemed to threaten his own power, Kissinger began a series of trips among Middle East capitals to work out a settlement. Despite two years of exhaustive efforts (his plane was tabbed the "Yo-Yo express" because it went up and down so often), the secretary of state worked out a cease-fire but could not find the key to a full settlement.

His diplomacy focused on two objectives. He wanted peace, but without Soviet participation. Resembling the nineteenth-century British statesmen he had studied as a historian, and also resembling Acheson and Dulles, Kissinger determined not to allow Russian strength to shape affairs in the Middle East. To block the Soviets, he and Nixon willingly took the chance of destroying détente. They also sought to end the danger that the Arabs might try to blackmail the West. This nearly occurred in 1973. When the United States supplied weapons to Israel, using NATO bases in Western Europe as transport points, the Arab-dominated Organization of Petroleum Exporting Countries (OPEC) imposed an oil embargo that threatened to strangle the Western and Japanese economies.

OPEC consisted of thirteen nations, including seven Arab countries, Iran, and Venezuela. It had been formed in 1960 to protest attempts of major oil companies (mostly owned by Americans, British, and Dutch) to reduce oil prices and payments to the producers. By the early 1970s the great international companies suddenly faced a unified bloc of producers. OPEC forced the companies to increase payments drastically, quadrupled the price of oil by 1974 to nearly $12 for a forty-two-gallon barrel, threatened nationalization of the companies' properties, and firmly believed that "we are the Masters."[33] Amidst a sudden energy crisis New York Stock Exchange shares lost $97 billion in value in six weeks.

Japan and Western Europe began switching from pro-Israeli to pro-Arab policies. This change further strained the alliance system, for the United States, which imported only 12 percent of its oil from the Middle East (compared with 80 percent for the Europeans and over 90 percent for Japan), remained staunchly committed to Israel. As the allies changed, Kissinger bitterly commented that they were "craven" and "contemptible."[34] Not only had hopes for the "year of Europe" turned to ashes, but he believed that Western Europe had become his "deepest problem."

The energy crisis would have occurred in the not distant future regardless of the Arab-Israeli conflict. Between 1945 and the late 1970s, the West and Japan consumed more oil and minerals than had been used in all previous recorded history. With 6 percent of the world's population, the United States used nearly 40 percent of that wealth.[35] The West could not continue to increase its energy use 5 percent annually, pay low oil prices, yet sell inflation-priced goods to the petroleum producers. This was emphasized by the shah of Iran, whose nation was the world's second-largest oil exporter, and who was Washington's most trusted Middle East friend, according to the Nixon Doctrine. "Of course [the price of oil] is going to rise," the shah declared. "Certainly! and how! . . . You [Westerners] increased the price of wheat you sell us by 300%, and the same for sugar and cement. . . . You buy our crude oil and sell it back to us, refined as petrochemicals, at a hundred times the price you've paid to us. . . . It's only fair that, from now on, you should pay more for oil. Let's say . . . 10 times more."[36]

---

[33]Gurney Breckenfeld, "How the Arabs Changed the Oil Business," *Fortune*, LXXXV (August 1971): 113–117. A superb analysis on the important books that have analyzed the background is Douglas Little, "America and the Middle East Since 1945," *Diplomatic History*, XVIII (Fall 1994): 513–540.

[34]*Washington Post*, March 17, 1974, p. A12.

[35]Richard Barnet, "The World's Resources," *The New Yorker*, April 23, 1980, pp. 45, 47; *Washington Post*, February 24, 1975, p. 1.

[36]*The New York Times*, December 12, 1973, p. 64; for the background, see James E. Akins, "The Oil Crisis: This Time the Wolf Is Here," *Foreign Affairs*, LI (April 1973): 470–472.

The Nixon-Kissinger policies were falling apart. They had focused on Russia and China, but the challenge now came from the Third World. American power was under attack even in Latin America, an area Kissinger had supposedly once dismissed as "a dagger pointed at the heart of—Antarctica." The Republicans devised no alternative to the moribund Alliance for Progress. As terrorism and guerrilla activities increased, Nixon's only major response was to propose doubling the amount of military arms sold by the United States and, in Chile, helping a military regime replace Allende. But Allende's overthrow did not remove a more fundamental danger. In 1975 the secretary of state worried that Latin Americans and other newly emerging nations were "tending to form a rigid bloc of their own," a development "particularly inappropriate for the Western Hemisphere."[37] Again his big-power diplomacy was being undercut by the Third World. Again the energy crisis made the challenge possible, for the Latin American bloc was organized and financed in large part by Venezuela and its oil revenues, which quintupled between 1970 and 1975. A similar danger appeared to the north. Canada's television, periodicals, banks, and half its industry were dominated by the United States. Canadians began playing their own balance-of-power game. Trade was opened with China. Pierre Trudeau became the first Canadian prime minister to travel in the Soviet Union, signing consultation and trade pacts with the Russians. In 1973 strict controls were placed on foreign investments for the first time. During the 1970s exports of Canadian oil and natural gas, upon which large sectors of the United States depended, rose dramatically in price, and then exports were cut back so that Canadians themselves could be assured of long-term cheap energy. While Kissinger searched for new relations with the four major blocs, hemispheric unity, which Americans tended to take for granted, fragmented.

U.S. officials could at least be relieved that the Soviets were not directly involved in the new developments in the Western Hemisphere and Middle East and did not immediately profit from the American troubles. In Africa, however, the superpowers nearly confronted each other in a crisis that typified the new Cold War that was

---

[37]*Department of State Bulletin,* March 24, 1975, pp. 365–366.

developing in the 1970s. Their confrontation in little-known Angola became a major reason for the death of détente.[38]

Since 1970 Kissinger had assumed that the Portuguese, through their colony in Angola, would help maintain stability in Africa. In 1974, however, the forty-year dictatorship in Portugal fell. Angola became independent and black revolutionaries vied for power. The Americans and Chinese supplied one faction, while the Soviets backed the group that ultimately won, the Popular Movement for the Liberation of Angola (MPLA). Most startling of all, the Russians flew thousands of Cuban troops into Angola in a move that Kissinger condemned as a dangerous escalation of the Cold War. He asked Congress for massive aid to stop this Soviet aggression "by proxy," but the legislators flatly refused to become immersed in a possible Vietnam-like conflict in Africa. The MPLA triumphed and then, in a wondrous turn of events, used the Cuban troops to protect the American-owned Gulf Oil refinery (one of the nation's most important facilities) and turned increasingly to Washington for technological help. Both superpowers were learning how little Africans cared about a Cold War that seemed to obsess some Americans and Russians.

But Kissinger did not draw that lesson. He believed that Americans, especially the young who "have been traumatized by Vietnam as we were by Munich," lacked the will to stand up to the Soviets.[39] His concern increased in 1974–1975, when the United States sank into its worst economic recession since the 1930s. He had hoped to use the nation's economic power to "manage" the Russians. Congress, however, had already undercut the 1972 trade treaty, and in 1975, when Kissinger tried to use an embargo on wheat exports as a weapon to make the Soviets behave in Africa, a tremendous uproar of protest from American farm communities forced him to back down. He reflected on how difficult it was for policymakers to protect what they considered to be the national interest when that job had to be done in a private enterprise economy.[40]

---

[38] Anatoly Dobrynin, *In Confidence* (New York, 1995), pp. 360–361. The best background and the key document are in Mohamed A. El-Khawas and Barry Cohen, eds., *NSSM 39: The Kissinger Study of Southern Africa* (Westport, Conn., 1976).

[39] Speech of April 17, 1975, *Department of State Bulletin*, May 5, 1975, p. 560.

[40] Remarks in Los Angeles, February 2, 1976, *Department of State Bulletin*, March 1, 1976, p. 272.

American foreign policy improved little after Gerald Ford replaced Nixon in August 1974. Appointed by Nixon to be Vice President after Spiro Agnew had to resign for taking illegal payments, Ford had been a leader in the House of Representatives. But he had little personal prestige and no background in foreign policy. When he made a serious error while discussing the Middle East, one journalist passed it off: "What the hell, it was just Jerry talking about things he doesn't understand."[41]

Ford became President as Vietnam was finally falling to the communists. The agreement that Kissinger negotiated in 1973 with North and South Vietnam had never worked. President Thieu attacked the communists emplaced in South Vietnam, and in late 1973 they began retaliating. Thieu's forces lost more soldiers in 1974 than during the height of the fighting in 1967. At the same time a recession-ridden United States cut its aid from $1 billion to $700 million. In early 1975 the South Vietnamese Army began to disintegrate. Thieu called for President Ford to provide the American "full force" promised by Nixon in 1973. But Nixon's 1973 promise was of no effect. He and Kissinger had not made the letter public (indeed, Kissinger publicly denied in 1973 that any secret understandings existed), and Congress had prohibited the reintroduction of American forces in Vietnam. In April 1975 South Vietnam fell into communist hands. The thirty-year war was over.

Kissinger asked Americans to put Vietnam behind them—a strange request coming from a former history professor, for the lessons to be learned were many and critical. The war demonstrated that militarily the United States could not single-handedly defeat nationalist movements in Asia. Nor did it have the economic and social resources to fight such a long, inconclusive war. The United States bore great responsibility for the downfall of South Vietnam. The involvement was not comparable to American responsibility for China in the 1940s. The governments of both South Vietnam and Cambodia were Washington's creations. Both depended upon the United States for their existence. Both collapsed after the American forces withdrew. In this sense the "domino theory" actually worked. (Dominoes is a game in which the pieces are laid flat. It requires special effort outside the rules to set them upright so that they can collapse.) American Presidents, supported in the early years by Congress and public

[41]Richard Reeves, *A Ford Not a Lincoln* (New York, 1975), pp. 174, 181, 200.

opinion, made a mighty effort to prop up the dominoes in Southeast Asia, and the collapse duly occurred.

Ford and Kissinger tried to reinvigorate foreign policy (and Ford's hopes for the 1976 presidential race) with two dramatic acts. They traveled to Russia in late 1974 and agreed with Brezhnev on the outline for a SALT II agreement that set new limits on nuclear arms. (Unknown to the Americans, Brezhnev suffered several seizures during and after the meeting. He began a rapid physical and mental decline but remained in power until his death in 1982.) The other drama occurred in May 1975, when Cambodian naval units seized an American cargo ship, the *Mayaguez*. The seizure occurred just after Vietnam fell, OPEC had quadrupled oil prices without an American response, and Kissinger had been unable to stop the MPLA in Angola. In this political climate Ford, with Kissinger's strong encouragement, did what Presidents have often done in similar situations: he used military force to show that he was decisive and not afraid to get tough with communists. Unknown to Ford, however, the Cambodian government had released the thirty-eight crew members. Forty American troops were killed in a needless raid on Cambodian territory. Public opinion polls nevertheless showed strong support for the President's use of military force.

The *Mayaguez* "rescue" and the arms agreement were not enough to save Ford's campaign in 1976. Indeed, Kissinger's foreign policy became an issue. Right-wing Republicans attacked détente until Ford outlawed using the word in his speeches. Kissinger remarked that détente "is a word I would like to forget."[42] Soviet activities in Angola and Cuba, and continued repression of dissidents within Russia, had soured many Americans on the idea that détente could work. Meanwhile, the Democratic nominee, Jimmy Carter, hit Kissinger from the liberal side for being too secretive, supporting dictatorial regimes, and arguing for higher defense budgets. In a style that was typical of Carter, he then blasted the administration from the other direction for giving away too much in the arms talks, and especially for Kissinger's work in the 1975 Helsinki agreements. At Helsinki, Finland, thirty-five countries, including the Western nations, accepted the East European boundaries as permanent; in return, the Soviets pledged to follow a more liberal human rights policy. Moscow leaders tried to modify their pledge ("We are masters in our own house," they declared), but, as a top Russian diplomat later noted, the Helsinki ac-

[42]*Department of State Bulletin*, December 1, 1975, p. 767.

cords "gradually became a manifesto of the dissident and liberal movement, a development totally beyond the imagination of the Soviet leadership." The stage was being set for the U.S.S.R.'s later collapse. Carter, however, condemned the deal for not doing enough to protect individual liberties inside Russia.[43]

The Democratic candidate took different sides on so many issues that unfriendly critics charged that Carter's image could never be carved in stone on Mount Rushmore because there was room on the monument for only one face. But his tactics worked. He lost most of his 30 percent lead over Ford in polls taken during late summer but held on to win by a slim popular vote.

Carter's triumph brought a remarkable decade to an end. Between 1966 and 1976 Americans had roller-coasted from heights to depths: from near victory in Vietnam to embarrassing defeat; from a powerhouse economy to a thieflike inflation; from an Imperial Presidency to the presidential humiliation of Watergate and the War Powers Act; from cheap gasoline to bending before demands of OPEC oil producers; from condemning Chinese communism to cooperation with it; and, most important, from détente to increasing confrontation with the Soviet Union. For at the heart of détente lay a fatal contradiction. On the one hand, the Soviet leaders saw détente as a form of class struggle in which they would employ the newly emerging nations to triumph over capitalism, while, of course, carefully avoiding a direct military confrontation with the United States. On the other hand, U.S. leaders viewed détente as a way to contain and manage Soviet power. "All in all," observed Soviet ambassador to the United States Anatoly Dobrynin, "one could say that détente was to a certain extent buried in the fields of Soviet–American rivalry in the Third World."[44]

U.S. power to contain and manage that Soviet power in the post-1960s world had dwindled. Frustrated Americans concluded that trying to manage Moscow through détente had been a great failure. The question now became whether a better approach could be devised. Jimmy Carter, Ronald Reagan, and—above all—Mikhail Gorbachev were to give quite different answers to that fundamental question.

---

[43]Henry A. Plotkin, "Issues in the 1976 Campaign." In Gerald Pomper, ed., *The Election of 1976* (New York, 1977), pp. 50–52; Dobrynin, *In Confidence*, p. 346.
[44]Dobrynin, *In Confidence*, pp. 468, 473.

CHAPTER 12

From Cold War to Old War: Reagan and Gorbachev (1977–1989)

In the late 1970s Americans finally emerged from the crises of Vietnam and Watergate only to confront a new Cold War. It was a conflict more dangerous and unmanageable than anything they had faced before. In the old Cold War Americans had enjoyed superior nuclear force, an unchallenged economy, strong alliances, and a trusted Imperial President to direct this incredible power against the Soviets. In the new Cold War, however, Russian forces achieved nuclear equality. Each side could only plan to destroy the other many times; the plan involved a military doctrine known as Mutual Assured Destruction, or MAD. The U.S. economy reigned supreme, but in such key areas as steel, automobiles, and textiles it no longer could compete in world markets. It certainly could no longer bear the crushing burden of satisfying Americans' demands to be both the globe's greatest consumers and its unquestioned policeman. Meanwhile the alliance system further cracked and the Imperial Presidency was overthrown. In the 1980s Ronald Reagan moved to solve these challenges by trying to roll back time to recapture the happier days of the earlier Cold War. But first, Jimmy Carter, after much indecision and confusion, launched policies that prepared the way for Reagan.

As a little-known Georgia governor in 1973, Carter appeared on the television show "What's My Line?" and none of the panelists could guess who he was or what he did. Three years later Carter turned this anonymity into a political weapon. He ran against the Washington scandals by emphasizing that he had never been associated with the capital's politics. Carter instead stressed his decency and religious beliefs, and promised, "I'll never tell you a lie." He was also a tough politician. The two sides of his character, the realistic politico and the caring Christian, combined in his appraisal of Nixon: "I despise the bastard, but I pray that he will find peace."[1]

The 1976 election produced no clear foreign-policy mandate. Carter often refused to take clear positions. Working both sides of the political street, he evoked the name of a famous Southern conservative when he described himself as "a Populist in the tradition of Richard Russell." (One observer commented that that made as much sense as saying he was "a socialist in the tradition of Herbert Hoover."[2]) With such wordplay, Carter received strong support from independents as well as regular Democrats, who applauded his fight against the Washington "establishment." Independents could recall the words of Carter's top aide, Hamilton Jordan: "If, after the inauguration, you find a Cy Vance as Secretary of State and Zbigniew Brzezinski as head of National Security [Council], then I would say we failed. And I'd quit. . . . You're going to see new faces, new ideas." Vance and Brzezinski, deeply rooted in the "establishment," became secretary of state and national security adviser, respectively. Jordan did not resign.

Carter's foreign policy quickly became confused as Brzezinski and Vance clashed. Brzezinski saw the world more in bipolar terms and believed that the Soviets posed immediate global dangers. An immigrant and the son of a Polish diplomat, Brzezinski had taught at Columbia University, where he wrote many books on communist systems. A fellow White House official only half-joked that Brzezinski enjoyed being "the first Pole in 300 years in a position to really stick it to the Russians." He had condemned the détente policies of Kissinger, a person with whom he had competed professionally since the early 1950s. Brzezinski both urged the "independence" of such bloc states as Rumania and criticized the SALT deals, especially if the Russians did not then behave in Africa or the Middle East. He refused, moreover, to believe "that the use of nuclear weapons would be the end of the human race. . . . That's egocentric."[3] (His view had its counterpart in official Soviet military doctrine that Russia could survive a nuclear exchange and, therefore, that blueprints for such an exchange be part of overall military planning.[4]) A close friend since 1972, Car-

---

[1]James Wooten, *Dasher* (New York, 1978), pp. 33–37.
[2]C. Vann Woodward, "The Best?" *The New York Review of Books,* April 3, 1980, pp. 10–11.
[3]Elizabeth Drew, "Brzezinski," *The New Yorker,* May 1, 1978, p. 126; *Washington Post,* February 18, 1979, p. C4; Ibid., February 5, 1977, p. A10.
[4]Harriet Fast Scott and William F. Scott, *The Armed Forces of the U.S.S.R.* (Boulder, Colo., 1979), pp. 44–45, 52–62.

ter called Brzezinski "my teacher" in foreign policy. Brzezinski explained the closeness by referring to a passage in *Sophie's Choice*, in which the author, William Styron, "describes a surprising affinity between Poland and the South, two peoples bred on a history that overcame defeat, on a code of chivalry and honor that proudly compensated for backwardness."[5]

Vance, on the other hand, agreed with the views of Marshall Shulman, his chief adviser on Soviet affairs and a former Columbia University professor who had been debating Brzezinski for a quarter century. Vance and Shulman believed that peace rested on negotiations and economic ties between the superpowers—not, as Brzezinski argued, by viewing any crisis anywhere in the world as a Soviet challenge. Unlike Brzezinski, Vance and Shulman saw SALT II as the central diplomatic issue and believed that no problem, even Russian aggressiveness in the Middle East, should be allowed to endanger arms talks. Shulman hoped to influence Soviet behavior through "soft linkage," saying quietly to Moscow officials that they had a greater chance of receiving badly needed American economic help if they better observed human rights within their country and peace elsewhere. Shulman's hope rested on those Russians he called "within-the-system modernizers," that is, young and middle-aged technicians and professionals who would work with the West to improve Soviet society. He saw the modernizers as a check on the older, neo-Stalinist factions, but Shulman understood that time and not a few funerals were required first. Vance and Shulman would never be given that time.

If trouble developed in the newly emerging nations, Vance and Shulman, unlike Brzezinski, believed it could usually be handled as a problem of new nationalisms, not a superpower confrontation. Their view received strong support from Andrew Young, the U.S. ambassador to the United Nations. Young believed profitable political and economic cooperation would develop between the United States and the newly emerging peoples, if they could be kept clear of great power conflicts. He later proved his point with major diplomatic successes in Zimbabwe and Nigeria. Finally, Vance and Shulman differed from Brzezinski in believing that Eastern European changes had to occur

[5]Zbigniew Brzezinski, *Power and Principle: Memoirs of the National Security Adviser, 1977–1981* (New York, 1983), pp. 20–21.

slowly. They believed that any rapid development of independent policies could produce a rerun of the 1968 Czech tragedy.

Between these two views stood the final decision maker. President Carter clearly wanted to hear conflicting advice, but he had to choose between these complex alternatives without having any significant personal foreign-policy background. Between 1973 and 1976 he had been the token Southern politician on the Trilateral Commission, a private group of Americans, Western Europeans, and Japanese that Brzezinski and banker David Rockefeller organized to discuss the mushrooming problems of industrial nations. A number of Trilateralists (including Vance and Young) joined the Carter team, but the commission seldom agreed on common policy. One member dismissed his colleagues as mere "boosters," "a bunch of very sophisticated Rotarians."[6] Even Brzezinski, a founder, grew disillusioned. By 1975 he had concluded that resolving the industrial world's problems was less important (and obviously more difficult) than facing up to the Soviets.

Carter learned no useful framework for a consistent foreign policy from the Trilateralists, and he was unable to devise such a framework himself. A trained engineer, he studied problems case by case, "like an engineering student thinking you can cram for the exam and get an A," as one official remarked. He had little historical knowledge and hence little sense of how to construct a comprehensive strategy. Carter admitted in 1979 that he had read more history since entering the White House than in all the rest of his life.[7] Sometimes he simply split the difference. When Vance and Brzezinski sent him quite different policy memoranda for an address on Soviet policy, Carter solved the problem by stapling the two memos together as the basis for his speech.[8]

Such an approach had worked with American voters, but it quickly failed in the world of U.S. foreign policy. Carter, for example, declared that his commitment to human rights was "absolute." In 1977 he openly encouraged Russian dissidents, who demanded more political freedoms. The gesture infuriated Brezhnev. The dissidents suffered under new crackdowns. Because Carter was simultaneously trying to negotiate arms reductions with them, the Russians

[6]*Washington Post,* January 16, 1977, p. A4.
[7]Interview by Don Oberdorfer, *Washington Post,* February 18, 1979, p. C4.
[8]James Fallows, "Zbig Without Cy," *New Republic,* May 10, 1980, p. 19.

speculated that his human rights policy was a mere "bargaining chip" to trade. In reality, as Andrew Young admitted, the policy was never "thought out and planned," so it remained ineffective.[9] Carter's tough line, which included sharply reducing aid, did cause military regimes such as those in Brazil, Chile, and Argentina to act more decently. The oppressive South Korean government was more important to U.S. security, however, so it received fewer public lectures and more arms. When Carter urged China to ease its dictatorial immigration rules in the interest of human rights, Vice Premier Teng Hsiao-p'ing (Deng Xiaoping) smilingly responded that he would be glad to do so and "send you 10 million immigrants right away." Carter dropped the issue.[10] Soviets soon noted that he said little about the thousands of political prisoners in China, even as he condemned holding such prisoners in Russia. The most glaring and costly inconsistency occurred in Iran. SAVAK, the shah's secret police, tortured and imprisoned upward of 50,000 Iranians. But on New Year's Eve 1977 Carter visited Iran, a vital link in U.S. defense plans. He toasted the shah for making Iran "an island of stability" and for deserving "the respect and the admiration and love which your people give to you."[11] A year later a revolution drove the shah from power.

Not all the confusion was Carter's fault. At home he inherited a political structure that had historically depended on a strong party system. He had not helped by running against party leaders and the "establishment," but in any case the system was in an advanced stage of disintegration before he appeared on the national scene. Into the vacuum rushed hundreds of private groups, many representing a single interest (for example, doctors, used-car dealers, educators, pro- or antiabortion advocates), whose members lobbied hard in Washington. No national consensus could be shaped out of these narrowly focused groups.[12] Special economic interests became ever more active as inflation skyrocketed to an annual rate of 13 percent in 1979–1980. In addition OPEC nations tripled oil prices to nearly $35 a barrel,

[9]See especially Stephen F. Cohen's comments in Fred Warner Neal, ed., *Détente or Debacle* (New York, 1979); and Stephen F. Cohen, "Why Détente Can Work," *Inquiry*, December 19, 1977, p. 16; author's interview in Moscow, November 14, 1980.

[10]*Washington Post,* February 4, 1979, p. A10.

[11]*Public Papers of the Presidents . . . Jimmy Carter, 1977* (Washington, 1978), p. 2221.

[12]Theodore Lowi, *The End of Liberalism* (New York, 1979), pp. 50–61; Joel Silbey, "The End of American Politics, 1980–1984?" unpublished paper, 1980, pp. 8–10.

draining the United States of $100 billion each year without any effective response by the President or a fragmented Congress. Severe economic recession set in. Allied leaders grew disenchanted with such disarray in the nation that supposedly led the noncommunist world.

Despite these problems and a lack of conceptual planning, Carter did score diplomatic victories. He did so most notably when he followed the Vance-Shulman-Young approach. In 1978 the Senate ratified the President's treaty that returned the Canal Zone to Panama over the next twenty-two years while protecting the American right to use and defend the waterway (see map, p. 207). Since 1947 the Panamanians had frequently rioted against the American zone that divided their country. When both sides lost lives in a 1964 outbreak, Lyndon Johnson began a new relationship that would recognize Panama's sovereignty in the Canal Zone. It took fourteen years to complete the arduous process. The decisive Senate figures were the leaders, Democrat Robert Byrd of West Virginia and Republican Howard Baker of Tennessee, who amended the two treaties submitted by Carter to make them acceptable to Republicans. Byrd and Baker took high political risks in fighting such opponents as Republican Senator S. I. Hayakawa of California, who proudly noted how the United States had seized the canal region in 1903 and then claimed, "It's ours. We stole it fair and square." Carter and the Senate scored the most important advance in U.S.–Latin American relations since the 1930s.

The President also followed Vance's suggestions about Africa, despite Soviet intervention and Brzezinski's opposition. When warfare erupted on a border between Zaire (a U.S. associate) and Angola (where Soviet advisers and 19,000 Cuban troops remained), Brzezinski urged direct involvement to teach the communists a lesson. Andrew Young urged instead that the United States help find "African solutions for African problems." Carter accepted Young's advice and the warfare subsided. The Soviets, however, did not show similar restraint. They intervened in the strategic Horn of Africa to aid Somalia, Sudan, and Ethiopia. But Somalia and Sudan soon threw out the Russians. Brezhnev and 15,000 Cuban troops then found themselves immersed in a costly, uncontrollable military campaign on behalf of Ethiopia. Until Young finally resigned as UN ambassador in 1979, his "cool" approach was effective in navigating the whirlpools of African nationalism.

A final Carter triumph occurred in the Middle East during September 1978. A year earlier Egyptian President Sadat had taken the historic step of personally flying to Israel to begin a peace process with Prime Minister Menachem Begin. Carter then invited the two leaders to his private retreat at Camp David, Maryland, where for thirteen nerve-racking days he helped them hammer out an agreement that ended the thirty-year war between Israel and Egypt. The pact provided for Israeli withdrawal from the strategic Sinai peninsula, which had been Egypt's until the 1967 war. Carter helped ease Begin's acceptance with $3 billion of military aid. It was the Georgian's proudest moment as President.

From that point in September 1978, the Carter presidency began a long decline, pulled downward by internal divisions and uncontrollable external events. Soviet-American relations became the most important victim of the confusion. Even the Camp David agreement worsened relations, for in 1977 Carter and Brezhnev had issued a joint statement on the Middle East. The Russians made significant concessions in return for the President's assurance that they could help construct a Middle East peace. The Egyptians, Israelis, and powerful pro-Israeli lobbying groups in Washington loudly protested reintroducing Brezhnev's unsubtle hand in the region. Awestruck by the reaction, Carter simply "walked away from the statement," to use Brzezinski's words.[13] Infuriated Soviet leaders rushed more arms to friends in the region, including Syria, Israel's archenemy.

Perhaps the crucial turn in the superpowers' relationship, however, occurred in May 1978, when Brzezinski, over Vance's objections, flew to Beijing and began the process that climaxed in the opening of formal diplomatic relations with China on New Year's Day in 1979. Brzezinski hoped to play this "China card" to trump Soviet policies in Africa and the Middle East, and on arms control. In Beijing he enthusiastically engaged in a game with Chinese leaders to see who was most anti-Soviet. Brzezinski was "so overwhelmed with the Chinese," Carter recorded later, that "I told him he had been seduced."[14] It is not seduction, however, when one travels halfway around the world to propose. Brzezinski's courtship produced immediate results. U.S. exports to China nearly doubled in 1979; thus

[13]Brzezinski, *Power and Principle,* p. 175.
[14]Jimmy Carter, *Keeping Faith: Memoirs of a President* (New York, 1982), p. 196.

Americans scored against their Japanese rivals in the game to see which would develop the long-fabled China market. Coca-Cola (a Georgia-based firm close to Carter) later opened its first plant in China, with guests drinking "Ke Kou Ke Le" (translated as "Tasty Happiness") as Beethoven's "Ode to Joy" played in the background.[15] (Pepsi-Cola, whose officials were close to Nixon, had earlier obtained a monopoly on the Soviet soft-drink market.)

In reality, China played an "American card" even more effectively against the Russians. Chinese leaders shrewdly timed the announcement of formal diplomatic ties with the United States so that it poisoned a meeting between Vance and the Soviets to discuss SALT II. The SALT process consequently was fatally delayed. Then China's powerful leader, Vice Premier Teng Hsiao-p'ing, visited the United States in early 1979. After his return home he launched an invasion of Vietnam, Russia's ally in Southeast Asia. By his timing, Teng made it appear as if the United States were a silent partner in the invasion. Moscow, at least, must have thought of it as collusion by Russia's two leading enemies. In Washington, however, Carter had no firm idea of where he was heading. "All sweaty in his tennis outfit," the President's top aide, Hamilton Jordan, stopped in Brzezinski's office in mid-1978 to observe that Carter's new toughness against the Soviets was "all a big accident, and who the hell knows whether the President will not veer in some direction tomorrow."[16] In retrospect mid-1978 marked a sharp turn in Soviet-American relations. Brzezinski's influence rose as Vance's fell, especially on Chinese affairs. The Soviets were locked out of the Camp David arrangements. Months later a high Chinese official captured the moment when, in splendid White House ceremonies, he praised Carter and Brzezinski, then turned to his translator and said publicly in Chinese, "I suppose I should also mention the Secretary of State; what's his name?"[17]

Brzezinski was amused by the incident; Brezhnev, no doubt, less so. Soviet leaders were still stunned by Nixon's resignation and the Senate's emasculation of the 1972 trade treaty that had undergirded

---

[15]*The New York Times*, April 16, 1981, p. A3; U.S. Department of State, *Gist*, November 1979, p. 1.

[16]Brzezinski, *Power and Principle*, p. 222.

[17]Brzezinski, *Power and Principle*, p. 418.

détente. Carter was becoming a political bedfellow of the hated Chinese. Evictions from Egypt, Somalia, and Sudan were sharp setbacks for the Russians. Brezhnev nevertheless moved cautiously.[18] Scuttling détente could involve paying a high price, especially in the economic and military realms.

The Soviet economic system became less efficient as official communist ideology (that "fig-leaf" of the system, as Kennan had called it in 1947) withered. Few people still shared the old hope that other revolutions would follow the Soviet model. Nor did anyone believe that a utopian communist community was just over the horizon—unless, as a Russian joke put it, "you understand that an horizon is an imaginary line that recedes as you approach it." But the ideology could not be disavowed because, bankrupt or not, it legitimized the Communist party's monopoly on power. After 1971 Brezhnev had attempted to solve these complex problems with a dual approach: increasing trade with the West to invigorate the Soviet economy, but treating dissidents brutally (while allowing more Jews to emigrate to Israel) to ensure the party's control. By the late 1970s this policy had failed. The expected economic payoffs from détente never appeared.

The Soviet Union actually outpaced the United States in coal, steel, and cement production, and was the world's largest oil producer, but a disproportionate share of the wealth went to nonproductive military budgets or disappeared in the floundering Cuban economy or devastated Vietnam economy. With the world's largest area of tillable land, Russia could not feed its own population. Equally embarrassing to the communists, under 3 percent of the farm area was privately owned, but it contributed as much as 40 percent of the meat, dairy goods, and vegetables. As computers, electronic items, and other high-technology goods became crucial for highly industrialized societies, a system run by narrow party officials and fearful bureaucrats gave little encouragement to innovation. Projections indicated that Russia might even have to import oil by the mid-1980s unless it could buy massive American or Japanese technology to exploit new fields.

The outlook was bleak. Since 1945 the Soviets had tended to increase their gross national product not through innovation but simply by employing more laborers. In the 1970s, however, Soviet growth

---

[18]Paul Marantz, "Foreign Policy." In Alexander Dallin, ed., *The Twenty-Fifth Congress of the CPSU* (Stanford, Calif., 1977), pp. 89–90.

rates declined from 5 percent annually during Brezhnev's first years in power to 0.8 percent in 1979. A sharp drop in the birthrate during the 1950s and 1960s meant fewer laborers after 1975. Astonishingly, death rates and infant mortality rose rapidly in the 1970s, the first time such increases had been noted in such a developed nation. Poor medical care, alcoholism, bad safety facilities, and the tendency of Soviet women to have several abortions before finally bearing children relatively late in life contributed to these embarrassing figures. Population increases occurred almost wholly in Central Asia among Moslem groups. But historic hatreds divided these peoples from the Great Russians who ruled the land. Soviet leaders feared giving the ethnic peoples extensive economic power.[19] Brezhnev and his closest associates meanwhile grew older, slower, and more enfeebled. Brzezinski remarked to Carter that "under Lenin the Soviet Union was like a religious revival, under Stalin like a prison, under Khrushchev like a circus, and under Brezhnev like the U.S. Post Office."[20]

In foreign affairs the Russians began to shiver from their old Stalinist fear of "capitalist encirclement"—only now it was communist as well as capitalist. Parts of the long Chinese-Russian border continued to be armed camps. A possible American-Chinese-Japanese partnership loomed on the Soviets' western flank. In Eastern Europe, economic crises and the energy crunch made the satellite states restless. Yugoslavia became unpredictable as Tito (who had cooperated with, as well as fought, the Soviets) became less active and then died in 1980.[21]

The most startling crisis suddenly appeared on Russia's own southern border. The shah of Iran's dynasty suddenly collapsed. Iran had been enduring terrible strains: half the population was younger than sixteen; the urban population was expected to quadruple to 20 million in just twenty-five years; an oil-dependent economy produced few jobs for an expanding population; 70,000 Iranians educated each

---

[19]Michael Binyon, *Life in Russia* (New York, 1983), pp. 39–40, 58–65; John P. Hardt, "Highlight: Problems and Prospects," in U.S. Congress, Joint Economic Committee, 97th Cong., 2nd Sess., *Soviet Economy in the 1980s: Selected Papers* (Washington, 1983), pp. vii–xiii; Marshall I. Goldman, *U.S.S.R. in Crisis: The Failure of an Economic System* (New York, 1983), especially pp. 100–102.

[20]Carter, *Keeping Faith*, p. 223.

[21]Paul Marantz, "Probing Moscow's Outlook," *Problems of Communism*, XXVIII (March–April 1979): 49–50; Ernest Kux, "Growing Tensions in Eastern Europe," *Problems of Communism*, XXIX (March–April 1980): 21–37.

THE NEAR EAST IN UPHEAVAL, 1980

U. S. S. R.

BLACK SEA

CASPIAN SEA

TURKEY

U.S.S.R. invasion of Afghanistan 1979-1980.

Soviet military buildup

SYRIA

Iraq-Iran border conflict

LEBANON

ISRAEL

IRAQ

JORDAN

• Tehran
IRAN

Moslem revolution overthrows pro-U.S. shah, 1979.

• Kabul

AFGHANISTAN

PAKISTAN

KUWAIT

PERSIAN GULF

EGYPT

SAUDI ARABIA

• Riyadh

Saudi kingdom threatened with internal uprising.

• Mecca

Muscat

OMAN

Strait of Hormuz. Key strategic passageway for oil to Western nations.

INDIA

SUDAN

YEMEN

SOUTH YEMEN

Marxist government

ETHIOPIA

DJIBOUTI

U.S.S.R.-supported Ethiopia in bitter border conflict with U.S.-supported Somalia.

• Berbera

SOMALIA

A R A B I A N

S E A

KENYA

• Mogadishu

Present or prospective U.S. bases.

• Mombasa

TANZANIA

I N D I A N

O C E A N

Diego Garcia

year abroad (35,000 alone in the United States) returned with liberal, often anti-shah ideas; and—of special importance—modernization threatened the country's ancient religious ties, especially the Moslem leaders (the mullahs), who were becoming implacable foes of the shah. The shah meanwhile squandered the nation's wealth by importing more arms from the United States in the 1974–1978 era than Iran had bought in its entire history. The shah used SAVAK, his secret police that had close ties to the CIA, to remove enemies. By 1978 he was nevertheless losing control to the religious leaders and political fanatics (moderate leaders were dead or in prison), and he was suffering from cancer.[22]

American, and probably Soviet, officials understood few of these developments. At the "King of Kings" demand, U.S. intelligence had virtually no contacts with opposition parties. As the revolution gathered force, Brzezinski and Vance split over a response. Brzezinski urged helping the shah establish a military regime to drown the revolt in bloodshed or, if that failed, mobilizing U.S. parachute troops for actual intervention. Vance urged Carter to contact the revolutionary leaders, distance himself from the shah, and assume that any military move could lead to the disintegration of the weakened Iranian Army. Carter again could not make a clear choice. On February 20, 1979, the leading religious figure, Ayatollah Ruholla Khomeini, led forces that drove the shah from power.[23]

U.S. foreign policy had suffered a major defeat. The Soviets publicly applauded this setback, but they could not take too much pleasure because Khomeini led a violently anticommunist Moslem group whose fanaticism could easily spread to the large and expanding Moslem population in Russia. As these revolutionary fires burned in the autumn of 1979, David Rockefeller, Henry Kissinger, and Brzezinski, all with close ties to the shah, convinced Carter to allow the fatally ill monarch into an American hospital.[24] Enraged mobs invaded the U.S. embassy in Tehran and seized sixty-nine hostages. Khomeini released sixteen women and African-Americans but would not free the remaining fifty-three, who, with their defiant captors, began to

---

[22]Abul Kasim Mansur [a pen name], "Why the U.S. Ignored a Quarter-Century of Warning," *Armed Forces Journal International*, January 1979, pp. 27–33.

[23]Brzezinski, *Power and Principle*, pp. 355, 388–393.

[24]Carter, *Keeping Faith*, pp. 452–453.

dominate television screens as the American presidential campaign got under way.

Carter's foreign policies began to unravel ever more rapidly. At a summit conference in Vienna during mid-1979, Carter and Brezhnev finally agreed on a SALT II pact that limited the number of nuclear arms launchers on each side to 2400 (with no more than 1320 to have MIRVs, the multiple warhead rockets). Each side retained its high card. For the United States the card was its small cruise missile, which could fly too low for Soviet detection; for the Russians it was their 300 huge land-based missiles. As Carter sent the treaty to the Senate, however, a group called the Committee on the Present Danger attacked the treaty. Established in 1976, the committee was headed by Paul Nitze and Eugene Rostow, both with long Washington experience, and both driven by the fear that Americans were losing their will to oppose communism. The seventy-two-year-old Nitze resurrected his old rhetoric from NSC-68 of thirty years before and lobbied the Senate incessantly until he and other opponents finally stalled the treaty. Nitze's highly theoretical arguments were picked apart by some arms experts, but Carter's relations with Congress were so poor, and the Cold War atmosphere in the country so tense, that Nitze and others against détente gained the upper hand. They did so even after Brezhnev suddenly allowed more than 50,000 Jews—the highest number in history—to emigrate from Russia in 1979. He thus met a key demand of the antidétente forces, but neither they nor Carter now reciprocated.[25]

The President was under attack from all sides. The Iranian debacle triggered a jump in oil prices. Western European allies blamed the United States for the jump, and they criticized Carter's indecisiveness in planning a weapons program to defend Western Europe. After a summit meeting with West European leaders in 1979, Carter recorded in his diary, "We then had a luncheon that was very bitter and unpleasant. [West German Chancellor Helmut] Schmidt got personally abusive toward me."[26] The President and his advisers also grew angry

[25]Fred Kaplan, *The Wizards of Armageddon* (New York, 1983), pp. 378–384; Adam Ulam, *Dangerous Relations: The Soviet Union in World Politics, 1970–1982* (New York, 1983), p. 250.
[26]Carter, *Keeping Faith*, p. 112.

over attempts by Schmidt and other West Europeans to profit from moving closer to Moscow. Secretary of Defense Harold Brown remarked caustically that the allies seemed to say, " 'Yes, there should be a division of task—we'll sell stuff to the Russians and you defend us.' " Brown added, "That's not what I mean by a division of task." Brzezinski glibly rationalized these failures by writing that the "world had entered a new post-Eurocentric era."[27] To paraphrase, this meant that his Trilateral approach was dead. The United States had few, if any, friends in the industrialized Western world who would fully cooperate in containing Soviet power or disciplining Third World revolutionaries.

Even the "American backyard" seemed unsafe. In July 1979 the revolutionary Sandinista forces overthrew the dictatorial Somoza dynasty that, with strong U.S. support, had been ruling Nicaragua since the mid-1930s. Named after the peasant fighter Augusto Sandino, who had successfully fought U.S. Marines in his country between 1927 and 1933, the Sandinistas had been battling Somoza's brutal national guard for nearly twenty years. By the late 1970s the dictator's greed (he personally owned 25 percent of Nicaraguan land) and the guard's terrorism had turned most Nicaraguans, including leading business figures, to the Sandinistas' side. As Anastasio Somoza was about to fall, however, Jimmy Carter tried to mobilize the Organization of American States to intervene so that the revolutionaries could not gain power. The President could not find a single significant Latin American supporter. He then tried to make the best of a bad situation by asking Congress for $75 million in aid to draw the Sandinista government closer to Washington. The new regime, however, did not want to move closer to the nation that had helped kill its supporters for two decades. The Sandinistas determined to follow a nonaligned foreign policy, but then drew close to Cuba, which had supported them in the final months of the war and now sent thousands of teachers, health experts, and military advisers.

Relations with Nicaragua approached the breaking point in 1980 as the Sandinistas supplied revolutionaries fighting to overthrow the military government in El Salvador. With one of the most inequitable societies and brutal militaries in the hemisphere, El Salvador was ripe for revolution. Carter actually cut off aid to the government after

---

[27]Brzezinski, *Power and Principle*, p. 515; the Brown quote is from *The New York Times*, December 7, 1980, p. 44.

four American Roman Catholic churchwomen were murdered (three had also been sexually assaulted) in late 1980 and Salvadoran officials did nothing. Their military forces, after all, had committed the crime. But the revolutionaries launched a major offensive in January 1981, and Carter quickly reopened aid channels. His Latin American policy, resembling his policy with the allies and the Soviets, lay in fragments.

Unable to devise coherent policies, in mid-1979 Carter seized the only alternative. He embarked on a major military buildup that, in retrospect, was the first chapter of the massive military spending program undertaken by the Reagan administration in the 1980s. The Defense Department budget began to grow as Carter built bases in the Persian Gulf region and authorized a so-called Rapid Deployment Force that (at least on paper) could strike quickly into Third World regions, especially in the oil-rich Middle East. Brzezinski later admitted that by this time, "There was neither dialogue nor deterrence in our relationship" with Moscow.[28] The relationship had been reduced to SALT II, and the pact was nearly dead because arms control proved too fragile, too politically exposed, to carry the entire burden of Soviet-American relations. It needed the kind of supporting political and economic structure that Nixon and Brezhnev had tried to create and that had now been dismantled.

As Carter turned to the military, so did Brezhnev. On Russia's border the Moslem state of Afghanistan began to move away from the control that the Soviets had wielded through puppet governments. In the nineteenth century British colonialists had talked about "the great game of empire" in the Near East, a game in which Afghanistan, because of its pivotal location, was a critical pawn. Now, to Soviet eyes, a hostile China and Iran run by Moslem fanatics threatened the country. In 1979 the Soviets decided the stakes were worth reopening the game. An ill Brezhnev was convinced by a few civilian advisers that strategic and ideological reasons demanded a war—which, they assured him, would be brief. He then overruled his uniformed military, who feared and strongly objected to the operation. On December 27 the Red Army invaded Afghanistan, executed the ineffective Marxist leader, and soon committed nearly 100,000 troops

---

[28]Two fine analyses are Melvyn P. Leffler, "From the Truman Doctrine to the Carter Doctrine," *Diplomatic History*, VII (Fall 1983): 245–266; and Stanley Hoffmann, "In Search of a Foreign Policy," *The New York Review of Books*, September 29, 1983, p. 54.

to a long, costly struggle with Moslem guerrillas. American experts speculated it would be the Soviets' Vietnam. To avoid such a disaster, the Russians used brutal force, including the killing of college students who demonstrated against the occupation. Brezhnev also ordered new arrests of Russian dissidents, including Nobel Prize winning physicist Andrei Sakharov, the leader of the Soviet human rights movement. A high State Department official believed that the invasion and arrests resulted in part from a "domestic crisis within the Soviet system. . . . It may be that the thermodynamic law of entropy has finally and fully caught up with the Soviet system, which now seems to expend more energy on simply maintaining its equilibrium than on improving itself. We could," he concluded, "be seeing a period of foreign movement at a time of internal decay."[29]

A beleaguered Carter, naively complaining that the Soviets had "lied" to him about their peaceful intentions, accelerated his military buildup, which had begun before the Afghanistan invasion. He withdrew SALT II from the Senate (where it was nearly dead anyway), began registering young men for the draft, embargoed U.S. wheat and technology exports to Russia, and ordered Americans to withdraw from the 1980 Olympic Games in Moscow. He promised to increase defense spending by 5 percent in real terms. Finally, the President dramatically announced a "Carter Doctrine" that pledged American intervention—unilaterally if necessary—if the Soviets threatened Western interests in the Persian Gulf region. Brzezinski persuaded Carter to announce the doctrine by directly comparing the crisis to Truman's in 1947. The Georgian, who revered the earlier President, now saw himself once again propping up the dominoes of Western civilization.[30]

Cyrus Vance refused to join the crusade. He believed that the Soviets had invaded Afghanistan because they had a "dangerous problem" on their border and, moreover, had little more "to lose in [their] relationship with the United States."[31] In April 1980 Vance finally resigned when, over his protests, Carter ordered a secret military mission to rescue the fifty-three American hostages in Iran. The complex

[29]Anatoly Dobrynin, *In Confidence* (New York, 1995), pp. 438–439; Charles W. Maynes, "The World in 1980," U.S. Department of State, *Current Policy*, April 1980, pp. 1–2.
[30]Brzezinski, *Power and Principle*, pp. 30–31, 444–445.
[31]Cyrus Vance, *Hard Choices* (New York, 1983), pp. 388–389.

mission failed as a collision between two of the helicopters and a transport plane killed eight American soldiers.

The President entered the 1980 presidential campaign with one of the lowest approval ratings in recent history (77 percent negative, with 82 percent negative for his handling of foreign policy). Spirits sank so low that when Carter stood up to Senator Edward Kennedy's challenge for the Democratic party nomination by replying "I'll whip his ass," Carter's staff told the President that it had done more for their morale than anything "since the Willie Nelson concert" of months before.[32] Carter tried to regain the initiative with his arms buildup. He signed Presidential Directive 59 (PD-59), which ordered massive new forces built to fight a prolonged, limited nuclear war. Critics quickly compared PD-59 with NSC-68 of three decades earlier when Soviet military power had been exaggerated.[33]

The nation's policy was taking a turn back to 1950. Unfortunately for Carter his political fortunes turned not at all. In his foreign policy he tried to outflank the Republican nominee, Ronald Reagan, from the right—a mission impossible. After several years of inconsistency and indecision, Carter tried to return to those simpler days of the Truman Doctrine and NSC-68 (see pp. 95–98). He again proved no match for Reagan in convincing Americans to embark on quests for the Holy Grails of America's Cold War.

Reagan received 51 percent of the popular vote but won overwhelmingly in the electoral college. Exit polls showed that most voters simply thought "it was time for a change"—that is, they wanted new leadership. They were especially disturbed by such domestic problems as inflation, but Americans were also angry over an apparent "loss of control" in foreign affairs. Of those polled, 84 percent believed the nation had sunk into "deep and serious trouble." They favored more money for defense and the use of force in crises.[34] Reagan rode these frustrations into power.

---

[32]Carter, *Keeping Faith*, p. 464; polls in *Washington Post*, July 30, 1980, p. A12.

[33]Fred M. Kaplan, "Our Cold-War Policy, Circa '50," *The New York Times Magazine*, May 18, 1980, p. 94; and Milton Leitenberg, "Presidential Directive (P.D.) 59," *Journal of Peace Research*, XVIII (1981): 309–317.

[34]Terry Deibel, *Presidents, Public Opinion and Power. The Nixon, Carter and Reagan Years* (New York, 1987), pp. 14–15; *The New York Times*, November 9, 1980, p. 28.

A former New Dealer, Reagan changed after dealing with communists in Hollywood, tiring of paying high personal income taxes, divorcing actress Jane Wyman, and marrying actress Nancy Davis, whose family was severely conservative. As television pitchman for General Electric in the 1950s and governor of California in the late 1960s, he blasted federal governmental powers. Governor Reagan also gained national attention for getting tough with antiwar and civil rights protesters on California campuses. In the 1970s he became the best-known spokesman for a neoconservative movement that demanded social order and reduced government spending at home but costly anticommunist military policies abroad. One neoconservative said that "the campus revolts of the 1960s, the rise of the counterculture, [LBJ's] Great Society," and the "takeover" of the Democrats by the liberal "McGovernite wing" had created the movement. But neoconservatism had also been spawned by millions of dollars given by business groups to establish such right-wing think tanks as the Heritage Foundation and the Hoover Institution. The neoconservatives took ideas seriously. Believing that liberalism had seen its day, they worked to come up with new programs. Reagan rode an intellectual as well as a populist wave into power.[35]

The new President's foreign policy was simple and direct: it rested entirely on opposing the Soviet Union. Gone were Nixon's sophisticated détente and Carter's earlier emphasis on North-South issues. Reagan instead took Carter's 1979–1980 anticommunist policies to an extreme. "Let's not delude ourselves," he declared during the 1980 campaign. "The Soviet Union underlies all the unrest that is going on. If they weren't engaged in this game of dominoes, there wouldn't be any hot spots in the world." If asked to be more specific, however, Reagan could seem vague and confused. He toasted his hosts in "Bolivia" while visiting Brazil, and in a critical national security meeting he mistakenly assumed the Soviet SS-19 missile was larger than the SS-18 because nineteen is a larger number than eighteen. By late 1981 his National Security Council (NSC) adviser found him so ignorant of foreign-policy fundamentals that he began showing the President simple government-made instructional movies. In

[35]Sidney Blumenthal, *The Rise of the Counter-Establishment* (New York, 1986), p. 250; *The New York Times*, December 28, 1980, p. E5; *Washington Post*, May 12, 1985, p. F4.

these sessions Reagan asked few questions except "What do I have to say?"[36]

But he devoted hours to preparing for public appearances in which he used his Hollywood training to sell his policies. "To grasp and hold a vision . . .—that is the very essence, I believe, of successful leadership—not only on the movie set where I learned it, but everywhere."[37] Reagan envisioned defeating the Soviet Union in the Cold War. He described the U.S.S.R. to fundamentalist religious leaders as "the evil empire," and he told the British Parliament in 1982 that "Marxism-Leninism" was doomed to "the ashheap of history." In 1981 Leonid Brezhnev, buffeted by war in Afghanistan, Chinese hostility, and a declining economy, sent a nine-page letter asking for talks on arms reductions. Reagan refused; he wanted instead to talk about Soviet "imperialism." His popularity remained firm. "He operates on a separate plane from the rest of us," a Senate leader noted. "We may find him flawed because he doesn't know the details. . . . But he can have a simple dialogue with the voters. . . . Jimmy Carter agreed with you and you didn't like it. This guy can disagree and you think he's great." The reasons for Reagan's effectiveness went beyond his personality and movie manners, however. His vision exploited Americans' anti-Soviet feelings, the roots of which went back to the 1940s, if not the 1890s. And he constantly assured them they were God's Chosen People to wage the great struggle according to what Reagan had called a "divine plan."[38]

His foreign-policy tactics for throwing the Soviets on history's "ash heap" were not as grand as his vision. Indeed, during the first five years of his presidency his foreign policy largely turned out to be his military budget. Reaganites charged that the 1970s arms race had been run only by the Soviets. Others, however, pointed out that during the 1970s Americans had modernized 500 Minuteman missiles; introduced the deadly MIRV missile, with its multiple nuclear

[36]*Time,* December 8, 1986, p. 34; Strobe Talbott, *Deadly Gambits* (New York, 1984), p. 274; *Washington Post,* March 27, 1988, p. C4; *Wall Street Journal,* June 3, 1980, p. 1.
[37]Terry Deibel, "Reagan's Mixed Legacy," *Foreign Policy,* No. 75 (Summer 1989): 50–51; Neil Postman, *Amusing Ourselves to Death. Public Discourse in the Age of Show Business* (New York, 1985), pp. 125–128.
[38]Blumenthal, *Rise of the Counter-Establishment,* pp. 252–253; Steven R. Weisman, "Can the Magic Prevail?" *The New York Times Magazine,* April 29, 1984, p. 41; *Washington Post,* November 21, 1983, p. A13; Ibid., March 29, 1981, p. A6; Strobe Talbott, *The Russians and Reagan* (New York, 1982), pp. 70–71.

warheads; launched Poseidon submarines, with their powerful and highly accurate Trident missiles; built 200 newly developed cruise missiles that could avoid Soviet radar tracking; and deployed a new strategic bomber more advanced than any the Soviets deployed. In reality, Reagan's military-force blueprint looked little different from Carter's. But there was to be much more of it: $1.6 trillion over five years instead of Carter's planned $1.2 trillion. In the 1990s, Pentagon investigators discovered that U.S. military and civilian officials had grossly underestimated costs—and grossly overestimated Soviet capabilities—to wring billions of dollars from Congress. For example, B-2 aircraft, costing $2 billion each, were demanded to penetrate certain Soviet air defenses—which did not exist. The money nevertheless flowed out from Congress, many of whose constituents wanted waste and fraud cut from government, but not if it affected their own profitable war contracts.[39]

Secretary of Defense Caspar A. Weinberger was nicknamed "Cap the Knife" because he had earlier fought for cutting government budgets. Now, however, he presided over plans to build vast forces that could fight three and one-half wars around the globe. (Nixon had thought the capability to fight one and one-half wars was enough.) The buildup also aimed to give Americans the capability of "prevailing" in a "protracted" nuclear war. Scientists and some military officers thought such planning absurd—the first nuclear exchanges could make much of the earth uninhabitable. Planning, nevertheless, went ahead until Weinberger's projected five-year budget seemed too small. The administration, moreover, repeatedly hinted it would disavow Carter's SALT II deal with Brezhnev (see p. 295) in order to build beyond the pact's limits. But just as often, U.S. military leaders warned that if SALT II were junked, the Soviets could build up faster than Americans. Reagan, who had roundly condemned Carter for the treaty, consequently now decided to abide by it.[40]

[39]Thomas J. Downey, "We Never Dropped Out of the Arms Race," *Washington Post*, November 29, 1983, p. A17; Hans A. Bethe, "The Inferiority Complex," *The New York Review of Books*, June 10, 1982, p. 3; *The New York Times*, July 13, 1980, p. 14; *Washington Post*, July 12, 1980, p. A8. The Pentagon investigations are noted in *The New York Times*, June 28, 1993, p. A10.

[40]Robert Dallek, *Ronald Reagan, The Politics of Symbolism* (Cambridge, Mass., 1984), p. 157; Ulam, *Dangerous Relations*, p. 248; Jeffrey Record, "Jousting with Unreality; Reagan's Military Strategy," *International Security*, VIII (Winter 1983/1984):3, 18; *Washington Post*, March 5, 1981, p. A1; Ibid., March 8, 1982, p. A1.

The buildup, however, continued and caused increasing concern. T. K. Jones, a Pentagon official, played down the concern. If a nuclear war began, he declared, "Dig a hole, cover it with a couple of doors and then throw three feet of dirt on top. It's the dirt that does it." One newspaper editor wondered if Jones was actually a character in the "Doonesbury" comic strip. Another Reagan official assured Congress that the U.S. mail would be delivered after a nuclear war "even if the survivors ran out of stamps." He further refused to change his mind after a congressman noted that delivering mail could be difficult when "there will be no addresses, no streets, no blocks, no houses." Others in the administration seemed similarly misinformed. In 1983 Reagan astounded aides by admitting he had just discovered that the Soviets had 70 percent of their strategic nuclear weapons on land-based missiles, while Americans had only 20 percent of theirs land based. Now he realized, Reagan added, why for two years the Russians had opposed his proposal to cut land-based systems drastically. But no reevaluation occurred. His team stubbornly clung to the scenario of "winning" a nuclear war.[41]

In 1983, as he prepared to run for a second term, Reagan tried to counter the criticism by proposing a Strategic Defense Initiative (SDI): a space-based, computer-controlled defense that would shoot down nuclear missiles before they reached their targets. Pentagon advisers had long discounted the possibility of "Star Wars," as this proposal was labeled. Reagan ignored them and also most American scientists, who believed that such a defense was not only impossible to build but dangerous even to suggest, because it could destabilize both U.S. and Soviet faith in mutual deterrence. The Soviets, for example, might build many times more missiles so that they could simply overwhelm any Star Wars defense. Nor were critics reassured when it was suggested that Reagan might have stolen the idea from his 1940 movie, "Murder in the Air," in which an imaginary "inertia projector" knocked down enemy planes.[42]

During his first term in office, Reagan's defense plans had little visible effect on Soviet policies. Each side understood that Russian

---

[41]Robert Scheer, *With Enough Shovels* (New York, 1982) is the standard source; Kaplan, *The Wizards of Armageddon*, p. 388; Dallek, *Reagan*, pp. 146–157; Weisman, "Can the Magic Prevail?" p. 48; *The New York Times*, March 19, 1982, p. A30.
[42]Garry Wills, *Reagan's America* (New York, 1987), p. 361; *Washington Post*, June 16, 1985, p. A14.

domination of Eastern Europe, or even Afghanistan, could not be dealt with by even the threat of nuclear war. More immediate, non-military tactics were needed to pressure the Soviets. Reagan, however, had surrendered to U.S. farmers' pressure and lifted the grain embargo Carter had imposed against the Russians. Conservative columnist George Will bitterly declared, "This administration evidently loves commerce more than it loathes communism." But worse occurred in Poland. That country had saddled itself with a $20-billion debt from badly managed 1970s industrial modernization plans. In 1980–1981 debts and food shortages led to widespread unrest. Next came the stunning appearance of Solidarity (an independent, noncommunist labor union). Then came the predictable crackdown by Polish communist military leaders, who decided they would do it before the Red Army did it for them. Reagan imposed economic sanctions on the Polish communist regime, but meanwhile he sent more grain to the Soviets. He found himself starving the oppressed and feeding the oppressors. Poland entered into that empty gray twilight that many Russians had long wished upon their neighbors.[43]

As the West Europeans watched all this in wonder, they became Reagan's next target. West Germany (by far the largest Western trading partner with the U.S.S.R.) had worked out a multibillion-dollar deal to help the Soviets build a 3600-mile pipeline that would carry natural gas from Siberia to six West European countries. U.S. officials condemned both European development of—and possible dependence on—Soviet resources. (West Germany planned to obtain 35 percent of its natural gas from Siberia.) The West Europeans replied that Soviet gas supplies were more dependable than the Middle East's. Moreover, they added, Reagan should believe his 1980 campaign oratory that government had to get "off the backs of the people" and not interfere in the marketplace. Nevertheless, Reagan declared "it's time we laid the wood to the Russians" and then announced that European corporations would not be allowed to use U.S.-licensed technology to help build the pipeline. Shocked European officials angrily responded that he had no business interfering with corporations in their countries. The President backed down in late 1982, and the pipeline was built. In 1962 President Kennedy had forced the West Germans and Italians to give up plans to build a So-

---

[43]Goldman, *U.S.S.R. in Crisis*, pp. 158–161; *Newsweek*, January 18, 1982, p. 100.

viet oil pipeline. Twenty years later, in the changed conditions of the third Cold War, Reagan no longer could dictate policy to Western Europe.[44]

He enjoyed better results, however, in 1983, when he worked closely with the West German conservative government to carry through Carter's promise of 1979 to install new Pershing intermediate-range missiles on German soil. The missiles were to counter Soviet weapons installed after 1977. Massive antiwar protests erupted in Europe, where fear grew that these were first-strike weapons that could start nuclear war. But with the European governments' cooperation, the Pershing deployment began. The Soviets walked out of arms talks in Switzerland in protest.

The Reagan administration's problems stemmed in part from its policies' contradictions. For example, the President could not get the government "out of the marketplace" and at the same time fight the Cold War by imposing economic sanctions. Moreover, after he declared that the massive Latin American debt (which approached $\frac{1}{2}$ trillion) must be resolved by private banks, he quickly reversed himself during a single weekend in 1982: the President allowed the U.S. government to send Mexico $3 billion to prevent the southern neighbor from defaulting on its $81-billion debt and possibly bankrupting U.S. banks to whom it owed money.[45]

Such policy contradictions, moreover, seemed worsened by questionable leadership. The administration focused on domestic issues, especially a tax cut. Reagan knew and cared too little to master foreign policy. Between 1981 and 1987 he went through five White House NSC advisers before he found one, General Colin Powell, who both understood foreign affairs and could successfully coordinate policy. In 1981–1982 Secretary of State Alexander Haig alienated the top White House staff with his abrasive personality, his undisguised ambition to control foreign affairs, and his policies. The White House maneuvered Haig into resigning. In June 1982 George Shultz became secretary of state. Nixon's secretary of the treasury, a tough Washington infighter, conservative economist, and multinational corporation ex-

---

[44]Superb accounts of the 1962 and 1982 pipeline controversies are in Bruce Jentleson, *Pipeline Politics* (Ithaca, N.Y., 1986), especially chapters 4 and 6; and in the final chapter in Frank Costigliola, *France and the United States; the Cold Alliance Since World War II* (New York, 1992).

[45]*Washington Post,* January 30, 1983, p. A1.

ecutive who passionately believed in freer marketplaces, Shultz soon talked Reagan into retreating on the pipeline issue.

Shultz became the dominant U.S. foreign policy–maker. "He was a Buddha, hard to read—and he looked like one," a White House official observed; with great energy, even in his late sixties, he "was beyond fatigue." Shultz had once been a proud U.S. Marine. The secretary of state fervently believed that the threat of force had to be clearly seen behind his diplomacy. As a staunch conservative, however, Shultz hated the idea of others using force to overthrow governments—unless the force was used to overthrow Soviet-supported regimes. He had no doubt about whose side history was on: "The Soviet system is incompetent and cannot survive," he had declared in 1979. Using force could give history a useful push, especially in the newly emerging nations. Shultz and Reagan's ambassador to the United Nations, Jeane J. Kirkpatrick, disliked each other personally, but she provided an important argument for the Reagan-Shultz policies. In a widely noted article Kirkpatrick urged that Americans strongly support "authoritarian" governments, such as the shah's in Iran, because they followed capitalist economic principles, cooperated with the United States, and were open to change. She wanted all-out opposition, on the other hand, to "totalitarian" regimes, such as the communists', because they abhorred capitalism, were anti-American, and were not open to liberal change.[46] She believed that communist-totalitarian regimes would never move toward real democracy unless pressured to do so by military force—a belief that was disproved in Eastern Europe before the 1980s were over.

Kirkpatrick's and Shultz's views about using force against Third World troublemakers fit with Reagan's belief that Americans had a mission to spread democracy throughout the earth. A belief in such a mission dated back to the seventeenth century and had found a twentieth-century champion in Woodrow Wilson. Thus Reagan drew on a deep vein of American faith. He stated his policy clearly in his "Reagan Doctrine" of 1985 when he declared: "Our mission is to nourish and defend freedom and democracy." Americans had to support those "on every continent, from Afghanistan to Nicaragua—to

---

[46]George P. Shultz, *Turmoil and Triumph* (New York, 1993), p. 6; Larry Speaks, *Speaking Out* (New York, 1988), p. 78; Jeane J. Kirkpatrick, *Dictatorships and Double Standards* (New York, 1982), especially pp. 23–52.

defy Soviet-supported aggression and [to] secure rights which have been ours from birth. . . . Support for freedom fighters is self-defense."

This policy, however, faced a major problem: since at least the Vietnam conflict, Americans disliked spending their money, not to mention their lives, to fight faraway conflicts. Reagan tried to overcome this problem by calling Vietnam "a noble cause," but many Americans disagreed. A 1982 poll revealed that 72 percent of those surveyed believed "the Vietnam war was more than a mistake; it was fundamentally wrong and immoral." The Reaganites dealt with this problem by supporting the strategy of "low-intensity conflicts" (LICs). Instead of Vietnam-type wars, LICs used small, specially trained counterinsurgency forces (native or U.S.) who through political action and guerrilla-type warfare could, over a long period, wear down opponents. LICs, moreover, were relatively cheap and so low-key that most Americans would pay little attention to them. In a sense, LICs aimed to turn communist revolutionary tactics against communist governments in such nations as Nicaragua, Afghanistan, Angola, and Kampuchea (Cambodia). But both the Reagan Doctrine and the LIC strategy soon came under attack. Critics warned that LICs could easily escalate (as in Vietnam) and that it was absurd to expend resources in distant areas (such as Kampuchea) where U.S. interests were, at best, vague. Military officers questioned LIC tactics for being imprecise and too open-ended.[47]

This division over LICs revealed a deeper, more dangerous split among Reagan's advisers. Shultz believed that the threat of force had to be used in dealing with foreign affairs and that, at times, force itself had to be used in newly emerging nations to make the threat credible. But Secretary of Defense Weinberger usually opposed using force or the threat of force. Weinberger's views reflected studies by top military scholars who had concluded that U.S. forces must never again be dragged into another Vietnam or detoured from their main

[47]Reagan's statement of the doctrine is in U.S. Government, *Weekly Compilation of Presidential Documents,* XXI (February 11, 1985): 145–146; Robert W. Tucker, "Reagan's Foreign Policy," *Foreign Affairs,* LXVIII, 1 (1989): 21; Richard E. Neustadt and Ernest R. May, *Thinking in Time* (New York, 1986), p. 305. On low-intensity warfare: Secretary George Shultz, "Low-Intensity Warfare," *Current Policy,* No. 783; D. Michael Shafer, "The Unlearned Lessons of Counterinsurgency," *Political Science Quarterly,* CIII (Spring 1988): 75, 77–78; Gabriel Kolko, "Foreign Policy After the Election," July 1988, manuscript in author's possession; Michael T. Klare, "The New U.S. Strategic Doctrine," *The Nation,* January 4, 1986, p. 697.

business of opposing Soviet (not Kampuchean or Nicaraguan) forces. In November 1984 Weinberger, in a remarkable speech, publicly announced that the United States should use military power only when certain conditions were met: an assurance of long-term public and congressional support, a guarantee that the commitment would be made "wholeheartedly" and with full intention of "winning," and a clear definition of the objectives that were to be sought.[48] An angry Shultz publicly questioned Weinberger's list of conditions and privately wondered why the military needed a $300-billion budget if it apparently did not intend to fight.

These contradictions and divisions in Reagan's Third World policies caused major disasters. The first, and one of the worst, occurred in the Middle East during 1982–1983. Fixated on keeping the Soviets out of the region, U.S. officials were uncertain of how to deal with the region's fundamental problem—the Israeli-Arab conflict. Reagan and Shultz stood by in mid-1982 when Israel invaded Lebanon to destroy the missiles of archenemy (and Soviet friend) Syria. The Israelis then drove into Lebanon's capital, Beirut, to destroy the Palestinian Liberation Organization, which represented Palestinians who vowed to return certain areas claimed by Israel to their own control. The Israelis became bogged down amid cutthroat Lebanese politics, the lack of a political consensus in Israel, and Syrian arms supplied by Moscow. When Israelis and Lebanese Christians carried out bloody massacres against Palestinians who lived in Israeli-controlled camps, Israel suffered a political crisis and—pushed by the United States—withdrew its troops. In 1982 (over Weinberger's objection) U.S. forces moved into Beirut to try to protect Palestinians, encourage Israeli withdrawal, and keep peace between Christian and Moslem factions inside Lebanon. In April 1983 lives were lost when the U.S. embassy in Beirut was bombed. Meanwhile U.S. troops, hunkered down near the Beirut airport, not only were open to sniper fire but were never clear about their mission. On October 23, 1983, a terrorist bomb killed 239 U.S. soldiers in their barracks. Reagan declared that keeping troops in Lebanon was now "central to our credibility on a global scale." But the President—facing strong public and Defense Department opposition, having no workable Middle East policy, and preparing to run for reelection—soon reversed himself. He pulled out the remaining 1600 soldiers.

[48]"The Use of Military Power," News Release, Office of Assistant Secretary of Defense (Public Affairs), November 28, 1984.

Lebanon became a bloody war zone in which Soviet-supported Syria gained the upper hand. Reagan's Middle East policy never recovered from the disaster.[49]

On October 25, 1983, two days after the Beirut barracks' bombing, Reagan and Shultz again deployed their military forces. They ordered an invasion of the Caribbean island of Grenada to destroy a regime that had close Cuban ties. The President declared he had acted to save 500 U.S. medical students and to aid neighboring governments who had asked for U.S. troops. The President's press secretary, Larry Speakes, later claimed that the White House believed the students were not endangered and that the invitation played little part in the U.S. decision. The real reasons were Reagan's desires to attack a pro-Cuban regime and to get American minds off the Beirut disaster. Again, the U.S. military had had severe reservations about the operation. And indeed, it became a close-run thing. Some 1900 badly prepared U.S. troops landed and finally overcame a small Grenadan force and 784 Cubans (most of whom were working to enlarge the island's airport), but only after the arrival of 4000 more U.S. troops and six days of fighting. Nineteen American soldiers were killed and 116 wounded. The Cubans counted 71 dead and 59 wounded. The Grenadans suffered 110 killed and 337 wounded. Five years after the invasion and $110 million of U.S. aid, Grenada's politics were anticommunist, but the economy was mired in depression and high unemployment.[50]

For Reagan, however, it proved to be an important political success at home. So were his encounters with Libya. That North African nation's pro-American monarchy had been overthrown in 1969 by Moslem army officers led by Mu'ammar Qaddafi. His expansionist plans, hatred of Israel, growing military ties with Moscow, and—especially—links with terrorists put Qaddafi on a collision course with the United States. In 1981 U.S. jets shot down two Libyan warplanes over disputed territorial waters. In April 1986 Reagan blamed Qaddafi for a bloody terrorist raid in West Berlin, called him "the mad dog of the Middle East," and ordered a bombing raid that killed Qaddafi's adopted daughter and injured at least a dozen other people. Libya, it

---

[49]Talbott, *Russians and Reagan,* pp. 34–36; *Washington Post,* October 30, 1983, p. C1; *The New York Times,* January 22, 1984, p. A1.
[50]Speakes, *Speaking Out,* p. 161; *Washington Post,* October 25, 1988, p. A23; *The New York Times,* May 2, 1994, p. A6.

turned out, had little connection with the West Berlin episode, although Qaddafi was intimately involved with other incidents of international terrorism.

The President's tough talk, his command of the media ("You'd be surprised how much being a good actor pays off," he observed), his limited but successful use of force in Grenada and Libya, and the booming (if debt-ridden) economic times enabled him to win forty-nine of fifty states in a landslide reelection victory over former Vice President Walter Mondale in 1984. His advisers later admitted they had urged him to avoid foreign-policy issues in the campaign because these were Reagan's main weaknesses. But he rode the crest of a "new patriotism" that reached its extreme with the popularity of "Rambo," a movie character who ignored the supposed appeasers in Washington and, in the best U.S. unilateral tradition, single-handedly returned to Vietnam, used new military technology, and taught the communists a lesson. The craze included a Houston nightclub, Rambose, where waitresses wore fatigues, issued .50-caliber machine guns, and served buffet from a military stretcher.[51]

But not even Rambo's and Reagan's rhetoric could mask the failure of the President's original policies. Taking Shultz's advice, Reagan finally broke down and met the Soviet ambassador to Washington, Anatoly Dobrynin. He told Dobrynin that "there are some problems that can and should be tackled now. Probably, people in the Soviet Union regard me as a crazy warmonger," Reagan continued, "But I don't want a war. . . . We should make a fresh start."[52] Kirkpatrick's advice to support "authoritarians" failed in both Haiti and the Philippines, where longtime dictators fell (despite Reagan's personal support of them until the last minute). In Haiti a bloodstained military group took over after the United States finally helped push the bloodstained "Baby Doc" Duvalier from power. In the Philippines U.S. officials finally helped replace the corrupt dictatorship of Ferdinand Marcos with Corazon Aquino's government in 1986. Even with U.S. aid, however, she was unable to stop the spread of both corruption and a communist-led insurgency. In South Africa, where 5

[51]Richard Barnet, *By the Rockets' Red Glare* (New York, 1990), Part IV; Elizabeth Drew, "A Political Journal," *The New Yorker*, December 3, 1984, especially p. 107.
[52]Dobrynin, *In Confidence*, pp. 517–518.

million whites ruled 21 million blacks through the brutal apartheid (enforced segregation) policy, Reagan followed a policy of "constructive engagement"—that is, using talk and economic ties rather than tough sanctions to ease apartheid. By 1986 the approach had failed. Congress, over the President's objections, imposed economic sanctions that began to squeeze the South African economy and helped convince more than half the 300 U.S. firms in the country to leave. In 1990 the besieged white regime finally freed the top black leader, Nelson Mandela, after he had spent 27 years in jail. But apartheid mostly remained.

Nor could the Reagan Doctrine and Kirkpatrick's approach save the President's policies in Central America. The 1980 Republican platform promised to replace Nicaragua's Sandinistas with a "free and independent" government. Reagan publicly declared he intended to make the Sandinistas cry "uncle." In November 1981 he signed the secret National Security Decision Directive 17 (NSDD 17), which authorized the CIA to spend millions to train and to equip Nicaraguan exiles, or "contras," who would fight the Sandinistas. In clear violation of U.S. neutrality laws, the CIA trained contras in the southern United States, then shipped them through Honduras to fight in Nicaragua. The Sandinistas, however, responded by building a force of 65,000 troops, strengthening their political hold on the country, and obtaining help from Western Europeans as well as the Soviet bloc. By late 1983 the contras' failures led the CIA to take over operations that destroyed oil refineries, mined Nicaraguan harbors, and aimed at assassinating Sandinista officials. A stunned U.S. Congress discovered these secret CIA missions, cut off military aid to the contras, and—as opinion polls indicated—received support from a large majority of Americans. U.S. military leaders again wanted no policy that might force them to fight an unpopular war in Nicaragua. Reagan's economic sanctions proved more effective. They helped make Nicaragua an economic basket case that lacked many necessities and, by 1989, suffered an unbelievable 33,000 percent inflation rate. The Sandinistas, nevertheless, held to power, despite the 40,000 killed by the contra war.[53]

In neighboring El Salvador Reagan suffered another defeat when

---

[53]Mary B. Vanderlaan, *Revolution and Foreign Policy in Nicaragua* (Boulder, Col. 1986), especially pp. 127–209; Barry Rubin, *Secrets of State* (New York, 1985), p. 219; *The New York Times*, December 24, 1981, p. A14.

he attempted to destroy the revolutionary Farabundo Martí National Liberation Front (FMLN) that tried to overthrow the U.S.-supported government (see p. 296). He refused to follow up the 1982 FMLN offer to negotiate and instead poured about $1 million into that small country each day over the next six years. Americans virtually took over the wrecked Salvadoran economy. The CIA tried to keep out of power both the left and the far-right groups that hired "death squads" to kill thousands of suspect civilians. In 1989, nevertheless, the far-right party, Alianza Republican Nacionalista (ARENA), won national elections. The country polarized. On the left, the FMLN's 7000 troops carried out bloody attacks even in the capital city. On the right, U.S.-trained and -supplied Salvadoran military massacred six Jesuit priests (who had led the attempt to end the war and its brutalities against civilians) and two women. U.S. officials, either because of ignorance or an attempted cover-up, at first blamed the FMLN for the massacre. When it became clear that army officers had ordered it, Washington demanded an investigation and convictions. The ten-year war had claimed 70,000 lives; at least two-thirds were civilians slaughtered by right-wing military-related death squads, but not a single military official had been convicted by the terrorized Salvadoran governments. In early 1990 U.S. military officials admitted that the FMLN could not be defeated. The war and the brutality nevertheless continued.

Recognizing the failure of U.S. policy, Costa Rican President Oscar Arias Sanchez won the Nobel Peace Prize in 1987 for stitching together a plan that tried to end the fighting in Nicaragua and El Salvador and to begin a process for democratic elections. U.S. officials disliked Arias's plan because it allowed the Sandinistas to remain in power but demanded that the contras disband. Arias's plan enabled Central Americans, not North Americans, to shape Central American affairs for the first time in a century. The Reagan Doctrine was not working well in what the United States liked to call its "backyard." Actually, the backyard and the house seemed to be much the same thing: more than 500,000 Salvadorans (or about one in eight) lived, illegally for the most part, in the United States to escape the bloodshed. Elsewhere in the neighborhood, General Manuel Antonio Noriega seized power in Panama during 1983. A longtime informant for the CIA, Noriega had also grown rich from the international drug traffic that flooded U.S. streets. Washington officials, including Shultz and Vice President George Bush, ignored Noriega's drug-running and political corruption. They even sent him millions of dollars because he helped fight the Sandinistas. When they finally tried to overthrow Noriega in 1987–1988, he defied them. As Arias feared, U.S. policy was making the neighborhood more, not less, violent.[54] (See map, p. 207.)

These Third World problems created Reagan's gravest crises. In 1984 Middle East terrorists, supported by Iran, seized U.S. citizens (including several CIA agents) as hostages. Reagan, who had condemned Carter in 1980 for negotiating the hostage issue, continually denied he would ever bargain with terrorists. In 1985, however, he secretly accepted an Israeli proposal to send antitank, and later antiaircraft, missiles to Iran. When the first U.S. weapons were sent, six hostages were being held; by mid-1987 nine Americans were held hostage. At the same time, Congress ordered that all military aid be cut off to the hapless contras in Nicaragua. Lieutenant Colonel Oliver North, of Reagan's National Security Council, proposed secretly to divert funds from the Iranian arms sales to supply the contras. Reagan later denied he knew about this act, made illegal by the congressional order, even though it was probably devised by his close friend William Casey, the CIA director. The President, Casey, and North were obsessed with overthrowing the Sandinistas. In late 1986, however, a Lebanese journal revealed the arms deals. A disclosure of the illegal contra aid followed. One independent investigation (by a commission headed by former Republican Senator John Tower of Texas) concluded that Reagan had failed to supervise his NSC staff or to properly oversee U.S. policy. North was brought to trial in 1989 and received a suspended prison sentence for lying to Congress, destroying documents, and accepting illegal payments. Casey died of a brain tumor before the scandal broke. When the scandal did break and fester in 1986–1987, Reagan's presidency reached its nadir.[55]

This political crisis coincided with economic dilemmas. The U.S.

[54]*Christian Science Monitor,* April 25, 1988, p. 1, reprinted in *Central America NewsPak,* April 25–May 8, 1988, p. 1; *The New York Times,* January 28, 1982, p. A10; Ibid., July 30, 1982, p. A6; Ibid., January 21, 1990, p. 21; Nora Hamilton et al., *Crisis in Central America* (Boulder, Colo., 1988), especially the Sharpe, Arnson, and Karl essays on El Salvador; *Washington Post,* April 5, 1988, p. A16; W. LaFeber, *The Panama Canal* (New York, 1989), pp. 193–215.

[55]U.S. House and Senate, 100th Cong., 1st Sess., *Report of the Congressional Committees Investigating the Iran-Contra Affair* (Washington, 1987), especially pp. 3–51 on Nicaragua, 157–209 on Iran, and 327–392 on North; I am indebted to Max Miller for a copy of this document.

arms budget approached $300 billion by 1986. The Soviets were spending nearly $250 billion. (Altogether the world's nations spent about $980 billion, or more than the combined income of the poorest half of the world, on arms in 1986.) Americans produced five nuclear warheads each day. The Soviets, according to CIA estimates, had actually leveled off their arms spending to no more than a 2 percent annual growth rate after 1976. The CIA's news arrived just as analyses disclosed that the $1.1 trillion of U.S. military spending between 1981 and 1985 had bought remarkably few new weapons. But corruption seemed rampant as $600 toilet seats and $7000 coffeemakers were discovered on the military ledger books. Forty-five of the nation's largest military contractors came under criminal investigation for illegal kickbacks and overcharges. Northrop Corporation was charged with buying parts from a local Radio Shack store to meet a deadline for producing a missile's incredibly intricate guidance system. One congressman wondered whether those missiles would hit "Washington or Moscow if we get into a war."[56] Reagan had demanded a 7 to 10 percent increase each year in the military budget. He had received less than half that amount by 1984 and only enough to cover the inflation rate by 1988.

Because of this spending and an inability to reduce domestic programs, the U.S. budget overflowed in red ink until more than $1 trillion of debt piled up in the Reagan years. At the same time, the U.S. economic machine became less competitive. In 1987 the Japanese outpaced the Americans in the amount of goods and services produced per person. Trade deficits hit record highs as Americans bought $171 billion more from abroad than they sold. (In addition, experts estimated that a booming $100-billion drug trade in the United States resulted in $5 to $25 billion being illegally sent abroad each year to pay for the drugs.) The astronomical deficit was made up in part by foreign investors: by 1989 they held $300 billion of U.S. industry, $400 billion of the $3-trillion national debt, and 21 percent of U.S. banking assets. Nearly all that money had arrived since 1974—that is, during the years of the third Cold War. By 1985 a historic watershed occurred. Just four years before, when Reagan had entered the White

---

[56]Raymond L. Garthoff, *Détente and Confrontation* (Washington, 1985), pp. 795–796; *The New York Times*, March 2, 1986, p. 8; Ibid., April 12, 1987, p. F3; Ibid., May 19, 1985, p. 28; the production figure is in *Washington Post*, April 23, 1987, p. A10; the Radio Shack quote and references are in Ibid., December 1, 1988, p. B22.

House, the United States had been the world's proud leading creditor nation, but now it had suddenly slid below Brazil and Mexico to become the world's largest debtor. One authority declared, "The United States has lost control of its financial markets to foreigners." In the 1980 race for the Republican nomination, George Bush had accused Reagan of following "voodoo economics." By 1985 a conservative columnist noted that "Reaganomics is giving voodoo a bad name."[57]

The two superpowers each had spent trillions of dollars on defense to checkmate the other, only to discover that they had gone far in undermining their own domestic societies. The Soviets found themselves much worse off than the Americans. In 1959 Khrushchev had promised that Soviet industry would surpass the American system in per capita production by the 1970s. By the mid-1980s the top Soviet leadership had to admit that this had been a pipe dream. Until the mid-1970s Brezhnev had built up his military by spending as much as 25 percent of the gross national product on it. (Americans spent about 6 percent of a much larger gross national product.) Brezhnev did so at the expense of the investment and civilian sectors. A corrupt, disheartening stagnation set in. The economy's growth rate flirted with zero percent increase. As the world's largest oil producer, and dependent on petroleum exports for 60 percent of its badly needed hard-currency earnings (dollars, yen, marks, etc.), the Soviets suffered severely as their production leveled off and world oil prices skidded downward in the 1980s. Consumer goods were shoddy; the U.S.S.R. was the world's largest producer of shoes, but the shoes fell apart in weeks or rotted in warehouses because so few wanted them. Producing twice as much steel as the United States, the Soviets were always short of steel because they wasted so much and produced so little of good quality. Male life expectancy continued to decline alarmingly (sixty-six years in 1964, sixty-two and one-half

[57]William Safire, "Reagan's Next Term," *The New York Times Magazine,* January 13, 1985, p. 22 has "voodoo" quote; *The New York Times,* March 26, 1988, p. 1; Ibid., September 11, 1988, p. F3; Ibid., August 22, 1989, p. D3; *Los Angeles Times,* December 6, 1987, p. 1; *Washington Post,* March 18, 1988, p. B1. Drug trade figures are drawn from Professor William Walker's work, and author's conversation with Professor Walker, September 19, 1989.

years by 1984), while female life expectancy remained about ten years longer. Infant mortality rates soared to levels unheard of in the industrialized world.[58]

Alcoholism, horrid hospital facilities (especially for women giving birth), and food shortages abounded. The aged, ill Brezhnev could find no solutions. A bitter joke circulated among Russians. Stalin, Khrushchev, and Brezhnev were riding on a train when it broke down. To solve the problem, Stalin advised shooting the engineer, Khrushchev suggested pardoning the crew and giving them another chance—and Brezhnev thought it would be best to pull down the window shades and pretend they were moving.

Brezhnev's incapacity also further undermined Soviet bloc strength. The bloc was economically linked by U.S.S.R. shipments of raw materials (especially oil) to such satellites as Poland and Czechoslovakia, who sent Soviets increasingly inferior manufactured goods. As oil prices sank and the quality of the manufactured goods worsened, the trade links frayed. Even militarily, the Warsaw Pact relations soured because the Soviets could not modernize their allies' forces. Hungary responded economically by trying to inject some private-market reforms. Hard-line regimes in Rumania, East Germany, and Czechoslovakia responded by jailing dissenters. Poland moved close to collapse and was finally propped up with martial law in 1981.[59]

Brezhnev died in 1982; he was followed by Yuri Andropov, who died in 1984, and then by an aged, ill, and inexperienced Konstantin Chernenko, who died in 1985. Andropov, the longtime KGB (secret police) chief, knew the system's weaknesses and tried to remedy them with fresh policies and younger, better-trained leaders, such as Mikhail Gorbachev. But both Andropov and Chernenko used the Stalinist tactics of seizing dissenters, such as Nobel Prize winning scientist Andrei Sakharov, and either exiling them or committing them as "insane" to psychiatric hospitals. Police limited the use of the relatively few copying machines and personal computers, because these

---

[58]Condoleezza Rice, "Gorbachev and the Military," *The Harriman Institute Forum*, II (April 1989): 1, 3; Goldman, *U.S.S.R. in Crisis*, p. 101; John P. Hardt, "Highlight: Problems and Prospects," in U.S. Congress, Joint Economic Committee, 97th Cong., 2nd Sess., *Soviet Economy in the 1980s . . . Selected Papers* (Washington, 1983), pp. vii–xiii; Seweryn Bialer, "Gorbachev's Program," *Political Science Quarterly*, CIII (Fall 1988): 412.
[59]*The New York Times*, February 19, 1984, p. 2F; Gordon A. Craig and Alexander George, *Force and Statecraft* (New York, 1983), p. 149; *Washington Post*, February 14, 1985, p. A23.

"forbidden fruit," as they were known, threatened the state's absolute control. That police action meant, however, that the stagnating economy fell further behind roaring Western systems that were fueled by the new technology. Only 50,000 personal computers were in the U.S.S.R. (Americans had 30 million), and they were generations behind Western machines. To copy an article, a Soviet scientist needed two or three days, if a photocopier could be found. Even the Soviet Foreign Ministry held up talks with U.S. diplomats for hours while typing out documents on carbon paper that could have been copied in seconds.[60]

By early 1985 the Russian system resembled a science-fiction movie's huge gray blob that looked threatening but moved ever more slowly. Soviet-American relations reached a dangerously low point. In March 1985 Chernenko died and was replaced as party leader (in a closely contested secret election) by Mikhail Gorbachev. Born in 1931 the new leader possessed remarkable political skills that had rapidly pushed him through the party ranks until in 1980 he became by far the youngest full member of the all-powerful politburo. But not only age made him unusual. Unlike the Brezhnev-Chernenko group, he had been well educated at Moscow State University, where he had read Western philosophy as well as the Leninist tracts and had studied at the elite school of law. His wife, Raisa, had received her doctorate in philosophy. In a regime that tried to destroy religious practices, Gorbachev's mother was a devout Christian who had baptized her son. (As Soviet leader in 1988, he removed many restraints on the Russian Orthodox Church as it celebrated its 1000-year anniversary.)

Gorbachev was not, however, an isolated, weird phenomenon. He represented a new Soviet generation that had become adult after Stalin's death, was well educated in the professions, had been inspired by Khrushchev's attempted reforms, was repelled by what it termed Brezhnev's repressive "stagnation," and understood how far the country was falling behind the West in technology. This new class's politics ranged from radical to reactionary, but numerically it was the largest professional class in the world. It was especially angry with the stagnant system that ruined chances for promotion and a better life. Gorbachev and this new class demanded what they soon

---

[60]Seweryn Bialer, "Danger in Moscow," *The New York Review of Books,* February 16, 1984, p. 6; Alex Beam, "The USSR: Atari Bolsheviks," *The Atlantic,* March 1986, pp. 28–32; *Washington Post,* January 16, 1984, p. A11; Ibid., January 16, 1986, p. A16.

called "new thinking"—not because they feared Reagan's military buildup but because they understood that the Soviet system they inherited could not keep up with, and adjust to, the technological changes (computers, satellites, instant international television coverage) that were revolutionizing Western societies. The Soviet Union, they knew, was an industrial society in a new, postindustrial age.[61]

Gorbachev sounded the theme: "Only an intensive, highly developed economy can guarantee the consolidation of the country's positions in the international arena." To achieve this goal, he proposed "perestroika" (a restructuring of the economy) and "glasnost" (publicity and political openness to encourage individual initiative). At the pivotal Twenty-seventh Communist Party Congress in February 1986, Gorbachev called for "radical reform." The reforms included more independence and even profit making for farm and industrial managers. It also included a slow revamping of the price and market systems so that they would more accurately reflect reality and force farm and industrial workers to meet marketplace demands. This new thinking even allowed previously impossible private "cooperatives"; between 1985 and 1988, 13,000 producing cooperatives and 300,000 family-owned businesses appeared. Some 50 percent of the service sector and 40 percent of agriculture were ultimately to be in private hands, Moscow officials announced. The initiative also allowed new partnerships with Western corporations. A Soviet economy closed to most capitalists suddenly had American Express building hotels, Baskin-Robbins selling its thirty-one flavors of ice cream along Red Square, Merck Pharmaceuticals working with Soviet research scientists, the world's largest McDonald's frying "bolshoi Macs," and Nabisco making Russian breakfast cereals.[62]

But Gorbachev's reforms ran into a stone wall of opposition made up of some politburo members (who feared such reforms in principle), the massive party and government bureaucracies (which feared loss of their own power and privileges), and many workers (it was

---

[61]Bialer, "Gorbachev's Program," pp. 407–408. This interpretation owes much to Bobby Herman's dissertation-in-progress at Cornell University, which is based on several years of research and interviews in Russia.
[62]Martin McCauley, ed., *The Soviet Union Under Gorbachev* (New York, 1987), especially pp. 1–9, 210–227; Serge Schmemann, "The Emergence of Gorbachev," *The New York Times Magazine,* March 3, 1985, especially pp. 44–46, 55–57; Hedrick Smith, "On the Road with Gorbachev's Guru," *The New York Times Magazine,* April 10, 1988, pp. 38, 42; *Washington Post,* February 27, 1986, p. A32.

estimated that 16 million could lose their jobs in perestroika). He fought back with a whirlwind of political changes. First he brought trusted advisers onto the politburo to replace many of his conservative opponents. In mid-1985 he appointed a longtime colleague, Eduard Shevardnadze, only fifty-seven, to replace the seventy-nine-year-old Andrei Gromyko as foreign minister. The new regime, moreover, publicly condemned key parts of Soviet history and opened that history to a reexamination that had (as does all historical analysis) enormous potential consequences. The regime declared that "the guilt of Stalin is enormous and unforgivable" because of his crimes against the people. Hundreds of political exiles, including scientist Andrei Sakharov and his wife, Yelena Bonner, won their release, although many more remained in prison.

By 1988 Gorbachev's economic reforms were not working. Productivity lagged. Food was scarcer than before 1985. He tried to raise productivity and stop rampant alcoholism by sharply limiting sales of wine and vodka. Gorbachev became known as "Lemonade Joe." His action led to loss of tax revenue and a severe sugar shortage as Russians began making home-brewed liquor (often with a poisonously high alcohol content). Sugar scarcity even led to a shortage of ice cream, one of the most loved foods.

Glasnost meanwhile resulted in sudden demands by ethnic minorities in provinces far from Moscow for more independence and freedom. Gorbachev had not anticipated these outbreaks, and the authorities put some of them down with force.[63] In mid-1989 more than 300,000 coal-mine workers went on strike. They were among the most favored of Soviet workers, but they lived in hovels and lacked necessities (for example, many received only one cake of soap every two months). Unrest spread across the country.

Throughout these crises Gorbachev's response was consistent: he purged political opponents and bureaucrats who, he claimed, were trying to use the crises to destroy his reforms. The climax of this policy came in March 1989, when he conducted nationwide elections for a new 2250-member People's Congress. Many Communist party leaders suffered humiliating defeats in the election. The ruling and secretive politburo, at the apex of the party structure, continued to have the final word. But now a new 572-member Supreme Soviet (elected

[63]Useful on the nationalities issues: McCauley, ed., *Soviet Union Under Gorbachev*, pp. 4, 86–95; Basile Kerblay, *Gorbachev's Russia* (New York, 1989), pp. 62–66.

by the People's Congress) replaced the old rubber-stamp Supreme Soviet and planned to meet six to eight months a year to debate legislation openly. Debates in this pioneering parliament were even carried on television to enthralled Soviets. Gorbachev thus tried to use glasnost, or openness, to kill opposition to perestroika. He played to intellectuals and encouraged openness in the arts. Orwell's *1984* and even some of Aleksandr Solzhenitsyn's bitterly critical novels of Soviet history were made available. Movies such as "Little Vera" and "Is It Easy to Be Young?" gave grim views of workers and alienated youths, as did stunningly popular rock music that emerged from underground.[64]

It was a remarkable performance—a performance topped in February 1990 by the previously unthinkable: Gorbachev and the Communist party leadership surrendered the party's seventy-three-year-old monopoly of power in the U.S.S.R. They had little alternative. Economic reform and decentralization required some political decentralization as well. The party was supposed to remain supreme, but it instead quickly divided between reformers and conservatives. To free himself further from party conservatives, Gorbachev moved toward a more Western-style presidency and cabinet system of government whose power was based on the popularly elected People's Congress. He was opening windows that had been sealed for seventy years.

Gorbachev's chances for success depended not only on his control of Soviet politics but also in cutting back wasteful, costly commitments abroad. Most immediately, his success depended on making arms deals with Americans so that he could reduce his runaway military budget.

The prospects looked grim when he came to power in 1985. U.S.-Soviet relations were tense. Reagan had once declared that the Chinese regime was "based on a belief in destroying governments like ours," but in 1984 the President suddenly reversed course. He visited China and returned to call it "this so-called Communist China." He even sent high-tech weapons to the Chinese as Sino-American trade

[64]Richard Stites, "Soviet Popular Culture in the Gorbachev Era," *The Harriman Institute Forum,* II (March 1989); a useful chronology of Gorbachev's reforms is in *Washington Post,* December 31, 1988, p. A14; *The New York Times,* July 24, 1989, p. A1.

boomed. The Soviets, obsessed with fear of a giant, well-armed Chinese neighbor, saw a Sino-American axis forming against them. Just before Reagan had gone to China, moreover, the Soviets had shot down a civilian Korean airliner that, they claimed, had intentionally flown over their highly sensitive eastern military bases. A U.S. congressman had been among the 269 people killed. Moscow called the flight a "deliberate provocation." Washington denied that the plane had been on an intelligence mission and called the August 1983 shootdown an inhuman act. One Soviet leader declared, "Comrades, the international situation at present is white hot, thoroughly white hot." A U.S. Marine Corps general announced that a U.S.-Soviet limited war was "an almost inevitable probability" in this generation. Reagan himself admitted, "There have been times in the past when people thought the end of the world was coming . . . but never anything like this."[65]

Then a slow but certain change began. Preparing to run for reelection in 1984 and aware that, as one poll revealed, more than one-third of Americans feared he would take them into a war, Reagan cooled his rhetoric. Moreover, at no time had even the most hawkish U.S. officials believed they could push the Soviets into a quick collapse. The secret National Security Decision Directive 75 of late 1982 planned only for "long haul" containment and the pious hope that the U.S.S.R. would somehow become more pluralistic. Reagan's rhetoric was more aggressive than his long-term policies. The turning point in the Cold War came when Gorbachev assumed power in March 1985. He had already publicly declared that a détente was possible. His economic plans now made détente necessary. Gorbachev simply reversed Soviet doctrine. Moscow had argued that only socialists would survive nuclear war; Gorbachev said it would spare no one—not even socialists. "Security," he announced, could "only be resolved by political means," not military face-offs. He further argued that the world's pressing problems, such as the environment and resource scarcity, had to be solved by cooperation, not confrontation: global "interdependence . . . is such that all peoples are similar to climbers

---

[65]Dallek, *Ronald Reagan*, p. 174; *The New York Times,* May 2, 1984, p. A1; Joel B. Harris, Bruce H. Turnbull, and Jeffrey P. Bialos, *Compliance with U.S. Export Control Laws and Regulations* (Washington, 1984), pp. 39–41; *Washington Post,* November 21, 1984, p. A1; Ibid., June 22, 1984, p. A15; *The New York Times,* October 21, 1984, p. 32 on "Armageddon."

roped together on the mountainside. They either can climb together to the summit or fall together into the abyss."[66]

To avoid the "abyss," Gorbachev pressed Reagan to meet him at the summit. The first summit meeting in six years occurred during November 1985 in Geneva. The two men agreed in principle on a 50 percent cut in strategic forces and to reopen cultural exchange programs. In a whirlwind fourteen-hour meeting at Reykjavík, Iceland, in October 1986, they shocked the world by agreeing to eliminate all intermediate missiles (such as the Pershings) in Europe. They nearly agreed on eliminating almost all other nuclear missiles. But this last stunning proposal collapsed when Gorbachev demanded that it be linked to the U.S. termination of its "Star Wars" program and Reagan refused.

A year later Gorbachev paid his first visit to Washington. The two men signed a treaty eliminating medium- and short-range nuclear missiles (that is, all those with a range of up to 3000 miles). This historic pact marked the first time an entire class of U.S. and Soviet nuclear weapons was not merely limited, but eliminated. In mid-1988 Reagan made a successful goodwill trip to Moscow. He and Gorbachev strolled arm-in-arm through Red Square. In December 1988 the Soviet leader returned to the United States and let the other, conventional-force, shoe drop: he announced that his armed forces would be reduced unilaterally by 500,000 men and 10,000 tanks in two years. Six tank divisions were to be withdrawn from East Germany. He also declared that Soviet law would be rewritten to ensure that no one would be persecuted for political or religious beliefs. As for "Star Wars," the United States had continued funding research, but Gorbachev concluded that Reagan's original plan was nearly dead—the victim of scientific realities, huge U.S. budget deficits, and the Pentagon's refusal to trust it with the nation's security.[67]

These arms deals were astonishing, but also important were Gorbachev's economic and human rights proposals. Reagan later joked,

---

[66]Most helpful are Raymond L. Garthoff, "Letters to the Editor," *Foreign Affairs, LXXIV* (May/June 1995): 198; Paul Marantz, *From Lenin to Gorbachev* (Ottawa, 1988); Marantz's "Gorbachev's New Thinking," *Current History,* October 1988, pp. 3–6; FBIS, *Daily Report: Soviet Union* (Washington, February 17, 1987), pp. AA15–AA16; *Washington Post,* December 26, 1983, p. A3.

[67]Strobe Talbott, *The Master of the Game: Paul Nitze and the Nuclear Age* (New York, 1988), pp. 362–368, 374–383; *Washington Post,* December 8, 1988, p. A1.

"When I told him we should put our cards on the table, he took out his Visa and his Mastercard." For his part, the President said in Moscow that he believed the Soviets were no longer "an evil empire." He added, "We can look with optimism on future negotiations." After their first meeting in 1985, Reagan whispered to Gorbachev, "I bet the hardliners in both our countries are squirming."[68]

One of those hardliners, Zbigniew Brzezinski (top adviser to former President Jimmy Carter), blasted people for "going bananas over Gorbachev simply because he happens to wear a clean shirt . . . and his wife does not look like a beast." But the persistent Gorbachev helped undercut hard-liners in both countries by allowing increased numbers of Soviet Jews to leave the U.S.S.R. Since 1969 the numbers of dissidents allowed to emigrate had fluctuated according to U.S.-Soviet relations and how badly Moscow wanted an arms deal and economic help:

1967: 4498	1980: 21,471
1971: 13,022	1984: 896
1972: 31,681 (Nixon-Brezhnev	1986: 914
SALT I agreement)	1987: 8155
1975: 13,221	1988: 19,286[69]
1978: 28,864	1989: 70,000 (estimated)
1979: 51,320 (Carter-Brezhnev	
SALT II arrangement)	

Gorbachev's decisions amazed Westerners. Some U.S. officials simply could not see what was happening. The CIA frequently underestimated Gorbachev and overestimated Soviet power, perhaps because it was trapped in a Cold War mentality, perhaps also because it had been penetrated by a Soviet agent, Aldrich Ames. The CIA's top Soviet expert, Robert Gates, told a highly doubtful Shultz in 1986 that Gorbachev was nothing new, and that "the Soviet Union is a despotism that works." Gorbachev soon proved Gates wrong. For example, since 1946 Americans and Russians had waged wars, both hot and cold, to control key newly emerging regions. When he assumed power, Gorbachev increased Soviet commitments to such divided,

[68]*Washington Post*, February 1, 1988, p. B8; *The New York Times* text of press conference, June 2, 1988, p. A16.
[69]*Congressional Quarterly*, February 25, 1989, p. 401; the Brzezinski quote is in Costigliola, *France and the United States*, p. 264.

war-wracked nations as Afghanistan and Angola. By 1986, however, he reversed course. These nations, along with Cuba, annually absorbed tens of billions of Soviet rubles with too little return for Moscow. Gorbachev disavowed Soviet-sponsored "wars of liberation" by declaring, "It is inadmissible and futile to encourage revolution from abroad." He angered Castro by repeating that policy in Cuba, then warned Castro to get his house in order because the Soviets could no longer pump in more than $10 million each day to keep the Cuban economy afloat.[70]

Peace began to break out on several fronts. Gorbachev supported a deal, patiently brokered by U.S. Assistant Secretary of State Chester Crocker, to stop the fourteen-year-old U.S.- and South African–supported revolt against the Marxist Angolan government. Some 215,000 had died in the conflict. In return, the 30,000 Cuban troops who had protected the Angolan regime were to return home. It was a defeat for the Reagan Doctrine but a victory for U.S. and Soviet diplomacy, and especially for the long-suffering Crocker. Gorbachev also visited China to strengthen ties. Most important, he pulled all 115,000 Soviet troops out of Afghanistan by early 1989. This "bleeding wound," as he termed it, had infected Soviet soldiers with drug addiction and alcoholism while claiming 15,000 Soviet (and 85,000 Afghan) lives. In the great triumph of the Reagan Doctrine, Washington had pumped in over $2 billion since 1979 to help the fundamentalist Moslem guerrillas fight the Soviet Army. The turn came in 1986 when, with strong support from Congress, the CIA gave the guerrillas Stinger antiaircraft missiles that could shoot down Soviet helicopter gunships. The irony was (as perhaps Gorbachev had calculated) that once the Red Army withdrew, the Afghans fell to fighting viciously among themselves. A U.S.S.R.-supported Marxist government managed to cling to power. "Everybody was against the Russians," a guerrilla leader observed, "but now people are confused."[71]

---

[70]Fred Kaplan, "Soviets Recasting Foreign Policy," *Boston Globe,* April 10, 1988; *Time,* July 27, 1987, p. 40; *The New York Times,* August 7, 1988, p. 11; Shultz, *Turmoil and Triumph,* p. 703.

[71]*Washington Post,* December 23, 1988, p. A14; Ibid., October 4, 1986, p. A14, lists the sanctions; Matthew Evangelista, " 'New Thinking' in Foreign Policy," *The Nation,* June 13, 1987, pp. 795–799; *The New York Times,* June 6, 1989, p. A4; Ibid., December 15, 1988, p. 27. Essential reading is John F. Burns, "Afghans: Now They Blame America," *The New York Times Magazine,* February 4, 1990, pp. 24–37.

Gorbachev not only escaped from these costly traps but redirected Soviet energies to profitable areas. Downplaying Angola and Nicaragua, he strengthened relations with India, Argentina, and Mexico—larger nations that offered economic as well as political benefits to him. Most significant (and perhaps most dangerous for U.S. interests), he launched a huge campaign to sweeten ties with Western Europe. Trips to Bonn, Paris, and London created "Gorby fever," and he used his popularity to call for "a common European home" that stretched from Great Britain through the Soviet Union.[72]

It was becoming clear that he intended nothing less than to pivot Soviet foreign policy from the half-century-old Moscow-Washington axis to a new Moscow-London-Paris-Bonn-Tokyo axis. He did so for three reasons. First, he believed American economic power was declining as European-Japanese strength increased. Americans had become less attractive business partners. Second, they were also less dependable. His closest adviser, Alexander Yakovlev, believed he knew the United States (he had attended Columbia University in New York City during the 1950s). Yakovlev saw the American community as infected with "chauvinism," "militarism," "horrible crimes," "the tendency toward fascism," a grindingly poor underclass, "McCarthyism," and a "Radical Right." He concluded that the Soviets could not work well with such a country. Third, the new alignment could undermine NATO if Gorbachev could link Soviets with Western Europeans in "our common European home," as he grandly called it.[73]

The world was changing at a dizzying pace. In the early 1900s the great historian Henry Adams played with laws of physics to prove (to his own satisfaction) that the very pace of history had accelerated during the 1870–1910 era of the industrial revolution and Western imperialism. If Adams had been alive in the late 1980s, amid the incredible Soviet transformation, the rising powers of Western Europe and Japan, and the revolution brought to daily lives by computers, satellites, and bioscience, even he would have been left in wonder-

---

[72]Neil MacFarlane, "The USSR and the Third World," *The Harriman Institute Forum*, I (March 1988): 4–5.

[73]Mikhail Gorbachev, *Perestroika* (New York, 1987), p. 190; Alexander Yakovlev, *On the Edge of an Abyss* (Moscow, 1985), pp. 12, 33, 39, 142–146; *The Economist*, July 15, 1989, p. 41; *Washington Post*, June 16, 1989, p. A29.

ment at the increased speed and depth of change. In one area, however, Adams would have felt at home. Between 1900 and 1914 he was one of the few prominent Americans who, fearful of an ultimate breakdown in Russia, wanted to cooperate with the Russians and help them adjust peacefully to a new world. Most officials in the new George Bush administration were in agreement with Adams.

CHAPTER 13

A New World Order—Or the Age of Fragmentation? (1989–)

On December 25, 1991, the seventy-four-year-old Soviet Union disappeared as if by the stroke of a magician's wand. No one had predicted the timing or the exact nature of the disappearance, but one person had prophesied the breakup:

> I cannot but think . . . that the future growth of Russia . . . [is] not a little overrated. Without a civiliz[ing] of the hordes nominally extending the Russian dominion over so many latitudes and longitudes, they will add little to her real force, if they do not detract from it; and in the event of their civiliz[ing], and consequent increase, the overgrown empire, as in so many preceding instances, must fall into separate and independent states.[1]

So wrote former U.S. President James Madison in 1821. But Madison's prophesy instructed post-1989 Americans in yet another way. As the most important author of the Constitution in 1787, Madison had insisted on creating a flexible (and, as it turned out, federal) political system that could expand across a vast "empire," as he and his generation termed it. In the 1990s the United States survived as incomparably the world's greatest power. Russia meanwhile began to emerge from a nightmare of economic breakdown, rampant crime, and even civil war, to pose new problems for the United States. The Cold War was over, but the roots of the century-long competition between Americans and Russians remained, not least because of the

---

[1]Madison to Richard Rush, November 20, 1821, in James Madison, *Letters and Other Writings of James Madison* (Philadelphia, 1867): III, 235–236.

thousands of nuclear weapons whose triggers were held by Moscow and Washington officials.

These two characteristics of the 1990s—the exceptional power of the United States and an increasingly frustrated, explosive Russia—were framed by a third theme: the political, ethnic, religious, and economic fragmentation of the global system. The divisions within the two superpowers' camps had begun in the 1950s (see p. 152), but with the end of the Cold War, the fragmentation seemed close to being out of control. The Soviet Union's fifteen members became a commonwealth of separate nations. Czechoslovakia and Yugoslavia splintered, African and Southeast Asian nations sunk into domestic warfare, and even industrialized nations such as Canada, Italy, and India were threatened by major splits. New York Democrat Senator Daniel Patrick Moynihan worried in 1993 that ethnic division "promises to get savage. Get ready for 50 new countries in the world in the next 50 years. Most of them will be born in bloodshed."[2]

In their moment of Cold War triumph, Americans loved to honor their principle of self-determination, but that principle threatened to become dangerously unpredictable. As Russian Vice President Aleksandr Rutskoi worried in 1992, "More than 130 . . . ethnic groups live on Russia's territory, so that if this right [of self-determination] is implemented in practice, we may end up with more than 100 'banana republics.' " Rutskoi became increasingly willing to use armed force to prevent the existence of such "banana republics."[3] One authority noted that although the United Nations recognized that some 185 countries existed, they contained about 250 ethnic-religious groups who could argue for statehood.[4]

Americans were not immune to the growing disorder. Once the domestic pressures of opposing communism lifted, the Democratic and especially the Republican political parties lacked cohesion. Third parties became more popular. As the economy lost some of its Cold War underpinning, the gap between rich and middle-class incomes widened, and frustration deepened. More violently, so-called militias,

[2]David C. Rapoport, "Interventions and Ethno-Religious Violence; Self-Determination and Space," Working Paper No. 8, The Center for International Relations, UCLA (Los Angeles, 1994), especially pp. 6–7.
[3]*Foreign Broadcast Information Service—Russia,* January 21, 1992, p. 52.
[4]The analysis by David Binder and Barbara Crosette in *The New York Times,* February 7, 1993, p. 14, is a useful overview of the developing ethnic wars.

which advocated using armed violence if necessary to oppose U.S. laws, grew to between 10,000 and 40,000 members. One such militia was allegedly responsible for the deadly explosion of the Oklahoma City federal building that killed 169 people in 1995. Evangelical Christians became politically powerful in many states as they waged "cultural warfare" (in the words of one of their leaders) on post-Cold War American society. The head of the Christian Coalition, Ralph Reed, explained the reason for this new, more fragmented America: "The truth is, the ends of wars bring the most divisive politics recorded in American history." Reed believed that "the old dichotomies of liberal-conservative, internationalist-isolationist, dove-hawk are breaking apart. There are some ideological categories being formed that don't have any history in the politics of the Cold War." He emphasized the pivotal point: "The end of wars don't [sic] bring stability. They [sic] bring chaos and recriminations. Postwar eras are periods of an enormous realigning of political lines."[5]

George Bush and Bill Clinton became the first U.S. Presidents who had to deal with this fragmenting world and a new, less predictable Russia, while facing a primary problem: quieting the anger and bridging growing divisions in American society so that the country could survive and prosper in an increasingly fragmented, but also interdependent, world.

Raised in wealth by an athletically talented mother and a father who had been an international banker and a U.S. Senator, George Herbert Walker Bush had been the Navy's youngest flier in World War II. He became a hero after being shot down and rescued, and then returned to fly 1200 more combat hours. Making his fortune in Texas oil, Bush used Houston as a base for helping to create the modern Texas Republican party. One of his closest friends, especially on the tennis court, was James Baker, a well-off scion of an old-money, politically powerful Houston family. Some work in African-American and Hispanic neighborhoods helped Bush broaden a virtually nonexistent party, and in 1966 he won election to Congress. A run for the Senate failed, but between 1971 and 1981 he gained wide experience as ambassador to the United Nations, U.S. representative in China,

[5]Sidney Blumenthal, "Christian Soldiers," *The New Yorker*, July 18, 1993, pp. 34–35.

head of the CIA, then Vice President. He earned the reputation of being in the moderate, pragmatic wing of Republicanism. In foreign policy, however, he had at times been an arch-Cold Warrior, as in 1965 when he declared that "I will back the President no matter what weapons we use in Southeast Asia," or in 1980 when at times his anticommunist rhetoric was actually stronger than Reagan's.[6]

Bush named Baker as his secretary of state. Baker had managed several of Bush's campaigns, including the politically brutal dissection of Democratic nominee Michael Dukakis in 1988. Known as "a political genius" with "the perfect Washington résumé" (White House chief of staff, secretary of the treasury, proven political operator, masterful manipulator of the press), Baker knew little about foreign affairs. Admitting he was "more interested in the game than in philosophy," and neither profound nor deeply reflective about foreign affairs, Baker was as fine a politician as anyone who had sat in the secretary's chair since William Seward in Lincoln's administration. "He is action-oriented—more so than Bush," said one senior official who knew both well. Bush's national security adviser, General Brent Scowcroft, was more reflective but highly cautious and a specialist in arms control—a subject of declining importance as Gorbachev disarmed. Baker had a tight group of four younger persons surrounding him whose political talents few disputed, but whose ability to shift forty-five years of U.S. foreign policy—and move a huge, stolid bureaucracy to shift with it—remained to be seen. A senior official warned, "Neither Bush nor Baker reads history." Much historical memory disappeared, moreover, when Baker rather savagely fired George Shultz's highly successful professional staff and replaced it with his own close associates, few of whom knew much about the U.S.S.R.[7] The question thus arose as to how well they would be able to understand the historical transformation that was radically reshaping the world of the 1990s.

Baker's political skills stunningly appeared when he dealt quickly with the Central American questions that had torn apart American politics, and, finally, the Reagan administration, in the 1980s. The

[6]Randall Rothenberg, "In Search of George Bush," *The New York Times Magazine*, March 6, 1988, pp. 29–49; David Hoffman's analysis in *Washington Post*, December 7, 1988, p. A26; Ibid., May 3, 1979, p. A2.

[7]John Newhouse, "Profiles: The Tactician," *The New Yorker*, May 7, 1990, pp. 50–51; Jack F. Matlock, Jr., *Autopsy on an Empire* (New York, 1995), p. 185.

secretary of state realized that the Nicaraguan contras, whom Reagan had created and lauded as "freedom fighters," were actually losers, and that they were not worth more struggles with Congress. Baker resolved to disband the contras in return for a Sandinista pledge to hold an open election in February 1990. It was a calculated gamble that the Sandinistas would lose the election, a gamble most observers thought Baker would lose. But he covered his bet by receiving Gorbachev's assurances that the Soviets would cut off arms aid to Nicaragua and pressure the Sandinistas to abide by the election results. Baker threw the dice—and won. The Sandinistas lost to a coalition led by Violeta Chamorro, a revered newspaper publisher, and surrendered power. In 1991 Baker scored a similar victory by pushing the bloodstained right-wing government in El Salvador to make peace with the leftist revolutionary FMLN. Again the Soviets cooperated. Another hero was the former Costa Rican President, Oscar Arias, whose 1987 peace plan Baker followed but seldom mentioned.[8]

Highly visible beneath this velvet-gloved diplomacy was an iron fist. On December 20, 1989, as Gorbachev was renouncing both the use of force and Soviet imperialism, Bush used massive force and raised memories of U.S. imperialism by invading Panama with 27,000 troops. It was the largest U.S. military operation since the Vietnam War. Bush said he invaded to shield the Panama Canal; protect U.S. citizens (a U.S. Marine had been killed on Panama's streets, and other Americans had been attacked); halt the vast drug traffic through Panama; and capture Manuel Noriega, the dictator who had defied Reagan and Bush. Critics doubted these reasons. No case was convincingly made that the Canal was threatened. U.S. citizens endangered in other countries were protected without overthrowing governments and losing between 250 and 1200 (mostly civilian) lives. Drug traffickers had other routes to out-of-control American drug users; indeed, drug traffic through Panama actually increased after the invasion. Other reasons seemed more important. Observers noted Bush's statement that Noriega was an "enormous" personal "frustration," recalled how the President had been termed a "wimp" for not removing Noriega when a chance arose several months earlier, and concluded that Bush's motives were personal and political.

[8]U.S. Department of State, "Secretary Baker: Democracy and American Diplomacy," *Current Policy*, no. 1266; Don Oberdorfer, *The Turn: From The Cold War to a New Era. The U.S. and the Soviet Union 1983–1990* (New York, 1991), pp. 268–270, 338–342.

Two results of the invasion were of special interest. First, the President had not consulted Congress before going to war with Panama, and neither the Senate nor the House ever cared enough to investigate thoroughly the causes and bloody consequences of his decision. Bush's foreign-policy powers approached those of the 1960s Imperial Presidency. Second, although the President and Congress promised much aid to the new Panamanian regime, little was forthcoming. The United States, as Bush admitted, had the "will" but not the "wallet." The nation's economic decline was affecting its ability to help its friends. The U.S.-installed Panamanian government meanwhile proved inept and depended on U.S. military help to put down its own army's revolts. Corruption, laundered drug money, and unemployment plagued Panamanians—so much so that they asked the U.S. military not to move its bases (and its dollars), out of the country on December 31, 1999, as the 1977–1978 treaties provided (see p. 288). With Cold War threats over, however, and the Canal losing its importance in a new age of supertankers and ship-railroad systems, Americans were also losing their interest in Panamanians.[9]

Unlike his handling of Panama, Bush approached Gorbachev and the rapidly evolving Soviet bloc with a caution that puzzled observers. His presidency seemed to become schizophrenic. One part was a "personal" presidency marked by a dizzying pace of meetings, globetrotting, golf, jogging, and fishing. The sixty-five-year-old Bush always seemed to be in motion. His hero was Theodore Roosevelt, whose picture now hung in the White House, and the new President clearly followed TR's booming call to "the strenuous life." But the other was a cautious, even passive presidency when it came to making complex policy decisions.[10] His attitude of "Let's wait and see whether it will work out on its own" became most noticeable on domestic issues. He took much the same approach as the most impor-

[9]Richard E. Cohen, "Marching Through the War Powers Act," *National Journal,* December 30, 1989, p. 3120; *The New York Times,* January 21, 1990, p. E3, February 11, 1990, p. 20, and January 18, 1992, p. 5; *Washington Post,* February 4, 1995, p. A14; Eytan Gilboa, "The Panama Invasion Revisited," *Political Science Quarterly,* 110 (Winter 1995–96): 551–559.
[10]Charles O. Jones, "Meeting Low Expectations." In Colin Campbell and Bert A. Rockman, eds., *The Bush Presidency; First Appraisals* (Chatham, N.J., 1991), pp. 37–59.

tant event of the last half of the twentieth century, the disintegration of the Soviet Empire, unfolded.

In March 1989, two months after Bush took office, Gorbachev held the first free elections in the Soviet Union since 1917. They resulted in humiliating defeats for the Communist party candidates running for the new national legislature. Discontent spread as perestroika did nothing to stop the sliding economy. One official tagged it the " 'Perestroikamobile': the key is in the ignition . . . but it has not moved." The danger grew that the Soviet Union itself would fall apart, creating chaos and the possibility that its 30,000 nuclear warheads would fall into the wrong hands. This danger had many sources, including the pluralistic, multiracial population that stretched across eleven time zones; the hatred of many of these people for the Great Russians, who had long dominated the central government; long-smouldering religious hatreds; and Gorbachev's reforms that decentralized power but produced economic disasters. Conservatives warned that only brutal Stalinist methods could force the Russian people to work harder. Others, including many in the West, argued that, to the contrary, the economy would improve only when Gorbachev turned completely to free markets and thus destroyed the Communist party—a move that the Soviet leader, a committed communist, refused to take.[11]

Amid this bitter debate, the three once-independent Baltic States (Lithuania, Latvia, and Estonia) prepared to break away from the Soviet Union. The world was then shocked in January 1990 by bloody fighting between Moslem Azerbaijanis and Christian Armenians who lived in a vital oil-producing region. The hatreds went back centuries. Azerbaijan threatened to leave the U.S.S.R. Gorbachev dispatched 30,000 troops, but despite the massive force, the revolt continued to simmer.

Bush's response to these dramatic events was to do little in early 1989. He declared that his advisers were carefully analyzing the situation. After five months the results were finally announced: U.S. policy would be "status-quo plus," an empty term, given the immense changes going on, that was quickly ridiculed. In a speech at Texas A&M University in May, Bush declared that the 1947 containment

---

[11]"The Nationalities Policy of the Party in Present-Day Conditions," *Reprints from the Soviet Press,* October 31, 1989, p. 22; Angela Stent, "Doctrinal Discord," *New Republic,* January 8 and 15, 1990, p. 17; *The New York Times,* January 1, 1990, p. 33.

policy had worked, but before the U.S.S.R. could be allowed into the Western community, Gorbachev had to meet a series of conditions—including sharply reducing Soviet involvement in Eastern Europe and the Third World. Bush offered nothing concrete (such as financial help) in return. He seemed confused. On the one hand, he valued his personal friendship with Gorbachev. (Bush often seemed to want to deal with foreign leaders as if they were old school chums.) He certainly did not want to see Gorbachev's central government dissolve. On the other hand, U.S. officials could not figure out how to help Gorbachev, given the growing demands on a stumbling U.S. economy and his commitment to communism. Bush's confusion grew for another reason: Gorbachev was ending the Cold War and, especially, the obvious need for the Americans' NATO military presence in Europe where "Gorbymania" was rampant. The United States had little other leverage over a booming Western Europe that was already moving away from Washington. As Secretary of Defense Richard Cheney admitted in 1989, the reduced Soviet threat "makes it more difficult for us to maintain the kind of cohesion and unity within the Alliance" that had existed.[12]

Gorbachev then stunned Bush in the autumn of 1989 by more than meeting the President's demands. In April the Solidarity movement became a legal noncommunist political party in Poland. Solidarity had clout; since 1981 it had been led by Lech Wałesa, a shipyard welder who had won the Nobel Peace Prize for trying to reform Poland nonviolently. In July Gorbachev publicly destroyed the Brezhnev Doctrine, and protected Wałesa, by declaring that it was "inadmissible" for one nation forcibly to "restrain the sovereignty" of another. He was admitting that the Soviets could no longer afford to fix the failures of the East European regimes. Their people lacked food while West Europeans enjoyed both food and VCRs—a gap in living standards glaringly shown in television and newspapers that filtered through the Iron Curtain. But Gorbachev also believed that left on their own, the East European reformers—good communists like himself—would triumph and keep the party in power in a better, happier Eastern Europe. The Brezhnev Doctrine, a Moscow official said,

---

[12]Michael Cox, "From Super Power Détente to Entente Cordiale?" in Bruce George, ed., *Jane's NATO Handbook*, 3rd ed. (Surrey, U.K., 1990), pp. 278–279; Oberdorfer, *The Turn*, p. 333.

was to be replaced with the "Sinatra Doctrine"—that is, East Europeans could do things "their way."[13]

The results were electric. Solidarity put Gorbachev to the test by demanding a dominant voice in the Polish government. Flustered Polish communists called Gorbachev for help and advice. There was no help, only advice: the Poles were on their own. The dam had been broken. Or, more accurately, the communist dominoes began to topple. As Solidarity won stunning election victories in Poland, fresh winds of change also blew in Hungary, which already had the bloc's most liberal economic system. Reformers drove out communists and free elections were set for 1990. When the new Hungarian regime opened its doors to the West in September 1989, East Germans flooded through Hungary into West Germany. The East German communists could not control the chaos, and this time, unlike 1953, Gorbachev ensured that the Red Army would not do it for them. Old regimes also collapsed in Czechoslovakia (where hundreds of thousands of young people lay siege to Prague streets for weeks until a noncommunist government gained power) and Bulgaria. The changes occurred with surprisingly little violence except in Romania,[14] where longtime dictator Nicolae Ceauşescu defied reformers and, along with his wife, was quickly executed. Most dramatically, on November 9, 1989, Communist East Germany suddenly opened the Berlin Wall, perhaps the Cold War's best known and most hated symbol. The twelve-foot-high barrier was then destroyed by workers, and pieces were sold for high prices by the new capitalists, while Germans sang their version of "For He's a Jolly Good Fellow." Under the "Sinatra Doctrine," Gorbachev had refused to use the Red Army, so East European communism collapsed. A surprised CIA director in Washington admitted, "It is going much faster than anyone might have anticipated."[15]

By the end of these surprising events in 1989, Bush had thrown

---

[13]The background is in *The New York Times,* December 11, 1989, p. D10; Richard Barnet, "After the Cold War," *The New Yorker,* January 1, 1990, pp. 66–69; and Larry Martz, "Into a Brave New World," *Newsweek,* December 25, 1989, p. 40; the "Sinatra" reference is in Oberdorfer, *The Turn,* p. 355.

[14]Through much of the post–1945 years, Rumania was the common spelling; following Ceauşescu's execution, the people of that country preferred Romania.

[15]Janine R. Wedel, "Lech's Labors Lost?" *World Monitor,* II (November 1989): 44–45; *Washington Post,* November 4, 1989, p. A4; Ibid., January 15, 1990, p. A12. The useful background account is in *The Chicago Tribune's* special publication, *Communism: A World of Change* (1989).

TURNING POINTS IN
EASTERN EUROPE, 1989

EAST GERMANY
Nov.

POLAND
Aug.

SOVIET UNION

WEST GERMANY

CZECHOSLOVAKIA
Nov.

SWITZERLAND

HUNGARY
Oct.

ROMANIA
Dec.

ITALY

YUGOSLAVIA

BULGARIA
Nov.

Key dates in the transition
from Communist domination

his political support fully behind Gorbachev. But this misled. The President could not deliver the massive economic aid that the Soviet leader needed. Indeed, although Secretary of State Baker admitted that the Soviet leaders were panicked and "men in a hurry" to solve their problems before they were destroyed by the onrushing chaos, the United States even refused to grant the U.S.S.R. most-favored-nation (mfn) trade status, which would give preference to Soviet goods in the U.S. market. Bush, however, did grant mfn status to China, even after the aged Chinese communists brought in tanks and bloodily smashed student demonstrations for democratic changes in June 1989. U.S. officials demanded immediate economic and emigration reforms before they would give similar trade preferences to the Soviets. The Bush administration, moreover, had no idea how to devise a policy that could replace the forty-three-year-old containment policy. In 1947 Mr. "X" (George Kennan) had argued that containment would lead to "the breakup or mellowing" of the Soviet Union (see p. 63). Now confronted by the "breakup" and potential chaos, U.S. officials grew worried. Even the eighty-five-year-old Kennan warned that the "disintegration," especially in East Germany, had to be stopped "one way or other."[16]

A broad debate erupted in the United States over how to respond to these shocks. One popular argument was Francis Fukuyama's "end-of-history" thesis. Fukuyama, who served in Bush's State Department, argued that the Cold War was over and "political liberalism" had totally whipped communism. The great historical struggles between competing ideologies had ended with capitalism's triumph. Critics, however, warned that far from meaning the "end of history," communism's fall could mean the return of the unpredictable, combustible history of pre-1945 that had produced two world wars. Other critics admonished that there was not a single capitalism, but many different kinds—and that in the past, as in the case of the United States and Japan, they had dangerously clashed. One U.S. official began to worry that the world was beginning to look more like "1939" than "1989." Another debate erupted over an essay by "Z" (later discovered to be Professor Martin Malia of the University of California–Berkeley). "Z" stressed that Gorbachev's reforms within a communist regime were doomed: "There is no third way between Leninism and the market, between Bolshevism and constitutional government." So Americans were not to help Gorbachev save his too-conservative reforms. But critics noted that "Z's" advice meant standing aside as the Soviet Union and its nuclear arsenal slid toward chaos.[17]

This vigorous debate did not seem to help Bush. He and Gorbachev did take major steps toward reducing the number of nuclear missiles and banning the production of chemical weapons. But they could not agree on how to deal with that historical dilemma sitting at the heart of Europe—Germany—which was rushing toward reunification now that the Berlin Wall was rubble. Gorbachev wanted no unified

---

[16]The late William Appleman Williams noted the links between containment and 1989–1990 affairs; and Paul Dukes's seminal *The Last Great Game: USA Versus USSR* (London, 1989), especially chapters 7 and 8, was most helpful. *The New York Times,* January 18, 1990, p. A8, has excerpts of Kennan's testimony. Oberdorfer, *The Turn,* pp. 369–370, has Baker's quote.

[17]Francis Fukuyama, "The End of History?" *The National Interest,* no. 16 (Summer 1989): 3–18; *Washington Post,* December 23, 1989, p. A11; "Z," "To the Stalin Mausoleum," *Daedalus,* CIL (Winter 1990): 295–340; Martin Sherwin, "Gorby and Z," *The Nation,* February 12, 1990, p. 189. Fukuyama acknowledged the multiplicity of capitalisms in his later book, *The End of History and the Last Man* (New York, 1990), especially pp. 122–128.

Germany and demanded that if it did unify, it must not be a NATO member. Bush's position was more complex. For decades Western leaders had said they supported German unification; they did so because they privately thought it would not occur. Now that it was about to happen, the leaders of France and Great Britain secretly begged Gorbachev not to allow it. Bush was also fearful. He quickly supported unification, but he also sent Baker to ask East German officials to slow their merger with West Germany. Matters, however, were out of all these leaders' hands. Germany's unification movement, propelled by history and a rich West Germany that offered to rebuild a devastated East, developed a momentum of its own. In July 1990 Gorbachev and West German leader Helmut Kohl made their own deals—some of which (such as forbidding NATO maneuvers in the former East German area) Bush did not like. The President nevertheless wisely decided to support a Germany that was "whole and free"—but to tie it to the West through NATO, as well as through the flourishing European Economic Community. Gorbachev had to agree; in return he demanded that the Germans limit their army to 370,000 troops, continue to swear off nuclear weapons, and give up former German lands once and for all by agreeing to the German-Polish border set in 1945. Gorbachev also now played down his "common European home" theme and literally begged Bush to retain U.S. power in Europe to keep a close eye on Germany.[18]

This agreement on the key problem of Central Europe marked another historic breakthrough. But it further froze the U.S. commitment to NATO, which was increasingly a huge military alliance in search of a purpose—unless that purpose was to be to watch over and control Germany, which was supposedly one of the closest allies of the United States. At a December 1989 summit Gorbachev happily announced the Cold War was over. When Bush was asked if it was, he turned testy: "If I signal to you there's no Cold War, then you'll say, 'Well, what are you doing with troops in Europe?' I mean, come on!" A State Department official added that NATO and its nearly 300,000 troops were needed now as in 1949—not for a Soviet threat, but so that the United States could shape "the emerging political and secu-

---

[18]Frank Costigliola, "An 'Arm Around the Shoulder': The United States, NATO and German Reunification, 1989–90," *Contemporary European History*, III, no. 1 (1994): 100–108; Oberdorfer, *The Turn*, p. 381; Cox, "From Super Power Détente," p. 281; Martz, "Into a Brave New World," p. 42.

rity architecture of Europe." NATO was thus a political weapon to keep Europeans sensitive to Washington's wishes. It was becoming clear that if the United States was to play a role in the new Europe, it might try to play it through the Conference on Security and Cooperation in Europe (CSCE), a thirty-five member group formed in 1975 to consider political and human rights problems. But CSCE was no alliance, and the United States was just one of thirty-five participants.[19]

Bush and Baker, along with other observers, watched with surprise in February 1990 when Gorbachev overrode bitter hard-line resistance and broke the Communist party's monopoly on power for the first time since 1917. In the spring, noncommunist parties won sweeping victories, including the election of Boris Yeltsin to the head of the Russian Federation, the largest by far of the fifteen Soviet republics. Gorbachev had purged Yeltsin from the Moscow party leadership in 1987 because the upstart demanded more rapid reforms. Yeltsin now had the beginning of his revenge: he had been legitimately elected by the people while Gorbachev, although the U.S.S.R.'s President, had not been. Gorbachev had been put in office by party functionaries. Hard-line communists now moved to stop the reforms. In January 1991 tough Interior Ministry troops killed fifteen people while using force to keep Lithuania in the U.S.S.R. Gorbachev tried to placate the hard-liners with appointments and his refusal to move rapidly toward free-market policies.

Some analysts later looked back on these months of mid-1990 to early 1991 as Bush's lost opportunity. Clearly, Yeltsin was legitimate, wanted to undertake far-reaching democratic reforms and arms reductions, and was surrounded by young advisers who were also tough and prodemocratic. The White House instead demanded that no U.S. government official build up Yeltsin or undercut Gorbachev. "It has become a Gorbachev-centered foreign policy," a U.S. diplomat observed, but there was no conceptual thinking about "where his disintegrating country might be headed." Bush had grown dependent on his personal friendship with Gorbachev and had grown deeply suspicious of Yeltsin, who threatened to break up Gorbachev's central control—and who also had appeared to be both an alcoholic and a boor during an unfortunate visit to Washington. U.S. ambassador

---

[19]Frank Costigliola, "NATO Theology," unpublished paper, 1991, pp. 14–15, in author's possession.

to Moscow Jack Matlock watched Gorbachev sinking and Yeltsin rising, then urged Baker to deal with both men. But White House "apologists" for Gorbachev, as Matlock called them, refused his good advice. Critics instead snickered that Yeltsin's most important American friend was Jack Daniel.[20]

Bush's inability to take advantage of the Soviet opportunities was not because of America's public opinion. Perhaps it was because Bush, Cheney, Baker, and Scowcroft had all been involved with Gerald Ford in 1976 when détente turned sour and Ford went down to defeat in the presidential election (see p. 281). Perhaps it was due to the administration's fear that if Yeltsin won, the Soviet Union could become so chaotic as to present new dangers. Amid growing demands from Americans that the military budget be cut so that they could enjoy a "peace dividend," Cheney in mid-1990 announced a 25 percent reduction in U.S. forces but noted that a new generation of military technology would have to be added—an addition that would also add tens of billions of dollars to the military budget later in the 1990s.[21]

A military crisis did arise, but it had little to do with the Soviet Union. On August 2, 1990, Saddam Hussein, the military ruler of Iraq, invaded the neighboring oil kingdom of Kuwait. Saddam was then poised, U.S. officials feared, for an invasion of Saudi Arabia, oil-rich and since the 1940s a close ally of Washington's. Saddam took Kuwait for many reasons. He hated the Kuwait-Iraq boundary line (actually imposed on Iraq by British imperial officials in 1922) because it largely cut him off from the sea. He hated the Kuwaitis for pumping large amounts of oil, and thus keeping prices low, when he needed to sell high-priced oil from his wells to pay off a huge debt he had incurred during an incredibly bloody eight-year war against Iran. He aimed ultimately at dominating the Arab world. And finally, he believed that the United States and its allies would not respond. After

---

[20]*Washington Post,* February 13, 1990, p. A1; privileged interview, February 11, 1992; John Morrison, *Boris Yeltsin* (New York, 1991), pp. 56–73; Stephen White, *Gorbachev and After* (New York, 1991), pp. 68–69, 167; Matlock, *Autopsy on an Empire,* pp. 508–509; Michael R. Beschloss and Strobe Talbott, *At the Highest Levels* (Boston, 1993), p. 105.
[21]*The New York Times,* December 2, 1989, p. 33; Ibid., February 3, 1992, p. A8; *Washington Post,* February 13, 1990, p. A1; Newhouse, "Profiles: The Tactician," p. 76.

all, they had given him $40-billion worth of arms in the 1980s to fight Iran, nearly all of it on credit. And until hours before the invasion, U.S. officials said privately to him and publicly to Congress that while Bush and Baker did not want force used, they would not take any position on the Iraqi-Kuwaiti boundary dispute and did not want to become involved. Not that Americans had illusions; they knew that Saddam had personally executed political opponents, had hung their bodies on meat hooks for public display, had publicly threatened "to make fire eat half of Israel" (the closest U.S. ally in the region), and had ordered tens of thousands of his young people to die in suicidal attacks against Iran. It was just that to Washington Iran seemed more of a danger. Reagan and Bush, moreover, sent billions of dollars of arms and food to the brutal dictator to keep him apart from the Russians. American farmers and arms dealers, who happily profited, raised no objections. "We looked like fools," a high U.S. State Department official admitted, for not anticipating the invasion.[22]

Bush again responded cautiously for several days. Kuwait, after all, had been the most pro-Soviet and anti-Israel state in the entire region. But Bush finally moved decisively. He was pushed especially by the tough British prime minister, Margaret Thatcher, whose country profited from billions of dollars of Kuwaiti investments and bank deposits. Both U.S. and British policies were dictated by domestic needs and interests. Bush also believed that the world's price of oil, and therefore the control of the world economy, was at stake. He decided, moreover, that it was 1938 and Munich all over again: if this "Hitler," as Bush called Saddam, succeeded, the world would be pushed back to a 1930s state of affairs, when aggressors ran rampant. He spelled out the meaning for the post-Cold War world: "What is at stake is more than one small country, it is a big idea—a new world order" where "peace and security, freedom and the rule of law" reign. With help from Gorbachev and, especially, the British, Bush mobilized the United Nations to resist, although he was actually in full command of the UN effort. Japan and Germany, who had cut their own deals with Middle East oil producers, were reluctant to help, but Bush

---

[22]A superb account in Bruce W. Jentleson, *With Friends Like These* (New York, 1994), pp. 14–16, 94–97, 132–171; Judith Miller and Laurie Mylorie, *Saddam Hussein and the Crisis in the Gulf* (New York, 1990), pp. 3–23; Daniel Yergin, *The Prize: The Epic Quest for Oil, Money, and Power* (New York, 1991), pp. 770–775; the U.S. official is quoted in *Washington Post*, October 28, 1991, p. A9.

extracted $13 billion from Tokyo and $11 billion from Bonn. He even went to Congress (unlike all other post-1945 U.S. Presidents) and after a hard-fought battle obtained a constitutional authorization for war. (Bush later spoiled this victory by declaring, incorrectly, that he had the "inherent right" to take the country to war without congressional authorization.) The President carefully reassured his able chairman of the Joint Chiefs of Staff, General Colin Powell, that this time—unlike in Vietnam—the military would be allowed to fight its war and fight to victory. Powell used U.S. airpower and technology spectacularly. After a month of bombing, 550,000 U.S.-UN forces unleashed "Operation Desert Storm" on February 27, 1991. In 100 hours they liberated Kuwait and occupied southern Iraq. Saddam had threatened to wage "the Mother of all battles," but instead faced massive defeat.[23]

Of the Americans 146 were killed; the estimated Iraqi death toll ran as high as 100,000, many of them civilian. Bush waited for Saddam to leave or for the Iraqis to overthrow him. Neither occurred. A blunder in U.S. military planning allowed most of Saddam's elite troops to escape. The dictator's chemical- and nuclear-weapons projects were not destroyed. A year later Saddam held a survival celebration in Baghdad. Bush had also held back in fear that if he obliterated Iraq, Iran's Islamic regime would emerge as the unchecked regional power. Bush and Powell had liberated Kuwait, but U.S. diplomacy had failed to anticipate or stop the invasion, and U.S. strategy had failed to remove the cause: Saddam. Secretary of State Baker did use the military success to forge a historic Middle East peace conference in which, for the first time, Israeli and Arab officials talked to each other about a lasting settlement in the war-torn region. Baker threw himself into his Middle East travels. (Bush joked, "Baker has a sign on his door. It reads '10 to 3.' They're not his hours, but his odds of not being there."[24]) For the first time, moreover, the United States made the Soviets a partner (albeit a very junior partner), in the Middle East peace process—a step that Nixon had refused to take in 1973 and which Gorbachev now gratefully accepted as a sign of his nation's continued great-power status.

During the Iraqi war Gorbachev had cooperated with Bush, but

---

[23]Theodore Draper, "Presidential Wars," *New York Review of Books,* September 26, 1991, pp. 64–74; Yergin, *The Prize,* pp. 775–779.
[24]William Schneider, "Vietnam Syndrome is Alive and Well," *National Journal,* April 13, 1991, p. 902; *Washington Post,* January 12, 1992, p. C1.

Soviet Army officers, who had helped equip and train the Iraqis, supported Saddam to the bitter end. One Soviet general even predicted that "The war in the Gulf will end in a major U.S. defeat." Embarrassed by the Iraqis' collapse, and humiliated both by Gorbachev's withdrawal from Eastern Europe and by German reunification (which seemed to throw into question even the great Russian victory in 1945), Soviet military officers moved closer to frustrated civilian conservatives who wanted to topple Gorbachev. Several opponents even charged that he was secretly dealing with Bush to make the U.S.S.R. totally dependent on the United States. Gorbachev, however, was also feeling pressure from his left, especially from Yeltsin and other leaders of the fifteen republics who were moving toward independence. In July 1991 Gorbachev agreed with nine of these republics on a treaty for a historic new, looser union in which the republics would be termed "sovereign," instead of "socialist," states as in the past. The treaty was to be signed on August 20, 1991.[25]

Hours before that ceremony, the hard-liners struck. They placed Gorbachev under house arrest and tried to clamp Stalinist restrictions on the press and people. Yeltsin and his Russian government held out in a Moscow building not far from the Kremlin. They defied the takeover. When the army was ordered to take control of the building and other outlying areas where opposition was rising, the military split. The army refused to fire on Yeltsin and several hundred thousand supporters (who were mostly older people—younger students did not appear in number to face down communist repression as they had in Czechoslovakia or China). Meanwhile the coup-plot leaders were disorganized, and, it turned out, some were quite drunk. Nor could they lie about their failures: the new technology of CNN television news, fax machines, and satellite pictures kept the world's eyes riveted on Moscow's streets. But Bush and his NSC adviser, General Scowcroft, were confused. The State Department, whose professionals Baker had largely shunted aside, were unable to help. The White House thus came close to recognizing the desperate right-wing

[25]*Wall Street Journal,* March 20, 1991, p. 8; *The New York Times,* December 26, 1991, p. A13; Ibid., October 7, 1991, p. A7; Cox, "From Super Power Détente to Entente Cordiale?" pp. 282–283; *Foreign Broadcast Information Service—Soviet Union—Economic,* April 24, 1991, p. 37.

344 Americans, Russia, and the Cold War, 1945-1996

coup when Scowcroft declared "we should not 'burn our bridges' with them." Bush was luckily saved from such foolishness when Gorbachev refused to join the plotters. The entire plan began to collapse. Some plotters tried to flee and were captured. Others committed suicide. Gorbachev reappeared in triumph, but Yeltsin emerged with the new, decisive power. Gorbachev was blamed for having placed the coup-plotters in their government positions. As Yeltsin began systematically to uproot Communist party strength, Gorbachev finally resigned from the party and moved to disband the powerful Central Committee.[26]

The hard-liners' perfect failure, and Gorbachev's beheading of the party, meant that communism had ended in the Soviet Union with a whimper, more in farce than tragedy. The larger question became whether Gorbachev himself could survive at the top. Bush seemed to be doing all he could to save his friend. While the White House issued stories about Yeltsin's boorishness and "ego," Bush, on August 1, 1991, stunned the Ukrainian legislature, which was set to quit the Soviet Union, by telling it that the 52 million Ukrainians (a population twice the size of Canada's) should remain under Gorbachev. (That comment, and the President's appeasement of China's brutal leaders, led conservative columnist George Will to charge that Bush preferred "order before freedom.") The U.S. leader tried to help his Soviet counterpart by slashing nuclear weapons costs; he pulled out nuclear artillery shells from Europe, tactical nuclear weapons from warships, and the nuclear-armed B-52 bombers from their round-the-clock airborne alert (where they had been since Eisenhower's presidency). Both sides further slashed the number of nuclear missiles and warheads, and also conventional forces, in Europe in 1991.[27]

Neither Gorbachev nor Bush, however, could revive the disastrous Soviet economy. A Russian's per capita annual income had dropped to one-tenth that of an American's $19,780, was about at the level of a Mexican's income, and was falling. In 1990 the U.S.S.R. had one of its greatest grain harvests, but starvation threatened because handling and transportation were so bad that 40 percent of the crop

[26]Matlock, *Autopsy on an Empire*, pp. 585–595; *The New York Times*, August 25, 1991, pp. 1, 16; *Washington Post*, August 30, 1991, p. A29; Ibid., August 23, 1991, p. A27; Richard Barnet, "Reflections: The Disorders of Peace," *The New Yorker*, January 20, 1992, p. 69.
[27]Will's quote is in *Washington Post*, January 12, 1992, p. C7; Ibid., June 21, 1991, p. A20; *The New York Times*, October 7, 1991, editorial.

Trying to Control Nuclear Weapons, 1963–1993

Date	Treaty	
August 1963	Limited Test Ban Treaty	Prohibits nuclear testing or any other nuclear explosions in the atmosphere, in outer space, and under water.
January 1967	Outer Space Treaty	Prohibits sending nuclear weapons into Earth orbit or stationing them in outer space.
July 1968	Nuclear Nonproliferation Treaty	Prohibits the transfer of nuclear weapons to other countries and prohibits helping countries without nuclear weapons to make or acquire them.
May 1972	Antiballistic Missile Treaty	Bans space-based defensive missile systems and limits the United States and the Soviet Union to one ground-based defensive missile site each.
June 1979	Strategic Arms Limitation Treaty	The first formal strategic arms treaty sets an initial overall limit of 2400 intercontinental ballistic missile launchers, submarine-launched missiles, heavy bombers, and air-to-surface missiles.
December 1987	Intermediate-Range Nuclear Forces Treaty	Provides for the dismantling of all Soviet and American medium- and shorter-range land-based missiles and establishes a system of weapons inspection to guard against violations.
July 1991	Strategic Arms Reduction Treaty—START I	Brings the number of Soviet long-range nuclear warheads down from 11,012 to 6163, and the number of United States warheads down from 12,646 to 8556.
January 1993	Strategic Arms Reduction Treaty—START II	Reduces the superpowers' arsenals to one-third of their current size, limiting them to 3000–3500 warheads and bombs.

rotted or was eaten by worms and rats. As production fell, the state paid bills by printing more money, which in turn triggered runaway inflation. As the ruble became worthless, Russians turned to a primitive barter economy. Vodka became a kind of exchange currency. Lacking money to purchase medicines, and as antiquated pharmaceutical plants were closed because they endangered the environment, even the most basic drugs such as aspirin often could not be found. The world's largest oil producer (11.5 million barrels daily in 1990) was about to become an importer of oil because of brokendown wells. Bush tried to help, especially at West European urging, but the United States could not afford to send much aid, and even the $4 billion of credit he offered for the purchase of U.S. food was dribbled out too little, too late. U.S. private investment did increase after the coup's failure. Pepsico (Pepsi-Cola, Frito, Pizza Hut) had more than $3 billion invested, General Motors had $1 billion, and Chevron continued its hunt for oil, while Colgate planned a toothpaste factory after noting that 280 million Russians are "a lot of teeth." But most U.S. ventures were dormant or losing money.[28]

Gorbachev had made several critical mistakes. He assumed the fifteen republics and 120-plus ethnic groups would remain loyal to the central government. He fatally underestimated the power of nationalism and ethnicity. Gorbachev also assumed that given some liberty and democracy, the Soviet people would work harder for the communist system—as he had. But they had been more terrorized or bought off by the system than loyal to it. Yeltsin quickly took power from the politically wounded Gorbachev. In December the Russian Federation, Ukraine, and Belarus declared their independence and formed a Commonwealth of Independent States (CIS). By the end of 1991 eleven of the fifteen former Soviet republics had joined the CIS. Only the Baltic States and Georgia's reactionary regime remained apart. When Yeltsin's Russia refused to pay Gorbachev's bills, the president found himself without a government. On December 25, 1991, he announced his resignation over national television. He had accomplished the historic task of opening his country to the democracy and openness of perestroika and glasnost. In the end, he was overwhelmed by the very forces he had let loose. As one Russian of-

[28]*The New York Times*, February 4, 1991, p. A1; Ibid., January 14, 1992, p. D2; Ibid., September 1, 1991, p. 6F; *Washington Post*, January 30, 1991, p. F3; Ibid., August 15, 1991, p. A41.

ficial remarked, Gorbachev "tried to reform the unreformable." Some thirty-three minutes after his speech, the Soviet Red Flag flying above the Kremlin was pulled down, and the traditional white-blue-red Russian flag was raised. The chimes on the Spassky Tower clock, which ring only on historic occasions, were heard. "Never before," observed the philosopher Sir Isaiah Berlin, "has there been a case of an empire that caved in without a war, revolution, or an invasion."[29]

In February 1992 Bush welcomed Yeltsin to Washington as the leader of the new Russia. Yeltsin's background differed from Bush's. Baptized (and nearly drowned during the ceremony) by a drunken Orthodox priest in a tiny Ural Mountain village, Yeltsin lived with five family members in a single-room hut where they slept huddled against the family's goat to keep warm. They had a cow and a horse, but both died. Yeltsin's father was arrested by Stalin's police. The son, however, rose through Communist party ranks after obtaining fine grades as an engineering student. He quickly gained power within the party, but he never forgot his roots and was (to Gorbachev's frustration) always pushing for more reform. Now, in early 1992, Bush and Yeltsin declared the Cold War over and planned further arms cuts. The Russian, however, wanted more. He presented a well-prepared, detailed list of proposals. But Bush either was not prepared to respond or felt the U.S. economic recession and his own upcoming reelection campaign gave him no room for a positive response. Yeltsin, as had Gorbachev, needed help quickly.[30]

Yeltsin pushed the economy toward free markets and privatization, but the gross national product continued to fall. One-third of Russia's people lived below the poverty line. Many of the old communist "apparatchiks" remained in place to slow reform and save their own jobs. During the winter of 1991–1992, a massive U.S.–West European airlift of food and medicines helped the people of Moscow, St. Petersburg (formerly Leningrad), and other cities avoid starvation. U.S. and European investors continued to show interest, not least McDonald's, which during the attempted coup had sent truckloads of hamburgers and coffee past Soviet tanks to the besieged Yeltsin and his allies. But the dangers that finally toppled Gorbachev also threat-

---

[29]*Foreign Broadcast Information Service—Soviet,* December 10, 1991, p. 56; *The New York Times,* December 26, 1991, p. 12; Ibid., December 15, 1996, p. 22; *Economist,* December 26, 1992–January 8, 1993, p. 67.

[30]Morrison, *Boris Yeltsin,* pp. 33–35; *The New York Times,* July 28, 1991, p. 10.

AREAS OF DISCONTENT, 1988–1994

ened Yeltsin. One was nationalism and ethnicism. Ukraine, for example, issued its own currency and created an army of 300,000. A right-wing reactionary movement, with deep roots in Russian history and vicious antiforeign feelings, also appeared.[31]

Bismarck once declared that Russia is never as strong or as weak as it appears. The Cold War's end proved that Bismarck was right about the "strong" part; Bush and other Western leaders hoped the nineteenth-century German was equally right about the "weak." Otherwise the growing chaos in Russia could, as it had in the past, spread to other regions. Announcing that "By the grace of God, America won the Cold War," Bush declared the United States "the undisputed leader of the age."[32] The "leader," however, had neither saved its

[31]*Foreign Broadcast Information Service—Soviet,* January 21, 1992, p. 52; Ibid., February 5, 1992, p. 50; *Washington Post,* February 2, 1992, p. A19; Dimitri K. Simes article in *Washington Post,* January 19, 1992, p. C4.
[32]The text is in *The New York Times,* January 29, 1992, p. A16.

closest Russian friend, Gorbachev, nor destroyed its sworn enemy, Saddam Hussein, in the 1991 war.

Bush paid for those failures in the 1992 presidential election. Seldom had a President fallen so far, so fast. Bush called Democratic presidential nominee Bill Clinton (the Governor of Arkansas) and his running mate Albert Gore (Senator from Tennessee) "two bozos" who knew less about foreign policy than did Millie, the Bushes' dog. But as an economic slump plagued the country, a Democratic bumper sticker appeared that read: "Saddam Hussein Still Has His Job. What About You?"[33] Bush flew to Japan in early 1992 to force that nation to buy more U.S. cars, only to get sick, vomit on the Japanese prime minister, and have the American automobile executives who were along condemn the trip as a failure. Clinton attacked Bush for refusing to cooperate with the world community at the historic Rio de Janeiro conference on the environment in 1992, for not stopping the killings in the civil war that erupted in the former Yugoslavia, and for stopping and returning refugees trying to flee military dictatorship in Haiti. Meanwhile the Republican party split. Since the 1950s it had united against the Soviets. With the U.S.S.R. no longer a threat, Republicans disagreed over foreign commitments and costs; some simply wanted to forget about foreign policy altogether. Foreign affairs played an important role in the election, as Bush, the supposed "foreign-policy President," went down to defeat.

The forty-six-year-old Clinton, the first baby-boomer (those born between 1946 and 1964) to reach the presidency, had an extensive agenda for domestic problems, but—despite his effective criticism of Bush—little idea of how to deal with the post-Cold War world. He named Los Angeles lawyer Warren Christopher as secretary of state. Christopher had been a successful State Department troubleshooter during Jimmy Carter's presidency, but he had little interest in rethinking and conceptualizing policy. Such rethinking was to come from Anthony Lake, the new director of the National Security Council. A longtime foreign service professional who had shown great courage in Vietnam, Lake had plotted Clinton's campaign attack on Bush. But Lake came up short in a September 1993 speech when he tried to construct a fresh approach. He argued that "we have arrived at neither the end of history nor a clash of civilizations [two popular

---

[33]Fouad Ajami, "Lucky Jim," *New Republic*, January 1, 1996, p. 35; Thomas Omestad, "Why Bush Lost," *Foreign Policy*, LXXXIX (Winter 1992–1993): 70–81.

characterizations of the post-Cold War problems], but a moment of immense democratic and entrepreneurial opportunity." He urged that post-1947 "containment" be replaced by "enlargement"—"enlargement of the world's free community of market democracies."[34]

Clinton's first attempt to apply this "enlargement" was a spectacular failure. It occurred in Somalia, the West African nation that Americans and Soviets had long competed for because of its strategic location. They had left so many weapons behind that one observer believed the Somalis had enough arms to fight one another for a hundred years. Wars did break out between rival clans. Americans paid little attention until December 1992 when their televisions showed grisly pictures of the starving and wounded. Bush and President-elect Clinton agreed to send a U.S.-led force, under UN authority, to distribute food and medicines. Television again covered the well-lit landings for a global audience. This intervention marked the first time that a UN force had intervened in a nation's internal affairs without the agreement of local authorities. In mid-1993 Clinton changed the mission. He decided that any enlargement of peace and aid could not occur until one militant clan leader was captured. That leader's forces struck back by killing eighteen U.S. soldiers in October. Stunned Americans now demanded that their sons and daughters be brought home. Clinton complied in late 1993.[35]

The Somalia debacle deeply affected Clinton's policies. During the 1992 campaign, he had demanded that the United Nations take more responsibility for policing the world. But after the Somalia tragedy, the United Nations, through some fault of its own, had a bad name. Clinton played to Americans' mistrust of the world organization by saying that the United States would learn to say "no" to UN requests. Television, especially CNN, had been more important in leading the United States into Somalia, then forcing it out. Clinton seemed to be at the mercy of the media, and he played to it. "Mr. and Mrs. Couch Potato want us to stop civil wars and save the hungry,"

[34]Anthony Lake, *From Containment to Enlargement* (Washington, 1993), pp. 3–5; Larry Berman and Emily O. Goldman, "Clinton's Foreign Policy at Midterm," in Colin Campbell and Bert A. Rockman, eds., *The Clinton Presidency: First Appraisals* (Chatham, N.J., 1996), especially pp. 296–299.
[35]*Washington Post,* November 19, 1993, p. A52; Michael Mandelbaum, "Foreign Policy as Social Work," *Foreign Affairs,* 75 (January–February 1996): especially 16–19.

one senior U.S. official groused. "They see the military as the best way to do that, but when people get killed they won't stand for it."[36]

The Pentagon's fear of becoming trapped in another Vietnam resurfaced. Clinton shared that fear. Thus when Liberia (founded by freed American slaves in 1837) suffered a civil war bloodier than Somalia's, Clinton would not intervene. Nor would he or the United Nations use enough force to stop even more disastrous tribal wars in Rwanda (where estimates of the dead ran to 800,000) or Burundi. As one observer concluded, the Cold War's end "set America free to pursue its own interests in Africa—and it found that it did not have any."[37]

Lake's plans for the enlargement of peace, democracy, and U.S.-UN cooperation largely disappeared. Remaining were his and Clinton's hope for enlarging economic opportunities. Their foreign policies were thereafter driven by two motors, both domestic: a determination to please the U.S. business community and, closely related, a commitment to pacify voters so that Clinton would be reelected in 1996. These two motors thus, for example, largely pushed out of the way such policy priorities as human rights and democratization.

China and Mexico provided examples. In the 1992 campaign, Clinton had condemned Bush for increasing trade ties with the booming economy of 1.2 billion Chinese while Beijing's communist leaders brutalized dissenters. But by 1994–1995 Clinton had bent to the $40 billion of bilateral trade (overwhelmingly in China's favor) and the demands of U.S. business groups who had formed a new China Lobby. He refused to impose economic sanctions even though by 1996 the Chinese military, growing more rapidly than any other in the world, threatened its neighbors. As for Mexico, Americans had long dreamed of creating a vast northern market comprising themselves, Canadians, and Mexicans. In 1988 Ronald Reagan had signed a treaty with Canada that would remove trade barriers over a period of years. In 1994 Clinton pushed to bring Mexico into this North American Free Trade Association (NAFTA). He did so despite strong opposition from some in his own Democratic party (especially union members who feared losing jobs to lower-paid Mexican labor). Opponents also

[36]*Newsweek*, December 27, 1993, p. 13.
[37]*The New York Times*, March 7, 1993, p. E3; Ibid., July 31, 1995, for op-ed, "Anatomy of a Massacre," by Milton Leitenberg.

warned that Mexico's one-party system was corrupt and its economy suspect. But with strong Republican support, the President passed the NAFTA treaty through the Senate. Shortly thereafter Mexico's economy nearly collapsed and its former president was sought for various alleged crimes. But Mexico, such as it was, nevertheless opened more fully to U.S. investment and trade.[38]

"I make no apologies for putting economics at the top of our foreign-policy agenda," Secretary of State Christopher declared in 1995.[39] That approach explained why the Clinton administration finally lifted twenty-year-long economic sanctions against Vietnam and discussed diplomatic relations with that recent enemy. The need to deal with growing economic competition in Southeast Asia, especially from Japan, overrode protests from military veterans and families of U.S. soldiers who were still unaccounted for by the Vietnamese.[40]

Economics and reelection plans also helped explain why Clinton maintained U.S. military spending at a rate nearly as high (85 percent) as it had been during the Cold War. Despite tremendous civilian demands on the budget, he kept military spending around $260 billion annually. Clinton even added expensive weapons systems that Bush had planned to cut. Congress then added more new weapons that the Pentagon did not want—all to keep people back home employed. Most Americans, including many who damned the federal government for being too powerful, gratefully took the money or looked the other way. The Pentagon helped justify such spending by developing a post-Cold War strategy that concluded that the military must be ready to fight two wars the size of the 1991 Persian Gulf conflict at the same time. That such a threat had never existed even during the Cold War, that most regional conflicts did not touch U.S. interests, and that allies existed to help deal with the crises—all these points made little difference to Clinton and the Congress. The Presi-

---

[38]Especially emphasizing this theme are Jim Hoagland, "Heeding the Voice of Silent Cal," *Washington Post,* February 9, 1995, p. A29; Melvin Small, *Democracy and Diplomacy* (Baltimore, 1996), with a useful final chapter on Clinton, and especially pp. 162–164 for the interesting Haitian example; *The New York Times,* December 18, 1995, p. A16; Berman and Goldman, "Clinton's Foreign Policies at Midterm," pp. 307–309.

[39]*Newsweek,* March 6, 1995, p. 34.

[40]A good, succinct argument is found in Kenton Clymer, "Lifting Vietnam Embargo Will Start Reconciliation Process," *El Paso Herald-Post,* February 9, 1994, p. B-5; and James C. Moore's "Twenty Years After the Fall," manuscript in author's possession, by a thoughtful Vietnam veteran.

dent also reversed Cold War policies by allowing sensitive dual use U.S. technology (that is, technology capable of being used for either civilian or military purposes) to flow abroad. In 1994 COCOM, the seventeen-member U.S.-led committee that since 1949 had policed and often prevented the sending of high-tech goods to potential enemies, was closed down.[41]

Smarting from the failure in Somalia, and accused of ignoring foreign policy, Clinton turned more attention overseas in 1995–1996. He began to emphasize that he was President "as the cold war gives way to the global village."[42] The "global village" theme was invented by Marshall McLuhan, who had predicted in the 1960s that radically new communications (computers, satellites) were inevitably making people and nations interdependent. The power of CNN had driven this point home. U.S. business and culture, moreover, were internationalizing at a breathtaking rate. Clinton and especially his secretary of labor, Robert Reich, warned that Americans were dividing into two cultures: those who had the knowledge so that they could prosper in the "global village," and those who did not and were therefore perhaps condemned to insecurity and low-paying jobs. Clinton downplayed enlargement of democracy to emphasize instead the enlargement of foreign economic opportunities. He also subordinated cooperation with the United Nations to a willingness to commit U.S. troops unilaterally to foreign crises so that these crises would not become costly political issues—as long, of course, as the commitments seemed relatively safe and lasted only for a specified (preferably short) time.

During 1994–1996, these new approaches were applied to two bloody trouble spots, Haiti and the former Yugoslavia. In Haiti, the elected President, Jean-Bertrand Aristide, had been overthrown by the military in 1991. The military acted as the agent for a small ruling elite that had ruthlessly exploited the Haitian people, turned the country into the hemisphere's poorest, and saw Aristide (a Roman Catholic priest who had condemned such exploitation), as a mortal enemy. Aristide took sanctuary in the United States. Clinton wanted to restore him to power, but U.S. officials also mistrusted Aristide. They viewed

[41]Ronald Steel, *Temptations of a Superpower* (Cambridge, Mass., 1995), pp. 59–62; Benjamin C. Schwarz, "The Arcana of Empire and the Dilemma of American National Security," *Salmagundi,* Spring 1994, pp. 182–210; *Washington Post,* December 11, 1993, p. D1.
[42]Text of speech on Bosnia, *The New York Times,* November 28, 1995, p. A14.

him as too radical and preferred that he compromise with the military. Clinton became embarrassed when Haitians began to flee in large numbers for Florida. To prevent a political uproar among Floridians, he ordered the capture and detainment of the refugees—the exact act for which he had condemned Bush in 1992. Finally, in 1994, under the threat of a U.S. troop landing, the military stepped down. They took large sums of money with them. Aristide meanwhile agreed to step aside for a duly elected successor in 1996. The elite and elements of the bloody-handed army, closely supported by the CIA with which the military enjoyed long ties, remained. But Clinton had prevented a refugee crisis and largely taken the issue out of the 1996 election.

Yugoslavia was both more dangerous and more complex. Its three major peoples—the dominant Orthodox Christian Serbs, the Roman Catholic Croats, and the Bosnians, who included some Serbians but especially many Moslems—stayed together until 1991. Croatia and Bosnia, with encouragement from Germany (and U.S. disinterest), moved toward independence. The Serb-dominated central government deployed force to protect Serbs living in the two breakaway areas. Conflict escalated. Both sides, especially the Serbs, began ethnic cleansing—that is, mass slaughter of those of a different religious and ethnic background. As European powers split over how to handle the crisis, Clinton and most Americans clearly wanted to stay out of this killing ground. They certainly had no appetite for joining small UN forces who tried unsuccessfully to separate the armies. In 1995, however, Serb defeats, well-timed NATO bombing, and Clinton's new interest in foreign policy led to an American-brokered peace agreement negotiated in Dayton, Ohio. The deal created a separate (if brittle) Bosnia, Croatia, and Serbia. Sixty thousand troops—not UN troops, but NATO troops—controlled in Washington and led by 20,000 U.S. military personnel moved into the ravaged area to enforce the peace. It was a huge but necessary gamble for Clinton. If Americans began to die in large numbers, the ghost of the former Yugoslavia would join the ghost of Somalia to haunt his political career.[43]

But if his gamble paid off, it would strengthen Washington's con-

---

[43]*The New York Times,* November 28, 1995, for Clinton's explanation of new policy; Ibid., November 1, 1995, p. A11, for a useful overview; Warren Zimmermann, "The Last Ambassador," *Foreign Affairs,* 74 (March/April 1995): 2–20.

THE BOSNIAN CRISIS, 1995–1996

HUNGARY

Zagreb

CROATIA
(Formerly part
of Yugoslavia)

EASTERN
SLAVONIA

	U.S. sector
	British sector
	French sector

Bihac

Banja
Luka

POSAVINA
CORRIDOR

Tuzla

SERBIA

BOSNIA

Srebrenica

Sarajevo

CROATIA
(Formerly part
of Yugoslavia)

Mostar

MONTENEGRO

Dubrovnik

AGREED ZONES OF CONTROL

Muslims ⎫
           ⎬ Muslim-
Croats   ⎭ Croat
           Federation

Serb Republic

ADRIATIC
SEA

ALBANIA

0   50 miles

0   50 kilometers

trol of NATO, the major institution for maintaining U.S. influence in European affairs. It would also project American power into the East Mediterranean region where it could link up with a growing U.S. military presence in the Middle East. Worried about growing instability in oil-rich Saudi Arabia, and concerned about both Iran's and Iraq's continued defiance, Clinton was injecting so much power into the area that critics termed it "the Third American Empire"—the first one being the U.S. overseas empire obtained after the war of 1898, the second after World War II in Europe and Asia.[44] Finally, and of notable importance, Clinton's gamble in Bosnia paid off by bringing Russian troops into the U.S.-directed peacekeeping effort. That event had been unthinkable just five years earlier.

Many Russians were unhappy about their troop deployment. For centuries the Orthodox Christian Russians had tried to protect their Serbian co-believers, but certainly not under U.S. direction. President Boris Yeltsin also took a gamble by cooperating with Washington because he wanted to appear to be a great power, even as his country sank into decline. Frustrated Russians turned against both Yeltsin and the West. Some observers believed that Russian-American relations were worse than at any time since bad Cold War days of the early 1980s. Russian resurgent nationalism, combined with great frustration and thousands of nuclear weapons, created considerable dangers. Yeltsin's armed forces declined rapidly in numbers, morale, and combat-readiness. As one authority observed, "They can do nothing much in Moscow, but they can wipe out New York."[45]

Yeltsin led a people who were wracked by economic chaos, frustrated by the sudden loss of an empire, and bedeviled by entrenched longtime communist bureaucrats who clung to power. Russia did still extend over ten time zones, but that empire's vast expanse threatened to pull the country apart, much as James Madison had prophesied 170 years earlier. The country had eighty-eight constituent regions, each led by local governments, as well as over a hundred ethnic groups. Trying to extend his control, Yeltsin was defied by both local officials and the conservative national parliament in Moscow.[46]

His political problems were surpassed by his economic headaches. The Soviet military-industrial complex had once swallowed fully one-third of everything the nation produced and had employed at least one of every five adults.[47] (The comparable U.S. fig-

---

[44]Jacob Heilbrunn and Michael Lind, "The Third American Empire," *The New York Times,* February 2, 1996, p. A15.

[45]*Washington Post,* March 24, 1993, p. A24.

[46]*The New York Times,* October 10, 1993, p. 12.

[47]Leon Aron, "Russia's Recent Political Developments. . . ." In The Aspen Institute, ed., *Russia, Ukraine, the Caucasus, and the U.S. Response* (Queenstown, Md., 1994), p. 38.

ures were approximately one-sixteenth of gross national product and about one of every 16 in the workforce.) To turn this complex into a market-based civilian economy without wrenching problems was beyond any mortal. In 1991 U.S. leaders helped open the channels for aid by bringing Russia and twelve of the other former Soviet republics into the International Monetary Fund and World Bank. In 1995 Russia also became a charter member of the new World Trade Organization (WTO) that replaced the forty-seven-year-old General Agreement on Tariffs and Trade. Massive aid, however, did not appear, least of all from the U.S. government. Lenders mistrusted Russian bureaucrats who tried to solve their dilemmas by printing more money. The fresh money generated runaway inflation as too much currency chased too few products. In 1986, under Soviet governmental rules, about two-thirds of one ruble bought a dollar; ten years later it took 4600 rubles.

Yeltsin appointed young market-oriented advisers, but they soon quit or were forced out in frustration. Their replacements were persons such as Viktor Geraschchenko, head of the powerful Central Bank that supposedly controlled the nation's money supply. "I understand the meaning of a bank," he told a group of Americans. "I like the words 'micro' and 'macro,' but not in economics. I don't understand all this stuff about micro and macro."[48] Not surprisingly, the Central Bank bent easily to political pressures for solving problems by printing rubles. As prices inflated, the elderly, the disabled, the military, and others on fixed incomes grew angry as their money became worthless for buying adequate food and medicines.

Westerners did continue to invest in Russia. Led by such giants as Proctor & Gamble, Chevron, and McDonald's (as well as Ben & Jerry's ice cream), Americans became the top foreign investors in the country. U.S. television shows, including a Russian version of "Wheel of Fortune" (called "Field of Wonders") and soap operas, invaded Russian television sets. But the investment was too small to help the mass of the people. Tremendous gaps arose between rich and poor, and while the nation was desperate for investment capital, perhaps $100 billion of Russian money was moved illegally to safer places abroad, often by mobsters.[49]

---

[48]*The New York Times,* January 23, 1994, p. F1.
[49]*The New York Times,* January 2, 1996, p. A3; Ibid., January 30, 1994, p. H31; Jack F. Matlock, "Russia: The Power of the Mob," *The New York Review of Books,* July 13, 1995, p. 14.

Mob crime seemed to be a fast-growing business. Police identified some 3000 gangs operating in Russia; nine or ten large mobs were competing in Moscow alone. FBI experts on organized crime signed agreements with Russian authorities so that they could help make the country safer for living and investing. An American who owned several restaurants in Moscow believed that "this country is going from Communism to recklessness overnight." Effects went far beyond individual crime. For example, mob leaders paraded their wealth with fancy cars, bodyguards, and women in short Lycra suits—exhibitionism that made ordinary citizens believe they could improve their own fortunes only through crime. Others associated Yeltsin's attempts to democratize with the glitz of the mobs and concluded that a strong Stalin-type government was preferable to this democracy. Crime in the streets, moreover, quickly translated into crime in disposing of dismantled nuclear weapons. Arrests occurred throughout Europe as groups tried to smuggle nuclear materials from Russia into such nations as Iran and Iraq. "The chaos scares me," said one former U.S. official from the Reagan-Bush years. "Here we have a 1930s situation in Chicago, except that Al Capone has access to nuclear weapons."[50]

Even as the economy improved somewhat in 1995–1996, and inflation dropped, the social effects of their new capitalism terrorized many Russians. Their life expectancy, already lower than that of any other developed country, dropped for men from sixty-four years in 1990 to fifty-seven years by 1994, while women's dropped from seventy-four to about seventy-one. (U.S. life expectancy was seventy-two for men and seventy-nine for women and had been steadily rising since 1900.) In 1991, 5300 women were murdered in Russia, a number three times higher than in most Central European nations. In 1993, 14,000 women were estimated to have been murdered by husbands, lovers, or former partners—twenty times the equivalent number for American women. Feminist groups formed to protest both such murder and the blatant economic discrimination that they experienced. The first major feminist political party, Women of Russia, won a surprising eleven percent of the vote in 1991.[51]

Other reaction was less democratic than this women's movement.

[50]*The New York Times,* August 16, 1993, p. A6; Seymour Hersh, "The Wild East," *Atlantic Monthly,* June 1994, pp. 61, 79.
[51]*The New York Times,* August 1, 1995, p. 1; *Economist,* August 12, 1995, pp. 44–45.

By 1992 Vice President Rutskoi, a powerful voice for conservatives, had become disgusted with the Western presence, especially the giant McDonald's in midtown Moscow, where, he charged, " 'Big Macs' with ketchup" overwhelmed the glory of "plain Russian meat pies," and where long lines of Russians seemed to be not merely "waiting for food" but "waiting for holy communion." Rutskoi condemned "the spiritual decline which has paralyzed our society." In 1993 Yeltsin tried to neutralize Rutskoi and his conservative colleagues in parliament. They responded in October by joining some communists, neo-Nazis, and extreme nationalists in an attempt to overthrow Yeltsin. The coup lasted only hours before being smashed, but it was a near miss, and Yeltsin's use of military units to blast the building in which the plotters holed up was seen globally on CNN. Reaction, however, had only begun. In December 1993 parliamentary elections, voters split between a coalition of prodemocratic parties led by Yeltsin, and extreme right-wing nationalist groups led by Vladimir Zhirinovsky, a populist demagogue who was bitterly anti-Western and at times appeared slightly unhinged.[52]

As unrest and anti-Westernism grew, Yeltsin shifted his ground. By 1996 he had forced out leading reformers, especially his foreign minister, Andrei Kozyrev, who (with a fine command of English) was identified with policies of cooperation with the West. Kozyrev was replaced by Yevgeny Primakov, a longtime Communist party operator, head of the Russian spy system, and friend of Iraq's Saddam Hussein. Yeltsin also tried to appease the conservatives with a move that turned out to be perhaps the worst mistake he made. In 1994 he ordered 40,000 troops to prevent the Chechnya region's separation from Russia. (See map, p. 348.) Living 1000 miles south of Moscow, the Chechens for centuries had gloried in defying the Great Russians. Bowing to nationalist pressures, Yeltsin sent helicopter gunships to destroy the separatists. Instead he found himself immersed in a Vietnam-like struggle, as Chechens seized thousands of Russian hostages and inflicted humiliating losses on Yeltsin's dispirited and underequipped troops. Nationalists attacked Yeltsin for not ending the war with massive force. The resurgent Communist party was led by Gennady Zyuganov, who separated himself from pre-1985 rulers by saying, "We are a new generation." But he also condemned capi-

---

[52]*Foreign Broadcast Information Service—Russia,* February 5, 1992, p. 50; Aron, "Russia's Recent Political Developments," pp. 37–38.

talism as "sweeping and arbitrary pillage" and praised Lenin for creating in 1917 a nation with "a mighty army and a strong ruble."[53]

Yeltsin's disasters embarrassed President Clinton. Having condemned George Bush for being too strong a supporter of a sinking Gorbachev, Clinton was now criticized for identifying U.S. interests too closely with a collapsing Yeltsin. Clinton's policy was actually better balanced than Bush's. Guided by his close friend, Russian expert, and Deputy Secretary of State Strobe Talbott, Clinton paid special attention beyond Russia itself to newly independent republics such as Kazakhstan, Ukraine, and Belarus—states that had severe internal problems, great natural wealth, and thousands of nuclear weapons. The Clinton-Talbott approach had payoffs. Chevron Oil, for example, developed a potential $20-billion joint venture with Kazakhstan. U.S. and Russian negotiators meanwhile agreed to a Strategic Arms Reduction treaty (START II), that, when ratified by the two nations' legislatures, reduced each country's nuclear stockpile to about 3500 weapons.[54]

But neither Clinton and Talbott nor anyone else could determine how to help Yeltsin solve his economic problems or protect him from the rising nationalists and communists. U.S. officials faced a terrible dilemma: they had to help support pro-Western, pro-capitalist Russians, but they had to do it so that these Russians would not appear to be Western stooges and thus bolster the nationalists' power.[55]

But that was not the only dilemma. Clinton pledged that in the near future NATO would be extended eastward to Poland, the Czech Republic, and perhaps Hungary, Romania, and Slovakia—that is, to the borders of Russia itself. His pledge came when these insecure nations asked for NATO membership, but also as U.S. officials (and former officials, such as Henry Kissinger) declared that Eastern Europe

[53]*The New York Times,* January 2, 1996, p. A6; *Washington Post,* January 10, 1996, p. A13, for a good chronology of the clash; *Washington Post National Weekly Edition,* January 1–7, 1996, p. 15.

[54]Nancy Lubin, "Central Asians Take Stock," *Peaceworks,* no. 2, of the United States Institute for Peace (Washington, D.C., 1995), pp. 1–24.

[55]Dimitri K. Simes, "America and the Post-Soviet Republics," *Foreign Affairs,* 71 (Summer 1992): 73, 77–78; Robert Legvold, "Political Developments in Russia," in The Aspen Institute, ed., *Russia, Ukraine, the Caucasus, and the U.S. Response* (Queenstown, Md., 1994), pp. 9–11.

could best be stabilized and protected under a NATO umbrella. As Kissinger warned about a possible resurgence of Russia, "Of course, history does not always repeat itself. But expansion extending over four centuries does reflect a certain proclivity." Selling large amounts of American equipment to these countries, moreover, would be highly profitable for the booming U.S. arms export industries. NATO extension could thus allow Americans to do well as well as to do good. On the other hand, even many pro-Western Russians bitterly protested NATO's plans as an intolerable military threat. Debate also erupted in the United States. Opponents predicted that NATO extension could drive Russians to turn fully against the West and to place militant anti-Western nationalists in power. They also feared that the United States would become responsible for keeping order in a region notorious for wars waged for centuries over ethnic differences and territorial disputes.[56]

Examining the world in the 1990s, Secretary of State Christopher noted that the United States was "at the end of the American century," but that if "we . . . continue to lead," then "the end of this millennium can mark the start of a second American century."[57] If Christopher is correct, Americans will have to deal with at least the following five questions:

1. *What kind of new power arrangement will replace the East-West competition of 1945–1989?* On one hand, British Prime Minister Margaret Thatcher believed in the late 1980s that the world would divide into a U.S. dollar bloc, a German mark bloc, and a Japanese yen bloc. The NAFTA agreement of 1994 seemed to support Thatcher's thesis. But otherwise her prophecy has not been fulfilled. Attempts to form a European free-trade area, for example, suffered a major setback in 1992 when Germany and Great Britain fought bitterly over currency rules.

---

[56]The debate is spelled out in Coit Blacker, Daniel Fried, and Alexander Vershbow, "U.S. Offers Moscow an Alliance," *Christian Science Monitor,* October 14, 1995, p. 15; for the other side, Owen Harries, "The Collapse of 'The West,' " *Foreign Affairs,* 72 (September–October 1993): 28–53; Kissinger's quote is in *Washington Post,* August 13, 1991, p. A17.

[57]Warren Christopher, "Leadership for the Next American Century," *U.S. Department of State Dispatch,* January 18, 1996, p. 4.

On the other hand, some thought a new world would be dominated by a "clash of civilizations"—that is, nations would divide along religious, ethnic, and cultural lines. Thus Western Christianity could be challenged by a rising Islamic world. The bloodshed in the former Yugoslavia between groups dividing along ethnic and religious lines gave some support to this thesis. In 1991 a U.S. official even testified that "the march of Islamic fundamentalism" was the problem most worrying policymakers. But the clash-of-civilizations thesis is suspect. Christianity, Islam, and other great religions are not monolithic. They deeply divide among themselves. For example, in the former Yugoslavia, Eastern Orthodox Christians in Serbia and Roman Catholic Christians in Croatia went out of their way to kill each other. Likewise, Iraq's Sunni Moslims and Iran's Shi'a Moslims slaughtered each other in large numbers during a six-year war in the 1980s. Moreover, by the mid-1990s the nation-state, not ethnic groups, continued to be by far the world's most important political unit.[58]

More likely the world was entering an age of fragmentation rather than a clash of civilizations. If information is power (and it especially has been in the post-1970s world), the rapid dissemination of information made possible by the computer, fax, and Internet meant that power was rapidly decentralizing. The world began to change not in 1990 with the end of the Cold War, but in the 1970s when the new communications of the postindustrial revolution began to take hold (see p. 291). When the Soviet Union could not adjust to these changes, it fell apart, then disappeared. New communications, moreover, allowed giant corporations to move money and other resources easily around the globe. The 1\frac{1}{2}$ trillion that flooded each day through the world's money exchanges was a deluge of wealth not even the most powerful nation's government could control.

The end of the Cold War thus allowed long-dammed-up money, ethnic rivalry, religious hatreds, and territorial disputes to burst out. Massive money flows enriched some regions but passed by others, such as impoverished African nations and even South Africa (which after 1990 finally destroyed its brutal segregation, or apartheid, system and came under control of its black African majority). Unre-

---

[58]Samuel P. Huntington, "A Clash of Civilizations?" *Foreign Affairs,* 72 (Summer 1993): 22–49; Fouad Ajami's critique in "The Summoning," *Foreign Affairs,* 72 (September–October 1993): 9; the U.S. official is quoted in *The New York Times,* January 1, 1992, p. 3.

strained capitalism became a major problem as well as a solution. George Soros, one of the richest and most agile of international capitalists, warned, "I don't believe markets are perfect. . . . I don't consider the survival of the fittest the most desirable outcome. I believe we must strive for certain fundamental values, such as social justice, which cannot be attained by unrestrained competition."[59]

2. If power is fragmenting, can ultimate power—nuclear weapons—be controlled? The United States and Russia agreed to reduce their nuclear arsenals from about 65,000 total weapons in 1988 to under 10,000 a decade later. Their success was offset to some extent by the spread of nuclear-weapons capabilities to a number of other states, including Israel, India, Pakistan, and North Korea. Older members of the nuclear club, especially China and France, developed their stockpiles. In addition the German government detected at least 350 cases of attempted nuclear smuggling, notably out of the collapsing Russian nuclear plants. Similarly, Libya, Egypt, Iran, Iraq, and China were charged with violating the 1972 Biological Weapons Convention by stockpiling germ weapons.[60]

The 1968 nuclear Non-Proliferation Treaty (NPT) barred acquisition of nuclear weapons by nonnuclear states. It also forbade nuclear states to export their capabilities to other nations. Iraq, Israel, India, and Pakistan remained outside the NPT. The United States led in trying to enforce the treaty, but its power proved limited. China, for example, joined the NPT, but despite U.S. protests sent vital nuclear materials to Pakistan, among other countries. Washington's moral authority was not helped when Americans continued to be by far the world's greatest supplier of conventional weapons (about $23-billion worth in 1991 alone).[61]

3. What then can be the role of international organizations, especially the United Nations, in helping to control the growing disorder and spread of nuclear arms? Since the 1980s the United Nations has been highly successful in helping end, or limit, conflicts in El Salvador, Angola (where the United Nations evacuated Cuban troops), and Cambodia, as well as the Iran-Iraq war. It has also been successful in monitoring

---

[59]Quoted in *Washington Post,* October 15, 1995, p. D2.
[60]*Washington Post,* April 7, 1993, p. A23; Ibid., August 17, 1995, p. A29.
[61]Richard J. Barnet, "Still Putting Arms First," *Harper's Magazine,* February 1993, pp. 59–62; *The New York Times,* July 16, 1995, p. E5; *Economist,* March 25, 1995, pp. 23–25.

the Soviet withdrawal from Afghanistan. The blue-helmeted UN peacekeeping forces deserved their Nobel Peace Prize in 1988. Other efforts, notably in Africa and Bosnia, were failures.

The United Nation's main problem, however, arose not from its peacekeeping, but from its members, especially the United States and Russia. Some Americans believed that the United Nations was an international conspiracy aimed at creating a world government to take over the United States. These Americans gained such clout that when a celebration was held in 1995 for the UN Charter's fiftieth birthday in the place of its founding, San Francisco, not a single elected Republican official, not even California's governor, attended. These U.S. critics were matched by some Russians, who, in the words of one communist leader, condemned "supranational organizations that claim the right to interfere in others' internal affairs."[62] But far from being a secret conspiracy aimed at taking over the affairs of, say, Idaho, Indiana, or Bashkiria, the United Nations by the mid-1990s was a near-bankrupt organization, suffering from numerous setbacks and burdened with a bureaucracy whose most efficient employees (according to one reporter) were "the short-order cooks in the cafeteria."[63]

After initially hoping that the United Nations could share some of the burden of U.S. policies overseas, President Bill Clinton grew critical of the organization. The United States, indeed, was the United Nation's biggest deadbeat and a major reason for its near-bankruptcy. Americans owed it well over $1 billion, but Congress refused to pay and several Presidents showed little interest in making restitution. One bitter British diplomat, remembering his own country's error in 1776, charged that Americans wanted "representation without taxation." Collective security, however, has never been popular with Americans, unless they can do the collecting and define the security. By the 1990s, as the world fragmented, the embattled United Nations moved to reduce its personnel and commitments.

   4. *Can the post-Cold War world then deal with perhaps its greatest danger, the destruction of the environment?* As the Cold War ended, world attention shifted to different but also highly lethal dangers: nuclear disasters (such as the 1986 tragedy at Russia's Chernobyl nuclear reactor, plus three more major radioactive leaks in Russia alone during

[62]*The New York Times*, February 1, 1996, p. A21; Ibid., July 9, 1995, p. E1.
[63]Barbara Crossette, "Sinister?" *The New York Times*, July 9, 1995, p. E1.

1993), disastrous oil spills, and the devastation of the Gulf War. ("Nearly apocalyptic" was the term used to describe the massive burning of Kuwaiti oil wells, lit by retreating Iraqis, that produced weeks of dark clouds over a vast region in 1991.) In Somalia and Rwanda tens of thousands of people were dead, victims not only of clan warfare but of multiplying populations facing starvation because of drought and, especially in Somalia, rapid disappearance of arable land.

Russia became an environmental catastrophe that threatened its neighbors. The distinguished Russian biologist A. V. Yablokov noted that regions in which more than half the population of the former Soviet Union lived were crises areas: "Every third man . . . has a cancer." In the southern Urals where atomic experiments were long conducted, four of five villagers suffered such chronic illnesses that one doctor believed the "genetic code of the Tatar people has so changed" that babies are often malformed or chronically ill from birth. "We do not have a future," she declared. "We have been so genetically harmed that our descendants will not be able to escape this curse."[64]

The United States was not exempt from such crises. U.S.-Canadian attempts to stop the flow of industrial and agricultural toxins into the Great Lakes, the world's largest freshwater source, largely failed. Scientists blamed the toxins for increased rates of sterility in males, physical disabilities in children, and breast cancer in women. The United States was also the leader in emitting waste gases such as carbon dioxide into the atmosphere. Despite the Rio agreement of 1992 to control such emissions, by 2010 Americans would continue to lead—and pump nearly 800,000 more tons into the air than in 1990. Corporations' attempts to move their dirtier industries into developing countries such as Mexico only compounded the crises in Mexico, while the toxins also drifted northward across the border.[65]

Environmental disasters were thus largely foreign-policy problems, especially as people in the global village became interdependent. Between 1960 and 1990, as resources disappeared, the world

[64]*International Herald Tribune*, March 26, 1991, p. 6; *Washington Post*, September 7, 1993, p. A12.
[65]Small, *Democracy and Diplomacy*, p. 150; *Washington Post*, October 5, 1995, p. A19; *The New York Times*, April 11, 1993, p. C4; Richard A. Johnston and Kenneth R. Meade, "Phaseout of Ozone Depleting Substances," paper for the 1993 Inter-American Bar Association, April 19–24, 1993.

population jumped from 3 to 5.3 billion. The number was expected to double to 10 billion by 2050, when many of the college students of the 1990s would have to live with the results. Only international efforts could effectively deal with such growth or help the more than one-half billion people who already existed in absolute poverty. Even in the 1980s a European expert figured that if the world were a village of 1000 persons, 240 would not have enough to eat.[66]

The Cold War had not been cold. More than 21 million people perished in wars between 1945 and 1990, mostly in the developing countries. Only the wars' causes, not the results, changed. "Many of the wars in this century were about oil," declared one expert, "but wars of the next century will be over water." As much as $800 billion over ten years would be needed for water projects globally, but the largest contributor, the World Bank, would be able to provide only about $40 billion.[67]

Meanwhile the developing world continued to demand more fossil fuel to industrialize. Thus more toxins would enter the air. China was expected to replace the United States as the main source for the "greenhouse" gases that were warming the atmosphere. Scientists argued over the exact cause of the significant global warming that occurred in the twentieth century. (Another possible cause was the destruction of forests, over an area the size of the state of Virginia, that continued to occur each year. Certainly this destruction helped explain the soil erosion that would annually take 17 million acres out of production, even as starvation increased.) Experts agreed, however, that whatever the cause, the warming could melt giant glaciers and snowcaps at the poles, then raise ocean levels until U.S. East Coast beaches could be under water within 25 years.[68] The related question was whether the world's richest and most scientifically advanced nation had the political skills to deal with such foreign-policy crises.

[66]Michael Kidron and Ronald Segal, *The New State of the World Atlas* (New York, 1984), figure 39. Secretary of State Christopher's important speech on the environment is noted in *The Washington Post*, April 15, 1996, p. A10. A pioneering paper on the necessary relationship between foreign policy and the environmental issues is Mark Lytle, "An Environmental Approach to American Diplomatic History," *Diplomatic History*, 20 (Spring 1996), pp. 279–300.

[67]*The New York Times*, August 10, 1995, p. A13.

[68]*The New York Times*, September 18, 1995, p. A1; *Washington Post*, May 15, 1990, p. A4.

Casualty Count: Number of U.S. Soldiers Who Died in Missions

Mission	Dead*	Wounded
1941–1945: World War II	405,399	671,846
1950–1953: Korean War	36,914	103,284
1964–1973: Vietnam War	58,174	153,303
1983: Grenada invasion	19	119
1983: Beirut bombing	241	79
1989–1990: Panama invasion	23	320
1991: Persian Gulf War	146[†]	465
1992–1993: Somalia mission	29	153
1994: Haiti intervention	4[‡]	3
1996: Bosnia[§]	1	3

*Combat-related and noncombat-related deaths.
[†]Thirty-five were the result of friendly fire.
[‡]Three were suicides.
[§]As of February 1996.

5. Are the American people prepared for the post-Cold War world?
After the Cold War ended, crises would be increasingly international
in scope, but Americans' ability to deal with them would still depend
upon the strength of their domestic society. The Soviet Union, after
all, rotted from the inside out. On the other hand, Japan's and Germany's rise to economic power occurred because of their educated
workforces, intelligent governmental guidance, ability to plan long-
term, and high savings rates (three to four times the rates of Americans) that created money for investment rather than a towering consumer indebtedness.

As Americans dealt with the new world, they came face-to-face
with several problems rooted in their history. The first was how to
adjust to the postindustrial technology that created instant communications, fragmentation of power, and extraordinary new multinational corporations. The last time they had to make such an adjustment occurred with the industrial revolution of the 1880s–1890s. The
results then were economic crisis, rising unemployment, intensified

racial tensions, populist uprisings, new political parties, and an imperialist foreign policy. If history were not to be repeated, people would need to learn from the past.

The second historical problem revolved around the nation's political system and how intelligently Americans could make it work both efficiently and fairly. The great French analyst of American society, Alexis de Tocqueville, observed in his *Democracy in America* some 160 years ago that the U.S. democratic system was near-perfect for settling and exploiting a continent, but it was much less adequate for conducting foreign policy. Tocqueville even thought it might be one of the poorest systems for handling diplomacy that he had ever studied. A successful foreign policy requires consistency, considerable secrecy, and a concern for the nation's larger interests. American democracy, Tocqueville noted, provides instead a notoriously inconsistent public opinion, a people who like to tell all they know, and persons whose primary concerns are individual economic interests rather than the national interest. A central question of the country's foreign policy for 200 years has thus been how a consensus can be created in such a democratic system to support foreign policy. During most of the years from 1947–1989, this was not a major problem because Harry Truman had solved it with his Truman Doctrine of 1947 (see p. 52). He brilliantly united the country behind the ideology of anticommunism. Every President from Eisenhower to Reagan used the Truman Doctrine to maintain popular support for their handling of foreign affairs.

George Bush and Bill Clinton were the first Presidents in the post-1945 era who could no longer use the Truman Doctrine; the communist threat had virtually disappeared. The long-term handling of the Tocqueville problem would depend largely upon Americans themselves. In the late 1940s U.S. officials devised effective foreign policies because Americans learned from the horrors of the 1929–1945 years, while creating the wealth to help others as well as themselves. In the 1990s a new world pressed in, a world that, for example, destroyed thousands of jobs in U.S. automobile plants and communications industries because of international rather than only domestic changes. The problem could be confusing. For example, the Greece, New York, town board vowed to "buy American" and so rejected the less expensive Komatsu dirt excavator to buy a John Deere product. The board then discovered that the Komatsu was made in the United

States, the John Deere was made in Japan, and both were produced by a U.S.-Japanese joint venture.[69] Americans had much to learn about the world they supposedly led. When asked whether more of the U.S. federal budget went to foreign aid (which many Americans saw as a mere giveaway), or Medicare, 58 percent answered foreign aid. Actually foreign aid amounted to much less than 1 percent of annual Medicare expenses. Only 50 percent of those questioned could identify the powerful speaker of the house, whose job was to help fix their taxes, but 64 percent recognized the judge in the O. J. Simpson murder trial, Lance Ito, who had no authority over the people polled. U.S. schoolchildren ranked as low as the bottom one-quarter in history, science, and math when measured against their peers (and future competitors) in Asia and Europe.[70]

Not surprisingly politicians reflected these weaknesses. Clinton's foreign policies stumbled badly in the first years of his presidency. When Republican conservatives won a landslide victory in the 1994 congressional elections, they ran on a "Contract with America" that was specific on numerous domestic issues but said virtually nothing about foreign policy—or, more important, on how the domestic and foreign-policy issues were interrelated. Thus the Republican House of Representatives, to show it was indeed a great power, voted overwhelmingly to extend NATO to the Russian border (see p. 360) but later—determined to cut back government—slashed funds needed for NATO by nearly two-thirds.[71]

Despite such foolishness, despite Clinton's warning that the country was turning "isolationist," many Americans were more internationalist in the mid-1990s than they had been during the Cold War. They were even willing to place U.S. troops under a UN commander for peacekeeping purposes. At the same time, U.S. corporations were requiring more knowledge of, and experience in, international affairs

---

[69]*The New York Times,* January 27, 1992, p. A15; Ibid., June 27, 1990, p. A23; *Washington Post,* February 4, 1995, p. A11.

[70]*Washington Post,* January 29, 1996, p. A1; Ibid., May 15, 1995, p. A6; *The New York Times,* June 20, 1991, p. A20; Ralph Nader and Mark Green, "Passing on the Legacy of Shame," *The Nation,* April 2, 1990, p. 444.

[71]Louis Fisher, "The 'Contract with America,' " *The New York Review of Books,* June 22, 1995, pp. 20–21; *Washington Post,* July 7, 1995, p. A1.

than ever before. Only 4 percent of their top job searches had such a requirement in 1990, but 28 percent did in 1995. Even every member of Tupperware's executive committee spoke between two and four languages.[72] The gap between these requirements and the foreign-policy ignorance revealed in polls could be explained. The United States was dividing between those who had studied and were adjusting to the new global village, and those who had not.[73] This division helped explain the growing income gap since 1973 between the richest and the middle to lower classes. The division could also lead to making disastrous choices, especially in the use of force.

A generation ago Reinhold Niebuhr worried that both Americans and Russians had too easily tried to escape political and economic dilemmas by placing their faith in military power:

> It is one of the mysteries of human nature that while most of us are unconscious of an inevitable mixture in our motives, we try to atone for this error by too constant emphasis on "the law in our members which wars against the law that is in our minds."[74]

As world affairs became less predictable and Americans continued to rely on their military superiority to deal with some of the unpredictability, Niebuhr's point remained crucial. It did not necessarily follow that with the end of the Cold War the earth was a safer place. The post-1945 world had lived with the threat of nuclear holocaust, but it had also assumed that the two great powers would maintain political stability. Now the world found itself living in an age of lessening nuclear threat but increasing political instability—especially in those historic seedbeds of war, Central and Eastern Europe, as well as in the newly emerging world.

The great and dramatic turn in world affairs that was represented by the ending of the Cold War was symbolized by Mikhail Gorba-

---

[72]John E. Reilly, "The Public Mood in Mid-Decade," *Foreign Policy*, no. 98 (Spring 1995): 76–77; Jessica Matthews, "The New Isolationism," *Washington Post*, February 5, 1996, p. A21.

[73]A useful starting place for understanding this problem is Lester C. Thurow, *Head to Head* (New York, 1992), especially the succinct analysis on pp. 15–16 that places the ne era in historical perspective.

[74]Reinhold Neibuhr, "Toward New Intra-Christian Endeavors," *Christian Century*, December 31, 1969, pp. 1662–1667.

chev's visit to Fulton, Missouri, on May 6, 1992. The former Soviet leader spoke at Westminster College, where in March 1946 Winston Churchill had sounded a rallying cry for Cold War against the Soviet Union by warning the West that "an iron curtain" had fallen across Europe (see p. 39). Gorbachev gently disputed Churchill's fear that the Soviets had been intent on world domination: "Stalin, as in 1939–41, was afraid of war," and the Soviet Union "was exhausted and destroyed." But Gorbachev admitted that the Soviets made a "major error" in misunderstanding and frightening the West, while, he claimed, the West gravely erred by launching a nuclear arms race. He pleaded that such mistakes not be repeated: "It would be a supreme tragedy if the world, having overcome the 1946 model [by having ended the Cold War], were to find itself once again in a 1914 model." Gorbachev especially warned about the explosive dangers in the growing gap between the wealthy North and poorer South around the globe, and in "an exaggerated nationalism" that "has already led to much bloodshed."[75]

As he pleaded for a stronger United Nations to maintain the peace and stop the spread of weapons around the earth—and as he warned Americans not to take a "monocentric" view that they had won the Cold War and could now dominate world affairs as they pleased—Gorbachev sounded much like Niebuhr. And above both loomed the spirit of James Madison warning about the fragmentation of empire. The Russian and the American, once bitterly locked in Cold War, now agreed that if the world's people did not use "their minds" to solve the growing disorder and fragmentation caused by burgeoning economic, political, and environmental problems, then—as not only the Cold War's history but the costly hot wars of 1989–1996 demonstrated—they could too easily resort to what Niebuhr had called "the law of our members."

[75]*New York Times,* May 7, 1992, p. A1, has the excerpts.

Bibliography for Additional Reading

(See also footnote citations in relevant chapters; most of those references are not repeated here.)

General Bibliographical Tools and Reference Works

Students must first consult Richard Dean Burns, editor, *Guide to American Foreign Relations Since 1700* (1983). It is so useful that the bibliography that follows does not repeat many of the Burns, *Guide*, references but instead attempts to update those references (especially for books published after 1981) as well as to provide a few standard volumes. For periodical literature, consult *Social Sciences and Humanities Index*. Soviet references for earlier years are in Thomas Taylor Hammond, *Soviet Foreign Relations and World Communism* (1965). U.S. government publications are listed in U.S. Superintendent of Documents, *Monthly Catalog of U.S. Government Publications* (since 1895); many of these now can be located by computer search. Good reference works include Thomas Paterson and Bruce Jentleson, editors, *Encyclopedia of U.S. Foreign Policy* (1997); Alexander DeConde, editor, *Encyclopedia of American Foreign Policy*, 3 volumes (1978), which has detailed bibliographies; John E. Findling, *Dictionary of American Diplomatic History* (1980); and, for the Russian and bloc events, the Hoover Institution's *Yearbook on International Communist Affairs*. Special bibliographical references are also listed in a number of the sections that follow.

Journals

Among many available journals, *Foreign Affairs*, *National Interest*, and *Foreign Policy* are especially influential. The government's view can be found in *Department of State Bulletin* and the State Department's *Current Policy*, in addition to the Department of Commerce's *Today*. *Bloc* is a new journal devoted to East-West trade. Good historical analyses can be found in *Diplomatic History*, *Journal of American–East Asian Relations*, *International Security*, *Political Sci-*

ence Quarterly, World Politics, International History Review, International Orga-nization, Journal of American History, and *American Political Science Review.* For the Soviet side, see *Current Digest of the Soviet Press, Problems of Communism, International Affairs* (Moscow), and *Slavic Review.*

General Works: United States and American-Soviet Relations

Indispensable is the Department of State, *Foreign Relations of the United States* (now available from 1861 to 1963); it is the well-edited set of State Depart-ment documents. The Department of State *Current Documents* series has two volumes on 1950–1955 and single volumes from 1956 through 1966; publica-tion of annual volumes recommenced in 1979. Especially valuable is the se-ries issued by the Government Printing Office, *Public Papers of the Presidents*— annual volumes that contain nearly all public utterances by Presidents since 1945. Ruhl J. Bartlett and David F. Long, editors, *A Documentary History of U.S. Foreign Relations, Volume II: The Mid-1890s to 1979* (1980) is a selection from and an addition to Bartlett's classic *Record of American Diplomacy.*

Important surveys of U.S. policies include Warren I. Cohen, *America in the Age of Soviet Power, 1945–1991* (1993), highly readable, especially strong on Asia, and with a useful bibliography; Thomas McCormick, *America's Half-Century* (1995), pioneering in its use of world-systems theory to interpret the Cold War; David Fromkin's stimulating *In the Time of the Americans* (1995), showing Wilson's and Theodore Roosevelt's influences on later generations; Henry Kissinger, *Diplomacy* (1994), a breathtaking multicentury sweep with special insights into the 1960s and 1970s; Richard Crockatt, *The Fifty Years War* (1995), which focuses on U.S.-U.S.S.R. competition; Melvyn Leffler, *The Specter of Communism, 1917–1953* (1994), a highly respected historian's analysis of a common theme; John Lewis Gaddis, *Russia, The Soviet Union, and the United States* (1990), which places the Cold War in a 200-year relationship; and Lloyd Gardner, *Covenant with Power* (1984), an imaginative, sweeping work that links Cold War figures with Woodrow Wilson. But start with Edward Crapol, "Some Reflections on the Historiography of the Cold War," in *History Teacher,* XX (1986–1987), a superb overview. Saul Landau, *The Dangerous Doctrine* (1988) well notes the distortions in the idea of national security, as does James Chace and Caleb Carr, *America Invulnerable* (1988), a stunning historical treat-ment; M. Boll, *National Security Planning* (1988); Lawrence Freedman, *Evolu-tion of Nuclear Strategy* (1983), an authoritative treatment; Gabriel Kolko's stimulating *Confronting the Third World: U.S. Foreign Policy, 1945–1980* (1988), and his bleak, powerful *Century of War* (1994); Goran Rystad, *Prisoners of the Past* (1982), on the "Munich syndrome"; and Richard E. Neustadt and Ernest R. May, *Thinking in Time* (1986), dissecting Cold War crises. Two standard accounts on the Western alliance are Lawrence Kaplan, *NATO and the United States* (1988), and David Calleo, *Beyond American Hegemony* (1987).

For surveys of the U.S.-Soviet relationship, Martin Walker, *The Cold War, A History* (1995) is by a respected British journalist; Dana H. Allin, *Cold War Illusions: America, Europe, and Soviet Power, 1969–1989* (1995) provides an important interpretation; as does Peter Boyle in *American–Soviet Relations* (1993); N. V. Sivachev and N. N. Yakovlev, *Russia and the United States* (1978) gives a Cold War perspective; and Paul Dukes, *The Last Great Game: USA Versus USSR* (1989) is stimulating and masterful, as is his earlier *The Emergence of the Super-Powers* (1970). Richard W. Stevenson, *Rise and Fall of Détente* (1985) traces 1953–1984 events; John Lewis Gaddis, *Strategies of Containment* (1982) suggests a conceptual framework; and Alexander L. George et al., *U.S.-Soviet Security Cooperation* (1988) contains twenty-one case studies on the search for stability in the arms race. Especially useful on East-West trade are Philip J. Funigiello, *American-Soviet Trade in the Cold War* (1988); Colin White, *Russia and America* (1988), a most important comparative study placed in long historical context; Philip Hanson, *Western Economic Statecraft in East-West Relations* (1988); and Bruce W. Jentleson, *Pipeline Politics* (1986), a justifiably prizewinning account.

Specific Topics in United States Policy Since 1945

As noted above, check first with Burns, *Guide,* and the footnotes in this book; those references are usually not repeated here, and therefore the following are largely post-1981 (that is, post-Burns, *Guide*) references. No text bibliography can duplicate Burns.

For the domestic scene, Lary May, editor, *Recasting America* (1988) is a superb collection of key essays; Stephen J. Whitefield, *The Culture of the Cold War* (1991) is essential; David P. Forsythe, *Human Rights and U.S. Foreign Policy* (1988) focuses on Congress; Tennent S. McWilliams, *The New South Faces the World . . . 1877–1950* (1988) is a useful specialized study; George C. Edwards III and Wallace Earl Walker, editors, *National Security and the U.S. Constitution* (1988) is pioneering; Louis Fisher, *Presidential War Power* (1995) is definitive; and Barry B. Hughes, *The Domestic Context of American Foreign Policy* (1978) remains important for both good introductory discussions and bibliography.

For individuals and elite groups, in addition to volumes listed below under specific presidential administrations, a useful starting point is Walter Isaacson's and Evan Thomas's readable *The Wise Men* (1986), on Acheson, Bohlen, Harriman, Kennan, Lovett, and McCloy, as is David Mayers, *Ambassadors and America's Soviet Policy* (1995). Mark Stoler, *George C. Marshall* (1989) is a fine short biography that builds on Forrest Pogue's four-volume study. Randall Wood's *Fulbright* (1995) is a superb biography covering the

1940s to 1970s. Two key figures were Clark Clifford, *Counsel to the President* (1991), and Loy Henderson, *A Question of Trust*, edited by George Baer. H. W. Brands, *Inside The Cold War, Loy Henderson* . . . is a fine biography. Wilfrid Sheed, *Clare Booth Luce* (1982) analyzes a shrewd, colorful woman. Dulles is given a definitive treatment by Ronald Pruessen—Volume I is *Dulles: The Road to Power* (1982); also useful is Mark G. Toulouse, *The Transformation of John Foster Dulles* (1985), an intellectual biography. Four excellent biographies of Kennan are also important histories of the Cold War: Anders Stephanson, *Kennan and the Art of Foreign Policy* (1989); Walter L. Hixon, *George Kennan: Cold War Iconoclast* (1989); Barton Gellmann, *Contending With Kennan* (1984); and David Mayers, *George Kennan and the Dilemmas of U.S. Foreign Policy* (1988). Kennan's critic of 1947 is given definitive treatment in Ronald Steel's magisterial biography, *Walter Lippmann and the American Century* (1980). Kennan's close friend and fellow Soviet expert Charles Bohlen wrote his memoirs, *Witness to History* (1973); he is well analyzed in Michael T. Ruddy, *The Cautious Diplomat* (1986). Important dissenters and catalysts are discussed in the following important books: Graham White and John Maze, *Henry Wallace* (1995); Joan Hoff-Wilson and Marjorie Lightman, editors, *Without Precedent. The Life and Career of Eleanor Roosevelt* (1984); Thomas G. Paterson, editor, *Cold War Critics* (1971); Justus Doenecke, *Not to the Swift* (1979); Ronald Radosh, *Prophets on the Right* (1975); and Doenecke's most useful bibliographical study, *Anti-Intervention* (1987), on pacifists and isolationists from 1914 to the 1950s. A later dissenter (and official) is George Ball, *The Past Has Another Pattern* (1982). Richard Fox has written the definitive study in *Reinhold Niebuhr* (1986). Pioneering on the key subject is Robert D. Schulzinger, *The Wise Men of Foreign Affairs* (1984), on the New York Council on Foreign Relations.

On cultural impact and influence, see Rheinhold Waganleitner, *Coca-Colonization and the Cold War,* (1994), a fine case study; Rob Kroes et al., editors, *Cultural Transmissions and Receptions* (1993), on U.S.-Europe; Morrell Heald and Lawrence Kaplan, *Culture and Diplomacy* (1977); Robert Dallek, *The American Style of Foreign Policy* (1983); Edward H. Berman, *The Influence of the Carnegie, Ford, and Rockefeller Foundations on American Foreign Policy* (1983); Sig Mickelson, *America's Other Voice*, on Radio Free Europe and Radio Liberty (1983); and Simon Serfaty, editor, *The Media and Foreign Policy* (1990), with good case studies.

For important surveys of defense and space policies, start with Freedman, noted above; Peter Maslowski and Richard Millett, *The Common Defense* (1984), a superb overview since 1776; Fred Kaplan, *The Wizards of Armageddon* (1983), on nuclear strategists; Matthew Evangelista, *Innovation and the Arms Race* (1988), on both U.S. and Soviet technology; Paul Brians, *Nuclear Holocausts: Atomic War in Fiction, 1895–1984* (1987); Jacques Gansler, *The Defense Industry* (1981); James Clayton, editor, *The Economic Impact of the Cold War*

(1970); Nicole Ball and Milton Leitenberg, editors, *The Structure of the Defense Industry* (1983); William D. Bajusz and David J. Louscher, *Arms Sales and the U.S. Economy* (1988); Ronald Powaski, *March to Armageddon* (1987), on the post-1939 nuclear arms race; Milton S. Katz, *Ban the Bomb: A History of SANE* (1986), on leading critics; and, on space, Walter A. McDougall's prizewinning *The Heavens and the Earth* (1985).

For recent cases especially, Louis Henkin et al., *Right v. Might: International Law and the Use of Force* (1989) is helpful, and Daniel Patrick Moynihan's *The Law of Nations* (1990) is highly important.

Excellent studies of the CIA have appeared: Rhodri Jeffreys-Jones, *The CIA & American Democracy* (1989); Peter Grose, *Gentleman Spy*, a superb biography of Allen Dulles; Thomas Powers, *The Man Who Kept the Secrets* (1979), on Richard Helms; and Joseph Persico, *Casey: From the O.S.S. to the C.I.A.* (1990). The new CIA Historical Intelligence Collection books are most useful, especially on the Truman years and the 1962 missile crisis.

For economic developments, Peter J. Katzenstein, editor, *Between Power and Plenty* (1978) and Herman Van Der Wer, *Prosperity and Upheaval: The World Economy 1945–1980* (1988) are basic; David P. Calleo, *The Imperious Economy* (1982) is especially important; Benjamin J. Cohen, *In Whose Interest? International Banking and American Foreign Policy* (1986) is a superb critique; Ian Skeet, *OPEC* (1988), by an oil insider, is revealing; and Alfred E. Eckes, *The U.S. and the Global Struggle for Minerals* (1979) is a useful analysis, while Eckes's *Opening America's Markets* is an excellent post-1776 overview of trade policies. Two differing overviews are important: Joan Edelman Spero, *The Politics of International Economic Relations* (1981), and Fred L. Block's devastating *The Origins of International Economic Disorder* (1977).

For U.S. relations with the United Nations, Seymour M. Finger, *American Ambassadors at the UN* (1987); Thomas M. Franck, *Nation Against Nation* (1985); and Toby Trister Gati, editor, *The United States, The United Nations and the Management of Global Change* (1982) are useful recent studies.

Starting places for the environment are Jessica Tuchman Mathews, editor, *Preserving the Global Environment* (1990); and John G. Clark, *The Political Economy of World Energy* (1991).

On the origins of the Cold War, see footnotes and especially Burns, *Guide*, as well as J. L. Black, *Origins, Evolution, and the Nature of the Cold War: An Annotated Bibliography* (1985) for starters. The standard, detailed study is now Melvyn Leffler, *The Preponderance of Power* (1992), on 1945–1952. Robert L. Messer, "World War II and the Coming of the Cold War," in John M. Carroll and George C. Herring, editors, *Modern American Diplomacy* (1996) gives the overview, as does David Reynolds, editor, *Origins of the Cold War in Europe* (1994); Warren Kimball, editor, *Churchill and Roosevelt: The Complete Correspondence*, 3 volumes (1984) is magisterial; Richard Rhodes, *The Making of the Atomic Bomb* (1987) is prizewinning, and Rhodes's *Dark Sun, The Making of the Hydrogen Bomb* (1995) opens new material; Lawrence Aronsen and Martin Kitchen, *The Origins of the Cold War in Comparative Perspective: American, British and Canadian Relations with the Soviet Union, 1941–1948* (1988) is unique; and Robert A. Pollard, *Economic Security and the Origins of the Cold War* (1986) is especially useful; as is Randall Woods and Howard Jones, *Dawning of the Cold War* (1990). Important for fresh perspectives is Melvyn P. Leffler and David S. Painter, editors, *Origins of the Cold War* (1994). For analyses of the key U.S.-British relationship, consult Terry H. Anderson, *The United States, Great Britain, and the Cold War, 1944–1947* (1981); Harry B. Ryan, *The Vision of Anglo-America* (1987), on 1943–1946; and John J. Sbrega, *Anglo-American Relations and Colonialism in East Asia, 1941–1945* (1983). Russell D. Buhite's *Decision at Yalta* (1986) is critical; John J. Bukowczyk, *And My Children Did Not Know Me* (1987) puts the Polish view in historical perspective; Hugh DeSantis, *The Diplomacy of Silence* (1981) interweaves personalities and policy to 1947; and Sivachev and Yakovlev, *Russia and the U.S.,* noted above, gives the Soviet view. In addition to Kimball and *Foreign Relations of the United States* on 1941–1945, Graham Ross, editor, *The Foreign Office and the Kremlin* (1983) provides key British documents for 1941–1945; U.S. Institute of Peace, *Origins of the Cold War: The Novikov, Kennan, and Roberts "Long Telegrams" of 1946* (1991) is essential.

For the Truman years first consult Richard Dean Burns, editor, *Harry S. Truman: A Bibliography of His Times & Presidency* (1984); Michael J. Lacey, editor, *The Truman Presidency* (1989); William E. Pemberton, *Harry S. Truman: Fair Dealer and Cold Warrior* (1989); and Robert J. Donovan, *Tumultuous Years* (1983), which covers 1949–1953. Paul Nitze, *From Hiroshima to Glasnost* (1990) is a key biography of the Cold War; Mark Lytle, *Origins of the Iranian-American Alliance, 1941–1953* (1987) is a critically acclaimed work standard on this key turn; Gregg Herkin, *The Winning Weapon* (1987) covers atomic diplomacy until 1950 and is important; Lawrence Wittner's superb *One World or None* (1993) is on the antinuclear movement to 1953; Robert L. Messer, *The End of an Alliance* (1982), and Patricia Dawson Ward, *The Threat of Peace* (1979) well analyze James Byrnes in 1945–1946; Deborah Welch Larson, *Origins of Containment: A Psychological Explanation* (1985) is fresh and pioneering; James L. Gormly, *The Collapse of the Grand Alliance, 1945–1948* (1987), a succinct overview, is useful for use of British materials; Anna Nelson, *The State Department Policy Planning Staff Papers, 1947–1949* (1983) is made up of three volumes of most significant documents; and Dan Tshirgi, *The Politics of Indecision* (1983) is a good recent study of the Israeli decision. Scott Bills, *Empire and Cold War* (1990) is essential for U.S.–Third World. On Europe, Ritchie Ovendale, *The English Speaking Alliance* (1985) uses many archives to analyze 1945–1951; Robin Edmonds, *Setting The Mould* (1987) is important on the U.S.-U.K. relationship; and Alan Bullock, *Ernest Bevin* (1983) is a fine biography, as is Thomas Schwartz's superb *America's Germany* (1991) on John McCloy. Carolyn Eisenberg, *Drawing the Line: The American Decision to Divide Germany* (1996) is a most important, detailed interpretation; Thomas T. Hammond, editor, *Witnesses to the Origins of the Cold War* (1982) gives good accounts of U.S. officials' views of Eastern Europe; Josef Becker and Franz Kipping, editors, *Power in Europe* (1986) is a stunning European view of 1945–1950; Robert Wolfe, editor, *Americans as Proconsuls* (1984) discusses U.S. military governors in Germany and Japan; John L. Harper, *America and the Reconstruction of Italy* (1986), and especially James Edward Miller, *The U.S. and Italy, 1940–1950* (1986) are two fine studies of the subject; and—of overriding importance— Michael J. Hogan, *The Marshall Plan* (1987), and Alan S. Milward, *The Reconstruction of Western Europe 1945–1951* (1984) are the two standard studies for our time. Key on the Greek affair are John O. Iatrides and Linda Wrigley, editors, *Greece at the Crossroads* (1995), authoritative on 1944–1947 and after; Lawrence Wittner, *American Intervention in Greece* (1982); Theodore A. Couloubis, *The U.S., Greece, and Turkey* (1983); Howard Jones, *A New Kind of War* (1989); and for a broader view, Chester Pach, Jr., *Arming The Free World* (1991). For useful perspectives on the most revealing secret document of the time, see Ernest R. May, editor, *American Cold War Strategy: Interpreting NSC-68* (1993). Thomas Borstelmann, *Apartheid's Uncle* (1993), on United States– South Africa to 1953 is important.

For Asia, and particularly Korea, until 1953 (and after), a superb regional overview is William Borden, *The Pacific Alliance . . . 1947–1955* (1984), key for its view of the Japan–Southeast Asia links; Lloyd Gardner, *Approaching Vietnam 1950–1954* (1988) is the best account of these years; Howard B. Schonberger, *Aftermath of War* (1989) is a major contribution on the Japanese occupation; Michael Schaller, *The American Occupation of Japan* (1985) provides the important context, as does his *MacArthur* (1989) biography, which focuses on Korea; and Kyoko Inoue, *MacArthur's Japanese Constitution* (1991). Marc S. Gallicchio, *The Cold War Begins in Asia* (1988) examines the roots of the Cold War and the role of John Carter Vincent; Kenneth Chern, *Dilemma in China, 1945* (1980) starts the story that Nancy Bernkopf Tucker's *Patterns in the Dust* (1983) continues definitively. The above two can be supplemented with Gordon Chang, *Friends and Enemies, 1948–1972* (1990); Paul G. Lauren, editor, *The China Hands' Legacy* (1987); June M. Grasso, *Harry Truman's Two-China Policy, 1948–1950* (1987), useful for the Truman-Formosa connection; Gary May, *China Scapegoat* (1982), a fine biography of Vincent; and David Allan Mayers, *Cracking the Monolith* (1986), which argues the wedge theory in detail (that is, how the United States tried to divide the U.S.S.R. and China). On Korea, an outstanding work is Rosemary Foot, *The Wrong War* (1985). William W. Stueck, Jr., *The Road to Confrontation* (1981); John Merrill, *Korea* (1989); and James I. Matray, *The Reluctant Crusade* (1986) are all major contributions, along with the books of Bruce Cumings, noted in the narrative of this book, and Stueck's new *The Korean War: An International History* (1995). See especially Cumings' magisterial *Origins of the Korean War, Volume II* (1990). Alexander Bevin, *Korea* (1987) is a fresh look at the war itself, and Roger Dingman, "Atomic Diplomacy During the Korean War," *International Security*, XIII (Winter 1988–1989) is most important. For the home front, consult Arthur A. Stein's fine analysis, *The Nation at War* (1980); David R. Kepley, *The Collapse of the Middle Way* (1988), on the Senate and bipartisan policy; and Ronald Radosh and Joyce Milton, *The Rosenberg File* (1983). See also many of Athan Theoharis's important books on the witch-hunting years, including *The Specter* (1974), which he and Robert Griffiths edited, along with Thomas C. Reeves, *The Life and Times of Joe McCarthy* (1982). Dorothy Borg and Waldo Heinrichs, editors, *Uncertain Years: Chinese-American Relations, 1947–1950* (1982) goes far beyond its title, as does William O. Walker, *Opium and Foreign Policy* (1991) on the United States and the British, 1912–1954.

The ever-expanding important literature on the Eisenhower years can be grasped at first with R. D. Bohanan, *Dwight D. Eisenhower* (1981), a major bibliographical study; William B. Pickett, *Dwight David Eisenhower and American Power* (1995); Richard A. Melanson and David Mayers, editors, *Reevaluating Eisenhower* (1987); and Stephen Ambrose's two major biographies, *Eisenhower: Volume Two: The President* (1984), and *Nixon* (1987), on the 1913–1962 portion of his career. On Dulles, see Pruessen's biography noted above, and Frederick W. Marks, *Power and Peace* (1995). See especially Peter G. Boyle, editor, *The Churchill-Eisenhower Correspondence, 1953–1955* (1990). Important interpretations include Robert Divine, *Eisenhower and the Cold War* (1981); Divine's *Blowing on the Wind* (1978), on the nuclear test-ban debate; and H. W. Brands, Jr., *Cold Warriors* (1988), a fresh look at key officials. Michael Beschloss, *Mayday* (1986) is important on the U-2 affair and its background; Robert W. Griffith, editor, *Ike's Letters to a Friend, 1941–1958* (1984) is most significant primary material; Burton I. Kaufman, *Trade and Aid* (1982), and Walt Whitman Rostow, *Eisenhower, Kennedy and Foreign Aid* (1985) are most important on these subjects; William Roger Louis and Roger Owen, editors, *Suez 1956* (1989) is now the best account because it uses recently declassified materials; and also see Peter Hahn, *The U.S., Great Britain and Egypt, 1945–1956* (1991). Richard Pfau, *No Sacrifice Too Great* (1984) is a pivotal biography of Lewis Strauss that deals with the Oppenheimer affair; David Carlton's important *Anthony Eden* (1981) is also worthwhile. The Guatemala intervention is well analyzed in Richard H. Immerman, *The CIA in Guatemala* (1982); Blanche Wiessen Cook, *The Declassified Eisenhower* (1981); and Piero Gleijeses, *Shattered Hope . . . 1944–1954* (1991). The Lytle volume noted above is standard on Iran. Madeleine Kalb, *The Congo Cables* (1982) is important for African policies in the 1950s and 1960s. For Vietnam, see Gardner, *Approaching Vietnam*, noted above, and David L. Anderson, *Trapped by Success . . . 1953–1961* (1991).

The books with which to start a study of Kennedy's policies are Thomas Paterson, editor, *Kennedy's Quest for Victory* (1989), written by some of the best younger historians who have used the primary sources; Warren I. Cohen, *Dean Rusk* (1980), a significant biography; Michael Beschloss, *The Crisis Years* (1991), on JFK and Khrushchev; James N. Giglio, *The Presidency of Kennedy* (1991); Thomas Brown, *JFK: History of an Image* (1988), fresh and revealing of the public as well as of JFK: Desmond Ball, *Politics and Force Levels* (1981), superb on the military buildup; and Montague Kern et al., *The Kennedy Crises: The Press, the Presidency, and Foreign Policy* (1983). Richard D. Mahoney, *JFK: Ordeal in Africa* (1983) is a major contribution. Trumbull Higgins, *The Perfect Failure* (1987) covers the Bay of Pigs. Robert A. Divine, editor, *The Cuban Missile Crisis* (1989); James G. Blight, *On the Brink* (1990); and Raymond Garthoff, *Reflections on the Cuban Missile Crisis* (1989) are very helpful. On Vietnam, start with George Kahin, *Intervention* (1986); Ellen J. Hammer, *A Death in November* (1987); and R. B. Smith, *An International History of the Vietnam War* (1986).

For the Johnson years, start with the essays in Warren Cohen and Nancy Tucker, editors, *Lyndon Johnson Confronts the World* (1994); Diane Kunz, editor, *The Diplomacy of the Crucial Decade* (1994); and Robert A. Divine, editor, *The Johnson Years: Volume One* (1986) and *Volume Three* (1994), which can be supplemented with Staff of the L. B. Johnson Library, *Lyndon B. Johnson: A Bibliography.* Key memoirs are Clark Clifford, *Counsel to the President* (1991); and Dean Rusk, as told to Richard Rusk, *As I Saw It* (1990), also important for the Kennedy years; as is Robert McNamara, *In Retrospect* (1995); and Deborah Shapley's *Promise and Power* (1993) on McNamara. The literature on Vietnam is rapidly proliferating, but a start should be made with Kahin, *Intervention,* noted above; George Herring, *The Longest War* (1996), standard and using recently declassified materials; Larry Berman, *Lyndon Johnson's War* (1989), a major study of the decision making; William C. Berman, *William Fulbright and the Vietnam War* (1988), important on a major dissenter; Brian De Mark, *Into the Quagmire* (1991), on escalation; David DiLeo, *George Ball* (1991), on the key dissenter within the administration; Melvin Small, *Johnson, Nixon, and the Doves* (1988), a fresh look at internal pressures; and Ole R. Holsti and James N. Roseneau, *American Leadership in World Affairs* (1984) and how it declined.

Along with the Nixon and Kissinger memoirs, indispensable for the 1969–1975 years are Walter Isaacson's *Kissinger* (1992); Seymour Hersh, *The Price of Power* (1983); and Theodore Draper, *Present History* (1983). Leonard A. Kusnitz, *Public Opinion and Foreign Policy: America's China Policy, 1949–1979* (1984) presents the background. Nathaniel Davis, *The Last Two Years of Salvador Allende* (1985) is the U.S. ambassador's view, to be used with James Petras and Morris Morley, *The U.S. and Chile* (1975) although Hersh is key on Chile also. Raymond L. Garthoff, *Détente and Confrontation* (1985) is a classic on post-1972 U.S.-Soviet relations, and it is encyclopedic as well. On Ford, see John R. Greene, *The Presidency of Gerald R. Ford* (1995); Christopher Jon Lamb, *Belief Systems and Decision-Making in the Mayaguez Crisis* (1989) is a fresh approach. Note especially Stephen Ambrose, *Nixon*, 3 volumes (1987–1992); Robert Schulzinger, *Henry Kissinger*, (1989); and Joan Hoff, *Nixon Reconsidered* (1994).

The Carter years have been revealed from the inside in the Carter, Vance, and Brzezinski memoirs listed in the footnotes. But also closely note Gaddis Smith, *Morality, Reason and Power* (1986); the relevant sections in Neustadt and May, *Thinking in Time*, noted above; Richard J. Barnet, *The Alliance* (1983), on how the administration began to unravel more rapidly in the late 1970s; and Gary Sick, *All Fall Down* (1985), an insider's view of what went wrong with Iran policy. Two insider accounts on the Central America crises are Anthony Lake, *Somoza Falling* (1989), and Robert Pastor's *Condemned to Repetition* (1987). Thomas J. Noer, *Cold War and Black Liberation* (1985) is pivotal for background as well as for 1970s events in Africa, and Henry Jackson, *From the Congo to Soweto* (1982) is key on the Nixon and Carter years. On human rights, Sandy Vogelgesang, *American Dream, Global Nightmare* (1980), and Lars Schoultz, *Human Rights and U.S. Policy Towards Latin America* (1981) are good starting points. Burton Kaufman, *The Presidency of . . . Carter* (1993) is a fine overview.

Material for the Reagan years is listed extensively in the chapter footnotes, which indeed are considerably longer for this chapter than the others. In addition, consult David Kyvig, editor, *Reagan and the World* (1990), which, with Cannon's biography, gives a good overview; Michael P. Rogin, *Ronald Reagan: The Movie* (1987), which is provocative; Garthoff's *Détente and Confrontation*, noted above, and his *The Great Transition*, (1994), which are superb on the Soviet relationship; Michel Tatu, *Eux et nous* (1985), which is a knowledgeable French correspondent's view of U.S.-Soviet relations from the early 1970s to 1984; Strobe Talbott's several books, especially *Deadly Gambits* (1984); George Shultz, *Turmoil and Triumph*, the most important record for the 1980s; Caspar Weinberger, *Fighting for Peace* (1990), a happy memoir; Joseph E. Persico, *Casey* (1990), on the CIA; Ronald V. Dellums (with R. H. Miller and H. Lee Halterman), *Defense Sense* (1983), a thorough critique that anticipates the later 1980s budgets; Martin Anderson, *Revolution* (1987), views of an early participant who notes the economic-military problems; Joel Krieger, *Reagan, Thatcher, and the Politics of Decline* (1986), on the presumed Atlantic conservative rise and fall; Mark P. Ligon, *The Reagan Doctrine* (1994), a good overview; and Robert M. Stern, editor, *Perspectives on a U.S.-Canadian Free Trade Agreement* (1987), important background on a historic pact. Itamar Rabinovich, *The War for Lebanon, 1970–1983* (1984) tells that sad story. Within the voluminous Central American material, good places to start are John Booth and Thomas Walker, *Understanding Central America* (1989); Booth's *The End and the Beginning*, 2nd ed. (1985), on Nicaragua; Tommie Sue Montgomery, *Revolution in El Salvador*, 2nd ed. (1992), the best single volume; Cynthia Arnson, *El Salvador* (1982), a major perspective; Raymond Bonner, *Weakness and Deceit* (1984), a detailed exposé on Salvadoran policy and its effects; and several books edited by Walker, as well as his own *Nicaragua, the Land of Sandino*, 2nd ed. (1986). A superb historical overview that provides the context for all this is Lester Langley, *America and the Americas* (1989). Especially important—and frightening—is Richard O. Curry's *Freedom at Risk: Secrecy, Censorship, and Repression in the 1980s* (1988).

On the Bush administration, the Iraqi War, and the end of the Cold War: Garthoff's superb *Great Transition*, noted above; Ambassador Jack F. Matlock's indispensable *Autopsy on an Empire* (1995); René Schwok, *U.S.-EC Relations in the Post-Cold War Era* (1991), especially its good historical chapters; Michael A. Freney and Rebecca S. Hartley, *United Germany and the United States* (1991), with good chronology, documents, and commentary; William G. Hyland, *The Cold War Is Over* (1991), a summing up; Lawrence Freedman and Efraim Karsh, *The Gulf Conflict* (1993), standard on the war; Bob Woodward, *The Commanders* (1991), the insiders' account of how the Bush administration ran the Iraqi war; Oles M. Smolansky, *The USSR and Iraq* (1991), on the 1950s through 1988; the Bruce Jentleson and Michael Beschloss–Strobe Talbott works cited in chapter footnotes; Kevin Buckley, *Panama* (1991); Michael Conniff, *The United States and Panama* (1992).

For the Clinton years, start with Ronald Steel's provocative *Temptations of a Superpower* (1995); the excellent Berman-Goldman essay in Colin Campbell and Bert A. Rockman, editors, *The Clinton Presidency* (1996); Elizabeth Drew, *On the Edge* (1994); Bob Woodward, *The Agenda: Inside the Clinton White House* (1994), especially on economic policy; also James Petras and Morris Morley, *Empire or Republic* (1995); and Tom Engelhardt, *The End of Victory Culture* (1995).

Area Studies

Latin America: See first the studies listed in the Reagan, Kennedy, and Eisenhower sections above. The Langley volume, *America and the Americas*, gives both an overview and good bibliographical guidance, as does Langley's *Mexico and the US* (1991). Gaddis Smith, *The Last Years of the Monroe Doctrine* (1994) is an important post-1945 analysis. Walter LaFeber, *Inevitable Revolutions* (1992) attempts to put the Central American crisis in a historical perspective. John A. Booth and Mitchell A. Seligson, editors, *Elections and Democracy in Central America* (1989) raises fundamental questions about U.S. policies; as does Abraham Lowenthal editor, *Exporting Democracy* (1991). Thomas M. Leonard, *The U.S. and Central America* (1984) is key on 1944–1949; and Philip L. Shepherd, *The Honduran Crisis and the U.S. Economic Assistance* (1989) is by a leading authority. Two major studies are Joseph Tulchin, *Argentina and the United States* (1990), and William F. Sater, *Chile and The United States* (1990). On the Panama crisis of 1964–1989, consult the footnotes in the chapters and also three works that provide historical contexts: J. Michael Hogan, *The Panama Canal in American Politics* (1986); David N. Farnsworth and James W.

McKenney, *U.S.-Panama Relations, 1903–1978* (1983); and Walter LaFeber, *The Panama Canal* (1989). On Cuba, start with Paterson, *Contesting Castro,* noted above; Jules R. Benjamin, *The U.S. and the Origins of the Cuban Revolution* (1990); Andrew Zimbalist and Claes Brundenius, *The Cuban Economy* (1989); Wayne S. Smith and Esteban Morales Dominguez, editors, *Subject to Solution* (1988); Peter Shearman, *The Soviet Union and Cuba* (1987); and Morris Morley's most important and well-researched argument, *Imperial State and Revolution* (1987).

Canada: See especially John H. Thompson and S. J. Randall, *Canada and the United States* (1994); Lansing Lamont and J. Duncan Edmonds, editors, *Friends So Different* (1989); and Lawrence Martin, *The Presidents and the Prime Ministers* (1982), a superb, readable account of post-1867 Canadian-U.S. relations.

Asia: In addition to books listed under presidential administrations above, consult M. S. Venkataramani, *The American Role in Pakistan, 1947–1958* (1982), a view of a pivotal era; Robert J. McMahon, *Colonialism and Cold War* (1981), the best study on U.S.-Indonesian relations; Warren I. Cohen, *New Frontiers in American–East Asian Relations* (1983), a fine collection; Stanley Karnow, *In Our Image* (1989), on U.S.-Philippine relations from McKinley through Marcos and Aquino; Nick Cullather's revisionist, pathbreaking, *Illusions of Influence* (1994) on U.S.-Philippines, 1942–1960; Yur-Bok Lee and Wayne Patterson, editors, *One Hundred Years of Korean-American Relations, 1882–1982* (1986); and Akira Iriye and Warren I. Cohen, editors, *The United States and Japan in the Postwar World* (1989), views of both U.S. and Japanese scholars; David Shambaugh, *Beautiful Imperialist* (1991), on China's America-watchers. Robert McMahon, *Cold War on the Periphery* (1994) is standard on US-India-Pakistan. When in doubt, consult ABC-CLIO's publication, *The United States in East Asia: A Historical Bibliography* (1985), with over 1100 references.

Vietnam: The overall perspectives are in the following standard studies: George Herring, *The Longest War* (1996); George Kahin, *Intervention* (1986); and Ronald H. Spector, *U.S. Army in Vietnam:* Volume I (1983), on 1941–1960. William Appleman Williams et al., *America in Vietnam* (1988) provides extensive documents and historical introductions. Lloyd Gardner, *Approaching Vietnam* (1988) is key on the 1950–1954 years, and Gardner's *Pay Any Price* (1995) is a detailed, invaluable interpretation of Johnson. Andrew Rotter, *The Path to Vietnam* (1987) examines the 1949–1950 context; and Neil Sheehan, *A Bright Shining Lie* (1988) is a magnificent biography of John Paul Vann and a magnificent account of the war. The background is in Gary R. Hess, *The United States' Emergence as a Southeast Asian Power, 1940–1950* (1986). Andrew F. Krepinevich, Jr., *The Army and Vietnam* (1986) counters with strong arguments the influential thesis advocated by Harry Summers, *On Strategy* (1981). Timothy J. Lomperis, *Reading the Wind* (1986) is superb on the novels, personal accounts, and oral histories of the war. Douglas Pike, *Vietnam and the Soviet Union* (1987) is standard. If you need more, consult Richard Dean Burns and

Milton Leitenberg, editors, *The Wars in Vietnam, Cambodia and Laos, 1945–1982* (1984), a bibliography with 6200 entries; Marvin Gettleman, *et al.*, editors, *Vietnam and America. A Documented History* (1995); and Marilyn Young's superb *Vietnam Wars* (1991).

Europe: Richard Barnet, *The Alliance* (1983) is thorough; Frank Costigliola, *France and the United States* (1992) is a superb and well-written analysis of post-1945 French-U.S. relations; Frank Ninkovich, *Germany and the United States* (1988), and Manfred Jonas, *The U.S. and Germany* (1984) are two fine accounts; Lawrence S. Kaplan and Robert W. Clawson, editors, *NATO After Thirty Years* (1985) is most important; Anton W. DePorte, *Europe Between the Superpowers*, 2nd ed. (1986) is a standard study; William Roger Louis and Hedley Bull, editors, *The Special Relationship* (1986) is valuable on U.S.-U.K. relations since 1945; Alfred Grosser, *The Western Alliance* (1980) is a distinguished European view; Audrey Kurth Cronin, *Great Power Politics. . . .* (1986) is valuable on Austria between 1945 and 1955; Alan Dobson, *The Politics of the Anglo-American Economic Special Relationship, 1940–1987* (1988) is pivotal on the economic as well as the bilateral aspects; and Wolfram F. Hanrieder, *Germany, America, Europe* (1989) is a detailed view of West German foreign policy. Peter Katzenstein, *Industry and Politics in West Germany* (1989) is superb.

Africa: In addition to the volumes noted especially in the Carter section above, consult Fred Mante, *Political Cycles . . . The Cold War and Africa, 1945–1990* (1995); Alfred O. Hero, Jr., and John Barratt, editors, *The American People and South Africa* (1981); Richard Leonard, *South Africa at War* (1983); Zaki Laidi, *The Superpowers and Africa, 1960–1990* (1990).

Middle East: In addition to the accounts listed above, especially in the Truman, Eisenhower, and Reagan sections, see especially Douglas Little's articles cited in footnotes; Burton I. Kaufman's important overview, *The Arab Middle East and the United States* (1995); Sandra Mackey, *Lebanon* (1989), a classic account; Richard W. Cottam, *Iran and the U.S.* (1988); Seth P. Tillman, *The U.S. and the Middle East* (1982), a most important study; Haim Shaked and Itamar Rabinovich, editors, *The Middle East and the United States* (1980), key on the 1970s; Steven L. Spiegel, *The Other Arab-Israeli Conflict* (1985), on U.S. political debates; William J. Burns, *Economic Aid . . .* (1985) on U.S.-Egyptian relations, 1955–1981; and James W. Harper, "The Middle East, Oil, and the Third World," in John M. Carroll and George Herring, editors, *Modern American Diplomacy* (1988), with a useful bibliography; Seymour Hersh, the *Samson Option: Israel's Nuclear Arsenal and American Foreign Policy* (1991); and William B. Quandt, *The U.S. and Egypt* (1990).

The Soviet Union and Eastern Bloc

Consult "General Works" above; the narrative and bibliography in R. Craig Nation, *Black Earth, Red Star: A History of Soviet Security Policy, 1917–1991*

(1995); the Reagan and Bush chapters with their fuller footnote references; and the presidential sections above. William J. Thompson, *Khrushchev* (1995), is a good overview, but see especially Anatoly Dobrynin's *In Confidence* (1995), an insider's account of the entire Cold War era. Much of the following relates to the 1980s: Moshe Lewin, *The Gorbachev Phenomenon* (1991), for the historical framework; Robert O. Crummey, editor, *Reform in Russia and the USSR* (1989), a major contribution and especially important on historical precedents; Robert Conquest, editor, *The Last Empire: Nationality and the Soviet Future* (1986); Carol R. Saivetz, editor, *The Soviet Union in the Third World* (1989), especially the Kanet, MacFarlane, and Duncan essays; Alexi G. Arbatov, *Lethal Frontiers* (1988), an intelligent Soviet view of nuclear weapons and diplomacy; Michael MccGwire, *Military Objectives in Soviet Foreign Policy* (1987), by a leading expert; Ben Eklof, *Soviet Briefing* (1989), a provocative look at Gorbachev reforms; Anders Aslund, *Gorbachev's Struggle for Economic Reform* (1989), an influential account; Robert C. Tucker, *Political Culture and Leadership in Soviet Russia: From Lenin to Gorbachev* (1987); R. W. Davies, *Soviet History in the Gorbachev Revolution* (1989), a fresh perspective; Ellen Jones, *The Red Army and Society* (1985); and Amy W. Knight, *The KGB* (1988).

For places to start on Eastern Europe and the communist bloc, see: the Winter 1990 issue of *Daedalus* (Vol. 149), entitled "Eastern Europe . . . Central Europe . . . Europe"; Gale Stokes, editor, *From Stalinism to Pluralism* (1991), useful documents; William E. Griffith, editor, *Central and Eastern Europe* (1989); Joseph Rothschild, *Return to Diversity* (1988), superb on post-1945; and Charles Gati, *Hungary and the Soviet Bloc* (1986), a prizewinning study; and Gati's *The Bloc That Failed* (1990). Timothy Garton Ash, *The Magic Lantern* (1990) is a near-magic journalistic account of the 1988–1989 changes.

Index

Acheson, Dean: on trade, 8; and Turkey (1946), 37–38; 1946 Baruch Plan, 42–43; 1947 views and Truman Doctrine, 50–58; Marshall Plan, 57–62; background and views, 80–81; NATO, 82–83; China (1949), 87–88, 91–92; Hiss, 93, 105; NSC-68, 96–98; Korean War, 98–99; 1950 initiatives, 105–110; McCarthy, 105–106; crossing 38th parallel, 114–118; 1950–1951 crisis, 118–120; MacArthur recall, 123–124; military aid (1951), 126; rebuilding European security, 127–128; Morgenthau, 130; 1957 debate, 199–200; Berlin (1961), 214; missile crisis, 222, 226; Rusk, 234; LBJ on Vietnam, 254; Kissinger, 258, 276; Nixon views, 266
Acheson-Lilienthal report, 42
Adams, Henry, 325–326
Adams, John, 133–134
Adams, John Quincy, 151
Adenauer, Konrad: background and views, 84–85; German independence, 128; Dulles, 150; EDC, 167; Dulles in late 1950s, 200–201
Afghanistan: USSR (1950s), 171; invasion, 297–298; Reagan, 306, 307; USSR retreats, 324
Africa: Truman Doctrine, 55; in 1950s,

174; Kennedy views, 209; 1957–1960s turn, 240; Johnson, 251; US (1974–1976), 273; post-1989 fragmentation, 328; US in 1990s, 351; see also individual nations
African-Americans, 257, 294
Agency for International Development (AID), 211
Agnew, Spiro, 255, 280
Albania, 225
Alekseyev, Aleksandr, 221
Aleutians, 91
Alianza Republican Nacionalista (ARENA) Party, 312
Allende, Salvador, 271
Alliance for progress: origins, 208, 211–212; Kennedy failure, 234; Johnson and Mann, 242
American Express, 318
American Federation of Labor, 266
American Legion, 5
American University, 225–226
Americans for Democratic Action (ADA), 46, 79, 112
Ames, Aldrich, 323
Ancient Greece and Rome, 265
Andropov, Yuri, 316
Anglo-Iranian Oil Company, 155–157
Angola: Nixon, 261; Kissinger, 279–281;

Carter, 288; Reagan, 307; USSR (1980s), 324, 325; settlement, 363
Animal Farm (book), 147
Antiballistic Missile Treaty (ABM), 268, 345
ANZUS pact (1951), 120–121
Ap Bac, 231–232
Apartheid, 240, 311, 362
Aquino, Corazon, 310
Arbenz, Jacobo Guzmán, 157–159
Arévalo, Juan José, 157
Argentina, 206, 208, 212, 287, 325
Arias Sanchez, Oscar, 312–313, 331
Aristide, Jean-Bertrand, 353–354
Armas, Carlos Castillo, 158–159
Armenians, 333
Arms control: 1972 agreements, 268; US and USSR, 340; post-1990, 344; chart of important treaties, 345; Clinton, 352, 360; 1988–1990s turn, 356, 363; *see also specific treaties*
Arms sales: Kennedy's policies, 210–211; Nixon's policies, 261; US in 1990s, 363
Aswan Dam, 181–186
Atlantic Conference (and principles), 8–10, 11, 12, 22, 29
Atomic bomb: origins, 24–25, 27, 28; Churchill's views, 39; and USSR, 40; 1946 debate, 42; in 1947, 55; Berlin crisis (1948), 77; Soviet bomb (1949), 84; during Korean War, 118; MacArthur view of China, 123; Dulles threatens Korea, 149; US threatens China and Soviets, 153; US capacity in 1950s, 154, 177; Vietnam (1954), 160; Germany in 1950s, 168, 199; Eisenhower proposal for control, 179; US stockpile by 1960, 194; in offshore island crisis, 197; French bomb, 215; US tests, 215; Missile crisis (1962), 222–224; Kennedy and fear of China, 228; China's bomb, 249; *see also* Hydrogen bomb, Nuclear war
Atomic Energy Commission (AEC), 177
Attlee, Clement: and Jewish vote, 78; in 1950 debate, 118–119
Auriol, Vincent, 128
Australia, 66, 120, 259; and SEATO, 164

Austria, 155, 170, 177–178, 202
Azerbaijan, 35, 333

B-52 aircraft, 302, 344
Baghdad pact, 153, 181, 188, 198, 199
Baker, Howard, 288
Baker, James: background, 329–330; Nicaragua settlement, 331; 1989–1990 end of Cold War, 336, 338, 340; Persian Gulf War, 342
Balaguer, Joaquín, 245
Ball, George, 222
Baltic States, 7, 333, 346; *see also* Estonia, Latvia, Lithuania
Bandung Conference (1955), 171–172
Baruch, Bernard, 9–10, 42–43
Baruch plan, 42–43
Baskin-Robbins, 318
Batista, Fulgencio, 203–204, 213
Battle Act (1951), 126
Bay of Pigs, 212–213, 219, 221
Baylor University, 54
Beard, Charles, 93–94
Beethoven, 290
Begin, Menachem, 289
Beirut bombing (1983), 308, 367
Belarus, 346, 360
Belgian Congo, 240–241; *see also* Zaire
Belgium, 16, 28, 206, 240–241
Ben & Jerry's, 357
Benelux, 74, 82; *see also* Belgium, The Netherlands
Beneš, Edvard, 72
Bentley, Elizabeth, 92
Beria, Lavrenti, 19, 143, 146
Berle, Adolf, 51
Berlin: 1948 blockade, 74–77, 81–82, 92; 1958–1960 crisis, 199–202; 1961 crisis, 214–215, 220–221
Berlin Wall, 214–215, 219, 335
Bevin, Ernest, 59, 109
Bidault, Georges, 59–60
Biological Weapons Convention (1972), 363
Bipartisanship: on NATO, 74; end of, 88–89
Bismarck, Otto von, 348

Black, Eugene, 181–183
Bogotá Conference (1948), 67
Bohlen, Charles, 53, 96, 137–138
Bolivia, 206
Bolsheviks, 3–4; *see also* Communism
Bond, James, 152
Bonner, Yelena, 319
Bosch, Juan, 243–244
Bosnia, 354, 362; map, 355
Boun Oum, 216
Bradley, General Omar, 83
Bradley University, 78
Brazil, 208, 212, 287; and Reagan, 300
Bretton Woods Conference (1944), 9
Brezhnev, Leonid: rise to power, 250–251; on Vietnam, 253; Czech crisis (1968), 256–257; Nixon views, 261; internal crises (1970s), 267; and China, 268; Nixon summit (1972), 268–270; Mideast crisis, 276–277; 1975 summit, SALT II, 281; declining health, 281; Angola policy, 288; 1978 Mideast agreement, 289; late 1970s crises, 291–292; Iranian Revolution, 294–295; Carter and SALT II, 295; Afghanistan invasion, 297–298, 304; Reagan relationship, 301; Poland, 304; Pershing missiles, 305; USSR military, 315; economic failures, 315–316; death, 316
Brezhnev Doctrine (1968), 256–257, 334–335
Bricker, John, 46
Bricker amendment, 176–177
Brinksmanship, 149, 187
Brodie, Bernard, 173
Brown, Harold, 296
Broz, Josip. *See* Tito
Brussels Treaty (1948), 74
Brzezinski, Zbigniew: views, 284–287; Angola, 288; pursues China, 289–290; fears USSR, 292, 297; Iranian Revolution, 292–294, 298–299; sees new era, 296; attacks Reagan policy on USSR, 323
Buddhists, 232
Budgets: Eisenhower's, 153–154; late 1950s, 193–194; Carter's military, 297; Reagan's military, 301–302, 314; *see*

also National Security Council paper 68
Bulganin, Nikolay, 143, 170–172, 178
Bulgaria, 12, 16, 70
Bundy, William P., 246
Burma, 50, 197, 216
Burundi, 351
Bush, George: Noriega relationship, 312; on Reagan's voodoo economics, 315; and Henry Adams, 326; background, 329–330; Panama invasion (1989), 331–332; Theodore Roosevelt as hero, 332; views USSR, 332–333; German policy (1990), 338; Gorbachev crisis (1990–1991), 339–340, 343–344; Persian Gulf War, 340–343; Yeltsin relationship, 347–348; end of Cold War, 348–349; Clinton (1992), 349; problem of governance, 368
Butler, John Marshall, 112
Byrd, Robert, 288
Byrnes, James F.: 1945 plans, 23–27; Iran policy, 37; views USSR, 40; 1946 German policy, 41–42; dislikes Wallace, 45–46

Cabral, Donald Reid, 243
Calley, Lt. William, Jr., 263
Cambodia, 162, 164, 165; map, 218; Nixon attacks, 262–263, 281; 1980s and after, 307–308, 363
Camp David Accords (1978), 289, 290
Canada: in NATO, 82; US in 1951, 121; US threats, 151; in Vietnam, 162; investment, 175; US influence and reaction (1970s), 278; threat of fragmentation, 328; US environment, 365
Capitalism: before 1917, 1; in 1918–1920, 3; Stalin views, 5, 14, 27–28, 39–40; Byrnes' view, 40; Niebuhr's view, 47–48; 1947 crisis, 50–51, 57–62; USSR views (1947), 69, 70–71; 1949 problems, 82; USSR views (1949–1950), 89–90; 1951 problems, 126; Stalin analysis (1952), 141; in Iran, 156; 1950s debate, 169, 173–175; Khrushchev views, 180–181; in Latin America,

203–207; Kennedy and Eisenhower, 210; Johnson's view, 235–236; effect of Vietnam on US, 264; in Chile, 272; Angola and Gulf Oil, 279; USSR contradictions, 282, 292; related to Carter political problems, 287–288; in Latin America (1980s), 305; Kirkpatrick's analysis, 306; in South Africa, 311; in US (1980s), 314–315; in USSR (1980s), 318–319; in Russia, post-1991, 346–347; Clinton administration, 351–353; Russian view, 358–360; three blocs, 361; 1990s changes, 362; Soros on, 363

Capone, Al, 358

Captive nations, 178

Carter, Jimmy: rise to power, 281–282, 283–284; views Nixon, 284; mediates Brzezinski versus Vance, 284–286; human rights policies, 286–287; Panama and Angola policies, 288; Mideast peace (1978), 288–289; China policies, 289–290; Iran Revolution, 292–294, 298–299; Nicaragua policy, 296; El Salvador policy, 296–297; USSR crises, 297–298, 323

Carter Doctrine (1980), 298–299

Casey, William, 313

Castro, Fidel: and Guatemala (1954), 159; background and 1959 revolution, 203–208; Bay of Pigs, 212–213; in missile crisis, 221–225, 229; Dominican Republic, 243–244; China relationship, 249; USSR retreats from (1980s), 324

Castro, Raul, 221

Ceaușescu, Nicolae, 335

Central America: map, 207; *see also individual nations*

Central Intelligence Agency (CIA): origins, 68; Eisenhower handles, 152–153; in Iran, 155–157; in Guatemala, 157–159; in Mideast, 188–189; in Cuba (1959–1961), 205, 212–213; in Laos, 230; in Belgian Congo, 241; Nixon's views, 259; in Chile, 272; in Nicaragua (1980s), 311; in El Salvador (1980s), 312; in Middle East (1980s), 313; aids Afghan rebels,

324; Bush relationship, 330; on end of Cold War, 335; relationship with Haiti (1990s), 354

Central Treaty Organization (CENTO) (1958), 199

Ceylon, 50

Chambers, Whittaker, 92–93

Chamorro, Violeta, 331

Chamoun, Camille, 198

Chechnya, 359

Chernenko, Konstantin, 316, 317

Chemical weapons, 168, 337, 363

Cheney, Richard, 334, 340

Chernobyl disaster, 364–365

Chevron, 346, 357

Chiang Kai-shek: power declines, 30–35, 65, 86–88; US supports (1950), 106–107; and MacArthur, 121; 1953–1954 crisis, 140, 149, 166; and Egypt, 182; dies, 266

Chicago: 1968 riots, 255

Chile: Nixon policies, 271–272; and human rights, 287

China: before 1917, 1–2; as policeman, 12; in 1945–1947, 30–33; map, 32; 1948 election in US, 78; 1949 turn, 84–85; USSR alliance (1950), 91; Vietnam relationship (1945–1950), 107; war with US (1950), 114–122; MacArthur views, 121–124; US debate over, 130–135; Eisenhower views, 140; compared with Latin America, 157; Vietnam in 1950s, 162–163; offshore islands crisis, 165–166; USSR (1954–1956), 171–172; Dulles on (1956), 172–173; and Egypt (1955), 182; USSR (1957–1960), 196–197; offshore islands crisis (1958), 197–198; Kennedy fears, 217–218, 228, 230–231; Khrushchev and missile crisis, 225; India dispute, 229; McNamara fears, 248–249; internal crisis, 249–250; A-bomb and H-bomb, 249, 254; USSR and Vietnam, 251; Nixon policies, 258, 264–265; USSR clashes, 265, 268; in Angola, 279; Carter and human rights, 287; Carter policy towards, 289–290; invades Vietnam, 290; Reagan policies, 320–321; 1989 crisis and Bush, 336, 344; Clinton policies, 351; nuclear policy, 363; environmental problems, 366

China lobby, 86, 87–88, 266

Christian Coalition, 329

Christopher, Warren, 349, 353, 361

Churchill, Winston: in 1942, 7; during World War II, 7–11; postwar plans, 12–14, 23–24, 35; Molotov attacks, 38; iron curtain speech (1946), 39–40, 43; on future of Pacific, 121; 1953–1955 policies, 147, 150, 161; Vietnam policy (1954), 160; Diem compared, 217; Gorbachev views, 371

Civil rights, 235

"Clash of civilizations," 362

Clay, General Lucius, 41; 1948 crisis, 72–73, 77

Clayton, William, 9, 10; on 1947 crisis, 50; shapes Truman Doctrine, 54

Cleveland, Mississippi, speech, 59

Clifford, Clark, 79

Clinton, Bill: background and 1992 election, 349–350; Somalia policy, 350; Liberia, 351; Burundi and Rwanda, 351; economy and policies, 351–352; China policy, 351; NAFTA and Mexico policy, 351–352; Yugoslavia fragmentation, 354–355; Russian policies, 360–361; view of UN, 364, 369; governance problems, 368–369

CNN, 350, 353; covers 1993 Russian revolt, 359

Coca-Cola, 290

COCOM, 353

Cohn, Roy M., 137

Cold War, The (book), 64

Colgate, 346

Collective security: US general view, 364

Collins, General J. Lawton, 163

Colombia, 119, 242

Cominform, 70–71

Comintern, 20

Committee on the Present Danger, 295

Common Market: origins, 201–202; development, 226–227

Commonwealth of Independent States (CIS), 346

Communism: compared, 1–2; in 1930s, 5–6; World War II plans, 13–21; in US, 20–21; in 1946, 39, 46; Zhdanov influence, 40–41; in France, 44, 50; views Wallace, 45–46; Niebuhr analysis, 47; use of in Truman Doctrine, 53–58; in Latin America, 67; by 1948, 81; 1949–1950 and China, 86–89; and McCarthyism, 93–95, 110–113; 1951 debate over, 130–134; in 1952 election, 136–137; Dulles views, 147, 173; in Asia, 159–165, 173–175; in Mideast (1958), 189; in Cuba, 204–205, 211–213; in Vietnam, 216–217; LBJ view of in Dominican Republic (1965), 244; Johnson view of in Vietnam, 248; by 1970s, 291–292; Reagan views, 300–301; economic failures, 316–317, 344; attempted reforms (1980s), 318–319; post-1991 Russian party, 359–360

Computers, 291; *see also* Technology

Conference on Security and Cooperation in Europe (CSCE) (1975), 339; *see also* Helsinki agreements (1975)

Congress. *See* United States Congress

Connally, John, 265

Connally, Tom, 83, 111

Constitution, 272; *see also* Presidential power

Containment: in 1946–1947, 53–54, 63–65; 1951–1952 debates, 130–135; Eisenhower reevaluation, 153–154; Nixon variations, 252–282; *see also* Kennan, George

Contract with America (1994), 364

Contras (Nicaragua), 311–313, 331

Costa Rica, 158, 206, 312

Cotton, 182

Council for Mutual Economic Assistance (COMECON), 69–70

Council of Economic Advisers, 59

Court of Arbitration, The Hague, 158

Croatia, 354, 363; map, 355

Crocker, Chester, 324

Cuba: in 1898, 151; 1959 Revolution, 203–208; map, 207; and USSR, 208; Bay of Pigs invasion, 212–213; 1962 missile crisis, 221–225; in Angola, 288;

in Grenada, 309; USSR retreats, 324; out of Angola, 363

Czar, 2–3

Czech Republic: post-1989, 335; NATO, 360

Czechoslovakia: in 1919, 3–4; 1930s, 5; in 1947, 70; 1948 crisis, 71–72; coup and US, 92; 1954 Guatemala arms sales, 158; 1955 Egyptian arms sales, 182; in 1960s, 225; 1968 crisis, 255–256, 261; in 1980s, 316; 1989 and after, 335; map, 336

Daily Worker (newspaper), 45–46

Dardanelles, 37, 38

Daughters of the American Revolution, 5

Dayton agreements (1995), 354

Debt: Latin American, 305; US in 1980s, 314–315; *see also* Capitalism

Declaration of Liberated Europe, 14–15

de Gaulle, Charles: in World War II, 10–12; after war, 139; returns to power (1958), 201–202; French atomic bomb, 215; challenges Kennedy over Germany, 226–227, 234; NATO pullout, 251

Democracy in America, 368

Democratic Party, US: 1948 election, 78–80; 1952 election, 135–136; 1956 election, 187–188; 1968 election, 255–257; weakening of, 259; in Watergate, 262; 1972 election, 270; 1980 election, 299; decline, 328

Denmark, 82, 202

Depression, economic, 5, 9, 26; Truman fears, 54; 1947 fears, 59–60; US in 1949, 82; post-1953, 174; *see also* Capitalism

Détente, 141–181; buried, 280, 282

Dewey, Thomas E., 78–79

Dhahran Airfield (Saudi Arabia), 182

Diem, Ngo Dinh: in 1954, 163; problems, 219; crisis and death, 231–233

Diem, Nhu Dinh, 232–233

Dien Bien Phu, 160–161, 173

Dirksen, Everett, 112

Disarmament: in 1953, 147; *see also* Arms control

Disengagement, 86; 1957 debate, 199–200

Dixiecrats, 79

Dobrynin, Anatoly, 282, 310

"Doctor's Plot," 142–143

Dominican Republic: 1965 crisis, 242–246

Domino theory: in 1946, 37–38; Berlin (1948), 76–77; Eisenhower and Vietnam, 161; Kennedy's view, 219; Kennedy and Vietnam, 231; assessed for Vietnam, 280–281

Doonesbury, 303

Douglas, Helen Gahagan, 113

Douglas, Paul, 112

Douglas, William, 39

Dreiser, Theodore, 137

Dr. Zhivago (film), 191

Drugs, 263; Panama conduit, 312, 331–332

Duclos, Jacques, 20–21

Dukakis, Michael, 330

Dulles, Allen, 159

Dulles, John Foster: and Hiss, 93; Japanese treaty and China (1951), 108, 120–121; on crossing 38th parallel (1950), 113; 1952 campaign, 136; McCarthyism, 137–138; Eisenhower relationship, 139–140, 191; on communism, 147–148; view of Asia (1953), 149; view of atomic weapons, 149, 153; German policy, 150–151; on Iran and nationalism, 155–156; on Latin American problems, 157–159; Vietnam policies, 159–165, 230; offshore islands crisis (1954), 166; EDC policy, 167–168, 178–179; on neutrals, 169–170, 172–175, 191; Suez-Hungary crisis, 181–186; 1956 election, 187, 188; Mideast crisis (1957–1958), 188–190, 198–199; views Sputnik, 192; on USSR in late 1950s, 196–198; on Lenin, 199; 1958 Germany turn, 200–201, 202; and Kissinger, 276

Dutch Shell, 156

Duvalier, "Baby Doc," 310

Eastern Europe: plans for in World War II, 11–21; map, 18; in 1946 turn, 40–41; 1948 crisis, 76; 1952 election, 136; *see also individual nations*

Economic Problems of Socialism, 141

Economy. *See* Capitalism, Debt, Depression, Gold, Oil, Trade

Eden, Anthony: in 1951, 128, 129; and Asia, 166; view of EDC, 167–168; at Geneva (1955), 178–179; Suez crisis, 181–186

Edwards, Jonathan, 46–47

Egypt: postwar, 50; in 1947, 70; and Farouk, 152; USSR relations (1950s), 171; 1955–1956 crisis, 181–186; map, 184; 1967–1974 crisis, 274–275; map, 275; 1978 peace, 289, 291; map, 293; biological weapons, 363

Einstein, Albert, 94

Eisenhower, Dwight D.: and NATO, 109, 126; Niebuhr views, 134–135; 1952 election, 135–136; deals with McCarthy (1953–1954), 138, 176–178; Dulles relationship, 138–140, 191; characteristics of, 139–140; 1953 policies, 147; and revolutions, 152–153; handles CIA, 152–153, 194–195; view of economy, 153–154, 194–195; view of nuclear weapons, 154–155; Vietnam policies, 159–165, 230; offshore island policy, 165–166; view of China, 174; view of intellectuals, 177; at Geneva summit (1955), 178–179; 1956 Suez-Hungary crisis, 181–186; wins 1956 election, 187–188; Mideast policies (1957–1958), 188–190; belittles missile gap, 193–194; farewell speech, 195, 210; offshore islands policy (1958), 197; 1958 Mideast crisis, 197–198; German policy (1958), 199–200; 1959–1960 crisis and Geneva summit, 202–203; deals with Cuban Revolution, 205–206; Latin American policies, 208; 1960 election, 209; policy toward Laos, 216

Eisenhower Doctrine (1957), 189–190, 245

Eisenhower packages, 148

El Salvador: in 1960, 206; Carter policies, 296–297; Reagan policies, 311–312, 363; UN mediates conflict, 363

Emperor of Japan, 25–26

England. *See* Great Britain

Enlargement, 350

Environment: Rio conference (1992), 349; crisis of, 364–365, 371; *see also* Population

Estonia, 7, 333

Ethiopia, 240, 288; map, 293

European Defense Community (EDC), 128–129, 150–151, 166–168

European Economic Community. *See* Common Market

Evansville College, 78

EXCOM, 222–225

Export–Import Bank, 174

Farabundo Martí National Liberation Front (FMLN), 312

Farouk, King, 152

Faure, Edgar, 178–179

Federal Bureau of Investigation (FBI): Truman's loyalty program, 68–69; and Russia, 358

Federalist, The, 93

Felt, Admiral Harry, 232

Finland, 6, 17, 70

Ford, Gerald: president (1974–1977), 280–282; Vietnam collapses, 280; USSR and SALT II, 281; *Mayaguez* crisis, 281

Ford Motors, 4

Foreign aid: Truman policies, 80; 1990s, 369; *see also* Loans

Formosa. *See* Taiwan

Forrestal, James: views USSR (1945), 15; Kennan relationship, 63; 1947 national security acts, 68; death, 68

Four policemen, 12

Fowler, Henry, 242

France: in World War II, 10–12; in 1995, 20; Molotov views, 38; German relationship, 41; 1946 crisis, 44; by 1947,

50, 70; in Marshall Plan planning, 59–62; and Franco, 65; Brussels Treaty, 74; German relationship (1949–1950), 85–86; Indochina to 1951, 107–108; German policy (1951–1952), 128–129; EDC involvement, 151; Indochina (1951–1954), 159–165; EDC accepted and changed, 166–168, 178–179; Suez crisis, 183–186; Dulles views, 189; de Gaulle returns (1958), 201–202; and EEC, 201; Kennedy relationship, 226–227; in Africa, 240; NATO pullout, 251; nuclear proliferation, 254; on Nixon, 265; fears Germany (1990), 338; nuclear arms, 363

Franco, General Francisco, 65, 127

Franklin D. Roosevelt (aircraft carrier), 38

Free Trade Association, 201–202

French Petroleum, 156

Frontier, US: Niebuhr view, 134

Fuchs, Klaus, 94

Fukuyama, Frank, 337

Fulbright, J. William: on Truman (1946), 46; evaluates Truman Doctrine, 49; Gulf of Tonkin sponsor, 239; rebels over Dominican Republic intervention (1965–1966), 245

Gaither, Rowland, 193

Gaither Report, 193–195

Gates, Robert, 323

Gavin, General James, 173

General Agreement on Tariffs and Trade (GATT), 357

General Dynamics Corporation, 211

General Electric, 4, 300

General Motors, 346

Geneva Conference (1954), 161–162, 164

Geneva summits: 1955, 178–179, 181; 1960, 202–203; 1985, 322

Georgia, 346

Georgia, University of, 78

Geraschchenko, Viktor, 357

Germans (in US), 137

Germany: before 1919, 3; in 1930s, 5, 9; invades USSR, 6; World War II, 7–23; map, 18; Potsdam conference policies,

23–25, 29; divided (1945–1946), 41–42; Niebuhr views, 47–48; Marshall Plan and Molotov view of policies toward West Germany, 58, 60–62; Kennan-Lippmann views, 65; West Germany 1948 crisis, 72, 74–75; 1949 turn toward West Germany's independence, 84–85; West German rearming, 109–110; West Germany's gains (1951–1952), 126–129; in 1951 US debate, 133; East Germany uprisings (1953), 148–149; Dulles' policies, 150–151; EDC includes West Germany, 167–168, 178; 1958–1960 crisis, 199–202; West Germany and EEC, 201–202; 1961–1962 crisis, 220; de Gaulle and West Germany, 226–227; West Germany and Carter, 295; Reagan sanctions on West Germany, 304; Pershing missiles in West Germany, 305; East Germany in 1980s, 316; USSR withdrawal, 322; post-1989 reunification, 335, 337–338; map, 336; Persian Gulf War problems, 341–342; policy on Croatia-Bosnia, 354; 1990s currency crisis, 361–362; economic power, 367

Gerö, Ernö, 185

Glasnost; 318, 320; assessed, 346–347

Glassboro summit (1967), 254

Global village, 353, 365

Goethe, 258

Gold, US, 242

Goldwater, Barry, 238, 259

Gomulka, Wladyslaw, 185–186

Gorbachev, Mikhail: views, 282; rise to power, 316–317; view of technology needs, 318; program, 318–319; Reagan turn toward, 321–322; summits, 322; US doubts about, 323; withdrawal from Angola and Afghanistan, 324; views Europe, 325; Nicaragua retreat, 331; 1989–1991 reforms, 333; German policies (1990), 337–338; Yeltsin relationship, 339; 1991 crisis, 339–340; Mideast policy (1991), 342–343; 1991 revolt, 343–344; assessed, 346–347; 1992 speech assessing Cold War, 371

Gorbachev, Raisa, 317

Gore, Albert, 349
Gottwald, Klement, 72
"Grand Design" of Kennedy, 227, 234
Great Britain: in 1914–1921, 3–4; in 1930s, 5–6; in World War II, 6–26; Molotov attacks, 38; 1946 crisis, 44; 1947 crisis, 50–58, 59–63; and Franco, 65; Brussels Treaty, 74; in Korean War debates, 118–119; Japan treaty, 120–121; Dulles' view in regard to Asia, 149; Egyptian relationship, 152; in Iranian crisis (1951–1954), 155–157; views Vietnam (1954), 161; EDC-NATO (1950s), 178–179; Suez crisis, 181–186; Dulles' views post-Suez, 189; 1958 Mideast intervention, 198; EEC relationship, 201–202; de Gaulle and EEC, 226–227; African relations, 240; and Afghanistan, 297; on German re-unification (1990), 338; currency crisis (1992), 361–362
Great Grain Robbery, 268
Great Lakes, 365
Great Leap Forward, 196
Great Society, 237, 252
Greece: postwar plans for, 12–13, 15–16; map, 36; 1946–1947 crisis and Truman Doctrine, 50–58; in NATO, 126; and USSR, 144
Greece, New York, 368
Grenada, 309, 310; US casualties, 367
Gromyko, Andrei, 104, 319
Gruening, Ernest, 239
Guatemala: and US (1954), 152; problems and revolution, 157–159
Gulf of Tonkin: attack and US Congress's resolution, 238–239; repeal of resolution, 273
Gulf Oil, 156, 279

Haig, Alexander, 305
Haiti: in 1980s, 310; Clinton policies, 349, 353–354; US casualties, 367
Halle, Louis, 11, n. 7
Harriman, W. Averell: in 1920s USSR, 4; 1944–1945, 14–15, 20, 28; on 1949 economic problems, 82

Hay, John, 165
Hayakawa, S. I., 288
Helsinki agreements (1975), 281–282, 339
Heritage Foundation, 300
Hiroshima, 24–25, 42, 270
Hiss, Alger, 92–93, 94, 95, 105, 111, 137, 138
Hitler, Adolf, 5–6, 11, 20, 37–38, 341
Ho Chi Minh: in 1945, 107; view of China, 107, 249–250; in 1950s, 159–165; and Kennedy, 216–217; and Johnson, 238–239; and USSR in 1960s, 251, 252; Tet offensive (1968), 254–255
Hoffman, Paul, 62
Honduras, 158, 311
Hong Kong, 118
Hoover, Herbert, 4, 16, 284
Hoover, Herbert, Jr., 156–157
Hoover, J. Edgar, 68
Hoover Institution, 300
Horn of Africa, 288–289; map, 293; *see also individual nations*
Hostage crisis, 292–294, 298–299
Hostages, 292–294, 298–299; and Reagan policies, 313
House, Colonel Edward M., 3
Hughes, Thomas, 237–238
Hull, Cordell, 23
Human rights: Kissinger view, 272; Helsinki accords and CSCE, 281–282, 339; Carter policies and USSR, 286–287; in 1990s, 339; Clinton policies and problems, 349–351, 353–354
Humphrey, George, 145, 149, 174–175
Humphrey, Hubert, 112, 255, 257
Hungary: in 1945, 16; in 1947 and Marshall Plan, 70; to 1956 revolt, 170, 181, 185–186; post-1989, 335; map, 336; NATO enlargement, 360–361
Hussein, King, 189
Hydrogen bomb: Truman orders development, 84; USSR view (1949–1950), 90; US decision and Einstein fear, 94; NSC-68 plans for, 97; first US bomb (1951), 125–126; USSR bomb, 146, 170; Oppenheimer view, 176–177; USSR in 1961, 215; China's bomb, 249; *see also* Arms control, *individual arms treaties*

Iceland, 82; 1986 summit, 322

Ickes, Harold, 46

Inchon (1950), 114

India: in 1946, 37; in 1947, 50; Zhadonov's view, 70; Korean War involvement, 114; regional and Southeast Asia, 162, 164–165; Dulles' views, 174; conflict with China (1962), 229; nuclear proliferation, 254; Gorbachev favors, 325; threatened with fragmentation, 328

Indochina: Molotov view, 38; US policies (1950–1951), 101, 207–108, 118; Eisenhower views, 147, 152–153; *see also individual nations*

Indonesia, 38, 70, 171, 172, 197

Inter-American Development Bank (IADB), 208

Intercontinental Ballistic Missiles (ICBMs), USSR's, 192–193, 196, 202, 203; in 1961, 215

International Monetary Fund (IMF): origins and development, 9, 40; and Russia, 357

International Telephone and Telegraph (IT&T), 272

Iran: in 1946 crisis, 30, 35–37; map, 36; Dulles' views, 139; US policies in 1953–1954, 152, 155–157; and CENTO, 199; role in Nixon Doctrine, 261; in oil crisis (1973–1974), 274–275, 276–277; Carter's views, 287; 1979 revolution, 292–294; map, 293; in 1990s, 355–356; Moslems, 362

Iran-Contra scandal (1986–1987), 313

Iraq: map, 36; in 1946, 38; 1958 crisis, 198–199; Persian Gulf War, 340–343; post-1991, 355–356; Moslems, 362

Irish, 137

Iron curtain, 39–40; Gorbachev's 1992 view, 371

Irony of American History (book), 130, 133–134

"Is It Easy to Be Young?" (film), 320

Islam and Islamic fundamentalism. *See* Moslem

Isolationism: redefined, 22; in 1950, 119;

and Eisenhower, 140; in 1954, 166–167; Nixon's views, 261

Israel: US recognizes, 77–78; and USSR, 144; 1956 crisis, 181–186; map, 184; 1967–1974 conflicts, 274–275; map, 275; 1978 peace agreements, 288–289; in 1980s, 308; nuclear weapons, 363; *see also* Jews, Palestine

Italy, 70, 81, 127, 304, 328; and Sputnik, 192; and EEC, 201–202

Ito, Lance, 369

Ivan the Terrible, 103

Jack Daniel, 340

Jackson State, 262

Jackson-Vanik amendment (1974), 273

Japan: before 1921, 2–3; in 1930s, 5, 9; by 1945, 24–26, 30; map, 32; Kennan views, 58, 63; 1947–1948 turn, 65–66; Acheson views (1950), 91–92; and Korean War, 99, 101; 1951 treaty, 120–121; 1951 Niebuhr analysis, 134; Stalin worry, 141; and Vietnam (1954), 161, 163; late 1950s economy, 194; and US arms, 211; in US defense, 219; JFK and Vietnam, 231; and Vietnam in 1960s, 251; role in Nixon Doctrine, 261; 1960s competition develops, 264; Nixon views, 264; seen as enemy by Nixon administration, 265; role in Mideast crisis (1974), 277; in trilateral approach, 286; and USSR, 292; 1980s and development of technology, 325; role in Persian Gulf War, 341–342; and Clinton policies, 352; economic power by 1990s, 367, 369

Jefferson, Thomas, 164, 209

Jews: in Russia before 1914, 2; in postwar era, 50; in USSR, 256, 295; emigrate from USSR, 323

John Deere, 368–369

Johnson, Louis, 97, 113

Johnson, Lyndon B.: and Bricker amendment, 176; role in Eisenhower Doctrine passage, 189; tries to exploit missile gap, 193–194; view of Vietnam

and Diem (1961), 217; background
and views, 233–237; Latin American,
especially Dominican Republic, policies, 242–246; Vietnam issue in 1964
election, 246–248; fears China, 248–
249; tries to play-off USSR and Vietnam, 251, 252; effect of Tet offensive,
decision not to run for reelection
(1968), 254–255; effect of Czech crisis
on policy toward USSR, 255–256; on
Vietnam, 263; Nixon goes beyond in
Vietnam, 266; Middle East crisis
(1967), 274–275; opens talks with Panama, 288; and Reagan, 300
Johnson Doctrine (1965), 244–245, 257
Joint Chiefs of Staff, US, 83, 88; role in
Korean War, 104, 109; MacArthur recall (1951), 122; view of Vietnam
(1954), 160–161; view of 1950s US
strategy, 173–174; view of 1958
Mideast crisis, 198
Jones, T. K., 303
Jordan, 189–190; in 1973–1974 crisis, 274;
map, 275
Jordan, Hamilton, 284, 290
Jou En-lai, 114, 116
Judd, Walter, 86
Jungle Warfare School, 211

Kaganovich, Lazar, 181, 190
Kampuchea. *See* Cambodia
Kansas City speech (Nixon) (1971), 264
Kassim, General Abdel Karim, 198
Katanga Province, 240–241
Kazakhstan, 360
Kem Amendment (1951), 126
Kennan, George: view of Truman Doctrine, 53–54; develops Marshall Plan,
58–59; 1947 crisis, 61–62; containment
theory and Mr. "X," 63–65; 1949 dissent, 85–86; on USSR-China, 91; opposes NSC-68 theories, 96; on crossing
38th parallel (1950), 113; 1957 debate
with Acheson, 199–200; view of communism, 291; on Cold War's end,
336–337

Kennedy, Edward, 299
Kennedy, John F.: tries to exploit supposed missile gap, 193–195; in 1960
election, 208–209; views on Cuba,
Vietnam, McCarthy, 208–209; policy
on Latin America, Alliance for
Progress, 210–212; Bay of Pigs disaster
(1961), 212–213; debates Khrushchev
at Vienna (1961), 213–214; Berlin crisis
policy (1961), 214–215; nuclear tests,
215; Southeast Asia policies, 215–216,
229–233; fears China, 217, 228; 1962
missile crisis, 221–227; nuclear test
ban (1963), 225–226; Grand Design for
Europe, 227; Sino-Indian war, 229; assassination of, 233, 255; relationship
with Johnson, 235–238; view of Trujillo, 243; Kissinger analyzes, 258
Kennedy, Joseph P., 209
Kennedy, Robert, 223, 255
Kent State, 262
KGB, 316
Khomeini, Ayatollah Ruholla, 294
Khrushchev, Nikita: and Stalin (1948),
81; in 1952–1953 internal crisis and
Stalin's death, 142–144; moves toward
power, 146; takes power, attacks
Stalin, 170–172, 180–181; at 1955
Geneva summit, 178–179; role in
Suez-Hungary crises (1956), 183–186;
in 1957–1958 transition, 190–191;
Sputnik and coexistence policy,
192–193; on arms control, 194; break
with China and 1957–1960 initiative,
196, 202–203; German crisis (1958),
199–202; Lunik, 203; Cuba, 203–204;
relationship with Kennedy, 213–214;
role in 1961 Berlin crisis, 214–215, 220;
ICBMs, 220; in missile crisis (1962),
221–227; fall from power, 225–226; relationship with Johnson, 235; view of
Stalin's foreign policy, 253; economic
promise not delivered, 315
Kim il Sung, 100–101
King, Martin Luther, Jr., 255
Kirkpatrick, Jeane J., 306, 310, 311
Kissinger, Henry: view of gray areas in

1950s, 155, 173; in 1961 Rockefeller analysis, 210; rise to power, 255; background and views, 257–258; relationship with Rogers, 260; on Nixon (1970), 262; on 1972 bombing of Vietnam and Nixon, 266–267; Moscow summit (1972), 268–269; peace-at-hand claim about Vietnam (1972), 270; policy toward Chile, 271–272; on doing the unconstitutional, 272; Nixon resignation, 273; attacks Congress, 274; 1973–1974 Mideast crisis, 276–277; belittles Latin America, 278; Angola policy, 279; odd assessment of Vietnam experience, 280; role in Ford policies, 280–282; SALT II policies, 281; on détente, 281; relationship with Brzezinski, 284; role in Iran, friendship for Shah (1979), 294; view of NATO and Russian expansionism, 361

Knowland, William, 46, 86, 87, 140, 148, 178

Kohl, Helmut, 338

Komatsu, 368

Korea: map, 32; North Korea's policies, 90; and Acheson, 92; North and South Korea in 1950–1953 war, 99–102; map, 103; South Korea and Vietnam, 251; South Korean airliner destroyed, 321; North Korea's nuclear policies, 363

Korean War: Acheson evaluates, 98; origins, 99–100; US crosses the 38th parallel and China enters war, 113–122; casualties, 116–117; 1953 truce, 125; USSR agrees to end, 144; Eisenhower views, 147; Dulles and atomic bomb threat, 149; truce talks, 149–150; compared with Vietnam War, 161; post-1953 economics affected by war, 174; US casualties, 367

Kosygin, Aleksey, 250, 253

Kozyrev, Andrei, 359

Kubitschek, Juscelino, 208

Kurile Islands, 31

Kuwait, 340–343, 363

Ky, Nguyen Cao, 247

La Follette, Robert, Jr., 95

Lake, Anthony, 349–350, 351

Lansing, Robert, 139

Laos, 162, 164, 165; in 1961–1962, 214, 215–216; map, 218; in 1962–1963, 229–231

Latin America: plans for in World War II, 21–22; US seminal policies of 1947–1948, 66–67; role in Korean War, 119; development in 1950s, 157–158; 1950s investment, 175; problems of development by 1960, 206; background of Eisenhower policy turn, 203–208; map, 207; Kennedy approach and Alliance for Progress, 210–212; Johnson retunes Alliance, 242–246, 251; Kissinger belittles, 278; *see also individual nations*

Lattimore, Owen, 95

Latvia, 7, 333

Leahy, Admiral William, 13, 15

Lebanon: in 1958 crisis, 198–199; in 1980s, 308; Reagan policies toward, 313

LeMay, General Curtis, 246

Lend-lease, 7

Lenin, Vladimir, 3–4, 64, 152, 360

Leningrad, 17

Liberals, US: in 1930s, 5; *see also* Americans for Democratic Action; Democratic Party; Great Society; Niebuhr, Reinhold; Wallace, Henry

Liberation: failure in 1953, 148–149; Eisenhower views, 155; in 1950s, 178

Liberia, 240, 351

Libya, 309–310, 363

Lilienthal, David, 42–43, 68

Limited wars, 173–174

Lin Piao, 249–250

Linkage, 267, 271

Lippmann, Walter: in 1919, 3–4; 1946 and Baruch, 42; view of Truman (1946), 46; in 1947 debate with Kennan, 64–65; 1957 debate on disengagement, 199

Lisbon Conference (1952), 127–129

Lithuania, 7, 333, 339

"Little Vera" (film), 320

Liu Shao-ch'i, 89
Loans: to British (1946), 10; to France (1946), 10–11; plans for USSR loan (1945–1946), 40; USSR to China, 90–91; USSR to Iran, 156; in US 1950s policy, 174–175; US to Dominican Republic, 243
Lodge, Henry Cabot, 233
Lon Nol, 262–263
Los Alamos, New Mexico, 24
Lovett, Robert, 74, 77, 234
Low-intensity-conflicts (LICs), 307
Lucas, Scott, 112
Luce, Henry, 31
Lumumba, Patrice, 241
Lunik (1959), 202

MacArthur, General Douglas: in Japan, 66; view of Pacific defense line (1949), 91; in Korean War, 102–105, 106; on crossing 38th parallel, 113–115; 1951 crisis and recall, 121–123; MacArthur hearings, 123–125; in 1951 debate, 132; and 1952 election, 136
Macmillan, Harold, 226–227
MacVeagh, Lincoln, 55
Madison, James, 93; foresees fragmentation, especially of Russia, 327, 356, 371
Majlis, 37
Malaya, 118, 147, 172
Malenkov, Georgy, 81, 89–90, 142; takes power, 145–146; loses power, 170–172
Malia, Martin ("Z"), 337
Malik, Yakov, 102
Malinovsky, Marshall Rodion, 220
Malone, George, 46
Manchuria: before 1917, 1–2; in 1945, 25–26, 30; 1945 rail system, 31–34; map, 32; in 1950 war, 91, 117; and Vietnam conflict, 163
Mandela, Nelson, 311
Mann, Thomas C., 242, 243, 245
Mao Ze-dong: in 1945, 31–34; 1949 triumph, 86–88; and Stalin (1950), 91; and Korea (1950), 100–101; shock over Taiwan (1950), 107; and US war in Korea, 114–122; on Vietnam conflict,

164; views new post-1957 forces, 196–197; offshore island crisis (1958), 197–198; Nixon opening, 258; Brezhnev relationship, 268
Marcos, Ferdinand, 310
Marshall, General George: and China (1945–1946), 33–35; Truman Doctrine formulation, 51–53; and Marshall Plan, 58–59; Latin American policy, 66–67; views 1947 crises, 71; victim of McCarthy, 111
Marshall Plan: formulation, 58–63; USSR reacts, 69–70; NATO's relationship, 83; possible Asian version, 101; failing in 1951, 126
Martin, Joe, 122
Marx, Karl, 64; and Reagan, 301
Marxism: in 1917, 3; in 1930s, 5; during World War II, 8–21, 26–27; *see also* Communism
Maryknoll Seminary, 163
Masaryk, Jan, 72
Massive retaliation, 154–155
Matlock, Jack, 340
Matsu, 165–166
Matthews, Herbert, 204
Mayaguez (1975), 281
McCarran, Pat, 127
McCarran Act (1950), 112
McCarthy, Eugene, 254
McCarthy, Joseph (and McCarthyism): legacy, 1; in 1946, 46; and Truman Doctrine, 53; origins and views, 94–95; during Korean War, 105; power grows, tactics (1950–1952), 110–113; and Truman, 117; views MacArthur recall, 122; 1952 elections, 136–137; during 1952–1954, 137–138; after 1953–1954, 146; end of, 175–177; Kennedy relationship, 209; USSR view, 325
McDonald's, 252, 318, 347, 353
McGovern, George, 270
McGrath, J. Howard, 111
McLuhan, Marshall, 353
McNamara, Robert: military efficiency, 211; view of missiles, 220; during missile crisis (1962), 222, 224; policies in

Vietnam, 231–232, 247–249; and Gulf of Tonkin episode, 238; fear of China, 248; to USSR about missiles, 254
Mekong Valley, 236
Mendes-France, Pierre, 161–162, 167–168
Merck, 318
Mexico: and US force, 152; and Guatemala, 158; by 1960, 206, 212; 1982 debt crisis, 305; US debt compared, 315; USSR in 1980s, 325; Clinton policy, 351–352; environmental problems, 365
Miami, University of, 78
Middle East: postwar situation, 35–37, 50; map, 36; Truman Doctrine view, 51–58; Suez crisis (1956), 181–186; during 1957–1958 transition, 188–190; 1958 crisis and US intervention, 197–198; 1973–1974 war and oil embargo, 274–275; during 1980s, 313; *see also individual nations*
Military-industrial complex, 210
Militias: in 1990s, 328–329
Miller, Arthur, 270
Missile crisis (1962), 221–227; legacy, 228, 229, 253
Missile gap, 208–209, 210
Mobutu, General Joseph D., 241
Molotov, V. M., 7, 14; and Truman encounter (1945), 16; views atomic diplomacy, 27; attacks US (1946), 38; views Germany (1946), 41; considers and rejects Marshall Plan, 59–60; own Marshall Plan, 69–70; in 1950s, 181, 190
Mondale, Walter, 310
Monroe Doctrine: viewed in 1945, 22; relationship to NATO, 83; applied to Guatemala (1954), 158–159; relationship to Vietnam, 165; in Mideast policy of Eisenhower (1957), 190; and Cuba (1960), 203
Morgenthau, Hans, 130–134
Morgenthau, Henry, Jr., 46
Morison, Samuel Eliot, 93–94
Morse, Wayne, 239
Moscow State University, 317
Moslems: in 1958 Mideast crisis, 198; in

Iranian Revolution (1979), 292–294; Soviets fear, especially in Afghanistan, 297–298; during 1980s, 308; in USSR, 333; during Persian Gulf War, 342; in former Yugoslavia and post-1991 crisis, 354, 362
Mossadegh, Mohammed, 155–156
Moynihan, Daniel Patrick, 328
Multiple Independently targeted Reentry Vehicles (MIRV), 268–269, 301–302
Mundt, Karl, 137
Munich (lessons of 1938 appeasement of Hitler at Munich): Stalin view in 1938, 5–6; Stalin view in 1946–1947, 70; Truman's views, 72; in 1952, 135; 1953 reference, 148; and Johnson, 237; Kissinger on, 279; Bush use of, 341
"Murder in the Air" (film), 303
Murray, Thomas E., 177
Muskie, Edmund, 255
Mutual assured destruction (MAD), 283
Mutual Defense Assistance Bill, 84
Mutual Security Program, 197
Mylai, 263

Nabisco, 318
Nagasaki, 25
Nagy, Imre, 170, 185–186
Nasser, Gamal Abdel: in Suez crisis, 181–186, 188–189; during 1958 upheaval and US intervention, 198–199; and China, 249
National Association of Manufacturers, 62
National Liberation Front (Greece), 51–52
National Liberation Front (Vietnam), 217
National Press Club speech (Acheson, 1950), 91–92
National Security Act (1947), 66
National Security Council: origin (1947), 68; in Korea (1950), 114; 1961 Berlin crisis, 215; Reagan use of, 313
National Security Council paper 68 (NSC-68): origins and content, 95–98; use of during Korean War, 106,

109–110, 117; effect on 1950 budgets, 117, 120; Gaither Report compared, 193; Carter policy compared, 295, 299
National Security Decision Directive, 17, 311
National Security Decision Directive, 75, 321
Nationalism: in USSR (1918), 3; Acheson views (1950), 92; in 1951–1952 debate, 135; post-1953 transition, 145; outbreak of mid-1950s, 169–170; and Sputnik (1957–1959), 192–193; in early 1960s, 227–228; Carter administration conflict over, 285–286; in 1990s, 328; in post-1991 Russia, 347–348, 360–361
Nazis, 5–6
Nehru, Pandit, 164–165, 183, 229
Nelson, Gaylord, 239
Nelson, Willie, 299
Neoconservatives, 300
Nepal, 50
Netherlands, The, 38, 50, 121, 128, 206, 276
Never-Again Club, 163, 217
New Deal: coalition in 1946, 46; Niebuhr views, 47; by 1950, 93; in 1952 election, 137; and Johnson, 235–236
New Look, 154
New York Times, The, 238, 262
New Zealand, 120, 164, 251
Newark, 255
Nhu, Madam Ngo Dinh, 216
Nicaragua: and Guatemala (1954), 158, 159; 1960 condition, 206; Carter policy, 296; Reagan intervention, 306, 307, 308, 311, 313; USSR retreat, 325
Niebuhr, Reinhold: views, theories applied (1946), 46–48; view of Marshall Plan, 62; in 1948, 78; Acheson compared, 81; in 1950s, 119; MacArthur controversy, 123; 1951 debate, 130–133; 1956 warning, 188; relationship with Kennedyites, 231; final warning, 370–371
Nigeria, 285
1984 (book), 320
Nitze, Paul, 295
Nixon, Richard: and Hiss, 93; 1950 victory, 113; and Eisenhower, 139–140, 145; view of Vietnam, 153; in Latin America (1958), 208; 1960 election, 208–209; rise to power (1960s), 255–257, 259–260; plumbers unit, 262; Cambodian policy and 1970 riots, 262; Kansas City Speech (1971), 264–265; China policy and trip, 266; bombs Vietnam, 267; 1972 USSR summit, 268–269; 1972 election, 270; supposed Vietnam peace, 270–272; Chilean policy, 271–272; resigns, 272–273; Vietnam falls, 280; Carter views, 284; and Reagan, 302
Nixon Doctrine, 261–262, 264, 277
Nonproliferation: in 1960s, 254; *see also* Arms control, *individual treaties*
Nonproliferation Treaty (1968), 363
Noriega, General Manuel Antonio, 312–313, 331–332
North, Lt. Colonel Oliver, 313
North American Free Trade Association (NAFTA), 351–352
North Atlantic Treaty Organization (NATO): origins, 73, 81–84; USSR view of, 90; 1951 buildup, 109–110; 1951–1952 tripwire theory, 125–126; and USSR (1950s), 171; Dulles' views (1956), 172–173; in late 1950s, 200; de Gaulle pullout, 251; Mideast crisis (1973), 276; Gorbachev views, 325, 334; Bush concern over, 338–339; in Bosnian crisis (1990s), 354; Clinton policy on expansion, 360–361, 369
Northrop Corporation, 314
Northwestern University, 78
Norway, 82, 202
Nuclear Test Ban, 225, 345
Nuclear war: Reaganites' view, 303; *see also* Atomic bomb, Hydrogen bomb
Oder-Neisse boundary, 41–42
Oil: USSR concern 1940s, 28; in Mideast crisis (1946), 35; in Truman Doctrine strategy, 54; in Marshall Plan, 61; 1948 Mideast crisis, 77; and Iran (1953), 155–157; Dulles' views, 172; Suez crisis, 183–186; US controls on (1959), 197; in Cuba-USSR relationship, 205;

Venezuelan, 206; 1973–1974 Mideast embargo, 274–277, 282; Canadian, 278; USSR, 291, 315–316; Iran crisis (1979), 292–294, 295–296, 297; pipeline and Reagan, 304–305; Bush policy, 329; Persian Gulf War, 340–343; USSR's (1990s), 346; compared with water's importance (1990s), 366

Okinawa. *See* Ryukyus

Oklahoma City bombing, 329

Olympic Games, 298

Open-door policy: in 1940s, 8–9, 12, 15–16, 26–27, 29; in Asia (1954), 165

Operation Desert Storm, 342

Operation Linebacker, 266

Operation Pan America, 208

Operation Solarium, 153–154

Oppenheimer, J. Robert, 55, 176–177

Organization of American States (OAS): origins, 67; in 1950–1951, 119; in Guatemala intervention, 157–158; in Dominican Republic invasion, 244; and Nicaragua, 296

Organization of Petroleum Exporting Countries (OPEC), 276–277, 282

Orwell, George, 147, 320

Outer Mongolia, 31, 91

Outer Space Treaty (1967), 345

Oz, 10–11

Pakistan, 50, 164, 199, 363

Palestine, 38, 50, 77–78

Palestinian Liberation Organization (PLO), 308

Panama: Canal Zone training for war, 211; Carter treaties with, 288; in 1980s, 312–313; US invades, 331–332; US casualties in 1989 invasion, 367

Paper tiger, 196

Pasternak, Boris, 191

Pathet Lao, 216, 229–230

Patton, General George, 30

Peace Corps, 211

People's Congress, 320

Pepsi-Cola, 290, 346

Perestroika, 318–319, 320; assessed, 346–347

Pershing missiles, 322

Persian Gulf: in 1950, 103; in 1979–1980 crises, 297–298

Persian Gulf War (1990–1991), 340–343; extent of destruction, 365; US casualties, 367

Pescadores, 166–167

Philippines, 91, 101, 118, 120, 134, 151; and SEATO, 164; in 1980s, 310

Phleger, Herman, 166

Pizza Hut, 346

Pleven Plan, 127

Plumbers, 262

Point Four (1949), 79–80

Poland: in 1919, 3; in 1930s, 6; during World War II, 7–8; postwar plans for, 13–15, 16, 22–23, 29; Molotov views, 38; in 1947–1948, 49, 70–71; to 1956 crisis, 181, 185–186, 190; in 1960s, 225; in early 1970s, 267–268; Reagan policies, 304; post-1989, 334–335; map, 336

Polaris submarines, 194

Politburo, 18–19, 142–144

Pompidou, Georges, 264

Popular Movement for Liberation of Angola (MPLA), 279, 281

Population: Dulles on, 172; Latin American (1960), 206; problems in USSR, 292, 315–316; US and Russia in 1990s, 358; projected, 365–366

Portugal, 82, 202, 240; and Angola, 279

Potsdam conference (1945), 23–24

Powell, General Colin: in Reagan NSC, 305; Persian Gulf War, 342

Prague Spring (1968), 256

Pravda (newspaper), 59

Presidential Directive, 59, 299

Presidential power: in 1947, 55–56; 1947 acts, 68–69; in 1948 crisis, 72–74; and NATO, 82; during Korean War, 102–103, 105; growth (1954), 165, 166; Bricker Amendment threatens, 175–177; growth (1957), 189; Kennedy and Vietnam, 232–233; during Gulf of Tonkin episode (1964), 239; Nixon use of, 259–260, 272; Carter, 290; Bush's use of, 332, 342; in 1990s, 368–369

Primakov, Yevgeny, 359

Proctor & Gamble, 357
Progressive Party (1948), 78–79
Public opinion, US: in 1945, 27–28, 29; shaped by Truman, 56–58; in 1948, 79; Acheson views, 80–81; NSC-68 shapes, 97–98; Eisenhower relationship, 140; Kennedy view, 209; Kennedy and press, 232; and Johnson, 237; Nixon during Cambodian attacks, 262; Nixon manipulates, 270–271, 272; during *Mayaguez* crisis (1975), 281; and Carter, 299; on UN, 364; in 1990s, 368–369
Punta del Este Conference (1961), 211–212
Purges: 1930s, 5; 1948–1950, 76

Qaddafi, Mu'ammar, 309–310
Quemoy, 165

Radio Shack, 314
Rambo, 310
Rambose, 310
Rapid deployment force, 297
Reagan, Ronald: and Eisenhower, 140; views, 282, 283, 299–303; Carter anticipates, 297, 300–302; SDI plans, 303; pipeline and USSR setbacks, 304–305; views Vietnam, 307; 1983 Mideast policy, 308; Grenada invasion, 309; Libya bombing, 309–310; 1984 election, 310; Nicaragua policies, 311, 331; El Salvador policies, 311–312; Middle East crisis, 313; Casey relationship, 313; Iran-Contra scandal, 313–314; and China, 320–321; turn on USSR, 321–322; summits with Gorbachev, 322; policy toward Iraq and Saddam Hussein, 341; NAFTA policies, 351–352
Reagan Doctrine (1985), 306–307, 312, 324
Red Army: in World War II, 12–14, 19–20, 28; by 1947, 49–50; Lippmann views, 64–65; during Korea (1950), 100; 1951, 141; early 1970s, 267; in Afghanistan crisis, 297–298; and Iraq, 343
Reed, Ralph, 329
Reich, Robert, 353
Reparations, 23–24
Republican Party: in 1946, 46; tax cuts and Truman Doctrine (1947), 51–58; views Marshall Plan, 61; 1947 anticommunism, 68; 1948 turn, 74, 78; in transition, 140–141; in 1956, 187–188; Kennedy fears, 228; in 1968, 255–257; emerging majority, 259; in 1976, 281; cohesion of, 328; 1994 victory and after, 369
Revolution: in Russia, 3–4; Stalin's views, 20–21, 31–32; in China (1940s), 30–35; in Greece (1940s), 37–38, 51–58; in 1951 US debate, 130–133; US views change in 1950s, 151–152, 155; Iranian and Guatemalan, 155–159; during 1954–1957 transition, 169–170; late 1950s China, 196–197; Cuban and Latin American (late 1950s), 203–208, 211; Kennedy's views, 209–210; in Laos, 215–217; Iranian, 292–294; Nicaraguan, 311; Salvadoran, 311–312
Reykjavik summit (1986), 322
Rhee, Syngman, 99–100, 105; prisoner crisis, 149–150
Ridgway, General Matthew, 160–161, 163, 173
Rio Conference (1992), 349, 365
Rio pact (1947), 66–67, 73
Rockefeller, David, 286, 294
Rockefeller, Nelson, 21–22, 139, 255
Rockefeller brothers' report (1961), 210
Rogers, William, 260
Rolling Thunder, 246
Roman Catholic Church, 5, 159, 297, 353, 354, 362
Romania. *See* Rumania
Roosevelt, Franklin D.: and Harriman, 4; recognizes USSR, 5; agonizes over second front, 7; postwar plans, 7–23, 31, 35; and Wallace, 45; and Acheson, 80; China policy, 89; 1950 legacy, 93; remains in Indochina, 107; influence on Johnson, 235; views Trujillo, 243

Roosevelt, Theodore, 2–3, 151, 332
Rostow, Eugene, 295
Rostow, Walt W., 217
Ruhr, 75, 85
Rumania (after 1989, Romania): in World War II, 7; 1944–1945, 12, 14, 16, 23, 24; in 1947, 49; moves away from Soviet model, 267; in 1980s, 316; 1989 and after, 335; map, 336; and NATO, 360
Rusk, Dean: in 1950, 113; and MacArthur, 123; need to control Pacific region, 124; and Kennedy, 234; views China, 249; on USSR and Vietnam, 253
Russell, Richard, 241, 284
Russia (pre-1917, post-1992): before 1917, 1–3; Mother Russia in World War II, 19; fragments, 328; map, 348; peacekeeping abroad (1990s), 356; nationalism in, 356; economy in 1990s, 356–357; mobs, economic woes, 358; politics, 358–359; 1993 revolt, 359; environmental crises, 365; *see also* Soviet Union
Russian Orthodox Church, 313
Rutskoi, Aleksandr, 328, 359
Rwanda, 351, 365
Ryukyus (including Okinawa), 91, 120, 219

Sadat, Anwar el-, 274–275, 289
Saddam Hussein, 340–343, 349, 359
Sakhalin, 31; map, 32
Sakharov, Andrei, 268, 298, 316, 319
Sandinistas, 296, 331
Sandino, Augusto, 296
SANE (National Committee for a Sane Nuclear Policy), 194
Saudi Arabia: and Suez crisis, 182; map, 184; and US arms, 211; in Persian Gulf War, 340–342; in 1990s, 355
SAVAK, 287, 294
Scammon, Richard, 259
Schine, David, 137
Schlesinger, Arthur, Jr.: 1949 liberal views, 94; rationalizes Bay of Pigs, 213; on Kennedy-Rusk, 234

Schmidt, Helmut, 295–296
Schuman, Robert, and Schuman Plan, 85–86, 109, 128–129
Scientists: Niebuhr views, 47; and USSR, 84; and Sputnik, 192; divided on test ban treaty, 226; in Reagan plans, 302
Scowcroft, General Brent, 330, 340, 343–344
Security Council, UN: in 1945, 21–22; and Iran (1946), 37–38; *see also* United Nations
Security Loyalty Program (1947), 68
Selective service, 73
Serbia, 354, 356, 362; map, 355
Seward, William, 330
Shah of Iran: threatened (1952–1953), 155–157; Nixon hopes for and arms sales to, 261; in 1973–1974 crisis, 277–278; human rights violations, 287; collapses, 292–294
Shevardnadze, Eduard, 319
Shulman, Marshall, 285–286, 288
Shultz, George: background and views, 305–306; opposes Weinberger, 307–308; and USSR, 310; and Noriega, 312; on USSR (1980s), 323; bad Baker relationship, 330
Siberia, 2, 3, 304
Sihanouk, Prince Norodom, 262
Simpson, O.J., 369
"Sinatra Doctrine," 335
Sinkiang, 91
Skybolt missile, 226
Slovakia, 360
Smith, Earl E. T., 204
Smith Act (1940), 112
Socony-Vacuum, 156
Solzhenitsyn, Aleksandr, 268, 320
Somalia, 288, 291; map, 293; in 1990s, 350, 365; US casualties, 367
Somoza, Anastasio, 296
Sophie's Choice (film), 285
Sorensen, Theodore, 209, 223, 234
Soros, George, 363
South Africa, 240; and Nixon, 261; in 1980s, 310–311, 324; post-1991, 362
Southeast Asia Treaty Organization (SEATO), 164–165; and Laos, 216

Southern Rhodesia, 240
Souvanna Phouma, 216
Soviet Union: 1917–1930s, 2–6, 9; in
1939–1941, 6; during World War II,
8–25; devastation of, 17; effect of US
atomic bomb, 24–25, 42–43; China
policies (1945), 31–35; Stalin views,
39–40; atomic bomb policies, 42–43;
Marshall Plan (1947–1949), 58–63;
Kennan views, 63–65; Lippmann
views, 64–65; NSC-68 analyzes, 95–97;
in 1949–1950 turn, 83–86; in Korean
War, 99–102; 1952–1953 crisis, 1953
views, 141–142, 146–148; post-Stalin
politics (1954–1956), 170–172;
1957–1958 politics of Khrushchev,
190–191; science and Sputnik, 192;
1950s economy, 193; Mideast (1958),
198–199; and Africa, 241; and Vietnam
(1960s), 250–254; economy sags, 253;
1968 Czech upheaval and invasion,
255–256; Nixon views, 261, 264; China
clash, 265–266; 1970s crises, 267–268;
map (1980s), 269; détente and economic collapse, 273; and Canada, 278;
in Angola, 279, 288; Helsinki human
rights challenge, 281–282; Carter administration views, 284–286; economic
problems (1980s), 314, 333; Reagan
turn toward, 321–322; and Cuba in
1980s, 324; self-destructs, 327–328,
343–344, 347; map, 348
Spain, 127
Sparkman, John, 138
Special Forces (US), 211
Sputnik (1957), 192–193
Stalin, Joseph: in 1920s–1930s, 4–5; in
World War II, 7–8; postwar plans,
11–25; motives, 19–20; atomic bomb
and Potsdam decisions, 23–25; Asia
(1945–1946), 31–32; and Middle East
policies, 35–37; 1946 speech, 39–40, 43;
army in 1947, 49; Marshall views, 58;
and Marshall Plan, 69–71; Tito and
1948–1949 turn, 75–76; Mao relationship (1949–1950), 87–91, 95; in Korean
War, 100–101, 103–104, 114–116;
1951–1953 debates and death, 125,

141–144, 145–146; Khrushchev attacks,
171–172, 180–181, 190, 253; warning
about US, 203; and computers, 256;
joke about, 316; repudiated (1980s),
319
Standard Oil (of California and of New
Jersey), 156
Star Wars, 303, 322
Stassen, Harold, 139
State Department. *See* United States De-
partment of State
Stettinius, Edward, 14
Stevenson, Adlai, 135–137, 187–188; at
UN, 213, 266
Stevenson amendment (1974), 273
Stimson, Henry, 15–16, 22, 23, 27, 48, 111
Strategic Arms Limitation Treaties
(SALT I, SALT II): initiated in 1972,
268–269; and Carter, 284–285; SALT II,
281; Carter and SALT II, 295, 297; Rea-
gan and SALT II, 302; chart of post-
1979 treaties, 345
Strategic Arms Reduction Treaties
(START): chart, 345; and Clinton, 360
Strategic Defense Initiative (SDI), 303
Stuart, J. Leighton, 88
Styron, William, 285
Sudan, 288, 291; map, 293
Suez: 1956 crisis, 181–186; map, 275
Sullivan and Cromwell, 139
Suslov, Mikhail A., 90
Sweden, 202
Switzerland, 202
Syria, 70, 182, 198, 274, 289; in 1980s,
308, 309; maps, 184, 275
Szilard, Leo, 84

Tachens, 165–166
Taft, Robert: in 1957, 55; attacks Lilienthal, 68; opposes Marshall Plan, 71;
views Korean War, 102, 110; and
Spain, 127; 1951 debate, 130–133; and
McCarthyism, 138; and Eisenhower,
140
Taiwan: 1949–1950, 88; in Korean War,
106–107; 1954–1955 crisis, 165–166;
1958 crisis, 197; and Nixon, 265

Talbott, Strobe, 360
Tariffs. *See* Trade
Tatars, 365
Taylor, Maxwell, 210, 217, 222
Technology: before 1917, 1; USSR
  (1980s), 316–318; US-China, 320;
  Henry Adams' views, 325; 1980s east-
  ern Europe, 334; in 1990s, 350, 353,
  362; US ability to control, 367
Television, 357; *see also* CNN
Teng Hsiao-p'ing, 287, 290
Terrorism: Libya (1980s), 309–310; in US,
  328–329
Tet offensive (1968), 254–255
Texaco, 136
Texas A&M University, 333–334
Thailand, 164, 216; and SEATO, 164; and
  Vietnam, 251
Thermonuclear weapons. *See* Hydrogen
  bomb
Thatcher, Margaret, 341, 361
Thieu, Nguyen Van, 270–271, 280
Tito, 52, 57, 292; 1948 split from USSR,
  75–76; and Nasser, 183
Tocqueville, Alexis de, 368
Tokyo, 24
Tolkien, J. R. R., 11 n. 7
Tower, John, 313
Trade: in 1920s, 4; World War II policies,
  8–10; 1945 plans for, 15–16; and Asia
  (1945), 30–31; in 1947 crisis, 50–51,
  59–63, 66; USSR and bloc (1940s), 70;
  Truman views, 79–80; USSR's (1950),
  90–91; controls on (1951), 126; mid-
  1950s US debate, 173–175; Cuban-US,
  204; USSR-Latin America, 206–207; ef-
  fect of Vietnam, 264; Nixon policies,
  265–266; US in 1970s, 268–269;
  Canadian-Chinese, 278; US-Poland
  (1980s), 304; US 1980s deficits,
  314–315; USSR bloc exchanges (1980s),
  316; US-China, 320–321; post-1989,
  336; post-1991, 361–362
Treaty of Friendship and Alliance
  (USSR-China, 1945), 31
Trilateral Commission, 286
Trudeau, Pierre, 278
Trujillo, Rafael, 243, 245

Truman, Harry S: damns USSR and
  Nazis (1941), 6; and FDR, 8; background of, 14–15; 1945 decisions,
  15–21; at Potsdam, 23–25; views
  atomic bomb, 24–26; on Japan peace,
  26; views Asia, 30, 33–35; policy toward Turkey, 38; atomic bomb policy,
  42–43; at Churchill speech (1946),
  43–44; clashes with Wallace (1946),
  45–46, 48; Truman Doctrine, 49–58;
  and Marshall Plan, 58–63; Latin
  American policy, 67; loyalty program,
  68; 1948 crisis, 71–73, 74–76; recognizes Israel, 77–78; 1948 elections,
  78–79; 1949 plans, 79–80; NATO creation, 82–83; views USSR bomb,
  84–85; views China (1949–1950),
  86–89; 1950 problems, 93, 94, 95; Korean War policies, 100–104; 1950 initiatives globally, 105–110; enters Vietnam, 107; McCarthy problems,
  111–112; decision to cross 38th parallel (1950), 114–118; 1950 debate,
  118–119; recalls MacArthur, 121–125;
  defense budgets, 125–126; in 1952
  election, 135; Eisenhower views, 153;
  in 1956, 187; Kennedy views, 228
Truman Doctrine: origins, 49–58; and
  Marshall Plan, 58–60; and UN, 104; in
  1951 debate, 131; related to Dominican Republic (1965), 244; Carter use
  of, 298; and de Tocqueville, 368
Tshombe, Moise, 240–241
Tupperware, 370
Turkey: in 1946, 30, 35–38; map, 36; 1947
  crisis, 50–58; and NATO, 126; and
  USSR, 144; USSR (1950s), 171; Sput-
  nik's effect, 192; and CENTO, 199
Twain, Mark, 2, 137
Twining, General Nathan, 160, 198
Two-camp view, 53–58, 70–71
Tydings, Millard, 95, 112
Tyler, William R., 228

U-2 plane, 203–204; in missile crisis, 221,
  222
Ukraine, 344, 346, 348, 360

United Arab Republic (UAR) (1958), 198–199

United Fruit Company, 157–158

United Nations: and Latin America (1945), 21–22; Molotov views, 38; Churchill views, 39; Rio treaty relationship, 66–67; and NATO, 74; Congress views, 80; Acheson belittles, 80–81, 87; in Korean War, 102; 1950 change, 104–106, 119; and Germany, 129; 1953 arms proposals, 179; and Suez (1956), 186; and Africa, 240; China enters, 266; Carter administration relationship, 285–286; splits, 328; in Persian Gulf War, 341–343; in 1990s, 363–364; US debt to and involvement with (1990s), 364; and Clinton, 369–370; Gorbachev views, 371

United Nations Atomic Energy Commission, 42

United States Congress: and atomic energy (1946), 43; postwar views, 44; Truman Doctrine debate, 52–57; Marshall Plan debates, 61–63; 1947 loyalty program, 68; 1948 crisis, 72–73; Acheson views, 81; NATO debate, 83–84; on China (1949), 86–87; bipartisanship ends, 88; House Un-American Activities, 92–93; and Korean War, 102–103; 1950 rearming, 110; McCarthyism, 112; and Spain (1949–1953), 127; restrains Vietnam policy (1954), 161; Bricker amendment debate, 176–177; Aswan Dam decision, 182; on Eisenhower Doctrine, 189; Gulf of Tonkin debate and resolution (1964), 238–239; on Dominican Republic debate, 245; and Nixon, 259, 263, 279; repeals Gulf of Tonkin resolution, 273; War Powers Act (1973), 273–274; Nicaragua debate, 311, 313; inept on invasion of Panama, 332; raises arms budgets (1990s), 352; UN debt, 364

United States Department of State: in 1930s, 5; 1941 views, 6; and de Gaulle, 10–11; postwar plans, 11–21, 23, 28; views Asia, 30–32; 1946 Middle East policy, 38; in 1947 crises, 50–52, 58–63;

1947 Asian turn, 65–66; on Germany, 85; and McCarthy, 94–95; and Korean War, 104; Acheson quotes, 118; 1952 McCarthyism, 136–138; and Foreign Service threatened (1953), 138; and Cuba, 205; Kennedy relationship, 234; Nixon belittles, 259–260; views Afghan crisis, 298

United States Information Service, 137

United States Marines, 296, 331

Uniting for Peace resolution (1950), 106

Universal military training, 73

Universal Suez Canal Company, 183

University of Chicago, 130

USS Nautilus (ship), 125

Vance, Cyrus: views, 284–287; policies toward Panama and Angola, 288; views China, 289, 290; Iran policies, 294–295; resigns, 298

Vandenberg, Arthur: 1945 turn, 21–22; and Wallace, 45; in 1947 debates, 55–57; on Latin America (1947), 67; views anticommunism, 68; supports NATO, 74–75; evaluates Acheson, 80; on NATO, 82; fears USSR atomic bomb, 84; illness, 88

Vandenberg Resolution (1948), 74

Varga, Eugene, 71

Venezuela, 22, 206, 211; and OPEC, 276–277

Verne, Jules, 29

Versailles Peace Conference (1919), 3

Veterans of Foreign Wars, 121

Viet Minh: in 1954, 160; in 1960s, 217, 219, 231–232

Vietnam: USSR views (1947), 70; US policies (1945–1951), 107–108; Eisenhower policies, 155, 159–165; USSR relationship (1950s), 171; Niebuhr fears for, 188; US aid (1957), 197; compared with Latin America, 206; Kennedy policies, 209, 216–218, 230–233; map, 218; Johnson policies, 235–238, 246–250; China mistrust, 249–250; USSR in 1960s, 251, 252–253; Tet offensive (1968), 254–255; Nixon-

Kissinger policies, 258–259; Mylai tragedy, 263; Nixon bombs, 266; 1972–1973 "peace," 270–271; South Vietnam collapses, 280–282; China invasion, 290; effect of war on 1980s, Reagan views, 307–308; US casualties, 367; *see also* Indochina
Vietnamization: Eisenhower's policy, 153; Nixon's policy, 262–263
Vincent, John Carter, 30
Vital Center, 94

Wake Island conference (1950), 115, 118, 121
Walesa, Lech, 334
Wallace, George, 257
Wallace, Henry A., 8, 44–45, 48, 55; opposes Marshall Plan, 62; views Marshall Plan, 71; in 1948 election, 78–79; in 1956, 188
War. *See individual wars*
War casualties (US), 367
War Powers Act (1973), 273–274
Warsaw Pact, 171, 185–186, 225, 316
Washington, George, 111
Watergate, 262, 270, 272–273, 274
Weinberger, Caspar A., 302, 307–308
Western European Union (WEU), 167–168
Westinghouse, 4
"What's My Line?" 283
"Wheel of Fortune," 357
Wherry, Kenneth, 86
White Paper (China 1949), 87
Whittier, John Greenleaf, 43
Why England Slept, 209
Will, George, 304, 344
Wilson, Woodrow, 3–4; and Dulles, 139; imperialism and order, 151–152; and Johnson, 235; and Reagan, 306
Winthrop, John, 27
Women of Russia, 358
World Bank (International Bank of Reconstruction and Development), 9; and USSR, 40; in 1950s transitions, 174, 181–182; tries to help Russia (1990s), 357; and water projects, 366
World Trade Organization (WTO), 357

Wyman, Jane, 300

"X," 63–65; *see also* Kennan, George

Yablokov, A. V., 365
Yakovlev, Alexander, 325
Yalta Conference (1945), 13–15, 16, 22, 25; McCarthy views, 111, 137–138; legacy in 1950s, 176
Yalu River, 114, 116
Yellow Peril, 117
Yeltsin, Boris: rise to power, rivalry with Gorbachev, 339, 347–348; 1991 crisis, 343–344; Clinton relationship, 356; post-1992 crisis, 356–357, 359; Chechnya disaster, 359; politics, 359–360; 1993 revolt, 359
Yemen, 182; map, 184, 198
Young, Andrew, 285, 286, 287, 288
Yugoslavia: in 1919, 3–4; 1947–1949, 52–57, 70; US policies (1948–1949), 75–76; in 1951, 126–127; and USSR, 144, 170, 171; in 1960s, 225, 292; fragments, 328, 354–355; map, 355

"Z" (Martin Malia), 337
Zaire, 261, 288
Zhdanov, Andrei, 40–41; analyzes international situation, 70–71; suspicious death, 81; legacy, 142
Zhukov, George, 170–172, 190–191
Zimbabwe, 285
Zyuganov, Gennady, 359–360

About the Author

Walter LaFeber was born and raised in Indiana, attended Hanover College, and then received his Master of Arts degree from Stanford University and his Doctor of Philosophy degree from the University of Wisconsin at Madison. His books include *The American Age: U.S. Foreign Policy at Home and Abroad Since 1750* (2nd ed., 1994); *Inevitable Revolutions: The United States in Central America* (2nd ed., 1993); *The Panama Canal: The Crisis in Historical Perspective* (2nd ed., 1989); and *The New Empire: An Interpretation of American Expansion, 1865–1898* (1963). He also wrote *The American Search for Opportunity*, Volume III of the *Cambridge History of American Foreign Relations* (1994). Since 1968, Professor LaFeber has been the Marie Underhill Noll Professor of American History at Cornell University, and in 1994, he was named a Stephen H. Weiss Presidential Teaching Fellow.